B2B PROFESSIONAL SALES VOLUME 1

THEORY | PROCESS | APPLICATION | TOOLS

Volume 1 and 2 Print-on-Demand (POD) Color Hardcover Editions

To accommodate the POD color hardcover services, the original B2B Sales textbook had to be split into two editions to meet the maximum of 550 page requirement for hardcover color books. Therefore, there are now two volumes available for purchase separately with the content as listed below:

VOLUME 1

VOLUME 2

People purchasing the POD color hardcover editions are invited to download a free copy of the entire textbook in color PDF format from **http://b2bprosales.com/txtbook_2021** and the complimentary resources folder from **http://b2bprofessionalsales.com/textbook/#textbook**

I hope you enjoy the book, and if you have any questions, please don't hesitate to contact me; thank you so much.

JP Amlin
B2B Professional Sales
jpamlin@b2bprofessionalsales.com

SALES TRAINING
& COACHING

First edition

JP Amlin, Sales Training and Executive Business Coach
Villa 61, Jalan Raya Tanah Lot, Kediri
Tabanan, Indonesia 82171
www.b2bprofessionalsales.com
jpamlin@gmail.com, jpamlin@outlook.com

ISBN 978-988-14088-2-2 (hard cover version)
ISBN 978-988-14088-4-6 (b/w paperback version w/ color cover)
ISBN 978-169-10056-2-8 (color paperback version)
ISBN 978-169-74153-8-4 (b/w paperback version)
ISBN 978-988-14088-3-9 (Kindle version)
ISBN 979-878-20136-2-2 (hard cover case laminate color Volume 1)
ISBN 979-879-08523-6-7 (hard cover case laminate color Volume 2)

Design and layout by Laura Brown.
Editing by Nanette Day.

Foreword

Salespeople are in the business of asking questions. The first two they're likely to ask are existential. They are "How did I get here?" and "How do I stay?"

The first question is trickier than it looks, as many salespeople arrive in the sales organization without knowing quite how, and perhaps even why. As college students, few plot a career trajectory by aiming for sales, though a whopping fraction of graduates land there—some after eliminating other options, some by rotational assignment, and many seemingly by serendipity alone. Sales managers' career paths aren't much more carefully chosen. Most are promoted for being a good salesperson, a qualification which, to the unfortunate surprise of many new managers, proves a fickle predictor of success.

These accidental salespeople and sales managers evoke Dirk Gently, the quirky investigator from Douglas Adams' comic detective novels. His "Zen" navigation technique involved simply finding "any car that looked like it knew where it was going and follow(ing) it." Dirk, like many salespeople and sales managers, discovers this technique results in outcomes more oft en surprising than successful, but is "worth it for the sake of the few occasions when it is both."[1]

However drawn to sales, whether through happy accident or some more purposeful route, many talented salespeople and sales managers find they want to stay. How they'll do so is a critical concern for them, and for their firms, who hope they'll not only stay but continue to thrive in the sales force. Staying requires finding a way to develop knowledge, skills, and ability in a field not well known for codifying its principles, or mapping the milestones for those traveling its route. There is no qualifying exam, no certification. Many will work for firms without meaningful training programs or with haphazard commitments to employee (let alone salesperson) development. And as if that weren't enough, they'll need to stay current in a field changing with breathless rapidity, adapting to the new models of buying and selling emerging in every industry.

This text is for them. Joe Amlin has assembled in this impressive book a sound foundation for professional sales development and an invaluable reference work useful to salespeople and sales managers at all career stages. It offers theory, processes, and specific applications of how professional salespeople manage their responsibilities. Practitioners will appreciate its focus on actionable techniques, including exercises that allow salespeople to apply concepts immediately after reading each chapter.

Joe's career in the oilfield services gives him unmatched experience in some of the most complex, challenging sales environments in any industry. That experience is evident in this text, with its focus on large opportunity management, competitive bidding and procurement, strategic sales messaging, and collaborative negotiation. Equally valuable for his readers is Joe's experience operating in seemingly every corner of the globe. A Canadian educated in Alaska (among other places), Joe is a long-time resident of Bali and spent much of his career traveling the world for a firm headquartered in Paris. His global citizenship and easy fluency in many cultures stand apart from others in our field, who mistake their own parochial success for a license to assume what works for everyone else.

Joe's commitment to sales education represents another happy accident for our profession; his contributions are, in true Dirk Gently fashion, equal parts surprising and successful. I met Joe through my efforts to start the Sales Management Association seven years ago. His interest, energy, and support of our fledgling enterprise—as a founding board member, advisor, and frequent contributor—were in no small way responsible for its success (the Sales Management Association now has more than 10,000 enrolled members in 40 countries).

I continue to be astonished by Joe's enthusiasm for the sales and sales management professions, and, like many others who've benefitted from Joe's work, remain immensely grateful for it. This text is an artifact of Joe's commitment, energy, and industriousness in developing our profession and offers ample evidence that as a sales effectiveness "thought leader," Joe's willing to do what so many others eager to claim that title ignore—carefully assess the best ideas, craft actionable insights, and present ideas focused on helping others improve.

In your own pursuits, whether those involve beginning or advancing a sales career, expanding your sales leadership ability, or simply developing a better understanding of the sales organization, I believe you'll benefit from the insights cataloged in this text. I wish you a journey full of as much success as surprise.

Robert J. Kelly
Chairman, Sales Management Association
Atlanta, Georgia

---

[1] Adams, D.: *The Long Dark Tea-Time of the Soul*

Preface

The cover represents a puzzle because this is how I viewed sales when I first started in 1983. As a young salesperson, I asked what I needed to do to be successful in sales. I got a lot of advice: some good, some not so good. To me, it was like putting together a puzzle. After some success and failures, I realized the best advice I received was from a very senior marketing manager. He told me "organize yourself for the task, look at all the pieces, set a strategy and execute. Do that and, like putting together a puzzle, all the pieces will come together to create a picture to be enjoyed." After that advice, I felt like I held the key to my success as a salesperson.

This textbook is my third book and, I believe, my best—not because the writing is better than before, but now the experiences are richer. I wrote my first book when still a young and keen mid-level manager thirsty for knowledge and looking for the pieces of the puzzle to manage a professional sales force in a B2B marketplace. My engineering degree did not provide me with the clues I needed. After earning my MBA, I realized there are a lot of very knowledgeable and generous people who were experts in the field of B2B professional sales. They have influenced my thinking and behavior as a professional salesperson. After many discussions with specialists in the B2B sales profession, teaching thousands of people on the sales skills and with the advice from my marketing manager now many years later, I believe I have a key. A key to being shared with today's sales professionals is wanting to be the best they can in their profession.

The structure of the textbook follows an academic model where each chapter begins with a list of learning objectives followed by the main text. As much as possible concepts start with a description of the theory to explain the concept, a process to be followed to apply the concept, applications of the process being applied to real sales examples, and tools that you can use to apply the concepts to your sales opportunities.

At the end of each chapter is a summary of the chapter objectives, which provides a method for readers to review and ensure that they have understood the main concepts presented in the chapter. There is also an "Applying the Concepts Section," for those who want to start using the tools that can be downloaded from www.b2bprofessionalsales.com. Finally, a reference section is included for each chapter , as is a suggested reading list for those who want to read more about B2B professional sales topics.

This textbook is not about shortcuts to sales success. The textbook is meant to be read from start to finish as each chapter builds on the previous chapter content. There are four sections in the textbook: Section 1: Sales Fundamentals, with nine chapters; Section 2: Consultative Selling Skills, with four chapters; Section 3: Selling in Competitive Markets, with four chapters and Section 4: Putting It All Together, with three chapters.

Not only is this textbook not a shortcut to sales success, but it is also not a guarantee of sales success. Rather, it is a starting point. The figure below is based on how adults learn and clearly shows that there are three phases in the process of learning as it pertains to achieving a desired level of competency.

The skills used to build the first puzzle add to your library of experience, making the next puzzle easier and faster. Like sales opportunities, everyone now and then there will be a puzzle that will challenge you and cause you to stop and work hard to see the picture and enjoy the success of winning.

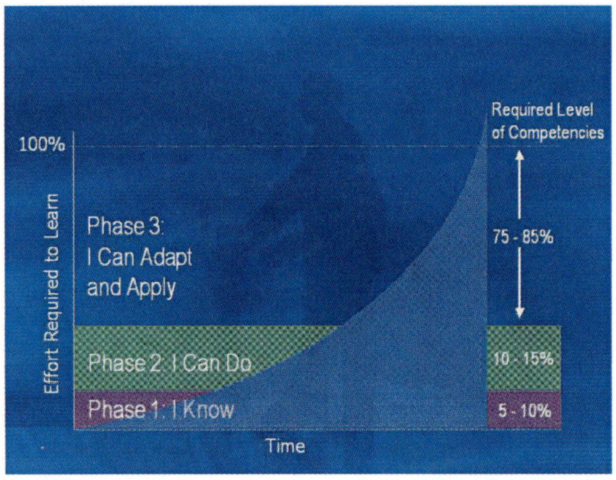

Readers of this textbook can expect to gain the foundation, or Phase 1: "I know." By studying the chapter highlights and completing the applying the concepts exercises at the end of each chapter, readers will be able to enter the next level, or Phase 2: "I can do." Reaching the professional sales level, or Phase 3, "I can adapt and apply," requires your commitment to adopting and applying the concepts to your sales responsibilities. A five-year study showed that the average time it takes a salesperson who enters the sales force after having sales training to reach the desired proficiency level of a professional salesperson is eight months to a year.[1] Those who reach the professional sales level become more efficient and effective over time. Efficiency is measured not by taking shortcuts, but by being methodical and thorough in the daily sales lifestyle. Effectiveness is measured by bringing increased satisfaction and value to your customers, your company, and your sense of personal satisfaction from that success.

I hope you find this book useful and that it contributes to your development as a professional salesperson. If you have any questions or comments, please do not hesitate to contact me.

J.P. Amlin

jpamlin@gmail.com, jpamlin@outlook.com, www.b2bprofessionalsales.com

---

[1]JP Amlin "From Sales Rookie to Professional" MBA report on sales effectiveness. University of Alaska Anchorage, Anchorage, Alaska (1987).

Acknowledgments

No book is the work of only the author. This book represents experiences, thoughts and ideas shared with my many clients and colleagues. I am particularly thankful to the companies I have had the sincere pleasure to work for either as an employee or privilege to deliver a sales training program. These companies include Archer, Baker Hughes, BGP Marine CNPC, Cummins, OiLSERV, Nucleus Software, Richardson, Schlumberger, Task Frontera Geoscience, TGT, and many more.

It is impossible to acknowledge individually all the people who contributed to the development of this material, although my debt to them is considerable, and I sincerely value their input and extend my gratitude. In particular, I want to thank my colleagues Ken Feather and Carlos Calad, two of the best sales and marketing professionals I had the pleasure to work with while at Schlumberger. I also want to thank Jason Jordan for his contribution to the field of sales effectiveness and Robert Kelly for being a champion of the sales profession.

I especially want to thank the more than 2,000 participants who attended my sales training seminars. Their questions, comments, and suggestions for improving the seminars, the first books, and teaching materials have been a rich source of ideas for this textbook. I look forward to their comments on this book and further suggestions for improving future editions.

Finally, I extend a special thanks to:

- Nanette Day for editing the final print copy, and
- Laura Brown for laying out and making changes to the draft and final versions of the chapters.

I hope as you read this book you find it interesting and useful. Your comments and suggestions on how to improve the book are greatly appreciated.

J.P. Amlin

jpamlin@b2bprofessionalsales.com
www.b2bprofessionalsales.com

Table of Contents

VOLUME 1

VOLUME 2 *Please note page numbering continues from Volume 1*

INDEX

Bold entries are in this volume, non-bold are in Volume 2.

A

B

C

D

E

F

G

H

I

J

K

L

M

N

O

P

Q

R

S

T

U

V

W

Y

Z

AUTHOR INDEX

A

B

C

D

M

N

O

P

R

S

T

U

V

W

Y

Z

IMAGE CREDITS

pg. 2, Golden Key and Puzzle © Sashkin

pg. 17, Man Shouting Megaphone © aslysun

pg. 89, Real Value Crossword Concept © pictafolio

pg. 91, Glossary Dictionary Definition © chris2766

pg. 93, Hand Drawing Blank Organization Chart © Hamza Turkkol

pg. 96, Portrait of Contemplative Businessman © Momentimages/ Tetra Images/Corbis

pg. 96, Close Up of Businessman Signing Document © Hero Images/Corbis

pg. 96, Businesswoman Reading Book in Office © Hero Images/Corbis

pg. 96, Business Colleagues in Meeting © Phil Boorman/Corbis

pg. 122, Communication Word Cloud © Mindscanner

pg. 126, Man Covering Ears © alamy.com

pg. 126, Stressed Businessman Putting His Fingers on his Temples © Wavebreak Media, Ltd.

pg. 126, Businessman with Mask © alamy.com

pg. 127, A Young College Intern at her Desk © Bobby Deal Real Deal Photo

pg. 127, Black African Businessman © Forgiss

pg. 140, Business Competition, Leadership and Key to Success © acarapi

pg. 140, Word Speech Bubble Illustration 50% Discount © kgtoh

pg. 154, Business People Group © toxawww

pg. 155, World Map in Polygonal Style © N-trash

pg. 156, Group of Business People © dreamstime.com

pg. 157, Retro Frame on String © Nik Sorokin

pg. 162, Donuts Isolated on White Background © Subbotina Anna

pg. 163, Referral Word on Three Arrow Signs © iqoncept

pg. 175, Vintage Inscription Made by Old Typewriter © Micha Klootwijk

pg. 176, Teamwork of People for Stable Growth in Business © Vladgrin

pg. 186, Law Book with Gavel on Top © txprofdev.org

pg. 190, Magnifying Glasses on Paper © alamy.com

pg. 193, Solution Business Concept © NiroDesign

pg. 196, Egyptian Pyramids © destination360.com

pg. 197, Babe Ruth © baberuthcentral.com

pg. 198, Magnifying Glass Success © shutterstock.com

pg. 198, Meeting Room Illustration © istockphoto.com

pg. 244, Man and Woman Signing a Business Contract © Bernie 123

pg. 344, Date Circled on Calendar © shutterstock.com

pg. 366, Vector World Map © broker

pg. 395, Forest Silhouettes © Oksanaok

pg. 403, Best Case Worst Case Signs © bigstockphoto.com

pg. 407, Questions © Tawng

pg. 520, Top Secret Envelope © bigstockphoto.com

pg. 551, Hand Signals © alamy.com

pg. 580, Customer Service Survey © nfsphoto

pg. 589, Friendship Hug © smamad

pg. 591, Businessmen Discussing © Dmitriy Shironosov

pg. 615, Paper Crown © dreamstime.com

pg. 626, Improve Definition © Kostyantin Pankin

SECTION 1

SALES FUNDAMENTALS

This section is the outside of the puzzle; it is the corners and flat edges that hold the puzzle together. In this section, you will discover that successful B2B sales efforts are not a cluster of ad hoc events culminating in the delivery of a price quote. Successful B2B selling is a structured process that effectively demonstrates how your company's products and services help customers meet their objectives better than your competition's. The first chapter is "Understanding the Role of Marketing and Sales." Valuable marketing and sales concepts are explained that will be referenced later in the textbook. The next two chapters are about the customer: "Value Drivers" and "Account Corporate Profile." Throughout the textbook, the focus of all the sales processes is on understanding the customer's value drivers and needs first and then selling. Chapter 4 "Opportunities Management" is the differentiating professional salesperson skill. The salespeople who are better at managing their opportunities win more often because they make time their advantage. The next chapter, "Communication Skills" emphasizes sales is in its simplest form as having a discussion with your customers. Communication skills for a salesperson can be called their most important tool. Chapter 6 "Sales Activities," the final chapter of this section, describes each of the key activity categories of what the professional salesperson does.

After reading this section, you are encouraged to complete the applying the concept exercises and become familiar with the tools described in the chapters and available to you from the www.b2bprofessionalsales.com website.

Understanding the Role of Marketing and Sales

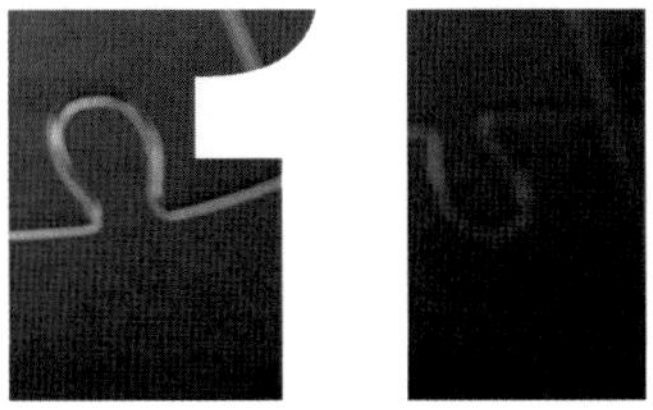

Value-Based Relationships

The goal of marketing is to create profitable customer satisfaction by building valuebased relationships with customers. In most organizations, the marketing position is the process owner of marketing strategies, and the sales staff are responsible for the successful implementation of the marketing strategies. This relationship is analogous to that of the Quality, Health, Safety and Environment (QHSE) function, where the QHSE manager is the process owner of QHSE policies and procedures, and managers are responsible for implementing those policies and practices. This chapter introduces basic marketing concepts and explains why these are important to the sales function. When a manager explains to their staff that everyone is in sales, it means that everyone—the support staff, operations staff and management—must focus on customer satisfaction. The marketing effort is the first step to customer satisfaction.

As a sales representative, it is important to understand the high-level marketing strategy and your role in the marketing process. Marketing strategy and tactics are continuously updated to reflect the changing needs of your customers. Marketing managers use a number of tools and analyses to manage your ongoing marketing efforts. This approach ensures your company's growth through new product offerings and the effective management of current products and services portfolio. Sales representatives play an important role in this effort.

After completing this chapter, you will have sufficient information to achieve the objectives listed in the "Chapter Objectives" sidebar. With this knowledge, you will be able to make a significant contribution to the marketing and sales efforts.

Chapter Objectives

After reading this chapter, you will be able to:

- Define marketing and its core processes.
- Explain how the sales position complements the marketing efforts.
- Understand six key marketing concepts that are used by sales teams in their day-to-day efforts to win business.

What is Marketing?

Simply put, marketing is the delivery of customer satisfaction at a profit.[1] Therefore, the marketing position must understand the needs of selected markets and determine the products and services required to serve those markets successfully. To select the markets and the products and services that fit those markets, the marketing professional follows the process shown in **Fig. 1.1.**

Fig. 1.1
The marketing process is used to select the markets in which your company will compete and identify what products and services to sell in the selected markets.

▶ ***Application Question:***
What is the corporate vision or mission of your company?

The Marketing Process

Every company exists to create a profit for its shareholders. Each company chooses from many options to achieve this objective. The chosen path is communicated to the company's shareholders, employees and customers through vision and mission statements. Guided by this vision, the marketing manager performs a strategic analysis of internal factors (strengths and weaknesses) and an analysis of external factors (opportunities and threats) to determine which markets to serve. This strategic analysis is called "SWOT." After completing this step, the marketing manager develops a formal marketing strategy, sometimes called a competitive strategy,[2] for the identified markets.

When selecting high-level marketing strategies, marketing managers must consider the competitive forces at work in the targeted market. In this way, managers first define the strategic advantages for your customers. Two possible advantages are low-cost leadership and differentiation.

Next, marketing managers pinpoint a strategic target or portion of the market to serve. They decide between serving a broad portion of the market or focusing on a particular niche. With the strategic advantage and target analysis complete, the marketing manager has sufficient information to choose one of the four generic marketing strategies as shown in **Fig. 1.2.**

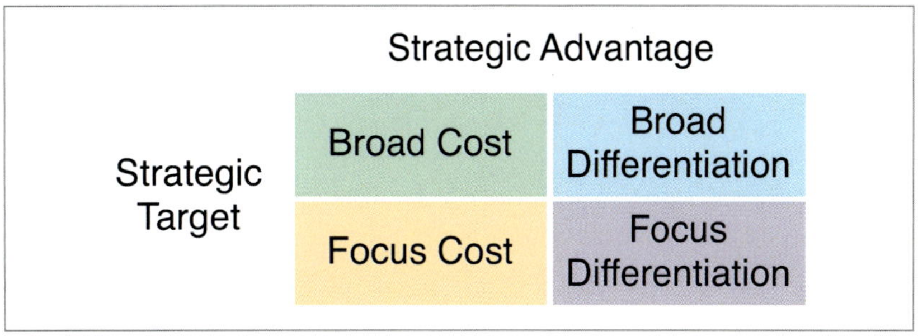

Fig. 1.2
Generic marketing strategies.

After identifying competitive forces, strategic advantages and target markets, marketing managers look at the marketing mix, commonly called the 4 Ps of the Marketing Mix:

- **Product** or service to be offered.
- **Place** where the product or service will be offered.
- **Promotion** activities, which clearly communicate the value of the offering to the market and its advantages over competitor offerings.
- **Pricing** strategy, which includes terms and conditions, price to customers, bundling incentives, credit terms and discounting policies.

Marketing and Sales Responsibilities Compared

As shown in Fig. 1.1, sales is the execution of the marketing strategy. To make decisions about future product development and to determine the viability of target markets, marketing managers seek input from customers, sales and other customer-facing staff. **Figure 1.3** defines marketing and sales responsibilities. Using input from customer and sales staff, the marketing group selects target markets; the sales staff then secures the desired market share at a designated level of profitability. Sales staff are challenged to strengthen customer relationships while negotiating, securing transactions and potentially handling difficult situations. Achieving the long-term objectives of the marketing strategy rests on effective, profitable sales. In other words, successful marketing requires successful sales.

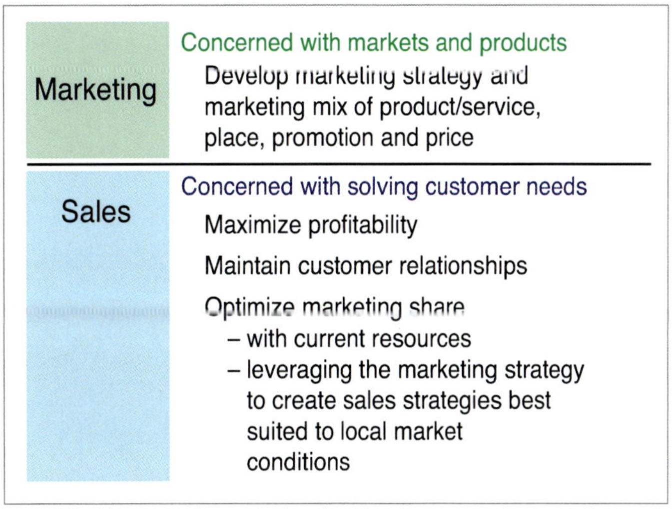

Fig. 1.3
Marketing and sales responsibilities.

A significant difference between the two roles is focus. **Figure 1.4** shows that marketing requires a longer focus to evaluate future market trends such as customer needs, technology developments and competitive threats. Gaps in current offerings must be understood through marketing in order to address those gaps with future offerings. The sales team, however, is much more focused on customers' current and near-term needs and on fulfilling those needs with present offerings.

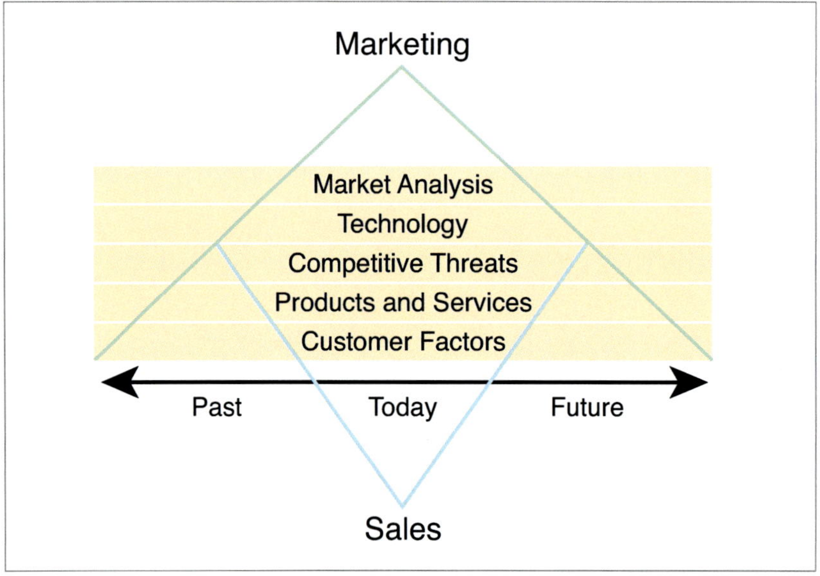

Fig. 1.4
Marketing and sales focus.

The sales team must also be aware of existing competitive threats in order to secure each sale. Several complementary tasks of each group are shown in **Fig. 1.5.**

Marketing	Sales
Business Trends	Client's Plans
Marketing Strategies	Sales Strategies
Market Surveys	Client Needs
Input to R&E	Input to Marketing
Technology Watch	Competitor Watch
Product Testing	Customer Satisfaction

Fig. 1.5
Marketing and sales tasks.

Long-Term Growth

One goal of the marketing function is to ensure the long-term growth of the company. In his article entitled "Marketing Myopia," Theodore Levitt discusses what steps companies can take to ensure long-term growth.[3] He believes companies that define their market too narrowly do not achieve long-term growth. As an example, Levitt describes the demise of the railroad business as the result of the belief that railroad companies were in the railroad business rather than the transportation business. Therefore, railroads saw their market share diminish as other, more efficient transportation alternatives developed.

Another common attribute of companies that do not attain long-term growth is what Levitt refers to as the "shadow of obsolescence." This shadow occurs when a company mistakenly believes it will continue to grow because an expanding market ensures growth. There are no competitive substitutes and the company is preoccupied with a product that lends itself to carefully controlled scientific experimentation. Levitt recommends companies define their markets more broadly to take advantage of growth opportunities.

Companies that do not achieve long-term growth also tend to believe that a superior product sells itself and that continued growth is a matter of continued product innovation and improvement. Such companies are oriented toward the product rather than the markets that use the product. All these biases suggest that, to capture growth opportunities, companies must adopt a customer approach to marketing.

In today's competitive marketplace, where there is less differentiation in offerings, the emphasis must start with the customers and focus on creating long-term, mutually valuable relationships with them. Two prime objectives of a relationship-centered marketing strategy are to increase net present value (NPV) and to extend the lifetime of key customer relationships. These objectives are supported by relationships with suppliers and alliances with competitors.[4]

Another factor that contributes to reducing long-term growth is what Levitt calls "a mirror, not a window." To sell technical products and services, companies often hold meetings with customers to explain the products and services and to offer assurance that outstanding service is part of the sale; however, many technical companies describe their products and services in their own terms when trying to make the sale. Such tactics are like looking at a mirror to present product and service attributes that reflect the company's technical management program rather than the customer's objectives. Levitt suggests that companies are challenged to discuss measurements of service in the customer's terms to demonstrate which business objectives are impacted by a particular product or service.

Marketing Philosophy

The marketing philosophy focuses strongly on the customer. Creating a strong customer focus across all of the company's business units will ensure a more efficient interface with customers. While the organization aids in customer interaction, the customer-focused marketing philosophy enables the marketing staff to effectively analyze potential markets and identify business opportunities. By selecting which segments of the market to serve, marketing staff can offer superior value to the chosen customers by way of products, services and core competencies that target customer needs.

In addition, the organizational structure and customer-focused philosophy provide a greater opportunity to leverage the assets of the entire organization, which further differentiates the company from its competitor companies. In a high-tech industry, the tendency is to develop good products without heeding the size and requirements of the market. By also leveraging the organizational structure, and keeping an eye on customer needs, a company can make better decisions regarding where to concentrate its resources.

▶ *Selling by Looking Through the Customer's Window*

Customers want to learn about actions taken that result in reducing their total costs, improving revenues, reducing risks, and improving return on investment (ROI).

Marketing as a Continuous Process

Just because a company provides its customers with products and services needed today, does not guarantee that it can meet customer needs in the future. Not only must a company have customer focus, it must be able to predict and position the company to meet future customer needs. In *Competing for the Future,* authors Hamel and Prahalad studied many companies in several industries and found that companies having an active program to think about the markets in which they operated, and how they would like to try to influence the shape of that marketplace, on average, provided higher returns to shareholders than peer companies in their industry.[5] **Figure 1.6** lists questions companies must answer in order to be positioned to capture future opportunities in their industry.

- Organizational transformation must be driven by a point of view about the future of the industry.
- How do we want our industry to be shaped in five to 10 years?
- What skills and capabilities must we begin building now if we are to be the industry leader in the future?
- How should we organize for opportunities that may not fit neatly within the boundaries of current business units and divisions?

Fig. 1.6
Strategic questions for competing in the future.

Figure 1.7 illustrates the decentralized organization, and the role of different groups with respect to the customer relationship. The sales organization is one of the primary interfaces with the customer. Two key roles of the local organization are service delivery and customer relationship management. The objective of the sales staff at the interface is to understand the customer's environment, business drivers and objectives, and then leverage the resources available from

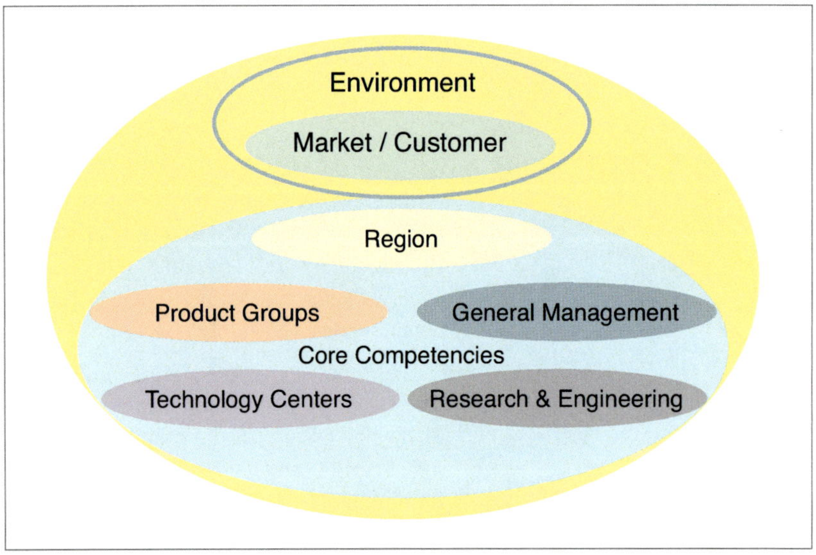

Fig. 1.7
The decentralized organization and customer relationship management.

the different groups in their organization to bring the most value to the customer while sharing in the value. (Concepts and processes regarding value pricing are discussed in detail in Chapter 11 "Competitive Bidding.") When a customer deals with sales staff, he or she works with people who are supported by his or her company's people and resources required to deliver on their promises.

Key Marketing Concepts for Sales

The first part of this chapter described the core processes of marketing and how the sales position complements the marketing efforts. In the remainder of the chapter, six key marketing concepts will be described as follows:

- Product life cycle
- New technology adoption
- Total product concept
- Marketing communications plan
- Buying center
- Buyer behavior

These concepts are used by business-to-business (B2B) sales organizations to enable them to compete effectively and win work in a complex marketplace.

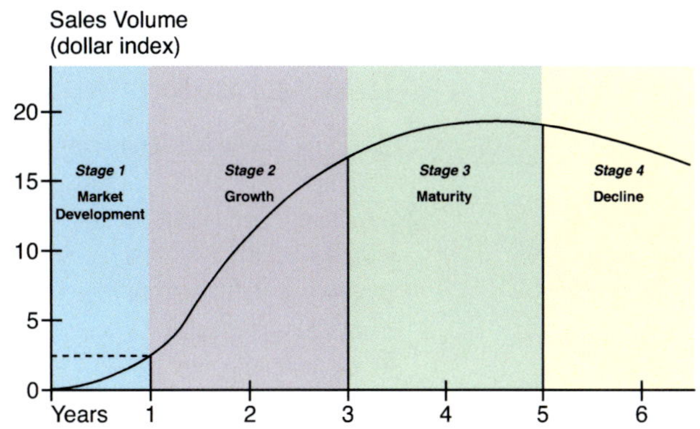

Fig. 1.8
Product life cycle stages.

Product Life Cycle

It is commonly accepted that products go through four stages after the product development stage **(Fig. 1.8)**, each requiring different strategies and tactics.

Market Development. Market development begins after the company has made the decision to commercialize a new product idea. Prior to market development, sales are zero, and the company's investment in costs mount. Then, in the market development stage, sales growth is slow as the product is introduced in the market; profits are typically negative or low because of low sales volumes and high start-up costs. In this stage, the promotional spending and demonstration runs are high in order to introduce customers to the new product and persuade them to try it. The company, especially if it is a market pioneer or leader, must choose a launch strategy that is consistent with the intended product positioning. The initial market strategy is just the first step in the total marketing plan for the entire life cycle of the product or service. The market position in the introduction stage is critical for ensuring the long-term profitability of the product.

Typically, competitive pressures are slight, because competitors often lack comparable products. The competitive edge in this stage comes from making sure the client understands the differences between the new product and those it is designed to replace or, in the case of a revolutionary new product, what it can do to benefit the client's business. Newly introduced products usually require careful explanation of features and benefits and, in many cases, ongoing consultation and support.

▶ ***Market Development Stage Important to Product Positioning***

In globally dispersed companies, the market development stage is a particularly sensitive time when many locations introduce the new product. In this stage, it is critical that the locations avoid creating spin-off strategies that could jeopardize the position of the product in the global marketplace. If locations deviate from the recommended pricing strategy, clients may communicate this to other operating areas, making it difficult to apply a global pricing strategy.

Growth. As the new product satisfies the market and demand increases, competitors begin to develop alternatives. In this stage, the competitive response is to present more relevant benefits. The more benefits the product delivers, the more valuable it is to the customer. Profits begin to increase during this stage.

Maturity. The product is well understood by clients and has been copied by many competitors. The key to additional sales during this stage is to differentiate the offering by customizing the solution to provide benefits that the competition does not offer. Profits tend to level off or decline due to increased costs of defending the product against the competition.

Decline. The product becomes a commodity, and price pressure is usually intense. The challenge here is to add sufficient value through customization and differentiation through service—how you provide it rather than just what it is—to command an acceptable margin, which is the main challenge in this stage.

The adoption of new technology has significant impact on the product life cycle and on strategies of differentiation. To understand the shape of the product life cycle, you must look at buyer behavior as it pertains to new technology adoption.

New Technology Adoption

Buyer willingness to adopt new technology can be described as shown in **Fig. 1.9.** The first groups to adopt new products are described as **innovators.** They account for a small portion of the purchasing population. They buy new technology for the sake of wanting to test it. Some organizations have groups who are given the responsibility of testing any new technology before it becomes widely used in the companies' operations. These groups and individuals are sometimes called gatekeepers in the buying center. These groups are usually good targets for field-testing campaigns during the product development stage and in the market development stage of the product life cycle.

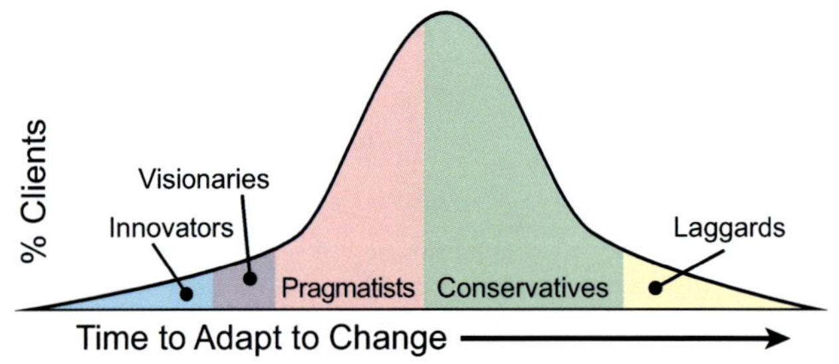

Fig. 1.9
New technology adoption life cycle. Pragmatists and conservatives represent the largest portion of the purchasing population and make up the majority of the purchases in stage two of the product life cycle.

▶ ***Visionaries at Work***

When logging while drilling (LWD) services were introduced in the 1980s, visionaries in drilling departments, such as BP and Exxon, were quick to adopt LWD as a way to shorten the drilling curve and reduce total evaluation costs.

After the new technology has been proven to work as advertised, the next groups to adopt the technology are **visionaries.** Visionaries, like innovators, buy into new product concepts very early in their life cycle, but unlike innovators, they are not technologists. They are people who find it easy to imagine, understand and appreciate the benefits of a new technology and to relate these potential benefits to their other concerns. Whenever they find a strong match, early adopters are willing to base their buying decisions upon it. Because visionaries do not rely on well-established references when making these buying decisions, preferring instead to rely on their own intuition and vision, they are key to opening up any high-tech market segment. Visionaries believe they will gain a competitive advantage by adopting new technology early. They believe they can gain a huge cost or revenue benefit from the new technology. These two groups—innovators and visionaries—are usually the ones who make purchases of new products during stage one, the market development stage.

The next groups to purchase a new product are the **pragmatists**. Pragmatists share some of the visionaries' ability to relate to technology, but ultimately they are driven by a strong sense of practicality. They know that many new products may not prove viable or practicable, so they are content to wait and see whether other companies successfully integrate the new technology before buying it. They want to see well-established references before making substantial investments. Because this group is the largest—accounting for roughly one-third of the whole adoption life cycle—winning their business is key to recovering investment and development costs of the new product.

The next groups to purchase are the **conservatives**. Conservatives share all the concerns of the pragmatists, plus one major additional one. Where pragmatists are comfortable with their ability to handle a new technology product once they finally decide to purchase it, members of the conservatives are not. As a result, conservatives wait until the product has become an established standard or has gained widespread industry approval and support. Even then, conservatives require a lot of proof and, therefore, tend to buy from large, well-established companies. Like the pragmatists, this group comprises one-third of the total buying population in any given market segment. Securing a large portion of this group is required if high levels of profitability are to be achieved.

The last groups to adopt new technology are the **laggards**. While small in size, the laggards are almost the same size as the innovators and visionaries percentage-wise. Laggards generally purchase new technology to protect investments and to replace worn-out products. An example of laggards are the companies who, in December 1999, purchased new UNIX machines to replace VAX 11780s, which would no longer run and were not upgradable due to Y2K issues.

New Technology Adoption Implications

What do the buyer categories mean to the marketing and sales staff that must sell new products in their markets? In the B2B environment, products and services may be heralded as successful during stage one, when innovators and visionaries prove the product or service meets advertised technical requirements. At this stage, field test participants are easy to find in the innovators. Then, after commercialization, sales are still made to the visionaries, but these sales are not sufficient to achieve the market penetration expected and projected after the successful field test. What happened? Part of the answer lies in the work from Moore.[6] As illustrated in **Fig. 1.10**, not all purchases from the additional groups in the technology adoption life cycle occur immediately one after another.

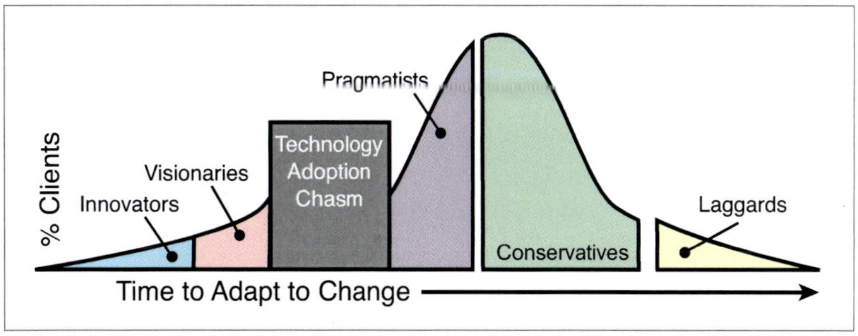

Fig. 1.10
Gaps in the technology adoption life cycle.

Significant time gaps may occur between the purchases made by groups, such as pragmatists and conservatives. If the innovators and visionaries are highly enthusiastic about the new product, competitors are encouraged to start work on similar offerings unless the technology is sufficiently protected by patents. As a result, the large group of visionaries and pragmatists may be shared with competitors, causing a delay in the payout of research and development and commercialization investments. In addition, pragmatists and conservatives may delay purchases unless their concerns are sufficiently addressed. In such cases, projected sales may never materialize, thereby jeopardizing the success of the new product.

The gap between visionaries and pragmatists—the **technology adoption chasm**—is what marketers must address in the initial marketing plan. How do you cross the chasm quickly and achieve the level of market share required to reach your levels of profitability for the product and service? The positioning of new products is critical in order to provide what each technology adoption group wants and determine which group can be used to support sales to another group, as shown in **Fig. 1.11**.

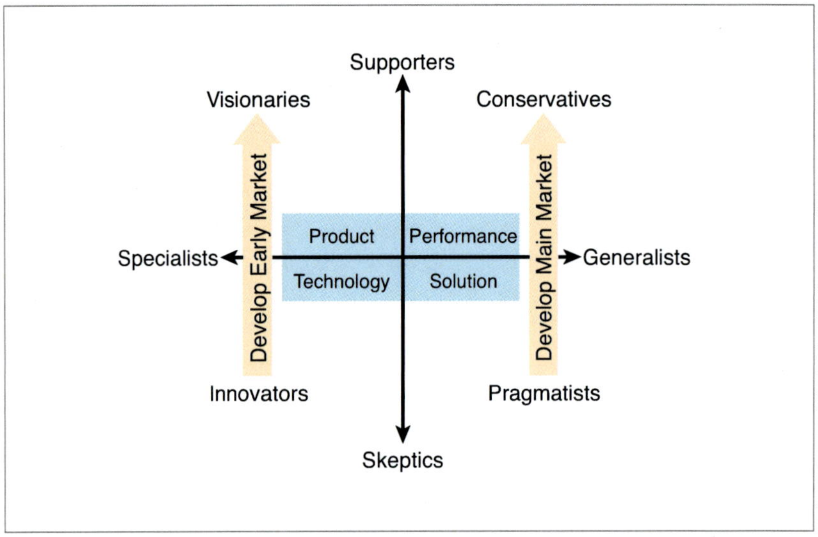

Fig. 1.11
Positioning of new products to new technology adoption life cycle groups.

Figure 1.11 shows that innovators can be used to help sell products and services to visionaries, but do not make acceptable references to pragmatists or conservatives. Successful marketing and field test programs should include plans that capture the required proof to sell to pragmatists and conservatives. Pragmatists can be used as proof to sell to conservatives. As pragmatists represent a significant share of the market, this in itself is sufficient proof to the conservatives that the industry has accepted the product or service. Thus, you must demonstrate a total solution to the pragmatists and industry acceptance of service and performance to the conservatives. **Fig. 1.12** lists specific sales-related factors for each technology adoption group and suggested sales aids to use when selling to these types of buyers.

Technology Adoption Group	What They Want	What They Buy	What You Should Sell (Concerns)	Sales Aids
Innovators	State of the art	Trials	Product excellence Concern Technical CT-50, Concern Service CS-5, Concern Financial CF-45	White papers Nondisclosure agreements Technology Center visits Field test Joint R&E
Visionaries	Revolution Recognition	Customized solution	Future competitive advantage CT-30, CS-60, CF-10	VIP seminars Technical journal articles
Pragmatists	Evolution Solve problems	Total solutions	Proven expertise in solving similar problems CT-20, CS-40, CF-40	SPE papers Testimonials
Conservatives	Not to be left behind	Industry standards	Return on investment CT-10, CS-45, CF-45	Industry reports Cost of ownership
Laggards	Status quo	Enhancement or extension of existing systems	Investment protection CT-5, CS-30, CF-65	Client-specific proposal

Fig. 1.12
New technology adoption life cycle groups and selling considerations.[7]

Total Product Concept

Theodore Levitt, a professor at Harvard University, best describes the challenge facing most marketing plans of new products in his work regarding product evolution and market expectations. Levitt describes the stages a new product goes through and what must be done to win and keep customers. He illustrates his ideas with the total product concept **(Fig. 1.13)**.

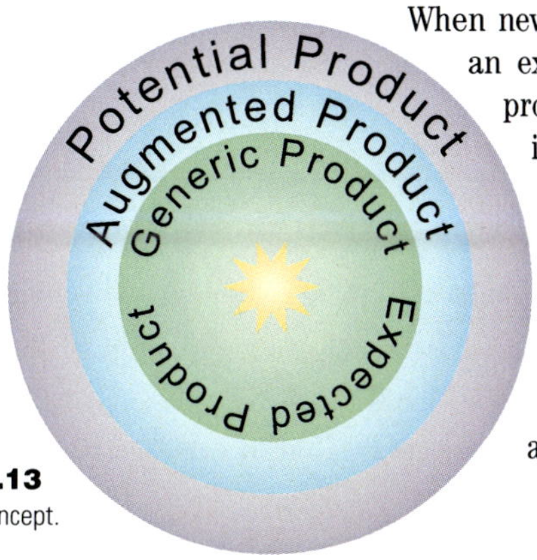

Fig. 1.13
Total product concept.

When new products are introduced, the consumer has an expectation of what the generic product will provide. This explains why selling to innovators is much easier than any of the other groups, especially the pragmatists and conservatives. Innovators buy or test a new product just to see if it works; they do not have any other expectations. This "easy sell" can produce false expectations in terms of being able to sell the product after field test to pragmatists and conservatives. The challenge of the marketing plan is to introduce and gain fast approval from the innovators and then help the visionaries integrate the product through augmentations that enable them to achieve their vision of using the product. These activities must be done while laying the strategy for taking the product to the next highest level, which is a product that is sufficiently differentiated so the pragmatist sees the product as a total solution with value compared to other alternatives. The total solution allows the product to reach its largest potential market before the decline stage sets in as replacement products or increased competition begin to have an impact later in the product life cycle.

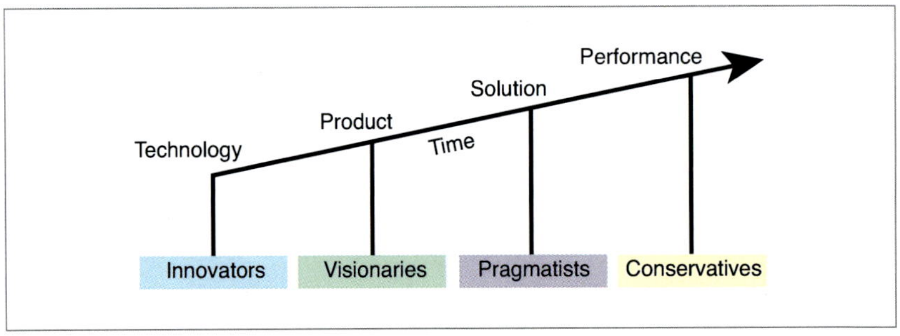

Fig. 1.14
Marketing strategy evolution for new products.

Figure 1.14 illustrates the evolution of the focus for the marketing and sales plans of a new product, and the key components of the marketing message in order to capture a particular group in the technology adoption life cycle as a function of time.

As a sales representative, you want to leverage the product progression to ensure fast and efficient introduction of new technology in the market. At the field test stage, you want to ensure that companies participating in the field test will release the data so you can offer the information as proof to the visionaries that the technology works. When you are in the commercialization stage and introducing the product to the visionaries, you want to learn from their application and augment your product offering so you can offer a proven product to the visionaries and solution for the pragmatists. As you gain more experience and jobs with the technology, keep good records and collect testimonials so that you can convince the conservatives that this is a proven and reliable technology or service. Over time, as you gain a better understanding of how the customer uses the product, you will be able to think of ways to evolve the product to its highest potential.

A key success factor for managing the product life cycle is the marketing communications plan. An effective marketing communications plan helps to keep your market informed and aware of your products and services and creates a buying environment.

Marketing Communications Plan

Two goals of the marketing communications plan are to:

- Create awareness among potential direct or indirect users of your products and services; and
- Have an accurate feedback mechanism in place to capture customer feedback.

▶ ***Are You Ready?***

The customer's decision to make a purchase is the result of a long process. In the industrial buying process, the purchase decision-making process is formalized and implemented by using an evaluation model. This is typically done in the customer's evaluation of options phase in the project management process. The project management process will be discussed in detail in Chapter 4 "Opportunities Management." From the sales perspective, you must also be aware of where the buyer is in the buyer-readiness stage, as depicted below.

Each ring's diameter represents the portion of the potential target market, with the bot-tom ring representing 100 percent of the target market. Typically, only a portion of the targeted market is aware of a new or existing company or product or service, as represented by the smaller awareness ring. A smaller portion will be knowledgeable about the company, product or service, and only a very few will actually make a purchase. The vertical position represents the sequence of the stage. For example, the first stage is awareness, followed by knowledge, liking, etc.

The stages buyers normally pass through in making a purchase decision include: **Awareness:** The buyer is aware the company, product or service exists. **Knowledge:** The buyer understands the benefits the company, product or service provides. **Liking:** The buyer has a favorable opinion of the company. The seller's company, product or service will be included on the qualified bidder's list. **Preference:** The buyer prefers to use the company or its products or services rather than other companies or their products or services. The seller's company, product or service will be selected for the short list of preferred suppliers. **Conviction:** The buyer is convinced and has evaluated the seller's company as the best match to the requirements. **Purchase:** The buyer makes the purchase decision from among the best competing alternatives.

Awareness

The first goal of the marketing communications plan is to create awareness in the market about your company's products and services and migrate potential users and buyers to the higher-level buyer-readiness stages (see the "Are You Ready" sidebar this page[8]). Marketing communication plans target a wider audience than the contacts you focus on during the pursuit phase of an opportunity. Marketing communications programs target groups of customers, such as geophysicist, geologists, petroleum and drilling engineers, and different types of projects, such as deepwater and high-temperature/high-pressure operations, in advance of the procurement phase for a particular sales opportunity. By being aware of the customers' strategies that make up the target market and their long-term plans, you can tailor the marketing program for the target market.

The marketing communications plan should be a structured, integrated program that makes use of a variety of marketing communication and promotional tools, including:[9]

- **Advertising:** Any paid form of non-personal presentation and promotion of ideas, goods or services by an identified sponsor.
- **Personal selling:** Personal presentation by the firm's sales force for the purpose of making sales and building customer relationships.
- **Public relations:** Building good relations with the company's various publics by obtaining favorable publicity, building a good "corporate image," and handling or heading off unfavorable rumors, stories and events.
- **Direct marketing:** Direct communications with carefully targeted individual consumers to obtain an immediate response. Direct marketing can be conveyed by numerous vehicles—mail, social media, telephone, fax, e-mail and other non-personal tools—to communicate directly with specific customers or to solicit a direct response.
- **Word of Mouth (WOM):** WOM is the number one influencer of B2B purchase decisions. Few B2B customers ever buy anything without first asking around about their experiences with the vendor and/or product. Shown in **Fig. 1.15** are the results of a survey of B2B decision makers by Forrester Research, 84% of respondents said WOM recommendations influence their purchase decisions. While nearly all B2B companies have blogs, only 24% of respondents said they trust blogs. Other research firms also have found that WOM rules in B2B.[10]

Chapter Highlight 1.1: Marketing Communications Programs describes some of the marketing communication tools used by companies. Each promotional tool can be targeted to take the user or buyer through one or several of the buyer-awareness stages. Effective account marketing communications programs focus on the lower level buyer-readiness stages so that when you are in the pursuit phase of a sales opportunity the sales team can spend more time building preference and conviction with the buying center to ultimately win the project.

Feedback

Gathering feedback and listening to your markets are as important as transmitting the message to the customer. They are a required part of excellent communications with your markets. The communications process is defined as sending a message and getting feedback. One rule to follow for effective communication is to always get feedback. If you are not getting feedback, you are not communicating. It is very dangerous for your company to rely only on your impression of the markets' satisfaction. **Chapter Highlight 1.2: Listening to Your Customers** discusses several listening strategies you can employ to develop a more accurate indication of your market's satisfaction.[11]

Chapter Highlight 1.1: Marketing Communications Plan

Are You Aware of That?

An effective marketing communications plan is a key component of a successful sales organization. Communications plans are an efficient, low-pressure method of creating awareness, educating your customers on how your company can assist them in achieving their business goals, and creating a buying environment for your products, services and solutions. Key features of a successful communications plan include the following:

- Remain high quality, current and relevant.
- Remain brief, precise and scheduled.
- Transfer best practices inside and outside the region.
- Include high-level meetings between customers and your company's upper management to discuss solutions to business issues.
- Include a monitoring system to know who is participating and make it easy for customers to receive additional information.
- Address each stage of the buyer-readiness stage.
- Include all components of the marketing and sales promotion tools.
- Include as many word-of-mouth testimonials as possible from satisfied customers.

Listed below are just a few of the successful sales communications plans that meet the above criteria. A successful market communications plan should leverage the available corporate programs and services as much as possible.

Personal Selling, Regular Company Informational Events

- Lunch and learns: Company-sponsored lunches with guest speakers discussing latest developments related to issues relevant to the target audience, such as deepwater completion techniques and fractured reservoir evaluation techniques.
- Participation at professional society conferences and meetings: Company speakers present technical papers on the latest technology developments and applications. Company booth in exhibition hall.
- Annual VIP seminars: Courtesy meetings between upper management teams demonstrating solutions to their business issues.
- Industry-sponsored training sessions: Company-sponsored training courses for products and services used within the specific market.

Direct Marketing and Sales Tools

- Regular document distribution: Complimentary copies of company publications to selected key customers in key accounts.
- Application-specific courtesy informational updates: Solutions page sent on a regular basis to selected customers highlighting specific market technical challenges solved with company products and services.
- Internet website: Company information portal for customers, employees and investors.

Advertising

- National and international advertising campaigns: Advertising programs in major trade journals and business magazines.

Public Relations

- Company-sponsored programs and donations supporting community development programs, educational institutions, sports-related programs, charities, community volunteer programs and annual celebrations. Effective public relations programs can make a significant impact on the liking buyer awareness stage.

Fig. 1.15
WOM is the number one influencer of B2B purchase decisions. Few B2B customers ever buy anything without first asking their peers or colleagues about their experiences with the vendor and/or product or service. In a survey of B2B decision makers by Forrester Research, 84% of respondents said Word of Mouth recommendations influence their purchase decisions. While nearly all B2B companies have blogs, only 24% of respondents said they trust blogs.

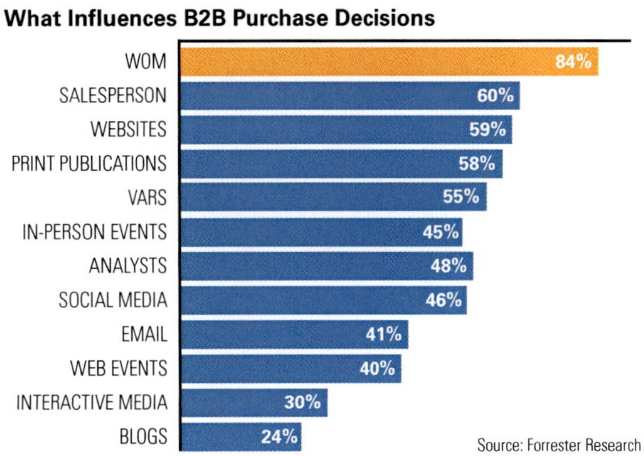

When you combine a marketing communications program with an effective feedback program, you establish communication links with your markets. Effective communication links make it easier and more efficient for your customers to contact you, discuss issues and leverage the relationship between their company and your company. Impaired communication is both a symptom and a possible source of future problems.

Buying Center

One of the main differences between consumer sales and B2B sales is the number of people involved in the purchase decision. Consumer sales normally includes one or two people, and B2B sales can have many people involved. In the article "Major Sales: Who Really Does the Buying?," [12] author T.V. Bonoma emphasizes that seemingly well-planned, well-executed selling strategies may fail if management does not understand the human side of selling. Marketing managers can get at the human factors of purchasing decisions by answering four questions:

- Who is in the buying center?
- Who are the powerful buyers?
- What does each buying-center member want?
- How do they perceive the seller?

On the next page is a list of the buying roles encountered in most B2B selling situations. In many buying centers, individuals may have multiple roles. For example, a user may be the evaluator and gatekeeper. There may also be approvers who do not work within the company, such as a government-approving department, as is the case in many countries that have a national oil company.

- **Initiator:** High-level manager proposes project that requires significant purchases.
- **Approver:** Manager or committee that reviews the decision maker's recommendation.
- **Decision maker:** Manager or committee that has the purchase decision.
- **Influencers:** Staff have important opinions for which others in the buying center will consult.
- **Gatekeeper:** Corporate purchasing and/or recognized experts who must

Chapter Highlight 1.2: Listening to Your Customers

At the heart of any successful strategy to manage customer satisfaction is the ability to listen to the customer. There are five major categories of approaches that companies can use to listen to their customers. Most highly successful companies employ several, if not all. Many average or poor performers either use very few or do a poor job of incorporating the results into their strategies. The five categories are:

Customer Satisfaction Indices

Surveying customers about their level of satisfaction and plotting the results can help managers understand how satisfied or dissatisfied customers are with both their dealings with the company in general and various elements of the company's product or service in particular. The fact that such indices are quantitative makes them a useful tool for comparing results from different time periods, locations and business units.

Feedback

Customers' comments, complaints and questions fall into this category. A company cannot implement a recovery strategy—a plan for making amends when something has gone wrong—if it does not know who has had a problem. Therefore, it is important to review the company's approach to soliciting feedback—good and bad—on product and service quality.

Market Research

Although companies traditionally invest significantly in this area, they often overlook two critical listening points. Customers should be interviewed both at the time of arrival (when they become customers) and at the time of departure (when they defect) about the reasons for their behavior. New customers should not only be asked, "How did you hear about us?" but also, "What major experiences influenced your decision to try our product or service?" The answers to the first question provide data about the effectiveness of the company's awareness advertising, and the answers to the second supply information about the specific factors that actually sparked the decision to try the product or service. It also is critical to understand why a customer defected.

Gleaning such information requires a high degree of sensitivity and skill because most customers will blame the price or some other relatively basic product attribute in order to avoid discussing the real issue. Carefully questioning departing customers is important for two reasons: to isolate those attributes of the company's product or service that are causing customers to leave and to make a last-ditch attempt to keep the customer. One company we studied found that it recaptured a full 35% of its defectors just by contacting them and listening to them earnestly.

Frontline Personnel

Employees who have direct contact with the customer provide a superb means of listening. However, to take full advantage of frontline employees' interactions with customers, the company must train them to listen effectively and to make the first attempts at amends when customers have bad experiences. They also must have processes in place to capture the information and pass it along to the rest of the company. Many companies that excel in satisfying customers have institutionalized one other practice. All employees—not just those with frontline jobs—spend a significant amount of time interacting in depth with customers.

Strategic Activities

Some companies go to extremes to involve the customer in every level of their business. MTV, the cable music channel geared to 18- to 24-year-olds, insists that most of its employees must belong to the demographic target group. Southwest Airlines actually invites frequent fliers to its first round of group interviews with prospective flight attendants and considers these customers' opinions in decisions to invite certain candidates back for individual interviews. Intuit, the financial software company, regularly brings in customers to participate in product development sessions.

approve new technologies or processes before widespread adoption within a company. Gatekeepers may also proactively analyze the company's future needs and recommend likely matches with potential suppliers.

- **Evaluator:** Corporate purchasing department or other assigned staff who evaluate offerings using an evaluation system. In most B2B purchases, the evaluators follow a procurement process that includes tendering and negotiation.
- **Users:** All employees who use the product or services and provide specifications to evaluators or gatekeepers
- **Partners:** It is also very important for the sales staff to determine if there are any partners who will have a role in the buying process. In some cases, the partners are not the operator of the project and as such may not be in direct contact with suppliers or managing the procurement process, but they could be providing the bulk of the financing of the project and therefore could be very influential in the buying process and need to be contacted.

Marketing and sales managers should listen to the sales force, emphasize homework and details and make productive sales calls the norm by focusing on people who will be in the buying center.

Buyer Behavior

Another very important marketing concept for B2B sales staff to consider is buyer behavior, which can be described as the level of importance the buyer gives to price differences and the level of importance given to product and services differences. Once this is understood, the buying behavior is used to classify buyers as one of four buyer types. This helps the sales staff identify what is most important to the buyer and adjust their sales conversations according to the buyer type. The buyer behavior and buyer types are shown in **Fig. 1.16**.[13, 14]

The upper left-hand corner of Fig. 1.16 shows buyers who seek to buy at the lowest price consistent with some minimum level of acceptable quality that several suppliers can meet. These **price buyers** do not make feature benefit trade-offs and cannot be convinced to pay more for the unique added value of superior features, service or supplier reputation. Price buyers' perception of value is the lowest price, without hassles, and consistent products. These buyers know exactly what they are buying and do not want any surprises.

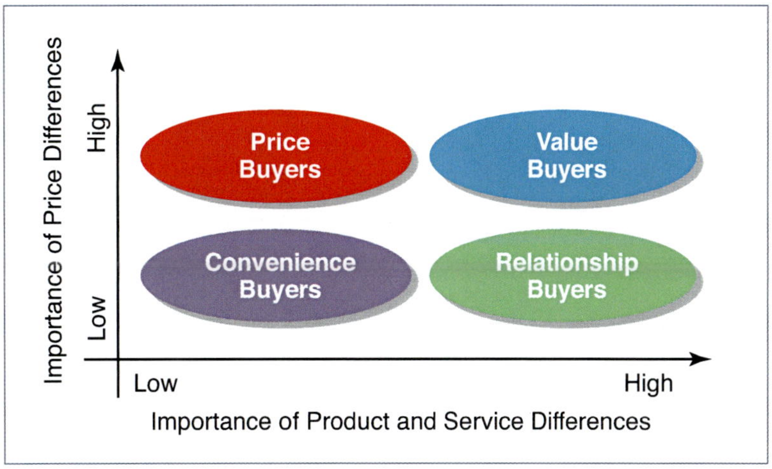

Fig. 1.16
Buyer price, product and service sensitivity classification and buyer type.

In the lower right-hand corner of Fig. 1.16 are the **relationship buyers** who already have a strong preference for one company, based on its unique reputation, its unique features or past experience with that company. If the prices of purchasing from that company do not exceed what they are willing to pay, these buyers will purchase from that company even if there are cheaper alternatives. Their perception of value is to buy the best total solution for their needs. They want to deal with experts so they can focus on other issues. While they know they are paying a premium, they are nonetheless convinced it is worth it.

Although these two segments are frequently considered the two ends of a price–quality continuum, Fig. 1.16 clearly reveals two other segments that do not fit within that linear view of buyers.

Many customers are price sensitive when they make large expenditures or have limited budgets, yet they are also sensitive to differences offered by various suppliers. These **value buyers**, shown in the upper right-hand corner of Fig. 16, may buy a relatively high-priced offering but will do so only after carefully checking the prices and features of the alternatives and concluding that the added value is worth the added cost.

Their opposites, represented in the lower left-hand corner, are **convenience buyers**. These buyers are not particularly concerned about the differences among brands. Any brand will do, but convenience buyers are also not particularly concerned about cost. Consequently, they buy whatever is most readily available, minimizing the search and evaluation of prices and features.[15]

The most common types of buyer behavior for most new B2B purchases are price, value and relationship buyers. Convenience buyer behavior can be important in B2B repurchases or when a customer has several contracts in place with different suppuliers and can buy from any supplier by simply placing an order to any of the approved suppliers.

Figure 1.17 shows what each of the three main buyer groups for new purchases perceive as value.[16]

Fig. 1.17
What the three main buyer segments say about value.

Buyer Migration

Conventional economic theory suggests that, over time, natural market forces create a migration of buyer behavior from loyalty and value to price. This happens when products and services become more similar over time, differences between suppliers become less obvious and the deciding purchasing factor becomes price. **Figure 1.18** illustrates this migration.

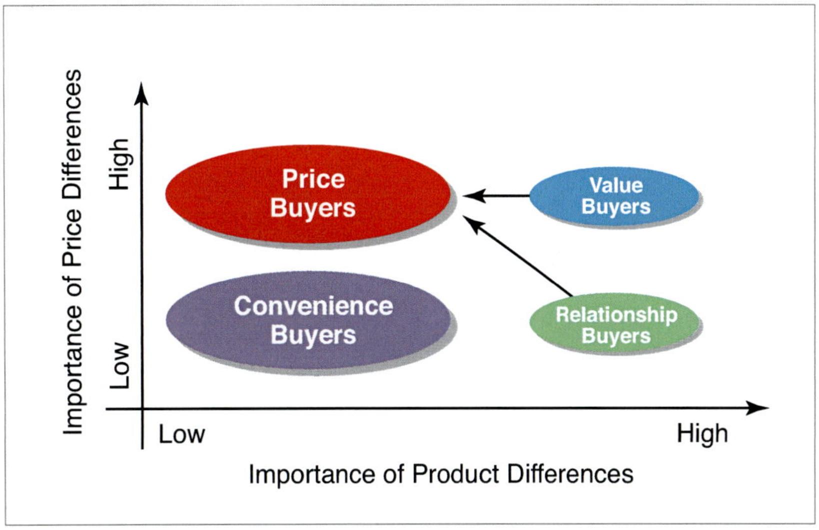

Fig. 1.18
Buyer migration over time.

This migration is observed as markets mature, even in markets where a company constantly introduces value-added products and services. In fact, some procurement departments would like you to believe that price is the only discriminating factor. Why does this happen in an industry that can benefit from more than just low prices?

Here are three common reasons:

- **Lack of customer focus.** This happens when a company's sales staff fail to explain the differentiating features and benefits that result in added value for the customer. Consequently, the customer views all or a selected group of companies and their offerings as the same. This lack of focus is particularly true when the customer does not have the time or internal expertise to quantify the benefits of the added features. As a result, the customer sees all products and services as equal and uses price as the key purchasing factor. **Figure 1.19** on the following page shows three different levels of focus and the main focal points for each level. For example, when sales staff talk to the customer about product features, they show a strong product focus. When they discuss general benefits, they show an application focus; when they discuss added value as it pertains to the customer's specific environment, they use customer focus. Customer focus, discussed more fully in Chapter 7 "Sales Call Skills," is the ideal focus for most sales staff.
- **Service does not justify a price premium over a competitor.** Many studies have demonstrated that customer loyalty is created by superior service, not just good service. When buyers select a supplier, they believe the purchase includes good service. Only total customer satisfaction gives a supplier an advantage over competitors.[17] Later chapters discuss the importance of delivering on the promise during the execution stage of projects, which directly impacts total customer satisfaction.

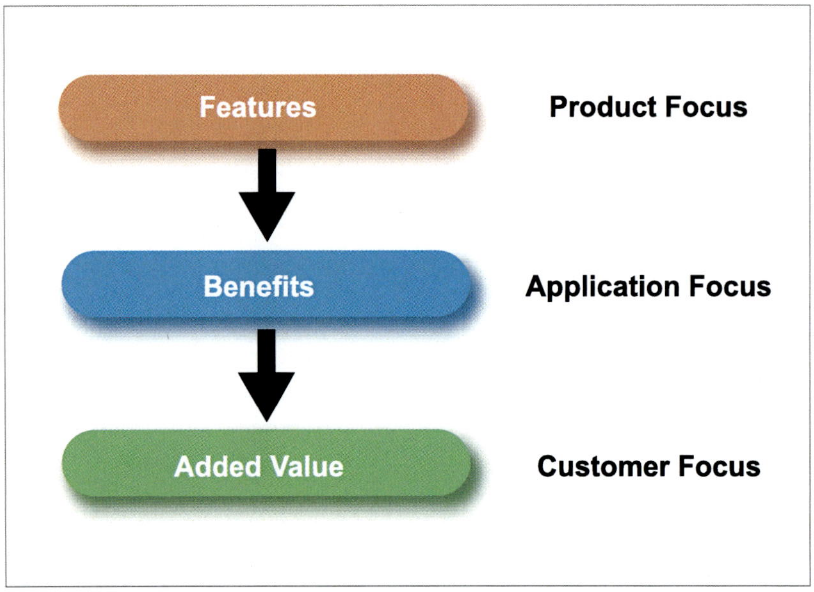

Fig. 1.19
Levels of focus.

- **Poor price management practices.** Such practices occur when a company has variable pricing policies that are not sufficiently justified based on the level of products or services offered, after-sales support or size of the customer commitment. As a result, the company rewards price buyers by giving them a better deal than the value or relationship buyers. Once the value and relationship buyers discover this, they ask for the same prices and behave like price buyers. This typically happens when companies try to increase market share by lowering prices.

This concludes this chapter on understanding the role of marketing and sales. In the discussion of marketing and sales, value was a frequently used word. In the next chapter, value drivers will provide a complete understanding of customer value drivers and how sales representatives can use this information to create a value-based relationship.

Summary of Chapter Objectives

Today's successful companies share a strong focus and heavy commitment to marketing.

Marketing seeks to attract new customers by promising superior value, and seeks to keep current customers by delivering satisfaction. Sound marketing is critical to the success of the organization. Sales organizations play an important role in the marketing efforts and employ key marketing concepts in their day-to-day sales responsibilities to secure business in a complex B2B marketplace.

1. Define marketing and discuss its core processes.

Marketing is the delivery of customer satisfaction at a profit. The processes marketing staff follow to construct corporate marketing strategies start with the company's vision. The final marketing strategy is a function of competitive market forces and a company's strengths and weaknesses, opportunities and threats in the targeted markets and customers' needs. The execution of the marketing plan describes the product or service, targeted markets (place), promotion (professional sales force) and pricing guidelines.

2. Explain how the sales position complements marketing efforts.

The marketing function creates the marketing strategy. The sales team executes the strategy. Feedback to the marketing function regarding the effectiveness of the strategy is a critical part of the sales effort. Feedback covers all aspects of the marketing mix—the product itself, how well it meets the expectations of the customer, whether the promotional aspects of the strategy are sufficient, whether the markets should be narrowed or expanded to whom a company offers the product (place) and whether the pricing achieves the profit levels. In addition, what is the customer feedback in terms of how to evolve the product to a higher level as described by Levitt's "Total Product Concept," and what are the competitor reactions? All this information goes into modifying the current strategy, leveraging the information to other target markets and formulating future strategies. When the sales force executes the marketing strategy successfully, the marketing group is considered successful. When the sales force cannot execute according to the plan, the marketing function is not successful.

3. Understand the importance of each product life cycle stage.

Products and services go through four distinct stages after the product development stage. Each state has different strategies and tactics to ensure that maximum profitability and sales volumes are achieved. The first stage is market development, in which sales are low and costs are high due to start-up costs. Next is the growth stage: Sales and profits begin to increase, and competitors with similar products may begin to appear. Then comes the maturity stage, when sales volumes peak and competitor pressure is the highest. The last stage is decline; now the once-new product or service becomes a commodity with many competitors, all competing with similar products. New products begin to replace the older products and services. Probability in this stage is low. To maximize profitability and usefulness of a product, there two very important marketing concepts–new technology adoption and the total product concept.

4. Describe how the technology adoption preferences of your customers impact their purchasing decisions.

Technology adoption preferences have a significant impact when customers are making first-time purchases. There are five types of buyers, as described by the technology adoption concept. First to purchase are innovators. These are technical experts who try anything new to decide for themselves whether it works. These customers are good targets for field tests. The next group to purchase are the visionaries. Once the technology has been proved to work, visionaries purchase because they are enthusiastic about new technologies and see technology as a way to improve. The next group to purchase are the pragmatists. Pragmatists purchase a solution to a problem. To convince pragmatists, you need to do more than just show proven technology; you have to offer a complete bundled solution. The next group to purchase are the conservatives. Conservatives will buy proven reliable technology. To sell to conservatives, security and dependability are more important than is the aspect of new and great technology. The last group to purchase are the laggards. They purchase new technology only when they have to. When buying products and services, they want what they had last time.

These customer profiles are extremely important to the sales representative when making proposals. The proposed solution is always one of many options. It is the sales representative's job to pick the best solution that is acceptable to the customer.

5. Use the total product concept to differentiate and compete more effectively with existing products and services.

Theodore Levitt uses the total product concept to describe the expectations of markets and customers when buying new products and how companies can differentiate their products and services by thinking about how to evolve their offerings. The total product concept has three levels: The first is generic, followed by augmented and finally potential. The objective for companies selling in the B2B environment is to quickly determine when to introduce new products at the generic level and how to augment to bring more value for the customer, while at the same time differentiating their products and services from competitors. This is key in the market growth and maturity stages. Competitors will always try to catch up by offering similar augmented products and services. Proactive marketing and sales organizations know this and always strive to continuously improve and enhance their offering as the highest potential value to the customer.

6. Identify the key components of the marketing communication plan.

There are two goals of the marketing communications plan: Create awareness, and establish an effective feedback mechanism for your customers. To create awareness, you follow the model described by the buyer-readiness stages. The marketing awareness plan targets all users and buyers of your products and services. Ideally, the plan uses all the marketing and communication tools to migrate users and buyers from the awareness level of the buyer-readiness stage to the preference level. When buying center contacts are at the preference level, the sales team can focus on building conviction and ultimately contact support in the purchase decision. The feedback mechanism completes the communication process, because without an effective listening system you may never determine how the customer perceives your services. Together, the marketing plan and feedback mechanism form the communication links, and most relationships are only as good as their communication links.

7. Identify the key roles in major B2B sales.

In major B2B sales, most purchase decisions are the responsibility of a buying center consisting of the following roles, which can be assigned to an individual or committee: **Initiator:** the high-level manager who proposes a project that requires significant purchases. **Approver:** a manager or committee that reviews the decision maker's recommendation. **Decision maker:** a manager or committee that makes purchase decisions. **Influencers:** staff who have an important say about which system and vendors the company will consider. **Gatekeeper:** corporate purchasing department and/or recognized experts who must approve new technologies or processes before widespread adoption within a company; gatekeepers may also proactively analyze the company's future needs and recommend likely matches with potential suppliers. **Evaluator:** corporate purchasing department or other assigned staff who evaluate offerings using an evaluation system; in most B2B purchases, the evaluators will follow a procurement process that includes tendering and negotiation. **Users:** all employees who use the product or services and provide specifications to evaluators or gatekeepers. It is also very important for the salesperson to determine if there are any partners who will have a role in the buying process. In some cases, the partners are not the operator of the project and as such may not be in direct contact with suppliers or managing the procurement process, but they could be providing the bulk of the financing of the project and, therefore, could be very influential in the buying process and need to be contacted.

8. Identify the four common buying behavior types.

Buying behavior and types are powerful concepts to help the sales staff focus on what the customer views as important. Buyers can be classified based on their perception of the relative importance of price differences and product and service differences. Price buyers view great prices as most important; value buyers will pay more if they believe they will receive more; relationship buyers know having the correct supplier is worth a premium; and convenience buyers will pay higher prices even if the products and services are similar, but the buying process is simpler and allows them to be more efficient when buying. In B2B, new purchases are a key factor for the sales staff to understand and focus on what is different between their offer and the competitor's and what is important to the customer. If the sales staff fail to do this, then value and relationship buyers migrate to price buyers.

Applying the Concepts

1. Visit the web page of your major competitor and identify what strategy they are applying. Determine which competitive marketing strategy your competitors are using.
2. As a salesperson, can you identify two specific times in which you have contributed to the marketing role?
3. Can you identify which stage of the product life cycle two of your key products or services are in?
4. Analyze your top three customers and classify them in terms of their technology adoption preferences. Give specific examples of why you classified them as you did. What are ways your sales effort could adjust to accommodate the different groups?
5. What are examples of situations in which you could augment a current offering that would put you in a stronger position for a future tender? How much would this cost and what would be the benefit to the customer? Do you think this would have a global application?
6. What major marketing communications event have you planned for your key customers? Should there be others?
7. Recall an important tender or bid you submitted. How many of the different buying center roles can you identify and who had those responsibilities?
8. In relation to your customers, what percentage are price, value and relationship buyers?

References

1. Kotler, P. and Armstrong, G.: *Principles of Marketing,* Upper Saddle River, New Jersey, Prentice Hall (1998).
2. For a more in-depth discussion of competitive strategy: Porter, M.E.: *Competitive Strategy*, New York, The Free Press (1980).
3. Levitt, T.: "Marketing Myopia," *Harvard Business Review* (July–August 1960) 45–56.
4. Center for Relationship Marketing, Goizuta Business School, Emory University (1992).
5. Hamel G. and Prahalad, C.K.: *Competing for the Future,* Boston, Massachusetts, Harvard Business School Press (1994); and "Competing for the Future," *Harvard Business Review* 72, no. 4 (1994) 122–128.
6. Moore, G.: *Crossing the Chasm*, New York, New York, Harper-Business (1999).
7. Levitt, T.: "Marketing Success Through Differentiation—of Anything," *Harvard Business Review* (January–February 1980) 1–9.
8. *Ibid.*, Kotler, P. and Armstrong. 425–437.
9. *Ibid.*, Kotler, P. and Armstrong. 425–437.
10. Fuggetta R.: "Top 5 Myths of B2B Word of Mouth" Zuberance Report (April 2010) 3–4.
11. Jones, T. and Sasser, Jr., W.E.: "Why Satisfied Customers Defect," *Harvard Business Review* (Nov.–Dec. 1995) 88–99.
12. Cespedes, F.V.: "Managing Major Accounts," Harvard Business School from notes prepared for classroom discussion (Oct. 26, 1989).
13. Yama, E.: "Purchasing Hardball, Playing Price," *Business Horizons* (September–October 2004).
14. Another very good source regarding pricing and buyer behavior is: Nagle, T. and Holden, R.: *The Strategy and Tactics of Pricing. A Guide to Profitable Pricing*, Englewood Cliffs, New Jersey, Prentice Hall (1994).
15. Convenience buyers are a significant group in consumer markets, where price does not play a significant part of the buying decision. Small convenience stores sell to these types of buyers, who will pay a premium to make a quick stop. The premium they pay is worth the added convenience.
16. Treacy, M. and Wiersema, F.: *Discipline of Market Leaders*, Cambridge Massachusetts, Perseus Books (1995).
17. Reichheld, F.: "Learning from Customer Defections," *Harvard Business Review* (March–April 1996).

Value Drivers

2

The Bottom Line

Sales representatives are often challenged to demonstrate to customers how you can contribute to their value drivers. Often, customers appear to be preoccupied with the bottom line and do not appear to value your additional capabilities. For customers to better understand and accept your value-added services, you must:

- Be involved when companies identify their value drivers during the corporate planning and execution stages, and
- Make a direct linkage between your product and services and how this benefits the customer on their specific project.

Chapter Objectives

After reading this chapter, you will be able to:

- Explain how and when value drivers are established.
- Know the most common corporate value drivers.
- Explain the purpose of the value proposition.
- Know the basic make-up and contents of an annual report.

Corporate Planning Stage

At the corporate planning stage, management defines the company's corporate vision or mission statement.[1] This vision drives the selection of long-term corporate goals. Management then identifies the critical success factors and value drivers required for meeting those long-term goals. Then, the company sets objectives and specific strategies. At this point, the company is ready to execute.

Corporate Value Drivers

Corporate value drivers are defined as:

Variables that directly or indirectly impact the market value of the corporation as measured by the combined value of the common stock, known as market capitalization.[2]

This definition can be broken into two parts: direct and indirect variables.

Direct corporate value drivers are variables that affect the value of the common stock or share price. Direct variables are stock market-related ratios such as earnings per share (EPS) and price-to-earnings ratio (P/E). What affects these ratios

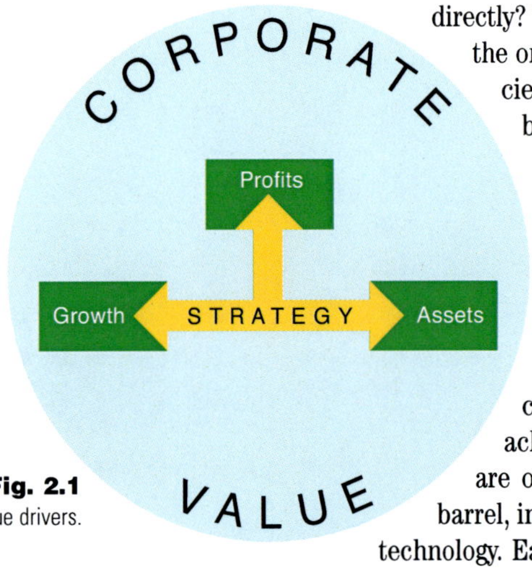

Fig. 2.1
Direct corporate value drivers.

directly? The obvious answer is increased profits, but this is not the only answer. Achieving optimum profit comes from efficient management using assets and identification of the best growth opportunities **(Fig. 2.1).**

Another set of direct corporate value drivers are profitability ratios such as return on equity (ROE) and return on capital employed (ROCE). These are discussed in more detail later. Your company can contribute to all the corporate value drivers.

Indirect corporate value drivers are initiatives or corporate policies that impact a company's ability to achieve its objectives. Examples of indirect value drivers are operational ratios, such as reducing lifting costs per barrel, improving QHSE performance and utilizing appropriate technology. Each company tracks a set of indirect corporate value drivers. These supplement the direct financial value drivers to ensure that day-to-day operations are on track to meet objectives. Both direct and indirect value drivers are typically included in management's key performance indicators (KPI). **Figures 2.2 and 2.3** are examples of technology indirect corporate value drivers for two E&P companies. Sales representatives must reach each account to uncover the direct and indirect corporate value drivers of those accounts.

Core Technologies
For all the clamor and glamour, technology's chief mission remains to support Chevron's core petroleum business. Inclusion, collaboration and leveraging are dominant themes.

Current examples:

Reservoir Optimization
Industry wide, an average 70% of oil remains locked in reservoirs, unrecovered by conventional techniques. Late in 2000, Chevron and an oil field services firm, launched a multiyear research project to provide the next-generation tools to increase recovery rates from existing reservoirs. The joint effort, says Technology VP Paul, "will allow you to develop a superior set of next-generation software products and modeling capabilities that neither would be able to accomplish individually."

Fig. 2.2
Indirect corporate value drivers—technology.[3]

Execution Stage

Corporate objectives lead to the selection of projects for execution. At this stage, the project manager identifies the project's critical success factors and value drivers that will influence the implementation, procurement and project management and review strategies. Project value drivers at the execution stage are focused on achieving the project objectives or producing the expected results. Project value drivers are defined as:

> Variables that directly or indirectly impact project results.

At the execution stage, sales staff must determine how to assist customers in achieving their project objectives. One answer is to minimize costs. The strategy to achieve project objectives, however, comes from project management's ability to achieve them while balancing the trade-offs among costs, results, and operating policy. At this point, you must research each project to ensure that you have a complete understanding of the project value drivers and then prepare a clear and concise value proposition statement.

The **value proposition statement** clearly communicates how your services or products contribute to corporate or project value drivers. For sales staff, the first task in the sales cycle is to gather sufficient information about the customer's objectives and value drivers at both the corporate and project levels. With this information, sales staff can then devise a strategy to support a proposal the customer will approve. The "Sales Call Skills" chapter clearly describes the steps needed to build an accurate and believable value proposition statement. Where there are two sets of value drivers, the one that delivers the most value to the corporation must be identified. The answers come at both the corporate value planning stage and the project selection stage. In **Fig. 2.4,** the customer project management process is reproduced from a presentation given by Chevron at an industry conference. The Chevron executive clarifies that the amount of value gained at the execution stage is minimal compared to the value of selecting the right projects in the planning stage.[5]

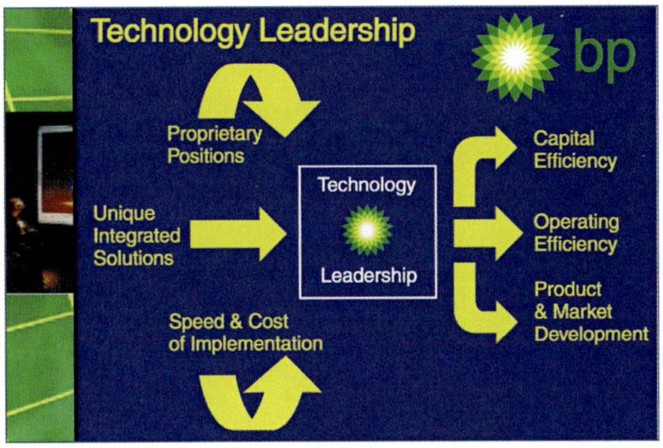

Fig. 2.3
Indirect corporate value drivers—technology.[4]

The ability of your company to impact and participate in the value identification stage is directly related to the quality of the relationship between your accounts and the customer-facing team in your organization. You and your management team should have conversations with your account's executives to generate awareness and understanding of their strategies as set out in phase 1 and ensure that you deliver the products and services in an efficient and effective manner to maintain the value through phases 4 and 5. All parts of your organization's business units should have the expertise needed to understand how projects are sanctioned in the project selection stage (phase 2). Then use this early information to fully analyze from the account's perspective and your company's perspective the best possible options in phase 3.

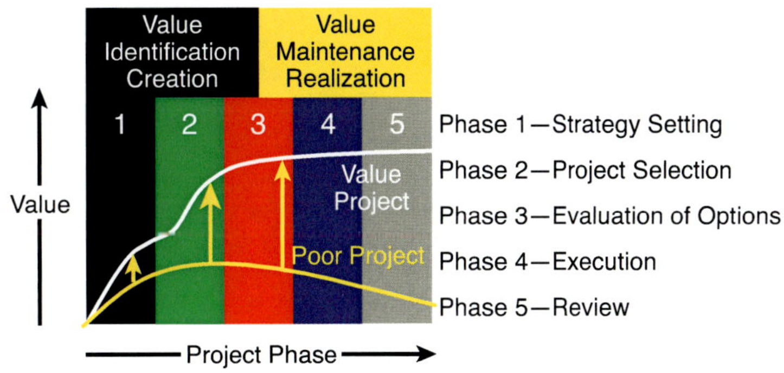

Fig. 2.4
Customer project management process.

Uncovering Company Value Drivers in the Annual Report

Sales representatives can study a number of documents to learn about a customer's value drivers. One of the most important of these is the annual report, the most common and regularly published vehicle a company uses to communicate to shareholders and stock analysts. Annual reports are typically broken into the following sections:

- Message to the shareholders
- Management's discussion and analysis of financial conditions and results of operations
- Financial review consisting of four basic reports: the balance sheet, cash flow statement, operating report (also called net income statement or profit and loss statement), and supplemental information on oil and gas producing activities
- Multiyear summary of financial and operating results

Message to Shareholders

This section of the annual report is typically written by the highest-ranking officer of the company and highlights major developments for the reporting year and future direction. In this section, the company officer gives a high-level review of the company's performance and major initiatives. **Figure 2.6,** shown on the next page, is an example of a high-level review taken from an annual report. This section is very helpful for beginning to uncover both direct and indirect company value drivers. It is typically followed by a tabular summary of financial and operating highlights. Examples of financial and operating highlights for an E&P company are shown in **Figs. 2.5 and 2.7.**

Financial Highlights

Millions of dollars, except per-share amounts	**2000**	1999	% Change
Net income	**$ 5,185**	$ 2,070	150%
Sales and other operating revenue	**$ 50,592**	$ 35,448	43%
Capital and exploratory expenditures*	**$ 5,153**	$ 6,133	(16)%
Total assets at year-end	**$ 41,264**	$ 40,668	1%
Total debt at year-end	**$ 6,232**	$ 8,919	(30)%
Stockholders' equity at year-end	**$ 19,925**	$ 17,749	12%
Cash flow from operating activities	**$ 8,662**	$ 4,481	93%
Common shares outstanding at year-end (thousands)	**$ 641,060**	$ 656,346	(2)%
Per-share data			
Earnings–basic	**$ 7.98**	$ 3.16	15.3%
Earnings–diluted	**$ 7.97**	$ 3.14	15.4%
Cash dividends	**$ 2.60**	$ 2.48	5%
Stockholders' equity	**$ 31.08**	$ 27.04	15%
Market price at year-end	**$ 84.44**	$ 86.63	(3)%
Total debt/total debt plus equity	**23.8%**	33.4%	
Return on average stockholders' equity	**27.5%**	11.9%	
Return on average capital employed (ROCE)	**20.8%**	9.4%	
Return on average capital employed, excluding special items	**21.8%**	10.2%	

*Includes equity in affiliates.

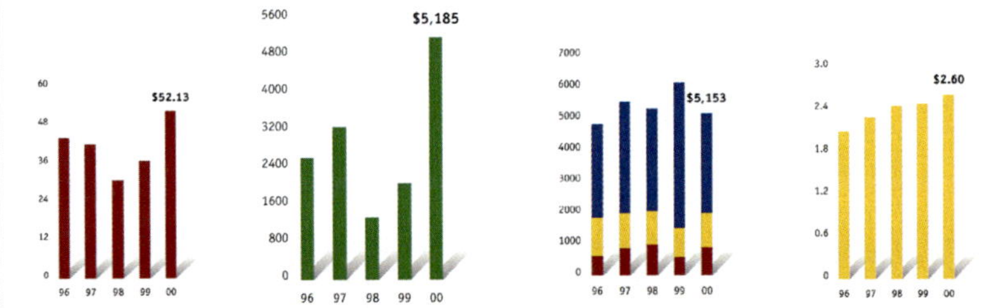

Total Revenues & Other Income
Billions of dollars

Revenue and other income increased sharply higher on prices for crude oil, natural gas and refined products.

Net Income
Millions of dollars

Net income of nearly $5.2 billion was the highest in the company's history.

Capital & Exploratory Expenditures
Millions of dollars

- *Exploration*
- *Refining, Marketing & Transportation*
- *Other*

Cash Dividends Paid
Dollars per share

Annual dividends increased for the 13th consecutive year.

Fig. 2.5 E&P company financial highlights, presented in an annual report's message to shareholders, clearly identifying this corporation's value drivers.[6]

CONOCO AT A GLANCE

Our vision is to be recognized around the world as a truly great, integrated, international energy company that gets to the future first. Conoco operates in more than 40 countries worldwide and at year end 1999 had approximately 16,700 employees. Conoco is active in both the upstream and downstream segments of the global petroleum industry. Power generation and carbon fibers, two developing businesses, are promising new areas for Conoco.

UPSTREAM—EXPLORATION AND PRODUCTION

Business Description | Conoco's Exploration and Production (E&P) activities cover the exploration, development and production of crude oil and natural gas, and the production of gas liquids through gas processing. Upstream is the company's largest business segment, with 1999 capital spending of $1.3 billion. The company is exploring in 15 countries and producing in nine. Conoco's E&P operations compete on a worldwide scale with other major integrated petroleum companies, such as ExxonMobil, BP Amoco, Royal Dutch/Shell, Texaco, Chevron and others, as well as national oil companies, and independent exploration and production companies. E&P customers and partners include host nations and national oil companies—such as Venezuela's Petroleos de Venezuela S.A., Statoil of Norway and the Sylvan Petroleum Company—with whom Conoco participates in major projects.

Operations | In 1999, E&P produced approximately 350,000 barrels of petroleum liquids and 1.7 billion cubic feet of natural gas per day from fields in North America, South America, Europe, Africa, the Middle East and Asia Pacific. Exploration activities are focused in five areas: the deepwater Gulf of Mexico, northern South America and the Caribbean, northwest Europe, East Africa and Asia Pacific. Business development activities are focused in South America, Asia Pacific, the Middle East and Russia. Natural gas and gas products operations include the gathering, processing, distribution and marketing of natural gas and natural gas liquids in North America, the United Kingdom, Norway and Trinidad. In 1999, Conoco marketed natural gas volumes in excess of 4.4 billion cubic feet per day in the United States and Europe, and also processed 64,000 barrels per day of natural gas liquids.

Strategy | E&P's strategy is to provide increasing earnings through profitable growth in high-potential areas around the world. E&P intends to fulfill this strategy by focusing on several key objectives.

- Develop at least two new core areas: Today, Conoco's E&P operations are focused in North America and the North Sea. In the future, Conoco intends to develop new core areas. particularly in northern South America and Asia Pacific, and perhaps in West Africa, the Caspian Sea region, the Middle East and, in the longer term, Russia.
- Maintain industry-leading productive growth: E&P is working to achieve its goal of 4% to 5% annual production growth through highly successful exploration, business development activities and selective acquisitions.
- Portfolio management and efficiency: Upgrading the quality and efficiency of Conoco's upstream portfolio substantially improved performance over the last several years. Conoco continually evaluates properties to ensure the portfolio is producing the maximum value. Proceeds from asset sales are being reinvested in large, early-stage, long-term projects in current and projected core areas.
- Maintain top-quality performance in the industry: Conoco was ranked number one among 14 major energy companies for the two-year E&P performance (1994–1996). The evaluation was conducted by Schroder & Co. Inc., an international banking firm.

Fig. 2.6
E&P company example of vision, objectives and strategies (from the Conoco 2000 Annual Report)

Operating Highlights

	2000	1999	% Change
Net production of crude oil and natural gas liquids (Thousand of barrels per day)	**1,159**	1,127	3%
Net production of natural gas (Millions of cubic feet per day)	**2,469**	2,513	(2)%
Sales of natural gas (Millions of cubic feet per day)	**5,261**	4,936	7%
Refinery input[1] (Thousand of barrels per day)	**1,358**	1,424	(5)%
Sales of petroleum products (Thousand of barrels per day)	**2,314**	2,324	–
Net proved reserves of crude oil, condensate and natural gas liquids (Millions of barrels)	**5,001**	4,784	5%
Net proved reserves of natural gas (Billions of cubic feet)	**9,552**	9,056	5%
Adjusted operating expenses per barrel	**6.06**	5.16	17%
Number of employees at year-end	**28,159**	31,459	(10)%

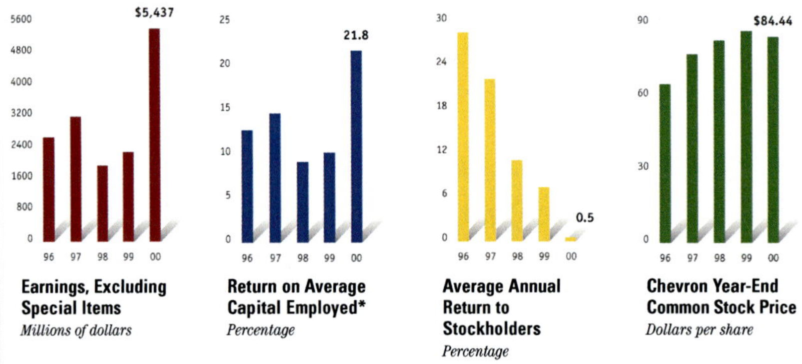

Fig. 2.7
Performance highlights, presented in the message to shareholders. The graphs at the bottom show additional value drivers for this company.[7]

Management's Discussion and Analysis of Financial Condition and Results of Operations

This section of the annual report gives a more detailed review of results as supported by financial and supplemental statements. It also includes a summary of each specific operating entity, often geographically. It usually highlights KPIs, such as net proved reserves and operating expenses per barrel.

Both the message to shareholders and management's discussion and analysis of financial results use horizontal, vertical and ratio analyses of results to:

- Evaluate past performance,
- Identify areas of focus or improvement,
- Describe future potential,
- Compare their performance to peers,
- Report on their corporate value drivers.

Financial Review

After the management discussion, the annual report presents a financial review that contains four basic reports. These reports constitute part of the company's annual reporting requirements and are presented in accordance with the general accepted accounting procedures (GAAP) required by the country in which the company is incorporated.[8] All companies must publish three standard financial reports: balance sheet, income statement and statement of cash flows. Oil and gas producing companies must also provide supplemental information on their activities.

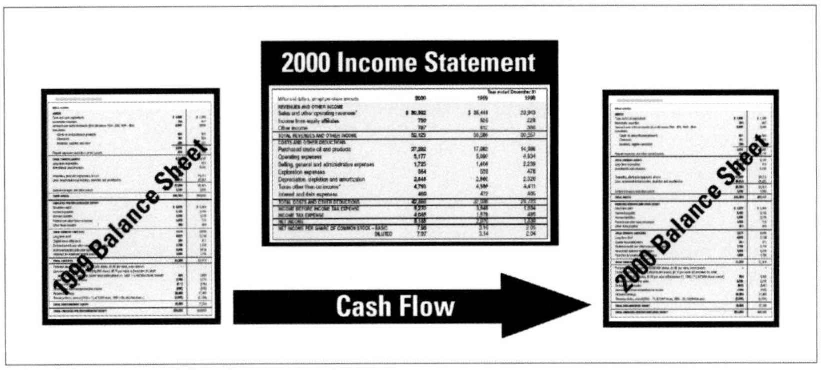

Fig. 2.8
The relationship of the three basic financial reports.

The three basic financial statements are not independent of each other, but are linked as shown in **Fig. 2.8**. Together, they give a full picture of the financial affairs of a business.[9]

Balance Sheet

The balance sheet can be considered the engine of the company. A snapshot of the economic condition of the company, it provides information about:

Assets: the physical resources except for intangibles such as goodwill. These are what the company owns and uses to generate its net.

Liabilities: the claims on those resources by both creditors and shareholders. These are what the company owes and also identify where the amounts owed come from.

Stockholders' equity: the owners' stake in the company.

Assets and liabilities are classified as current or long-term information. In the basic accounting model, assets match the sum total of liabilities and stockholders' equity. An example of an E&P company balance sheet is shown in **Fig. 2.9** on the next page.

Assets

Cash and cash equivalents are cash items that will be used within the operating cycle. Cash is principally all unrestricted, non-interest–bearing funds available on demand.

Short-term investments are classified as available for sale and are in highly liquid debt or equity securities. Those investments that are part of the company's cash management portfolio with original maturities of three months or less are reported as "cash equivalents." The balance of the short-term investments is reported as "marketable securities." Short-term investments are market-to-market, with any unrealized gains or losses included in other comprehensive income.

Inventories include crude oil in storage; petroleum products and chemicals are stated at cost, using a last-in, first-out (LIFO) method. In the aggregate, these costs are below market. Materials, supplies and other inventories are generally stated at average cost.

Long-term receivables are receivables that will not be collected within one year.

Investments and advances are in stock of nonconsolidated entities, joint ventures or trade accounts not collectible within one year.

Property, plant and equipment (PP&E) are carried at cost. Depreciation of PP&E, other than oil and gas properties, is generally computed on a straight-line basis over the estimated economic lives of the facilities, which for major assets range from 14 to 25 years.[10]

Millions of dollars		
ASSETS		
Cash and cash equivalents	$1,896	$1,345
Marketable securities	734	687
Accounts and notes receivable (less allowance 2000 – $30, 1999 – $36)	3,837	3,688
Inventories:		
Crude oil and petroleum products	631	585
Chemicals	191	526
Materials, supplies and other	250	291
	1,072	1,402
Prepaid expenses and other current assets	674	1,175
TOTAL CURRENT ASSETS	$8,213	$8,297
Long-term receivables	802	815
Investments and advances	8,107	5,231
Properties, plant and equipment, at cost	51,908	54,212
Loss: accumulated depreciation, depletion and amortization	29,014	28,825
	22,894	28,825
Deferred charges and other assets	1,248	1,006
TOTAL ASSETS	$41,264	$40,668
LIABILITIES AND STOCKHOLDERS' EQUITY		
Short-term debt	$1,079	$3,434
Accounts payable	3,163	3,103
Accrued liabilities	1,530	1,210
Federal and other taxes or income	1,479	718
Other taxes payable	423	424
TOTAL CURRENT LIABILITIES	$7,674	$8,089
Long-term debt	4,872	5,134
Capital lease obligations	281	371
Deferred credits and other noncurrent obligations	1,768	1,739
Noncurrent deferred income taxes	4,908	5,070
Reserves for employee benefit plans	1,836	1,796
TOTAL LIABILITIES	$21,339	$22,919
Preferred stock (authorized 100,000,000 shares, $1.00 per value, none issued)	–	–
Common stock (authorized 2,000,000,000 shares, $0.75 per value at December 31, 2000, and 1,000,000 shares, $1.50 per value at December 31, 1999; 712,487,068 shares issued)	534	1,069
Capital in excess of par value	2,758	2,215
Deferred compensation	(611)	(546)
Accumulated other comprehensive income	(180)	(115)
Retained earnings	$20,909	$17,400
Treasury stocks, at cost (2000 – 71,427,097 share; 1999 – 56,140,994 shares)	$(3,385)	$(2,134)

Fig. 2.9
E&P company balance sheet.

Capitalization of exploration costs can be treated using either the full cost method or successful efforts method. With the full cost method, all exploration costs are taken in the financial period in which they occur. With the successful efforts method, which is the most common, the costs for all development wells, related plant and equipment, and proved mineral interests in oil and gas properties are capitalized. Costs of exploratory wells are capitalized pending determination of whether the wells found proved reserves. Costs of wells that are assigned proved reserves remain capitalized. Costs are also capitalized for wells that find commercially producible reserves that cannot be classified as proved.[11,12]

Deferred charges and other assets are purchased goodwill (excess of cost over net assets of an acquired business), patents, know-how, and intellectual property and contract rights originating in the acquisition of a business. These costs are amortized over the estimated life of that specific asset.

Liabilities

Liabilities are amounts due to parties external to the company.

Short-term debt will be settled within the next year through the use of a current asset or by incurring another current liability for the portion of long-term debt due within one year.

Accounts payable are amounts owed to suppliers, such as your company.

Accrued liabilities are amounts owed to others, interest on borrowings, legal fees, insurance premiums and similar items.

Federal and other taxes on income are accruals for taxes payable within one year.

Other taxes payable are taxes such as production taxes in some countries.

Long-term debt owed, but not due within the year, could be in the form of debentures (bonds backed by the credit of the corporation), secured debt (collateralized loans) and mortgages (debt secured by land or buildings).

Capital lease obligations are liabilities for lease commitments.

Concurrent deferred taxes on income reflect the cumulative difference between tax expenses and taxes payable resulting from transactions in current or past periods that is taxable in future periods.

Reserves for employee benefit plans are liabilities such as pensions and deferred post-retirement benefits.

Stockholders' Equity

Stockholders' equity includes all claims by the owners of the business. It consists of three main components.

Issued preferred and common stock for cash consideration is the main mechanism for bringing owners' capital into the business.

Capital reserves are all surpluses accruing to the common shareholders that have not arisen from normal business trading transactions, such as the revaluation of assets or premiums on shares issued in excess of par value. It may also include debits such as deferred compensation and other accumulated comprehensive income.

Revenue reserves are earnings retained by the company after dividends have been paid to the shareholders. Over time, these reserves build up and are usually used by companies to fund growth. They may also include treasury stock, which is stock the company has repurchased from the market.

Common Values Referred to on the Balance Sheet

These values are typically compared from one year's balance sheet to the next:

Total assets refer to the sum of current and fixed assets.

Capital employed is the balance of total assets less current liabilities. From the example in Fig. 2.9, capital employed for the year (FTY) 2000 is $33,590 [$41,264 (total assets)–$7,674 (total current liabilities)]. Capital employed is the long-term foundation of the company.

Net worth is total assets less total liabilities, which is another way of expressing stockholders' equity except that this definition puts emphasis on the validity of the asset values.

Working capital is total current assets less total current liabilities. This is a measure of the company's liquidity, which is an indicator of cash availability. From the example in Figure 2.9, working capital FTY 2000 is $539 [$8,213 (total current assets)–$7,674 (total current assets)].

Statement of Income Report

The statement of income report records the financial performance of the business over a specified period of time. Produced monthly by management, it includes financial data and statistics and is reported on an annual basis in the annual

Millions of dollars, except per-share amounts	2000	1999	Year ended December 31 1998
REVENUES AND OTHER INCOME			
Sales and other operating revenues	$ 50,592	$ 35,448	$ 29,943
Income from equity affiliates	750	526	228
Other income	787	612	386
TOTAL REVENUES AND OTHER INCOME	52,129	36,586	30,557
COSTS AND OTHER DEDUCTIONS			
Purchased crude oil and products	27,292	17,982	14,036
Operating expenses	5,177	5,090	4,834
Selling, general and administrative expenses	1,725	1,404	2,239
Exploration expenses	564	538	478
Depreciation, depletion and amortization	2,848	2,866	2,320
Taxes other than on income	4,793	4,586	4,411
Interest and debt expenses	460	472	405
TOTAL COSTS AND OTHER DEDUCTIONS	42,859	32,938	28,723
INCOME BEFORE INCOME TAX EXPENSE	9,270	3,648	1,834
INCOME TAX EXPENSE	4,085	1,578	495
NET INCOME	5,185	2,070	1,339
NET INCOME PER SHARE OF COMMON STOCK–BASIC	7.98	3.16	2.05
DILUTED	7.97	3.14	2.04

Fig. 2.10
Statement of income report.

report. This statement is the link between the opening and closing balance sheets of a specified period. It identifies total revenues earned and total costs incurred over the period. The difference is the operating profit or income. An example income statement for an E&P company is shown in **Fig. 2.10**.

Revenue and other income are invoiced during the period specified and includes any income from equity affiliates.

Other income includes gains from sales of assets and interest earned from investments.

Costs and other deductions are those costs that relate directly to revenue, such as the purchase of crude oil, gas and products. Operating expenses include costs that relate to the time period covered by the accounts, such as administrative expenses, expenses resulting from unsuccessful exploration activities, depreciation, depletion and amortization, non-income tax expenses, and interest and debt expense.

Income tax expense is the tax paid on taxable income.

Net income is measured from normal operating transactions.

Common Values Referred to on the Income Statement

These values are typically compared from one year's income statement to the next. Each of these values relates to the way profit is distributed to the major interests in the company—namely, lenders, government and shareholders. These values are as follows:

- Profit before interest and tax **(PBIT)**
- Profit before tax **(PBT)**
- Profit after tax **(PAT)**
- Retained earnings **(RE)**

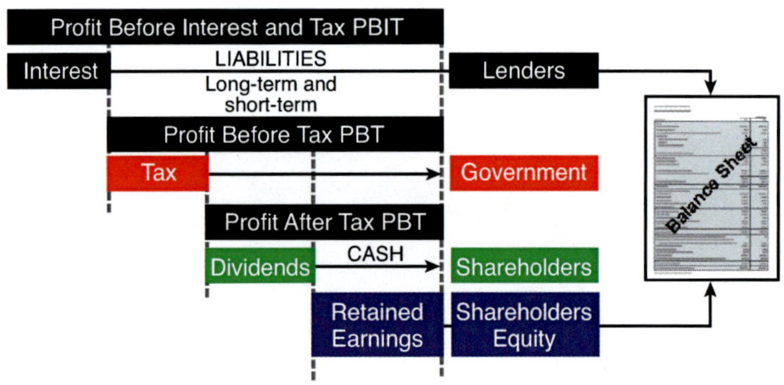

Fig. 2.11
Profit flow and stakeholders.

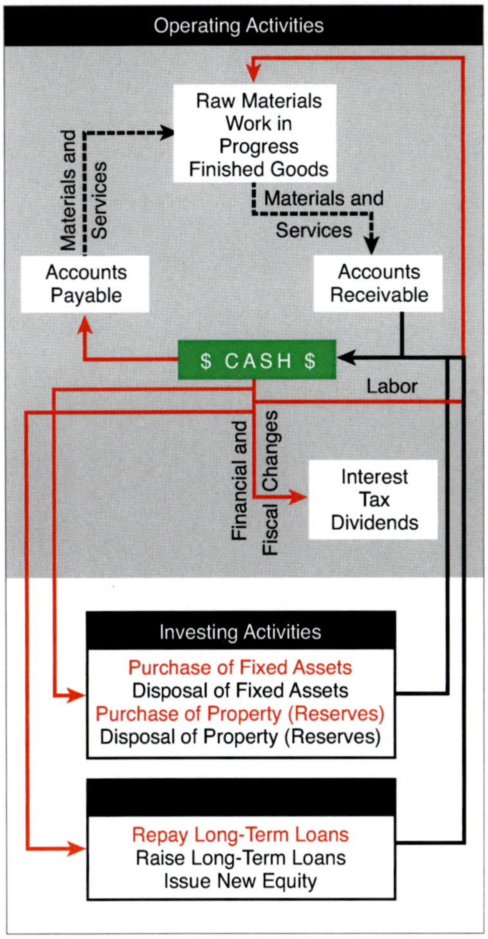

Fig. 2.12 (above)
Main components of corporate cash flow report. The red lines represent uses of cash, and the black lines represent sources. The CASH box consists of profits plus any non-cash flow items such as depreciation of fixed assets, depletion credits for produced hydrocarbons, and expenses taken for unsuccessful exploration programs from previous years. One of the main differences for an E&P company from other companies such as a services company is the additional non-cash flow items to depreciation that an E&P company adds back in to compute operating cash flow.

The order reflects the order of appropriation of the profits, as depicted in **Fig. 2.11.**

Cash Flow Statement

The cash flow statement records changes in cash and equivalents resulting from the following:

- Operating activities
- Investing activities
- Financing activities

Figure 2.12 (left) illustrates the basic components of cash flow as found on the corporate cash flow statement.

Figure 2.13 (below) is a cash flow statement for an E&P company. The individual components of the statement of cash are described below.

Operating activities are the net operating income and any adjustments (gains or losses) made for Depreciation, Depletion and Amortization (DD&A)[13], previous years' dry hole expenses, distributions from any equity affiliates, sales of assets, net change from foreign currency exchange, changes in operating capital resulting from changes in accounts and notes receivable, inventories, prepaid expenses and current assets, accounts payable and accrued liabilities, and other income or non-income taxes payable, and provisions made.

Investing activities include capital expenditures, proceeds from asset sales, sales of marketable securities, purchase of short-term investments, and distributions from any other affiliates.

CONSOLIDATED STATEMENT OF CASH FLOWS	Year ended December 31		
Millions of dollars	2000	1999	1998
OPERATING ACTIVITIES			
Net income	$ 5,185	$ 2,070	$ 1,339
Adjustments			
Depreciation, depletion and amortization	2,848	2,866	2,320
Dry hole expense related to prior years' expenditures	52	126	40
Distributions (less than) greater than income from equity affiliates	(154)	(258)	25
Net before-tax gains on asset retirements and sales	(236)	(471)	(45)
Net foreign currency (gains) losses	(67)	23	(20)
Deferred income tax provision	408	226	266
Net decrease (increase) in operating working capital[1]	846	636	(809)
Decrease (increase) in Cities Service provision	–	(149)	924
Cash settlement of Cities Service litigation	–	(775)	
Other, net	(220)	187	(309)
NET CASH PROVIDED BY OPERATING ACTIVITIES[2]	8,662	4,481	3,731
INVESTING ACTIVITIES			
Capital expenditures	(3,657)	(4,366)	(3,880)
Proceeds from asset sales	524	992	434
Net sales (purchases) of marketable securities[1]	35	262	(183)
Net purchase of other short-term investments	(84)	–	–
Distribution from Chevron Phillips Chemical Company	835	–	–
Other, net	(73)	32	(230)
NET CASH USED FOR INVESTING ACTIVITIES	(2,420)	(3,080)	(3,859)
FINANCING ACTIVITIES			
Net (repayments) borrowings of short-term obligations	(3,657)	(4,366)	(3,880)
Proceeds from issuances of long-term debt	524	992	434
Repayments of long-term debt and other financing obligations	35	262	(183)
Cash dividends paid	(84)	–	–
Net (purchases) sales of treasury shares	(73)	32	(230)
NET CASH USED FOR FINANCING ACTIVITIES	(5,693)	(626)	(308)
EFFECT OF FOREIGN CURRENCY EXCHANGE RATE CHANGES ON CASH AND CASH EQUIVALENTS	2	1	(10)
NET CHANGE IN CASH AND CASH EQUIVALENTS	551	776	(446)
CASH AND CASH EQUIVALENTS AT BEGINNING OF YEAR	1,345	569	1,015
CASH AND CASH EQUIVALENTS AT YEAR-END	$ 1,896	$ 1,345	$ 569

Fig. 2.13
An E&P company statement of cash flows.

Financing activities include net borrowings of short-term loans, proceeds from the issuance of long-term debt, repayments of long-term debt and other financing obligations, dividends paid, and net purchase or sales of treasury shares.

Net change in cash and cash equivalents[14] are the total of the above activities.

Cash and cash equivalents at the beginning of year are the balance as of the end of the preceding year.

Cash and cash equivalents at year-end is the balance of cash and cash equivalents for the reporting year.

Supplemental Information on Oil and Gas Producing Activities

Evaluating the economic performance of oil and gas producing companies cannot be achieved using financial statements alone. The information contained in these reports can be reviewed to gain insight into upstream investment in terms of upstream capital expenditures and production replacement, which measures attempts to replace produced volumes of hydrocarbons.[15]

The reporting requirement provides supplemental information on oil and gas exploration and producing activities of the company in six separate tables. Tables I through III provide historical cost information pertaining to costs incurred in exploration, property acquisitions and development; capitalized costs; and results of operations. Tables IV through VI present information on the company's estimated net proved reserve quantities, standardized measure of estimated discounted future net cash flows related to proved reserves, and changes in estimated discounted future net cash flows. Examples of these tables are shown in **Figs. 2.14 through 2.20** on the subsequent pages.

Costs Incurred in Exploration, Property Acquisition and Development

This table includes all costs for both consolidated companies and affiliates, broken down by major operating areas. Costs included are those incurred in exploration, property acquisitions and development presented with the previous two years' results for comparison. The table includes all costs, whether capitalized or expensed. Table I (Fig. 2.14) gives a breakdown of capitalized costs. Brief descriptions of each major cost category are listed below.

Exploration costs are incurred in identifying areas that may warrant examination and in examining specific areas that are considered to have prospects containing oil and gas reserves, including costs of drilling exploratory wells and exploratory-type stratigraphic test wells.

Property acquisitions include costs for acquisitions of proved properties, such as costs incurred to purchase or otherwise acquire proved oil and gas reserves in place. Costs for acquisition of unproved properties include costs incurred to purchase, lease or otherwise acquire a property, including costs of lease bonuses and options to purchase or lease properties.

Development costs are costs incurred to obtain access to proved reserves and to provide facilities for extracting, treating, gathering and storing oil and gas. More specifically, development costs include the depreciation and applicable operating costs of support equipment and facilities, as well as other costs of development activities.

TABLE I – COSTS INCURRED IN EXPLORATION, PROPERTY ACQUISITIONS AND DEVELOPMENT							
	Consolidated Companies				Affiliated Companies		
Millions of dollars	U.S.	Africa	Other	Total	OPS	TCO	Worldwide
YEAR ENDED DECEMBER 31, 2000							
Exploration							
Wells	366	40	129	535	5	–	540
Geological and geophysical	30	25	149	149	14	–	163
Rentals and other	36	11	65	112	–	–	112
Total exploration	432	76	288	796	19	–	815
Property acquisitions							
Proved	24	1	–	25	–	–	25
Unproved	61	9	175	245	–	–	245
Total property acquisitions	85	10	175	270	–	–	270
Development	737	395	356	1,488	168	240	1,896
TOTAL COSTS INCURRED	1,254	481	819	2,554	187	240	2,981
YEAR ENDED DECEMBER 31, 1999							
Exploration							
Wells	258	40	120	418	3	–	421
Geological and geophysical	37	25	85	147	17	–	164
Rentals and other	30	7	60	97	–	–	97
Total exploration	325	72	265	562	20	–	682
Property acquisitions							
Proved[4]	9	–	1,070	1,079	–	–	1,079
Unproved	27	11	1,202	1,240	–	–	1,240
Total property acquisitions	36	11	2,272	2,319	–	–	2,319
Development	532	518	375	1,425	182	148	1,755
TOTAL COSTS INCURRED	893	601	2,912	4,406	202	148	4,756
YEAR ENDED DECEMBER 31, 1999							
Exploration							
Wells	350	108	101	559	3	–	562
Geological and geophysical	49	31	112	192	16	–	208
Rentals and other	44	23	53	120	–	–	120
Total exploration	443	162	266	871	19	–	890
Property acquisitions							
Proved	12	–	–	12	–	–	12
Unproved	58	–	14	72	–	–	72
Total property acquisitions	70	–	14	84	–	–	84
Development	680	561	411	1,652	156	120	1,928
TOTAL COSTS INCURRED	1,193	723	691	2,607	175	120	2,902

Fig. 2.14
Cost incurred in exploration property acquisitions and development.[16]

Capitalized Costs Related to Oil and Gas Producing Activities

Table II (Fig. 2.15, next page) gives a breakdown of the original capitalized costs for oil and gas producing activities for both consolidated companies and affiliates, broken down by major operating areas for the current reporting period and the previous two years' data for comparison. In this table, the data are presented for unproved and proved properties. A brief description of what each major cost category includes is listed.

Gross capitalized costs include the original depreciation, depletion and amortization costs booked. Capitalized costs for proved and unproved properties include the costs as described in Table I. Support equipment is the capitalized cost of equipment used in operations for both proved and unproved properties. Deferred exploratory wells are the capitalized costs of exploration activities for properties that have yet to be determined as containing producible reserves. Other capitalized costs are for uncompleted exploration projects.

Accumulated depreciation costs include the accumulated credits taken against revenue for items in the gross capitalized costs.

TABLE II – CAPITALIZED COSTS RELATED TO OIL AND GAS PRODUCING ACTIVITIES

	Consolidated Companies				Affiliated Companies		
Millions of dollars	U.S.	Africa	Other	Total	OPS	TCO	Worldwide
AT DECEMBER 31, 2000							
Unproved properties	337	78	1,459	1,874	–	378	2,252
Proved properties and related producing assets	16,713	4,621	8,346	29,680	1,370	1,158	32,208
Support equipment	469	308	280	1,067	906	254	2,217
Deferred exploratory wells	101	204	95	400	–	–	400
Other uncompleted projects	348	640	476	1,464	255	136	1,865
GROSS CAPITALIZED COSTS	17,968	5,851	10,656	34,475	2,541	1,.926	38,942
Unproved properties valuation	128	59	219	406	–	–	406
Proved producing properties							
Depreciation and depletion	11,991	2,363	3,774	18,128	751	131	19,010
Future abandonment and restoration	778	400	227	1,405	63	13	1,481
Support equipment depreciation	315	127	172	614	535	97	1,246
Accumulated provisions	13,212	2,949	4,392	20,553	1,349	241	22,143
NET CAPITALIZED COSTS	4,756	2,902	6,264	13,922	1,192	1,685	16,799
AT DECEMBER 31, 1999							
Unproved properties	317	69	1,441	1,827	–	378	2,205
Proved properties and related producing assets	16,662	4,034	7,318	28,014	1,158	689	29,861
Support equipment	478	268	321	1,067	902	243	2,212
Deferred exploratory wells	136	132	66	374	–	–	374
Other uncompleted projects	354	758	664	1,775	335	405	2,516
GROSS CAPITALIZED COSTS	17,947	5,301	9,810	33,058	2,395	1,715	37,168
Unproved properties valuation	133	53	157	343	–	–	343
Proved producing properties							
Depreciation and depletion	11,953	1,993	3,071	17,017	681	99	17,797
Future abandonment and restoration	835	371	208	1,414	60	10	1,484
Support equipment depreciation	317	104	142	563	476	80	1,819
Accumulated provisions	13,238	2,521	3,578	19,337	1,287	789	20,743
NET CAPITALIZED COSTS	4,709	2,780	6,232	13,721	1,178	1,526	16,425
AT DECEMBER 31, 1998							
Unproved properties	390	58	235	683	–	378	1,061
Proved properties and related producing assets	16,759	3,672	6,253	26,684	1,015	629	28,328
Support equipment	432	182	307	961	768	232	1,961
Deferred exploratory wells	51	51	91	193	–	–	193
Other uncompleted projects	700	893	383	1,975	408	245	2,629
GROSS CAPITALIZED COSTS	18,372	4,856	7,269	30,497	2,191	1,434	34,172
Unproved properties valuation	151	49	110	310	–	–	310
Proved producing properties							
Depreciation and depletion	11,808	1,719	2,705	16,232	689	32	16,993
Future abandonment and restoration	851	337	187	1,385	57	8	1,450
Support equipment depreciation	315	90	127	532	373	67	932
Accumulated provisions	13,135	2,195	3,129	18,450	1,189	347	19,725
NET CAPITALIZED COSTS	5,237	2,861	4,140	12,038	1,072	1,337	14,447

Fig. 2.15
Capitalized costs related to oil and gas producing activities.

Results of Operations for Oil and Gas Producing Activities

Table III has two parts (Figs. 2.16 and 2.17). The first part (Fig. 2.16) gives a breakdown of the operating performance for oil and gas producing activities for both consolidated companies and affiliates, broken down by major operating areas for the current reporting period and the previous two years' data for comparison. Interest income and expenses are excluded from the results. The costs, which are included in each line item, are as described in the earlier tables. Line items not yet described are listed below.

The second part of Table III (Fig. 2.17) lists the average sales price obtained for oil and gas sales and the average production costs per barrel of oil equivalent for the current and previous two years. It also shows the average price received for oil and gas as of the end of the year for the current and previous two years.

Sales are the revenues received for the sales of oil and gas.

Transfers are the company's shares of revenue received from minority interests in non-operated fields.

Production costs[17] are the costs incurred to operate and maintain wells and related equipment and facilities, including depreciation and applicable operating costs of support equipment and facilities, and other costs of operating and main-

TABLE III – RESULTS OF OPERATIONS FOR OIL AND GAS PRODUCING ACTIVITIES

Per-unit average sales price and production costs.	U.S.	Africa	Other	Total	CPI	TCO	Worldwide
	Consolidated Companies				Affiliated Companies		
YEAR ENDED DECEMBER 31, 2000							
Average sales price							
Liquids, per barrel	$ 26.35	$ 26.75	$ 26.67	$ 26.59	$ 22.41	$ 20.14	$ 25.63
Natural gas, per thousand cubic feet	4.04	0.03	2.98	3.65	–	0.13	3.55
Average production costs, per barrel	5.37	2.99	3.80	4.27	5.67	2.91	4.28
YEAR ENDED DECEMBER 31, 1999							
Average sales price							
Liquids, per barrel	$ 15.73	$ 17.27	$ 17.69	$ 16.82	$ 13.40	$ 10.53	$ 15.90
Natural gas, per thousand cubic feet	2.17	0.05	2.21	2.14	–	0.38	2.10
Average production costs, per barrel	4.73	2.81	3.32	3.84	4.47	2.39	3.79
YEAR ENDED DECEMBER 31, 1998							
Average sales price							
Liquids, per barrel	$ 11.27	$ 11.49	$ 11.21	$ 11.34	$ 9.73	$ 5.53	$ 10.68
Natural gas, per thousand cubic feet	2.02	0.07	2.26	2.04	–	0.57	2.01
Average production costs, per barrel	5.30	2.94	2.93	4.12	3.10	2.32	3.91
Average sales price for liquids ($/Bbl)							
December 2000	$ 25.41	$ 23.23	$ 24.87	$ 24.43	$ 22.33	$ 24.39	$ 24.21
December 1999	22.25	24.88	24.06	23.68	23.68	11.55	22.65
December 1998	8.86	9.55	9.04	9.17	8.33	3.69	8.58
Average sales price for natural gas ($/MCF)							
December 2000	$ 7.70	$ 0.04	$ 4.16	$ 6.47	–	$ 0.25	$ 6.19
December 1999	2.02	0.04	2.41	2.23	–	0.38	2.18
December 1998	2.23	–	2.47	2.29	–	0.57	2.26

Fig. 2.16
Results of operations for oil and gas producing activities.

SUPPLEMENTAL INFORMATION ON OIL AND GAS PRODUCING ACTIVITIES

TABLE III – RESULTS OF OPERATIONS FOR OIL AND GAS PRODUCING ACTIVITIES

Millions of dollars	U.S.	Africa	Other	Total	CPI	TCO	Worldwide
	Consolidated Companies				Affiliated Companies		
YEAR ENDED DECEMBER 31, 2000							
Sales	$ 2,496	$ 2,804	$ 2,351	$ 7,653	$ 50	$ 710	$ 8,413
Transfers	2,762	506	952	4,220	831	–	5,051
Total	5,260	3,310	3,303	11,873	881	710	13,464
Production expenses	(1,112)	(378)	(520)	(2,010)	(223)	(114)	(2,347)
Proved producing properties depreciation, depletion and abandonment provisions	(862)	(316)	(619)	(1,797)	(129)	(53)	(1,979)
Exploration expenses	(265)	(62)	(237)	(564)	(14)	–	(578)
Unproved properties valuation	(22)	(6)	(82)	(110)	–	–	(110)
Other income (expenses)	(26)	61	243	278	(2)	(56)	220
Results before income taxes	2,973	2,609	2,088	7,670	513	487	8,670
Income tax expense	(1,100)	(1,942)	(924)	(3,956)	(258)	(146)	(4,370)
RESULTS OF PRODUCING OPERATIONS	$ 1,873	$ 667	$ 1,164	$ 3,704	$ 255	$ 341	$ 4,300
YEAR ENDED DECEMBER 31, 1999							
Revenues from net production							
Sales	$ 1,449	$ 1,156	$ 1,415	$ 4,620	$ 24	$ 356	$ 5,000
Transfers	1,626	299	597	2,522	592	–	3,114
Total	3,075	2,055	2,012	7,142	616	356	8,114
Production expenses	(1,005)	(340)	(411)	(3,756)	(206)	(88)	(2,050)
Proved producing properties depreciation, depletion and abandonment provisions	(764)	(311)	(433)	(1,508)	(109)	(47)	(1,664)
Exploration expenses	(161)	(91)	(214)	(538)	(17)	–	(555)
Unproved properties valuation	(22)	(5)	(36)	(63)	–	–	(63)
Other income (expenses)	(358)	(53)	5	(406)	(2)	(9)	(417)
Results before income taxes	759	1,249	863	2,871	282	212	3,365
Income tax expense	(257)	(848)	(416)	(8,521)	(143)	(63)	(3,327)
RESULTS OF PRODUCING OPERATIONS	$ 502	$ 401	$ 417	$ 1,350	$ 139	$ 149	$ 1,638
YEAR ENDED DECEMBER 31, 1998							
Revenues from net production							
Sales	$ 1,368	$ 1,118	$ 757	$ 3,261	$ 28	$ 175	$ 3,465
Transfers	1,185	212	458	1,855	454	–	2,309
Total	2,571	1,330	1,215	5,116	482	176	5,774
Production expenses	(1,132)	(346)	(304)	(1,822)	(153)	(76)	(2,051)
Proved producing properties depreciation, depletion and abandonment provisions	(714)	(301)	(316)	(3,338)	(106)	(40)	(1,477)
Exploration expenses	(213)	(53)	(212)	(478)	(96)	–	(494)
Unproved properties valuation	(20)	(8)	(16)	(44)	–	–	(84)
Other income (expenses)	54	48	85	187	2	(7)	182
Results before income taxes	506	670	452	4,608	209	53	1,890
Income tax expense	(163)	(328)	(323)	(814)	(102)	(16)	(932)
RESULTS OF PRODUCING OPERATIONS	$ 343	$ 342	$ 129	$ 814	$ 107	$ 37	$ 958

Fig. 2.17
Results of operations for oil and gas producing activities, part 2.

taining those wells and related equipment and facilities. They become part of the cost of oil and gas produced. These costs are also referred to as lifting costs.

Reserve Quantity Information

Table IV (Fig. 2.18) gives a breakdown of the net proved reserves for combined crude oil, condensate and natural gas liquids combined and in separate columns for natural gas. These volumes are shown for both consolidated companies and

TABLE IV – RESERVE QUANTITY INFORMATION

	NET PROVED RESERVES OF CRUDE OIL, CONDENSATE AND NATURAL GAS LIQUIDS Millions of barrels							NET PROVED RESERVES OF NATURAL GAS Billions of cubic feet						
	Consolidated Companies				Affiliates		World wide	Consolidated Companies				Affiliates		World wide
	U.S.	Africa	Other	Total	CPI	TCO		U.S.	Africa	Other	Total	CPI	TCO	
RESERVES AT DECEMBER 31, 1998	1,196	1,131	519	2,846	578	1,082	4,506	4,991	223	3,187	8,401	161	1,401	9,963
Charges attributable to:														
Revisions	(1)	106	28	133	110	7	250	(151)	77	13	(61)	7	(17)	(71)
Improved recovery	38	88	36	160	25	–	185	7	–	–	7	12	–	19
Extensions and discoveries	43	92	7	142	2	16	160	372	–	3	375	1	21	397
Purchases	5	–	30	35	–	–	35	32	–	5	37	–	–	37
Sales	(12)	–	(22)	(34)	–	–	(34)	(119)	–	(50)	(189)	–	–	(189)
Production	(119)	(117)	(77)	(313)	(62	(30)	(405)	(635)	(12)	(175)	(822)	(30)	(21)	(873)
RESERVES AT JANUARY 1, 1998	1,148	1,300	521	2,969	653	1,075	4,697	4,497	288	2,963	7,768	151	1,384	9,303
Charges attributable to:														
Revisions	(23)	3	(24)	(44)	(98)	115	(27)	(426)	49	30	(347)	2	126	(219)
Improved recovery	44	62	20	126	30	–	156	7	–	8	15	1	–	16
Extensions and discoveries	50	45	17	112	2	76	190	347	–	86	433	5	98	536
Purchases	1	–	213	214	–	–	214	35	–	372	407	–	–	407
Sales	(33)	–	(2)	(35)	–	–	(35	(74)	–	–	(74)	–	–	(74))
Production	(115)	(120)	(84)	(319)	(59)	(33)	(411)	(598)	(15)	(248)	(861)	(25)	(27)	(913)
RESERVES AT DECEMBER 31, 1999	1,072	1,290	661	3,023	528	1,233	4,784	3,788	322	3,231	7,341	134	1,581	9,056
Charges attributable to:														
Revisions	(5)	56	4	55	35	106	195	(29)	450	140	561	8	126	695
Improved recovery	58	20	9	87	16	–	103	12	–	6	17	–	–	17
Extensions and discoveries	46	92	65	203	2	7	212	405	1	371	777	4	9	790
Purchases	5	131	3	139	–	–	139	18	12	–	30	–	–	30
Sales	(8)	–	–	(8)	–	–	(8)	(131)	–	(1	(132)	–	–	(132)
Production	(114)	(53)	(212)	(478)	(96)	–	(494)							
RESERVES AT DECEMBER 31, 2000	1,054	1,465	644	3,163	528	1,310	5,001	3,493	768	3,486	7,747	122	1,683	9,552
Developed Reserves														
At January 1, 1998	1,025	721	293	2,039	435	532	3,006	4,391	223	1,695	6,309	145	688	7,142
At December 31, 1998	982	891	342	2,215	436	646	3,297	3,918	283	2,074	6,255	135	832	7,222
At December 31, 1999	906	940	489	2,334	340	750	3,464	3,345	272	2,243	5,860	131	1,011	7,002
AT DECEMBER 31, 2000	981	943	460	2,284	327	795	3,406	3,109	290	2,929	6,328	121	1,019	7,468

Fig. 2.18
Reserve quantity information.

affiliates, broken down by major operating areas for the current reporting period and the previous two years' data for comparison. The last section shows the volumes of developed reserves. Line items are described below.

Proved oil and gas reserves[18] are the estimated quantities of crude oil, natural gas and natural gas liquids, which geological and engineering data demonstrate with reasonable certainty to be recoverable in future years from known reservoirs, under existing economic and operating conditions (i.e., prices and costs as of the date the estimate is made). Prices include the consideration of changes in existing prices provided by fixed contractual arrangements, but not escalations based upon future conditions (e.g., inflation).

Reservoirs are considered proved if economic producibility is supported by either actual production or conclusive formation test. The area of a reservoir considered proved includes 1) that portion delineated by drilling and defined by gas–oil or oil–water or both contacts, if any, and 2) the immediately adjoining portions not yet drilled, but which can be reasonably judged as economically productive on the basis of available geological and engineering data. In the absence of information on fluid contacts, the lowest known structural occurrence of hydrocarbons controls the lower proved limit of a reservoir.

Reserves that can be produced economically through the application of improved recovery techniques (such as fluid injection) are included in the "proved" classification when successful testing by a pilot project, or the operation of an installed program in the reservoir, provides support for the engineering analysis on which the project or program was based.[19]

Changes in proved reserves include the following:

Revisions of previous estimates. Revisions represent changes in previous estimates of proved reserves, either upward or downward, resulting from new information (except for an increase in proved acreage) normally obtained from development drilling and production history or resulting from a change in economic factors.

Improved recovery. This improvement refers to changes in reserve estimates resulting from the application of improved recovery techniques.

Extensions and discoveries. These additions are to proved reserves and result from the extension of the proved acreage of previously discovered (old) reservoirs through additional drilling periods subsequent to discovery and the discovery of new fields with proved reserves or of new reservoirs of proved reserves in old fields.

Developed reserves. These reserves can be expected to be recovered through existing wells with existing equipment and operating methods. Additional oil and gas expected to be obtained through the application of fluid injection or other improved recovery techniques for supplementing the natural forces and mechanisms of primary recovery should be included as "proved developed reserves" only after testing by a pilot project or after the operation of an installed program has confirmed through production response that increased recovery will be achieved.[20]

Standardized Measure of Discounted Future Net Cash Flows Related to Proved Oil and Gas Reserves

Tables V and VI look at the standardized measure of discounted future net cash flows as related to proved oil and gas reserves (Figs. 2.19 and 2.20). The first table is a standardized measure of discounted future net cash flows, related to the above proved oil and gas reserves, broken down by major operating areas for the current reporting period and the previous two years' data for comparison.

TABLE V – STANDARDIZED MEASURE OF DISCOUNTED FUTURE NET CASH FLOWS RELATED TO PROVED OIL & GAS RESERVES

	Consolidated Companies				Affiliated Companies		
Millions of dollars	U.S.	Africa	Other	Total	CPI	TCO	Worldwide
AT DECEMBER 31, 2000							
Future cash inflows from production	$ 60,830	$ 33,950	$ 27,490	$ 122,270	$ 12,700	$ 30,350	$ 165,320
Future production and development costs	(13,610)	(7,740)	(6,410)	(27,760)	(8,560)	(7,250)	(43,570)
Future income taxes	(16,590)	(15,690)	(7,720)	(40,000)	(1,720)	(6,440)	(48,160)
Undiscounted future net cash flows	30,630	10,520	13,360	54,510	2,420	16,660	73,590
10 percent midyear annual discount for timing of estimated cash flows	(12,340)	(4,130)	(5,210)	(21,680)	(930)	(11,180)	(33,790)
STANDARDIZED MEASURE OF DISCOUNTED FUTURE NET CASH FLOWS	$ 18,290	$ 6,390	$ 8,150	$ 32,830	$ 1,490	$ 5,480	$ 39,800
AT DECEMBER 31, 1999							
Future cash inflows from production	$ 31,650	$ 31,830	$ 23,690	$ 87,170	$ 11,950	$ 24,380	$ 123,500
Future production and development costs	(11,350)	(6,030)	(5,420)	(22,800)	(7,830)	(4,900)	(35,530)
Future income taxes	(7,050)	(16,490)	(6,200)	(29,740)	(1,820)	(4,980)	(36,540)
Undiscounted future net cash flows	13,250	9,310	12,070	34,630	2,300	14,500	51,430
10 percent midyear annual discount for timing of estimated cash flows	(5,480)	(2,920)	(4,590)	(12,990)	(900)	(10,400)	(24,290)
Standardized measure of discounted future net cash flows	$ 7,770	$ 6,390	$ 7,480	$ 21,640	$ 1,400	$ 4,100	$ 27,140
YEAR ENDED DECEMBER 31, 1998							
Future cash inflows from production	$ 19,810	$ 12,560	$ 13,010	$ 45,380	$ 6,020	$ 8,360	$ 59,760
Future production and development costs	(12,940)	(6,980)	(4,930)	(24,850)	(4,470)	(5,860)	(35,180)
Future income taxes	(1,970)	(2,110)	(2,850)	(6,930)	(660)	(200)	(7,790)
Undiscounted future net cash flows	4,900	3,470	5,230	13,600	890	2,300	16,790
10 percent midyear annual discount for timing of estimated cash flows	(1,880)	(1,070)	(2,190)	(5,140)	(390)	(1,990)	(7,520)
Standardized measure of discounted future net cash flows	$ 3,020	$ 2,400	$ 3,040	$ 8,460	$ 500	$ 310	$ 9,270

Fig. 2.19
Discounted future net cash flows.

TABLE VI – CHANGES IN THE STANDARDIZED MEASURE OF DISCOUNTED FUTURE NET CASH FLOWS FROM PROVED RESERVES

	Consolidated Companies			Affiliated Companies			Worldwide		
Millions of dollars	2000	1999	1998	2000	1999	1998	2000	1999	1998
PRESENT VALUE AT JANUARY 1	21,640	8,460	13,110	5,500	810	1,890	27,140	9,270	15,000
Sales and transfers of oil and gas produced, net of production costs	(9,863)	(5,385)	(3,294)	(1,254)	(679)	(429)	(11,117)	(6,064)	(3,723)
Development costs incurred	1,488	1,425	1,652	408	330	275	1,896	1,755	1,928
Purchases of reserves	1,154	2,811	208	–	–	–	1,154	2,811	208
Sales of reserves	(1,020)	(344)	(347)	–	–	–	(1,020)	(344)	(347)
Extensions, discoveries and improved recovery, loss related costs	5,147	2,886	813	132	385	49	5,279	3,271	862
Revisions of previous quantity estimates	(1,093)	(503)	262	1,281	84	280	188	(419)	542
Net changes in price, development & prod. costs	17,105	25,457	(11,321)	625	6,938	(2,159)	17,730	32,195	(13,480)
Accretion of discount	3,672	1,165	2,096	817	135	289	4,489	1,300	2,385
Net change in income tax	(5,400)	(14,332)	5,281	(539)	(2,503)	614	(5,939)	(16,835)	5,895
Net change for the year	11,190	13,180	(4,650)	1,470	4,690	(1,080)	12,660	17,870	(5,730)
PRESENT VALUE AT DECEMBER 31	32,830	21,640	8,460	6,970	5,500	810	39,800	27,140	9,270

Fig. 2.20
Changes in future net cash flows.

Estimated future cash inflows from production are computed by applying year-end prices for oil and gas to year-end quantities of estimated net proved reserves. Future price changes are limited to those provided by contractual arrangements in existence at the end of each reporting year. Future development and production costs are those estimated future expenditures necessary to develop and produce year-end estimated proved reserves based on year-end cost indices, assuming continuation of year-end economic conditions. Estimated future income taxes are calculated by applying appropriate year-end statutory tax rates. These rates reflect allowable deductions and tax credits and are applied to estimated future pretax net cash flows, less the tax basis of related assets. Discounted future net cash flows are calculated using 10% mid-period discount factors. Discounting requires a year-by-year estimate of when future expenditures will be incurred and when reserves will be produced.

It is important to note that this information does not represent management's estimate of the company's expected future cash flows or value of proved oil and gas reserves. Estimates of proved reserve quantities are imprecise and change over time as new information becomes available. Moreover, probable and possible reserves, which may become proved in the future, are excluded from the calculations. Also, the calculation requires assumptions as to the timing and amount of future development and production costs. The calculations are made as of December 31 each year and should not be relied upon as an indication of the company's future cash flows or value of its oil and gas reserves.

Table VI, detailing the changes in the standardized measure of discounted future net cash flows from proved reserves, lists the changes in present values between years, which can be significant, and reflects changes in estimated proved reserve quantities and prices, and assumptions used in forecasting production volumes and costs. Changes in the timing of production are included with "Revisions of previous quantity estimates."[21]

Analyzing the Annual Report

From the annual report, you can derive the value drivers used and reported by companies[22] and begin to understand the data used by your customers to calculate those drivers.

Horizontal Analysis

Horizontal analysis compares two or more years of financial data. It highlights areas of focus and typically includes both dollar and percentage changes, as a single measurement may lead to false conclusions. Below are some of the more common items compared on a horizontal basis with previous years.

- Operating earnings income are generated by ongoing operations of the company, excluding special items or adjustments caused by changes in accounting principles. Oil and gas price fluctuations have tremendous effects on operating earnings compared from one year to another. In a good year, there will be additional monies for capital expenditures; in poorer years, cost management will take a higher profile in the following year.
- Capital and exploratory expenditures total the amount spent on related projects and should ensure future earnings growth if managed properly. Decreasing trends could be an early warning of future problems.

Vertical Analysis

Vertical analysis is also used on financial statements and supplemental statements. Annual report discussions use vertical analysis, which involves the expression of items in the statement as a percentage of the "base amount," such as balance sheet items as a percentage of total assets and expense items as a percentage of the total revenue on the income statement. Vertical analysis is a good technique for comparing results for competitors with industry averages.

Ratio Analysis

Ratio analysis allows for the measurement of the relationship between two single amounts. Examples include the following:

- Liquidity ratios
- Asset management ratios
- Profitability ratios
- Debt management ratios
- Market value ratios
- Liquidity ratios
- Operating ratios

Liquidity Ratios

Liquidity ratios show the firm's ability to meet its current obligations as they fall due. There are three common liquidity ratios:

- **Current ratio** measures the cover provided by current assets for current liabilities.

  Current ratio = current assets / current liabilities

  When a company is struggling, it slows payment to creditors and borrowings increase. A falling current ratio indicates trouble.
- **Quick ratio** measures the company's ability to pay off short-term obligations without relying on the sale of inventories.

  Quick ratio =
  (current assets – inventories) / current liabilities
- **Working capital to total assets ratio** indicates relative liquidity of total assets.

  Working capital to total assets =
  working capital / total assets

  where:

  Working capital = current assets – current liabilities

When looking at the liquidity of a company, these ratios are only the starting point of liquidity analysis. Other factors to be considered are the nature of the business, composition of the current assets, seasonal nature of the business and its effect on liquidity, probability of market values deviating materially from book values, and credit rating and ability to refinance short-term debts.

From this point, it is easy to see how your customers need to react decisively whenever there is a large negative price swing in oil and gas prices as their liquidity will be severely affected with large price changes from one year to the next.

Debt Management Ratios

This group of ratios measures the company's ability to manage debt or the solvency of the company. These ratios are a measurement of the risk to long-term creditors and shareholders. Commonly used ratios include the following:

- Gearing ratio
- Debt to total assets
- Times interest earned.

Gearing ratio is the relationship among different types of funds in a company, such as loans and equity. The higher the amount of loan funds, the higher the amount of fixed interest charge in the profit and loss account. Where interest charges are high, a small change in operating profit will have an increased result in return to equity for shareholders. This is compared on a horizontal basis with previous years.

Gearing ratio = total debt / total debt + total equity

Debt to total assets ratio is the percentage of assets financed other than by stockholders.

Debt to total assets = total liabilities / total assets

The lower the ratio, the greater the cushion for creditors. Shareholders, in contrast, can benefit from higher leverage because it magnifies earnings.

Times interest earned (TIE) ratio measures the extent to which operating income can decline before the company is unable to meet its interest costs. Significant levels of interest on debt relative to the company's annual operating income suggests that the company's borrowings are too high.

Times interest earned =
income before interest and taxes / interest charges

Profitability Ratios

This group of ratios shows the combined effects of liquidity, asset management and debt management on operating results. Commonly used ratios are as follows:

- Return on equity
- Return on capital employed
- Total stockholder return

Return on equity (ROE) is a measure of the percentage return generated by a company for the equity shareholders. It is calculated by expressing profit after tax as a percentage of shareholders' funds. Some experts argue that ROE drives company value.

Return on capital employed (ROCE) includes all long-term funds in the balance sheet—that is, shareholders' funds plus long-term loans plus miscellaneous long-term funds. ROCE is calculated by dividing net income before tax by the average of total debt and stockholders' equity for the year.

Total stockholder return is the return to stockholders from stock price appreciation and reinvested dividends for the reporting period.

Market Value Ratios

This set of ratios relates the company's stock price to its earnings and book value per share. These ratios are applicable for publicly traded companies. Commonly used ratios include the following:

- Price/earnings ratio
- Earnings per share
- Market/book ratio

Price/earnings (P/E) ratio shows how much investors are willing to pay per dollar of reported profits. The P/E ratio is calculated by dividing price per share by earnings per share. Generally, P/E ratios are higher for companies with high growth prospects, other things held constant, but they are lower for riskier companies.

Earnings per share (EPS) is the profit earned for the ordinary shareholder as shown in the profit and loss account divided by the number of issued ordinary shares. It is calculated by dividing net income by the total number of outstanding shares.

Market/book ratio gives an indication of how investors regard the company. Companies with relatively high rates of return on equity generally sell at higher multiples of book value than those with low returns. The market/book ratio is calculated by dividing the market price per share by the book value per share, whereas the book value per share is calculated by dividing common equity by outstanding shares.

Operations-Related Measurements

Each industry has a set of standard operating measures used to evaluate the performance of a business year-on-year and against peers and part of the annual report. In this section, the operations-related measures are specifically for oil and gas producing companies.

Operations-related measurements fall into three main categories:

- Reserves replacement costs (RRC)
- Reserves replacement ratio (RRR)
- Lifting costs

Reserves replacement costs include the following four main measurements.

Reserves replacement costs (RRC) are defined as the costs of proved reserves added through all means including all costs and all reserve additions related to extensions and discoveries, revisions, improved recovery and purchases of proved reserves. They are calculated by dividing the ratio of the costs described above by the additional proved reserves. The units are dollars per barrel of oil equivalent added.

Finding and development costs (FDC including revisions) are defined as the cost of proved reserve additions from extensions and discoveries, improved recovery and revisions, but excluding the effect of proved reserve purchases. FDC, including revisions, provides a separate and useful measure of performance in adding reserves with the drill bit, exclusive of costs and reserves added through proved property acquisitions. The units are dollars per barrel of oil equivalent added.

Finding and development costs (FDC excluding revisions) are defined as the cost of proved reserve additions from extensions and discoveries and improved recovery, but excluding the effect of revisions and proved reserve purchases. FDC, excluding revisions, provides another measure of adding reserves through the drill bit. The units are dollars per barrel of oil equivalent added.

Proved reserve acquisition costs (PRAC) are defined as the calculated cost of proved reserves added through purchases of proved properties. They are calculated by dividing the ratio of the costs described above by the additional proved reserves. The units are dollars per barrel of oil equivalent added.

Reserve replacement rates (RRR) are the ratio of added proven reserves divided by the annual production. RRR is a percentage of the additional reserves to the annual production.

Lifting costs per barrel or production costs are a key performance measure calculated by taking operating, selling, general and administrative expenses; adding own-use fuel costs; subtracting special items and expenses of divested operations; and then dividing by production and sales volumes. The units are dollars per produced barrel of oil equivalent.

WORLDWIDE PROVED RESERVE ACQUISITION COSTS (PRAC), FINDING & DEVELOPMENT COSTS (FDC) AND RESERVE REPLACEMENT COSTS (RRC). ALL COSTS IN $ PER BOE. PRODUCTION REPLACEMENT RATES IN %.

	2009	2010	2011	2012	2013	3-Year	5-year
PRAC	$ 4.28	$ 9.53	$ 8.85	$ 10.59	$ 5.20	$ 6.14	$ 6.48
FDC	12.84	17.82	16.88	21.77	22.00	20.13	18.30
RRC	11.68	16.24	15.93	20.69	14.19	16.33	15.54
RRR Oil (All sources)	119%	119%	147%	139%	219%	169%	149%
RRR Gas (All sources)	152%	139%	139%	72%	143%	118%	128%
PRODUCTION COSTS	$ 11.58	$ 13.93	$ 18.33	$ 18.89	$ 19.58	$ 18.94	$ 16.52

Fig. 2.21
Worldwide—proved reserve acquisition costs (PRAC), finding and development costs (FDC) and reserve replacement costs (RRC).

2013 PERFORMANCE MEASURES

	Worldwide	Africa/ Middle East	Asia Pacific	Canada	Europe	South/Central America	United States	Other/ Unspecified
Proved reserve acquisition costs	$ 5.20	$ 64.49	$ 3.85	$ 8.69	$ 20.65	$ 19.56	$ 17.58	$ 9.85
Finding and development costs	22.00	44.45	19.78	21.01	71.17	20.94	16.58	31.62
Reserve replacement costs	14.19	45.07	8.28	17.95	57.22	20.91	16.70	28.55
Oil production replacement rates								
All sources	219%	65%	380%	242%	10%	96%	217%	16%
Excluding purchases & sales	115%	65%	101%	249%	40%	97%	225%	48%
Gas production replacement rates								
All sources	143%	41%	174%	141%	22%	136%	210%	89%
Excluding purchases & sales	152%	65%	136%	161%	41%	135%	231%	162%
PRODUCTION COSTS ($/BOE)	$ 19.58	$ 13.90	$ 24.21	$ 21.71	$ 19.88	$ 17.94	$ 14.87	$ 17.78

Fig. 2.22
2013 worldwide regional performance measures (costs in $ per BOE; production replacement rates in %).

Figure 2.21 shows the worldwide historical trends averages for several E&P performance indicators. **Figure 2.22** shows the worldwide and regional performance indicators for 2013.[23]

Using Value Drivers to Advantage

Once the value drivers—corporate direct and indirect, and project value drivers—have been identified, sales representatives have the foundation for planning a sales strategy. This understanding also provides the basis for a compelling value proposition statement that clearly justifies using your company.

This chapter has described how to use the annual report to uncover corporate value drivers. Other sources include corporate speeches, presentations and strategy reports. Often the best source of information for discovering project value drivers is the company contact. The "Sales Call Skills" chapter discusses specific techniques used in sales calls to discover this type of information from contacts.

Corporate value drivers do not change drastically from year to year as they are based on long-term goals that support the corporate vision. Value drivers are important for all sales people to understand. This includes discovering information such as corporate vision, long-term goals, value drivers, objectives and strategies that, once known, are best recorded for each account and then shared with other individuals who work with the account. This information should be maintained in your company's CRM database and stored in the "Account Profile," the topic of the next chapter.

Summary of Chapter Objectives

1. Explain how and when value drivers are established.

In the corporate planning stage, when the company establishes its long-term vision for the company, it will also set its long-term goals. The long-term goals then will set the critical success factors and value drivers for achieving the long-term goals and company vision. With the long-term goals set, then short-term objectives are established, and projects are selected to achieve the objectives. You classify value drivers into two classes: corporate and project value drivers. Corporate value drivers are defined as variables that directly or indirectly impact the market value of the corporation as measured by the combined value of the common stock, known as market capitalization. This definition can be broken into two parts: direct and indirect variables. Direct corporate value drivers are variables that affect the value of the common stock or share price, such as EPS. Indirect corporate value drivers are initiatives or corporate policies that impact a company's ability to achieve its objectives. Examples of indirect value drivers are operational ratios, such as reducing lifting costs per barrel. Project value drivers are for projects in the execution stage, which are focused on achieving the project objectives or producing the expected results. Project value drivers are defined as variables that directly or indirectly impact project results. An example of a direct project value driver is production rate. An indirect project value driver might be a faster and more efficient analysis of logging data. At the execution stage, sales staff must determine how to assist customers in achieving their project objectives. Both corporate and project direct and indirect value drivers are typically included in the management's KPI. Sales representatives must do their research on each account to uncover the direct and indirect corporate value drivers of those accounts.

2. Know the most common corporate value drivers, both direct and indirect.

The two classes of common corporate value drivers are profitability ratios, such as return on equity, return on capital employed, and total stockholder return, and market value ratios, such as price/earnings ratio, earnings per share, and market/book ratio. The most common corporate indirect value drivers are production, lifting costs per barrel, reserves replacement ratio and proven reserves.

3. Explain the purpose of the value proposition.

The value proposition statement clearly communicates how your company's services or products contribute to corporate or project value drivers. For sales staff, the first task in the sales cycle is to gather sufficient information about the customer's objectives and value drivers at both the corporate and project levels. With this information, sales staff can then devise a strategy to support a proposal the customer will approve. The next chapter clearly describes the steps needed to build an accurate and believable value proposition statement.

4. Know the basic make-up and contents of the annual report.

Annual reports are typically broken into the following sections: message to the shareholders, management discussion and analysis of financial conditions and results of operations, and financial review. In the message to shareholders, the highest-ranking officer of the company highlights major developments for the reporting year and future direction. In this section, the company officer gives a high-level review of the company's performance and major initiatives. This section is very helpful for beginning to uncover both direct and indirect company value drivers. Management's discussion and analysis of financial condition and results of operations gives a more detailed review of results as supported by the financial and supplemental statements. It also includes a summary of each specific operating entity, often geographically. It usually highlights KPI, such as net proved reserves and operating expenses per barrel. The financial review contains four basic reports. These reports constitute part of the company's annual reporting requirements and are presented in accordance with GAAP. All companies must publish three standard financial reports: balance sheet, income statement and statement of cash flows. Oil and gas producing companies must also provide supplemental information on their activities.

Applying the Concepts

1. For one of your key accounts, search it's websites for speeches, presentations and strategy documents. Download documents that improve your understanding of its long-term goals, critical success factors and value drivers. Using this information, summarize your findings and describe the account's:
   - Corporate mission,
   - Long-term goals,
   - Critical success factors,
   - Value drivers both direct and indirect,
   - Current objectives and strategies.
2. Which of the value drivers do you believe you can impact with the product and services you sell?
3. Make a value proposition statement for this customer's value driver(s).

References

1. See insets for Conoco vision statement taken from the *1999 Annual Report.*
2. For companies that are not publicly traded, the same concepts apply, except that there are fewer owners of the company.
3. Taken from Chevron's 1999 and 2000 annual reports.
4. Taken from BP Technology Seminar, D. Oliver, Managing Director (June 2001).
5. Adopted from the speech "Capital Efficiency—Importance to a Major Petroleum Company," J. N. Sullivan, Chevron Corporation (1998).
6. Taken from *Chevron 2000 Annual Report.*
7. *Ibid.*
8. For example, in the U.S., the GAAPs are the Financial Accounting Standards Board (FASB) and Securities Exchange Commission (SEC).
9. For a more detailed discussion of financial reports, see C. Walsh, *Key Management Ratios,* London, England, Prentice Hall Publishing (1996).
10. When assets that are part of a composite group are retired, sold, abandoned or otherwise disposed of, the cost—net of sales proceeds or salvage value—is charged against the accumulated reserve for depreciation. Where depreciation is accumulated for specific assets, gains or losses on disposal are included in period income. Maintenance and repairs are charged to expense; replacements and improvements are capitalized.
11. Classification of proved reserves is pending one or more of the following: 1) decisions on additional major capital expenditures, 2) the results of additional exploratory wells that are under way or firmly planned, and 3) the securing of final regulatory approvals for development. Otherwise, well costs are expensed if a determination cannot be made within one year following completion of drilling as to whether proved reserves were found. All other exploratory wells and costs are expensed.
12. Long-lived assets, including proved oil and gas properties, are assessed for possible impairment by comparing their carrying values with the undiscounted future net before-tax cash flows. Impaired assets are written down to their estimated fair values, generally their discounted cash flows. For proved oil and gas properties, the company generally performs the impairment review on an individual field basis. Impairment amounts are recorded as incremental depreciation expenses in the period in which the event occurs. Depreciation and depletion (including provisions for future abandonment and restoration costs) of all capitalized costs of proved oil and gas producing properties, are expensed using the unit-of-production method by individual fields as the proved developed reserves are produced.
13. DD&A: A method of accounting associated with the acquisition, exploration and development of new oil and natural gas reserves. Depreciation is a means of allocating the cost of a material asset over its useful life, such as operating equipment.

14. Cash equivalents represent investments with maturities of three months or less from the time of purchase. They are carried at cost plus accrued interest, which approximates fair value.

15. The presentation of this information is not as consistent as the three previously discussed basic financial reports. Each country has its own GAAP regarding the additional reporting requirements for an E&P company. For example, in the U.K., the reporting requirements are covered in the UK Statement of Recommended Practice "Accounting for Oil and Gas Exploration, Development, Production and Decommissioning Activities." In the U.S., it is the Statement of Financial Accounting Standards No. 69, "Disclosures About Oil and Gas Producing Activities" (FAS No. 69). The reports shown here are per U.S. standards, as they are the most comprehensive.

16. Figures 4.14 through 4.19 were taken from the *Chevron 2000 Annual Report.*

17. Examples of production costs are labor to operate the wells and related equipment and facilities, repairs and maintenance, materials, supplies and fuel consumed and supplies utilized in operating the wells and related equipment and facilities, property taxes and insurance applicable to proved properties and wells and related equipment and facilities, and severance taxes.

18. Descriptions of reserve quantity line items taken from *Arthur Andersen Global E&P Trends 2000.*

19. Estimates of proved reserves do not include oil that may become available from known reservoirs, but which is classified separately as "indicated additional reserve"; crude oil, natural gas and natural gas liquids, the recovery of which is subject to reasonable doubt because of uncertainty as to geology, reservoir characteristics or economic factors; crude oil, natural gas and natural gas liquids that may occur in undrilled prospects; or crude oil, natural gas and natural gas liquids that may be recovered from oil shales, coal, gilsonite and other sources.

20. Proved undeveloped reserves are reserves that are expected to be recovered from new wells on undrilled acreage or from existing wells where a relatively major expenditure is required for recompletion. Reserves on undrilled acreage shall be limited to those drilling units offsetting productive units that are reasonably certain of production when drilling. Proved reserves for other undrilled units can be claimed only where it can be demonstrated with certainty that there is continuity of production from the existing productive formation.

21. The description of the standardized measure of discounted future net cash flows and the changes in standardized measure of discounted future net cash flows were taken from the *Chevron 2000 Annual Report.* These last two reports are in accordance with the requirements of FAS No. 69.

22. More in-depth information on commonly used financial analyses can be found in C. Walsh, *Key Management Ratios*, London, England, Prentice Hall Publishing (1996).

23. Reserve replacement ratio data and performance data taken from *Ernst and Young Global Oil and Gas Reserves Study*, 2014.

Account Corporate Profile

3

Your Basic Research

Chapter Objectives

After reading this chapter, you will be able to:

- Complete an account corporate profile for your key accounts.
- Know how to leverage the account profile in your day-to-day sales activities.

Professional sales organizations complete their basic research on the accounts they want to build a relationship with before they ever think about what to sell to a specific account. It clearly demonstrates that you, as a professional salesperson, have taken an interest in your accounts and, before you start to sell, you want to understand their company. The account profile is the report based on your research that holds this information and is a document you can share with the rest of the Account team.

The account profile sections hold information regarding the account's business environment, goals, value drivers, strategies, and objectives. This information is then easily shared with others who will be involved with the account. In this chapter, you will learn how to complete the profile information to create the account corporate profile.

Corporate-level information about an account is the main input for an account profile. The accounts profile contains information about the account's products and services, markets, competitors, mission, philosophy, critical success factors, short- and long-term business strategies, and account and industry conditions. Taken together, information in the account profile provides an overview of the account's business and value drivers, which can be used for many purposes:

- **Account briefing:** Provides an introduction to the account that can be used for making contacts or giving presentations.
- **Managing sales stages:** Stage 1 provides an understanding of business drivers in the sales cycle; stage 2 identifies customer needs in the sales cycle. Each of the sales stages will be discussed in depth in the next chapter.
- **Account management planning:** Provides input for making or reviewing account development plans.

The account profile requires corporate headquarters information and, when appropriate, information regarding any subsidiary accounts operating in the region.[1] Account profile sections can be completed by referring to the account's annual report, corporate website, and strategy reports as well as by entering information learned during personal contact with the account executive.

▶ **References:**

When completing the account profile, be sure to state all sources of information and include any supporting documents for the account in the attachments area of your corporate CRM system.

Completing an Account Corporate Profile

The account profile sections contain information from the account's perspective. This information is updated annually soon after the account's annual planning meeting. As part of the ongoing business relationship, someone from your company should be assigned the responsibility of updating the account profile annually. The account profile sections are described below.

Business Description

This section consists of eight parts, as follows:

Revenue, Profit, and Fiscal Year End: This information should reflect the most recent reported period for the account. If the account is a subsidiary, this information can usually be found in the management discussion section of the account's annual report and from contacts within the account.

Account Trend: This section is the header for the Account Condition section and is a short description of the account's current growth condition. The recommended options are *Emerging* if the account is new, *Growth* for revenue growth or asset expansion, and *Stable* and *Declining* if the account is starting to limit or reduce its operations in the region. This input should support the situation described in the Account Condition section.

Executive Summary: This section provides a summary of the key information found in the other sections of the account profile. It should be completed after all other sections for the account profile have been completed. The information in this section should be included in any strategic sales plan prepared for the account. Anyone who is participating in a review for a specific opportunity but not familiar with the account can use the executive summary as a quick introduction to the account.

Account's Mission: This section describes the account's stated mission or vision. It usually contains the position the account has stated it wants to achieve or maintain. For example:

> "Our vision is to be recognized around the world as a truly great, integrated, international energy company that gets to the future first."[2]

Account's Philosophy: This section describes what the account believes its unique strengths are and its guiding principles for doing business, which are often called "core values." The Account's Philosophy can also contain a description of the account's culture.[3] For example:

> "The most important thing companies can do is to adhere to some basic principles of doing business. This is not intended to lecture, but rather to emphasize the importance of good fundamentals in pursuing and engineering the enormous challenge ahead. These principles include: Placing the highest priority on the safety and health of employees and the environmental well-being of the areas and communities in which you operate. Operating with an understanding that yours is a long-term business and that therefore you must be committed to 'stay the course' through the ups and downs of the business environment—and making certain you have the financial strength to do so.

Said another way, 'thrive on adversity.' Following a selective, highly disciplined financial approach that does not waste money or pursue uneconomic projects. Ensuring that you can put the highest-quality people in the right place at the right time to get the job done in an effective and highly ethical manner. Having an experienced management team to direct these activities and to work with host governments to achieve mutual objectives. And maintaining an active and substantial program to develop new technology to meet business needs and to solve unforeseen problems on the run."[4]

Account's Critical Success Factors: This section describes the critical success factors the account believes are required to achieve its stated mission. Corporate executives, when addressing investors, stock analysts, and public forums, frequently state the critical success factors, and these are usually stated clearly in the annual report. For example:

> "This Annual Report describes Chevron's year 2000 accomplishments and explains your plan for achieving long-term goals. Essential is the set of strategies you call 4 plus 1. The foundation is the 'plus 1'—organizational capability—a system of competencies that when linked together form a unique capability. We intend to achieve this unique capability in four drivers of business success—operational excellence, cost reduction, capital stewardship and profitable growth. Thus, 4 plus 1. Success with this strategy will drive Chevron to world-class performance."[5]

Account's Goals—Long Term/Qualitative: This section describes stated long-term/qualitative goals as found in the account's mission statement. The excerpt below illustrates information that could be included in this section:

> ". . . goals for the five-year period 2000 through 2004: to be No. 1 in total stockholder return relative to your peers and to achieve a minimum 12% return on capital employed while continuing to grow. Success requires profitable earnings-per-share growth greater than your competitors' . . ."[6]

Account's Corporate Strategies: This section contains specific actions and projects the account plans to undertake to achieve its long-term goals. These strategies usually result in opportunities for your company to supply value-added services.[7]

Account and Industry Condition, and Account Goals and Objectives

Account Condition: The Account Condition section describes the account's current condition and major areas of focus. It also includes information regarding year-to-year trends in income and the balance sheet and cash flow statements. Trends in key performance indicators (KPI's) such as reserves, reserve replacement ratio, and lifting costs per barrel are included, as are any other KPI's the account tracks, such as cost per foot drilled and gearing ratio. Typically, the corporate strategy will target any KPI's that are worsening or falling significantly below industry average. If possible, this section should include the account's assumptions for economic analysis, such as supply and demand and price range. The following excerpt from the *Chevron 1999 Annual Report* illustrates information that could be included in the Account Condition section. In this case, the Account Condition would be growth:

> "In late 1998, crude oil prices were at near-record lows, and recovery was uncertain. At that time, you announced plans to reduce capital spending in most of your businesses and to launch a company-wide effort to reduce your

cost structure by $500 million. These moves allowed you to continue funding your growth in international exploration and production. We've more than met your commitments. In the first quarter of 1999, you acquired Rutherford-Moran Oil Corporation, which gives you a new growth platform in Southeast Asia's natural gas market. In September, you purchased Petrolera Argentina San Jorge S.A., a company with excellent prospects in two key geologic basins in Latin America."[8]

Industry Condition: This section describes the general industry condition within the region. At minimum, the description should include a three-year trend of supply and demand, investment levels, reserve and production levels, exploration and development activity, number of operators, gross expenditures, and upcoming lease sales. In countries where a national oil company operates, the description should include any major government programs and give the number of active petroleum agreements. Good sources of information for completing this section are industry reports published by oil companies,[9] governments, and research groups such as the International Energy Agency (IEA).[10, 11]

Account's Corporate Objectives: This section describes the account's highest-level stated corporate objectives for the current year. These objectives usually state the targets for cost-reduction programs, capital investments, return on capital, and investments in major projects. For example, this input section for BP Indonesia would show the BP corporate objectives from the most recent annual report. Subsidiary objectives are also noted in this section. Strategic sales plan users are encouraged to complete the account profile input, then generate the strategic sales plan–Corporate Profile. This profile can be shared with the subsidiary executive to obtain input for modifying the objectives to better reflect the subsidiary's specific objectives.

Products/Markets/Competition

Account's Products and Services: This section, which describes the account's products and services at the corporate level, should include both oilfield and non-oilfield businesses.

Account's Major Markets: This section describes the account's major markets both inside and outside the oilfield and should include past, present, and future markets. In this section, strategic sales plan users can learn about the organization of the company and names of business units—useful terminology when discussing the account with an account executive. This section also identifies which markets are considered the leading contributors to income and production and notes in which markets the company will invest in the near and long term as well as in which markets the company may withdraw from or reduce its investments.

Account's Competitors: This section describes the account's major competitors. This information can be obtained from corporate presentations from financial conferences, strategy reports, industry reports, and individual conversations with account contacts.

Using Account Profile Information

Account profile information can be used for many purposes: account briefing, sales stage management, and account development, as described below.

▶ **Briefing Document:**

The account profile report information is commonly used to brief newly assigned account representatives or others who are contacting the account or making presentations to the account.

Account Briefing

After the account profile has been completed, all account team members should be sent a copy of the report. When any company executives are going to visit the account, he or she should be sent a copy as part of the pre-visit briefing package.

Managing Sales Stages

By completing the account profile information, sales representatives have access to enough information to complete Stage 1—Understanding Business Drivers of the sales cycle. This stage is common across all opportunities for each account.

A complete and thorough analysis of the Trends and Objectives section of the account profile provides excellent preparation for upcoming account projects and allows sales representatives to position their company as the supplier of choice.

Information gathered for the account's Critical Success Factors (CSF's) and Corporate Strategies sections can be used to align your solution to a newly initiated account project or to build a sound business case to recommend an expenditure to address the account's CSFs and Strategies. This information is required to customize and align sales proposals and to clearly state the value proposition for the account.

Account Planning

All account profile information can be used when reviewing your account strategy or account development plans. These plans should complement the account's philosophy and goals.

For example, if your account plan objective is to migrate the account from a price buyer to a value buyer, the role of technology should be stated as a high priority for the account's projects. If this is not the case, your plan would have to address this point before investing in new technologies or adding product development staff.

If your account plan objective is to introduce one of the advanced pricing models, the importance of involving contractors earlier in the planning cycle should be stated as a high priority for the account's projects. If this is not the case, your plan would have to address the difference.

▶ **Alignment:**

Your approach to the people in the account needs to be aligned with the philosophy and objectives of the account. The account corporate profile is an excellent tool for an introduction to the account plan discussed later in the textbook.

The Biggest Benefit of Completing the Account Corporate Profile

The greatest benefit of working through the process to complete an account profile is the awareness gained of what your customers believe they require to succeed. The process of completing an account profile includes working with the account representative to fully understand the account's business drivers. Completing and regularly updating account profile information enables you to become involved early in the project life cycle to prepare for, rather than simply react to new account opportunities.

This concludes the "Account Corporate Profile" chapter. Although short, it nonetheless outlines a very important process of the professional salesperson. The next chapter will describe in detail the center point of all professional sales activities opportunities management. In fact, completing the account corporate profile is the first stage of opportunities management.

Summary of Chapter Objectives

1. **Complete an account profile for your key accounts.**

To complete an account profile, you must have a thorough understanding of the account's business environment, goals, value drivers, and objectives. In addition, you need to determine what is the account's current condition and the industry in which they operate. The account profile should be stored on the corporate CRM system. Anyone in the sales position should be familiar with this information before they start to pursue sales opportunities or provide day-to-day support. This level of knowledge of the account is required in order to prioritize and tailor our activities to provide value added services for the account. Before anyone makes contact with the account for the first time, it should be a minimum requirement for them to review the account profile.

2. **Know how to leverage the account profile in your day-to-day sales activities.**

This report is also an effective tool to brief anyone who will make contact with the account but who is not familiar with the account. Such situations include high-level visitors from outside the region or support personnel who will be assisting to service the account. This can be done prior to contacting the account. Each sales opportunity that you pursue should be checked to understand how it contributes to the account's goals and objectives described in the account corporate profile in the early stages of the sales cycle. This will ensure that you are aligned with the account. The research that you do to complete an account profile prepares you to make value propositions that are specific to the account. It is good practice to show the account corporate profile report to a high-level contact in the account organization to get their feedback regarding the accuracy of the report. You can then use the contact's feedback to improve the quality of the account profile. This approach also demonstrates to the account that you are not just interested in selling to them, but are very much interested in how to assist them to achieve their objectives. Your interest in their business will differentiate you from other sales representatives who wait for a request for proposal to be sent to them before making contact.

Applying the Concepts

1. In the "Applying the Concepts" section of the "Value Drivers" chapter, you were asked to collect information about your account. Using that information, complete an account profile using the template in Appendix A.
2. Complete the account profile and review the profile with one of your key contacts in the account and consider their input to improve the profile.
3. On a rating of 1–5, where 1 is significant and 5 is none, how would you rate the impact an up-to-date and validated account profile would have on effectiveness to work with the customer? Ensure that you consider both long and short terms.
4. Are there any changes or additional information that you would suggest to be included in the account profile?

References

1. If there is an HQ and regional account, the account profile information from the HQ account can be used in the regional account profile and expanded to include the specifics of the regional account for each section. For example, the BP account profile information for the worldwide BP account can be used for the Indonesian BP account profile and expanded to reflect BP Indonesia's specific account profile information, such as objectives and key performance indicators.
2. Taken from the *Conoco 1999 Annual Report.*
3. Note this may be different from the philosophy applied by people in the buying center, which will be discussed in the Strategic Sales Plan chapter.
4. Taken from *Getting From Here to There: Meeting the Oil and Gas Needs of 2010,* presented at the Cambridge Energy Research Associates Executive Conference, remarks by Harry J. Longwell, Senior Vice President, ExxonMobil Corporation.
5. Taken from the *Chevron 2000 Annual Report.*
6. *Ibid*.
7. A good example of a strategy report is the *BP 2001 Strategy Report* by Sir John Browne. The report is downloadable from the BP website.
8. Taken from the *Chevron 2000 Annual Report.*
9. One example is the *BP Statistical Review of World Energy.* This report is typically published each June and made available free of charge on BP's corporate website.
10. The *IEA World Energy Outlook* report examines energy demand and supply for 13 world regions up to the year 2020. The *World Energy Outlook 2000* can be purchased at http://www.iea.org.
11. *Ernst and Young Global Oil and Gas Reserves Study, 2014* is an excellent source of information regarding industry trends for the energy industry.

Appendix A

Account Profile

Account Name: ____________________

Sales Representative Name: ____________________ **Date:** __________

Business Description: Revenue:______ **Profit:** ________ **Trend:** _______ **Fiscal Year-End:** _____

Executive Summary: This is a concise summary of all the other fields read this after reading the other parts of the profile.

Mission: Defines a position the Account is attempting to reach.

Philosophy: What the Account believes its unique strengths are and its guiding principles for doing business, or "core values."

Critical Success Factors: Critical success factors the account believes are required to achieve its stated mission. Corporate executives, when addressing investors, stock analysts and public forums, frequently state the critical success factors, and these are usually stated clearly in the annual report.

Long-Term Goals: Long-term/qualitative goals.

Strategy: The portfolio of projects or initiatives the Account plans to undertake to achieve the long-term goals.

Objectives: Corporate objectives or key performance indicators (KPIs) for the current year, for example targets for cost reduction, capital investments, return on capital, and investments in major projects.

Account Condition: What is a three-year trend for the: main line items in the income statement, balance sheet and cash flow statements? What is is a three-year trend for KPIs such as reserves, reserve replacement ratio and lifting costs per barrel? Include any other KPIs the account tracks, such as cost per foot drilled and gearing ratio. If possible, this section should include the account's assumptions for economic analysis, such as supply and demand and price range.

Industry Condition: For the geographic regions, the Account operates what is a three-year regional trend for key performance indicators (KPIs) such as reserves, reserve replacement ratio, production, and lifting costs per barrel? What is a three-year trend for investment levels in exploration and development in the region? How many operators are in the region? Are there any significant incentive programs or upcoming lease sales in the current reporting year?

Products and Services: What are the Account's upstream and downstream businesses and any other businesses, not in the oilfield?

Major Markets: What are the Account's major markets that it has business?

Competitors: Who does the Account consider its major competitors?

Opportunities Management

4

Make Time Your Advantage

Chapter Objectives

After reading this chapter, you will be able to:

- Describe the sales phases and stages in the opportunities management process and understand the more significant factor in each stage.
- Understand which opportunities management tool to use at the appropriate time in the process.

This chapter describes the opportunities management process used to effectively manage the sales processes that both complement and are focused on your customer's project management process.

Each phase in the opportunities management process has specific objectives that drive your sales activities and strategies. The opportunities management process is designed to organize your sales efforts and identify the customer's needs and value drivers. Followed from beginning to end, the opportunities management process makes time your advantage. The graphic on the right is a representation of opportunities management as a clock, with the main stages of opportunities management on the face of the clock. The key success factor of all time management is prioritizing and identifying the important activities that must be done. Opportunities management for the sales professional is the key to prioritizing the most important sales activities. Opportunities management eliminates surprises and allows you to develop and deliver a value-added solution that is significantly better than the competition. The process also helps secure the project at the desired profitability level.

The customers' project management process described in Chapter 2 "Value Drivers" was used to develop the sales professionals' opportunities management process. One modification was made to the customer's project management process. Although the oil company executive quoted in Chapter 2 did not consider the procurement as a separate phase in their project management process, the procurement phase is nevertheless a phase that each project management team must complete to select their suppliers for their project. Therefore, it is very important for the sales professional to understand. Phase 3–Evaluation of Options has been expanded to include Phase 3a–Evaluation of Options as described in Chapter 2 and Phase 3b–Procurement consisting of five procurement stages shown in **Fig. 4.1** on the next page.

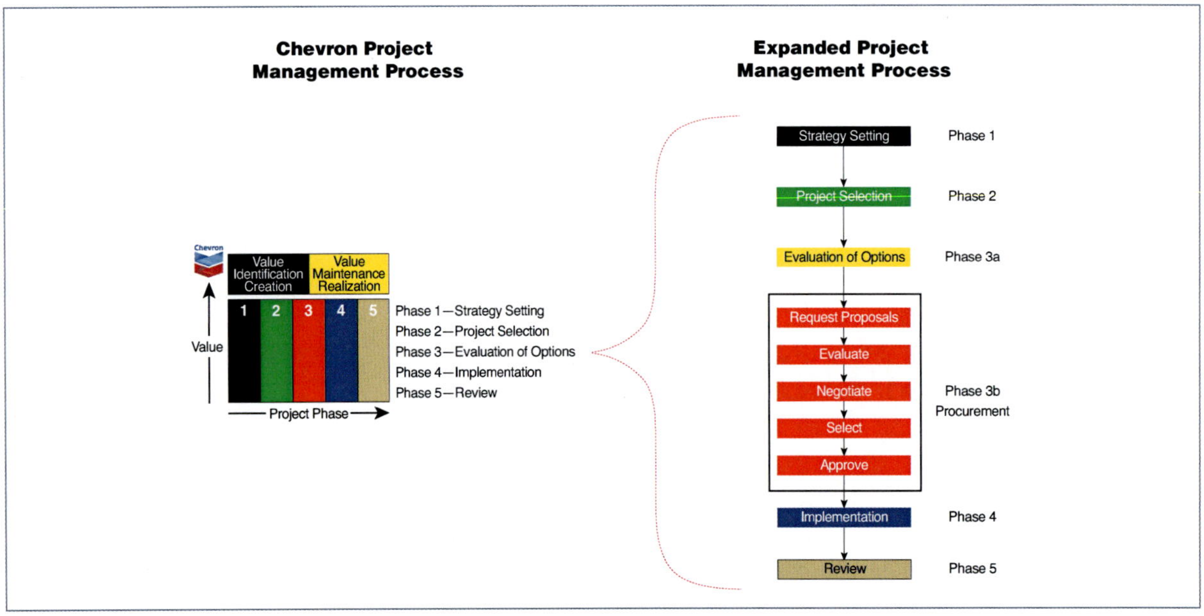

Fig. 4.1
Chevron Project Management Process shown on the left. Expanded Customer Project Management Process shown on the right.

The expanded customer project management process drives the sales opportunities management process, as shown in **Fig. 4.2** below. It is important to realize early in a salesperson's career that the customer's project management process does not wait for a seller's involvement. Each customer management phase you fail to exploit can reduce your chances of winning the project. Sales staff often say their major challenge is overcoming the lack of time available to accomplish all their sales and non-sales tasks. One way to get more time for sales-related tasks is to become involved earlier in the customer management process and not wait to receive the tender. As T. J. Wilson, founder of IBM, once said, "Make time your ally and time will make you." Each opportunities management process phase and stages is discussed in more detail on the following pages.

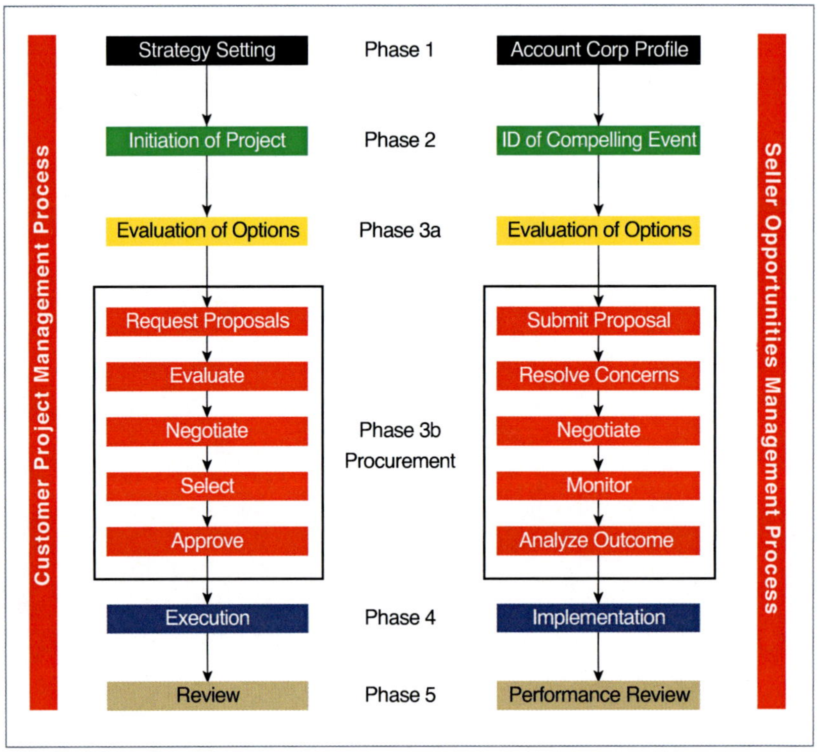

Fig. 4.2
Customer Expanded Project Management Process and Seller Opportunities Management Process.

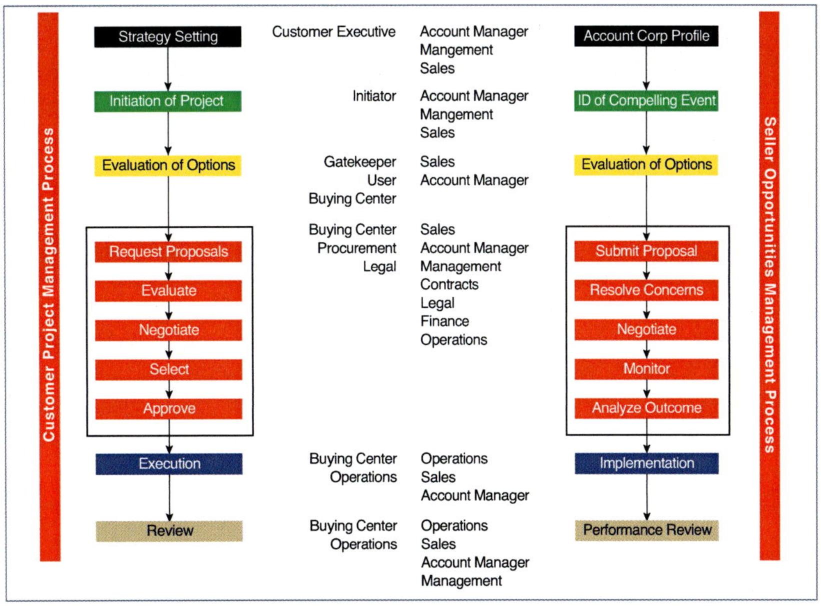

Fig. 4.3
Customer Project and Seller Opportunities Management Processes.

Sales Phases in the Opportunities Management Process

The opportunities management process has five phases. Each sales phase corresponds to a customer project management phase. In each sales phase, you will identify the important issues for the customer and the objectives and issues for sales staff. **Figure 4.3** above shows the most commonly involved people in both the customer project management process and seller opportunities management process. The opportunities management cycle can take from months to many years to complete. Participants from the customer and seller may change with the phases and stages, which makes close team coordination essential.

In large sales, the seller's representatives may be involved in multiple phases from start to finish in the opportunities management process. Preparatiovvn and effective management are essential to securing projects. A key difference between large and small sales is the length of the sales cycle. The "Large versus Small Sales" sidebar shows some other key differences.[1] Most of the time, sales representatives deal with large sales and buying centers made up of many members. From the buyer's perspective, large purchases also carry greater risks than smaller ones, so the sales objective is to clearly demonstrate the value proposition and address any negatives that might concern the buying center during implementation.

▶ *Large versus Small Sales*

Large sales require different strategies and selling techniques than small sales for five reasons:

- Length of the selling cycle
- Size of the commitment
- Relationship
- Risks
- Consequences of the purchase

Most marketing and sales literature discusses sales techniques for consumer markets, which are mostly small sales. Key aspects of large sales, such as those in the business-to-business environment, are shown in the table below.

Factor	Small	Large
Needs	Implicit	Explicit
Sales skill	Closing	Probing
Relationship	Personal	Business
Buying center	Few	Many

Phase 1: Corporate Account Profile

Creating a corporate account profile is the first sales phase of the opportunities management process, which corresponds to the customer's strategy-setting phase. In this phase, the customer frames business strategies and objectives to align with business goals and the corporate mission. The customer also sets the criteria for project selection and defines the corresponding budgets.

During the customer's strategy-setting phase, your objective is to acquire a thorough understanding of the customer's corporate profile. The corporate profile includes corporate-level information about the account's products and services, markets, competitors, mission, philosophy, critical success factors, short- and long-term business strategies, account and industry conditions, and corporate value drivers.

In this phase, you must understand the customer's strategies and the criteria used to select projects for implementation. With this information, you then create a strategy that aligns you with customer objectives and that positions you in favor over your competitors. You may also be able to uncover opportunities to assist the customer in previously unconsidered ways.

The second objective is to stay in close contact with the sponsors and initiators of the customer's projects so you know when a new project has been approved. This objective requires an organized effort to arrange meetings with the account's upper management. Meetings with high-level contacts should be held after the account's annual budgeting or planning process or soon after the annual report is published. This phase is critical to the opportunities management process and is common to all opportunities for any specific account. Carrying out this phase thoroughly and sharing the information across your company through the CRM program gains efficiencies for both customer and seller organizations.

Phase 2: Identification of a Compelling Event

Phase 2 begins when the customer initiates a project. In this phase, the customer identifies projects that meet the criteria developed in the strategy-setting phase. Projects are initiated for many reasons, including:

- Approval through the corporate planning process (for example, an exploration program or new field development project);
- Identification of a problem that warrants action (for example, an outdated evaluation system or increasing water production in an existing field); and
- New knowledge learned from a service provider about products or services that would advance company objectives (for example, a reservoir optimization project to increase production).

In phase 2, you discuss the proposed project with the initiators or sponsors in order to qualify and better understand project drivers and critical success factors. To qualify the project, you must ask questions about what is compelling the customer to spend money and resources on this project and other related project questions, such as:

- Why does the customer have to act?
- How does this project fit into the customer's business strategy?
- What are the customer's key issues and objectives for the project?
- What is the measurable impact on the customer's business?
- What are the consequences if the project is delayed?
- What is the payback if the project is completed ahead of schedule?
- What is the priority for this project compared to others?
- What are the key customer milestones for the project? What events clearly mark the end of each phase of the project management process and the start of the next? This information helps you determine how much time you have for each of the preceding sales phases to prepare and execute your sales strategy.
- Who are the people in the buying center? See the "Major Sales: Who Really Does the Buying?" sidebar for a brief description of the buying center concept.[2] Who has been assigned responsibility for implementing the project, and who has the power to make decisions or influence implementation of the project?
- What is the customer's total budget for the project?

▶ *Major Sales: Who Really Does the Buying?*

In the article "Major Sales: Who Really Does the Buying?," author T.V. Bonoma emphasizes that seemingly well-planned, well-executed selling strategies may fail if management does not understand the human side of selling. Marketing managers can get at the human factors of purchasing decisions by answering four questions:

- Who is in the buying center?
- Who are the powerful buyers?
- What does each buying-center member want?
- How do they perceive you?

Sales managers should listen to the sales force, emphasize homework and details, and make productive sales calls the norm.

At right is a list of the buying roles encountered in every selling situation as illustrated in the purchase or upgrading of a telecommunications system. In many buying centers, individuals may have multiple roles. For example, a user may be the evaluator and gatekeeper. There may also be approvers who do not work within the company but in a government-reviewing department, as is the case in many countries that have a national oil company.

Initiator: High-level manager proposes to replace the company's telecommunications system

Approver: Manager or committee that reviews the decision-maker's recommendation

Decision-maker: Vice president of IT department has final decision on which system will be purchased

Influencers: Staff have important say about which system and vendors the company will consider

Gatekeeper: Corporate purchasing and corporate telecommunications departments analyze the company's needs and recommend likely matches with potential suppliers

Evaluator: Corporate purchasing department completes the purchase to specification by negotiating and bidding

Users: All division employees who use the telecommunications equipment

Overall, the main goal of phase 2 is to maintain regular (preferably semi-annual) contact with the account's high-level managers or others who initiate projects. Each new project must be subjected to the questions outlined in this section in order to fully define the compelling event and get a head start on the next opportunity management phase evaluation of options. A very effective tool for having a focused conversation with the customer to uncover this information is the project summary shown in **Chapter Highlight 4.1: Be Like Nike and "Just Do It!"**.

At this point, the customers, as part of their overall corporate strategy, have selected a project and now are in their evaluation of options phase. The seller's focus at this time is to retrieve information to understand the high-level drivers for the project and contact the customer's project team assigned to carry out the remaining phases of the customer's project management process. At this time, the salesperson completes a level 1 review of the opportunity. The seller's objective is to assess five factors regarding the sales opportunity:

- Is there a sales opportunity?
- Can we compete?
- Can we win?
- Is it worth winning? and
- What next?

To assess the five critical factors, the salesperson answers a series of questions for each factor. By completing the level 1 review, the salesperson identifies what the seller knows and does not know about the opportunity. By identifying the missing information, the salesperson can prioritize what actions to take in the time remaining before submitting a proposal or response to an invitation to tender from the customer. A level 1 review form is shown in **Chapter Highlight 4.2: "Tell Me Doctor, Do I Have An Opportunity?"**. The level 1 review will be discussed in detail in Chapter 9 "Strategic Sales Plan."

Chapter Highlight 4.1: Be Like Nike and "Just Do It!"

The Golden Rule: Understand First, Then Sell

In a sales training seminar for opportunities management, the instructor recommended that the students use a structured approach when having a conversation with their customers. At this point in the lecture, the instructor was referring to qualifying the compelling event for new projects. What the instructor recommended was using the Project Summary Worksheet (shown on the next page). The instructor called it the professional salesperson's checklist and compared it to a pilot's pre-departure checklist. The instructor said a characteristic of real professionals is using the right tool for a job. The amateur will try to use one tool for every job; some salespeople not trained in the professional sales processes will use a blank page from their day timer. The instructor's advice was to use the worksheet in the meeting with the customer and always offer to give the client a copy at the end of the meeting. Much to the instructor's surprise, one senior student Joao claimed his customers would not like a formal approach because his clients liked a more relaxed approach. The sales trainer, who was also very experienced in sales, doubted the student's claim. The sales instructor told a similar story about a salesperson who was skeptical about the worksheet, but when he used the sheet, his customer was pleased and asked for a copy. The instructor suggested Joao be like Nike and "Just Do It!"—that is, try using the worksheet once before drawing any conclusions about the effectiveness of the project solution worksheet. Joao agreed, and the result is shown below in an email to the instructor.

-----Original Message-----
From: Joao Senior Student
Sent: Tuesday, December 19, 2006 2:27 AM
To: JP Amlin Instructor
Subject: Lessons learned. . .

JP,

As per my "IDEAS list" from the seminar, I used the Project Worksheet format for the first time. It is true I edited it a bit, but it was essentially the same info (see attached).

I remembered when you said the story about a salesperson who was skeptical about the project solution worksheet. Well, today my client (Mr. VP International Exploration) was VERY complimentary about the way the meeting went and how the sheet helped the conversation to be focused. He asked me to send it to him and volunteered to review/edit it in case I missed some info.

I'd like to say thanks for the good teaching and I would like to take the opportunity to wish you and your lovely wife a MERRY XMAS and a great 2007!

Regards,

Joao

The lesson from this student's experience is customers do appreciate having conversations they believe will add value. Structured interviews using professional sales tools like the worksheet will give the client the impression they are dealing with a professional. However, it is the responsibility of the salesperson to use the information from the conversation to return to the customer with useful recommendations.

Another lesson for salespeople is to ensure that they understand what the client is trying to do and what they consider are the important factors before starting to sell. The project summary worksheet is designed to uncover the relevant facts about the customer's project. Having this conversation early in the customer's project management process will be very beneficial when it comes time to make a value-added proposal in the later stages of the opportunities management process. By understanding the client's needs before starting the selling process, the salesperson builds credibility with the customer. The Golden Rule is to understand first, then sell.

Having the Right Conversation with the Right Person about the Right Things at the Right Time!

Project Summary

Date: ______ Contact: ______

Company: ______

Business/service unit(s): ______

Project: ______

Description: ______

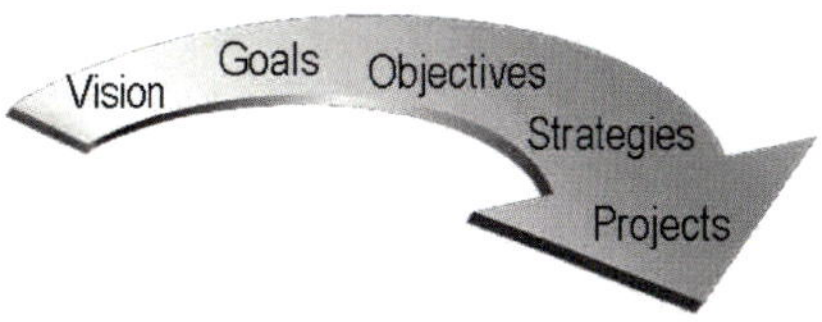

Project Objectives

Project Manager

Budget

BUSINESS DRIVERS

CRITICAL SUCCESS FACTORS

MANAGEMENT TEAM

Operations

Technical

Finance

Procurement

Partners

Government

CONCERNS/EXPECTATIONS

Customer Project Management Schedule

Dates

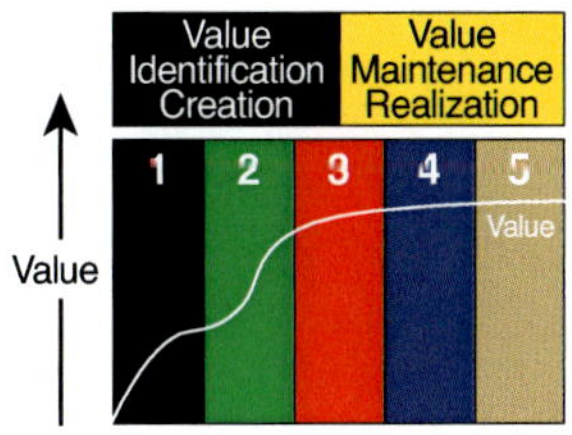

Phase 1—Strategy Setting ______

Phase 2—Project Selection ______

Phase 3a—Evaluation of Options ______

Phase 3b—Procurement ______

Phase 4—Implementation ______

Phase 5—Review ______

The project summary worksheet is used in the meeting with the customer to discover the important factors, timing, and people participating in the client's project team. The sheet is completed starting from the top, guiding the salesperson to use open questions to the customer about their project. The worksheet can be customized to include the client and seller logos, as well as the client's specific project management process phases. It is best practice to use the sheet in paper form when having the conversation with the customer. A PDF version of the project solution worksheet and other sales tools can be downloaded from http://www.b2bprofessionalsales.com

Chapter Highlight 4.2: Tell Me Doctor, Do I Have an Opportunity?

What You Don't Know Can Be Fatal. Have Regular Check-Ups to Nip the Problem Early

Good advice from your doctor is to get regular check-ups, identify problems, and take action to avoid potentially fatal results. The same goes for sales opportunities. The level 1 review is a periodic check-up for the salesperson. The level 1 analysis is completed early in the opportunities management process—ideally at the start of phase 3a–Evaluation of Options and at several other times during the process that will be discussed later in this chapter.

The story below is, unfortunately, repeated too often in the sales world, and in many cases the salesperson could have prevented the situation by completing the level 1 review before making a proposal to the customer. The review is completed by answering the questions for each factor. Responses to the questions can be "+" for a strong position, "-" for a weak position, and "?" when the seller does not know the answer. This assessment is typically done for the salesperson's company and at least one or two competitors. This story is a real case of one salesperson we will call Wayan.

Sales Opportunity Level 1 Review Form

Account:		Date:	Reviewed by:	
Factors and Assessment Questions		Opportunity:		
Is there an opportunity? ❑ Yes ❑ No ❑ ?				
Account corporate profile	+ Completed – Not done	+	The first four questions are assessed from the customer's point of view. The remaining level 1 factors and assessment questions are answered from the perspective of your company and your competitors.	
1. Customer's application or project	+ Defined – Undefined	+		
2. Customer's business profile	+ Strong – Weak	+		
3. Customer's financial condition	+ Strong – Weak	+		
4. Access to funds	+ Yes – No	?		
5. Compelling event	+ Defined – Undefined	?		
Can we compete? ❑ Yes ❑ No ❑ ?		Our Company	Competitor 1	Competitor 2
Requirements diagram Vulnerability analysis Customer value analysis	+ Completed – Not done	–		
6. Formal decision criteria	+ Defined – Undefined	?	?	
7. Solution fit	+ Strong – Weak	?	?	
8. Resource requirements	+ Low – High	+	?	
9. Current relationship	+ Strong – Weak	+	?	
10. Unique business value	+ Strong – Weak	?	?	
Can we win? ❑ Yes ❑ No ❑ ?		Our Company	Competitor 1	Competitor 2
Buying center analysis	+ Completed – Not done	–		
11. Inside support	+ Strong – Weak	?	?	
12. Executive credibility	+ Strong – Weak	+	?	
13. Cultural compatibility	+ Good – Poor	+	?	
14. Informal decision criteria	+ Defined – Undefined	?	?	
15. Political alignment	+ Good – Poor	?	?	
Is it worth winning? ❑ Yes ❑ No ❑ ?		Our Company	Competitor 1	Competitor 2
Business case?	+ Completed – Not done	+		
16. Short-term revenues	+ High – Low	+	+	
17. Future revenue	+ High – Low	?	?	
18. Profitability	+ High – Low	+	?	
19. Degree of risk	+ Low – High	+	+	
20. Strategic value	+ High – Low	–	?	

What next?

What has to happen for you to win this sales opportunity? The Action field identifies the sales tactic being used (e.g., retrieve information, emphasize strengths, minimize weakness, prove value, insultate against competition). Make sure to consider all opportunity management stages. If early in the evaluation of options phase, you should retrieve information from any level 1 factors that have "?'s". The last two actions are the most important actions for Competitor 1 and 2.

Action	Description of action, name of customer, contact from your company, and completion date.
1.	Gathered requirements from contact. Submitted proposal.
2.	
3.	
Competitor 1	?
Competitor 2	

Wayan was about to go on a sales call with his manager and was waiting in the reception area of the customer's office for the meeting. Wayan asked his manager not to bring up a recent sales opportunity that Wayan had just been informed was awarded to the competitor. The manager was surprised and upset and asked what had happened? Wayan said he did not know; he was also surprised as he thought the work was supposed to be awarded to him. After the meeting, the manager asked Wayan to go through the level 1 review; perhaps the results could highlight what went wrong. Shown to the right is the completed review. What is apparent from the analysis is there were far too many "?'s" in this review.

Wayan was correct when he told his manager that he did not know. Unfortunately at the time Wayan submitted his proposal for the work, he did not realize that there were so many unknowns or the level of uncertainty related to him winning the work.

A blank level 1 review form is included in the appendix and can be downloaded from http://www.b2bprofessionalsales.com

Chapter Highlight 4.2: Tell Me Doctor, Do I Have an Opportunity? (cont.)

Sun Tzu was a Chinese military general, strategist, and philosopher who lived in the Spring and Autumn Period of ancient China. He is traditionally credited as the author of *The Art of War*, an extremely influential ancient Chinese book on military strategy. One of his many famous quotes from the Art of War is:

> "If you know the enemy and know yourself, you need not fear the result of a hundred battles. If you know yourself but not the enemy, for every victory gained you will also suffer a defeat. If you know neither the enemy nor yourself, you will succumb in every battle."

Applying Sun Tzu's interpretation for the level 1 review would result in something like what follows if he ever decided to become a sales consultant.

Sales Opportunity Level 1 Review Form

Account:	Date:	Reviewed by:		
Factors and Assessment Questions	Opportunity:			
Is there an opportunity? ❑ Yes ❑ No ❑ ?				
Account corporate profile	+ Completed – Not done	+	The first four questions are assessed from the customer's point of view. The remaining level 1 factors and assessment questions are answered from the perspective of your company and your competitors.	
1. Customer's application or project	+ Defined – Undefined	+		
2. Customer's business profile	+ Strong – Weak	+		
3. Customer's financial condition	+ Strong – Weak	+		
4. Access to funds	+ Yes – No	?		
5. Compelling event	+ Defined – Undefined	?	?	
Can we compete? ❑ Yes ❑ No ❑ ?		Our Company	Competitor 1	Competitor 2
Requirements diagram Vulnerability analysis Customer value analysis	+ Completed – Not done	–		
6. Formal decision criteria	+ Defined – Undefined	?	?	
7. Solution fit	+ Strong – Weak	?	?	
8. Resource requirements	+ Low – High	+	?	
9. Current relationship	+ Strong – Weak	+	?	
10. Unique business value	+ Strong – Weak	?	?	
Can we win? ❑ Yes ❑ No ❑ ?		Our Company	Competitor 1	Competitor 2
Buying center analysis	+ Completed – Not done	–		
11. Inside support	+ Strong – Weak	?	?	
12. Executive credibility	+ Strong – Weak	+	?	
13. Cultural compatibility	+ Good – Poor	+	?	
14. Informal decision criteria	+ Defined – Undefined	?	?	
15. Political alignment	+ Good – Poor	?	?	
Is it worth winning? ❑ Yes ❑ No ❑ ?		Our Company	Competitor 1	Competitor 2
Business case?	+ Completed – Not done	+		
16. Short-term revenues	+ High – Low	+	+	
17. Future revenue	+ High – Low	?	?	
18. Profitability	+ High – Low	+	?	
19. Degree of risk	+ Low – High	+	+	
20. Strategic value	+ High – Low	–	?	

What next?

What has to happen for you to win this sales opportunity? The Action field identifies the sales tactic being used (e.g., retrieve information, emphasize strengths, minimize weakness, prove value, insultate against competition). Make sure to consider all opportunity management stages. If early in the evaluation of options phase, you should retrieve information from any level 1 factors that have "?'s." The last two actions are the most important actions for Competitor 1 and 2.

Action	Description of action, name of customer, contact from your company, and completion date
1.	Gathered requirements from contact. Submitted proposal.
2.	
3.	
Competitor 1	?
Competitor 2	

Assessment Analysis: Many question marks for your assessment issues and the competitors.

Sun Tzu's Interpretation: If you know neither the enemy nor yourself, you will succumb in every battle.

Assessment Analysis: Plusses and some minuses for seller's assessment, many question marks for competitors.

Sun Tzu's Interpretation: If you know yourself but not the enemy, for every victory gained you will also suffer a defeat.

Assessment Analysis: Plusses and minuses for seller's assessment and plusses and minuses for competitors.

Sun Tzu's Interpretation: If you know the enemy and know yourself, you need not fear the result of a hundred battles.

What Wayan needed to do before submitting his offer was ask more questions to assess the strength of his position and then take actions to win the opportunity.

The next section of this chapter, Opportunities Management Phase 3a–Evaluation of Options, addresses the issue of how to prepare to be in a winning position when you submit your offer.

Phase 3a: Evaluation of Options

This phase starts with the customer's evaluation of options. By this stage the customer has already sanctioned the project, purchase, or repurchase and is searching for the best product or service to meet their requirements. The evaluation of options phase is the most critical in the opportunities management process as this is when competitive battles are fought and won.

In this phase preparations are made for proposal submission and negotiations that will come in the procurement stage. Your active involvement in this phase positions you more favorably in the procurement process. See **Chapter Highlight 4.3: Understanding Why It is Risky to Wait for the Tender to Come Out**. In this phase you must answer the remaining factors of the level 1 review:

- Can we win?
- Can we compete?
- Is it worth winning?
- What next?

> ▶ ***Apostles and Terrorists: A Company's Best Friends and Worst Enemies***
>
> In a paper entitled "Why Satisfied Customers Defect," T. Jones and E. Sasser explain the importance of customer loyalty and understanding buying center members' unique behavioral attributes (prior individual biases), intensity of satisfaction or dissatisfaction (attitude), and ability to act on their perceptions (competitive market dynamics). As a result of these factors, customers behave in one of four basic ways: as loyalist, as defector, as mercenary, or as a hostage. Turning as many customers as possible into the most valuable type of loyalist, the apostle, and eliminating the most dangerous type of defector, or hostage, the terrorist, should be every company's ultimate objective.
>
> Supporting the valuable buying center members and converting the dangerous types of buying center members are two of the objectives of the implementation phase and account management.
>
> In the evaluation of options phase, you want to determine which buying center members are already aligned with you as mentors and supporters. Later, in the procurement phase, you will rely on their assistance to help you convert the neutral and non-supporters to supporters. If you cannot motivate the non-supporters, you have to devise strategies to help your mentors neutralize them.

The first two questions are significantly different. "Can we win?" is concerned with informal decision criteria and your alignment with the powerful and influential people in the buying center (see "Apostles and Terrorists: A Company's Best Friends and Worst Enemies"[3] in the sidebar.) "Can we compete?" asks how you stand compared to the competition with respect to the decision-making criteria. To answer these questions, one must complete the following five objectives:

- Identify and make contact with key buying center members.
- Determine the decision criteria, evaluation model, and procurement stages that will be used in the procurement phase.
- Ask each buying center member if he or she has the requirements for what he or she will buy from you. What have they identified as the critical success factors or issues? Do they have any concerns or expectations about the purchase or your company? Moreover, how do they rank the decision criteria factors from the most crucial to incidental?
- Formulate a strategy that maximizes a perceived fit.
- Establish the dollar amount of the customer's perceived differential value.
- Address customer concerns and consequences.

Make Contact with Buying Center Members

To win an opportunity you must be in a strong position when you submit your proposal. This requires you to have focused conversations early in the evaluation of options phase with the buying center members before you select your sales strategy. Not having sufficient information can lead to bad decisions and disappointments when you discover you lost the sure bet. The professional salesperson uses the request for proposal worksheet to have these conversations. See **Chapter Highlight 4.4: Get Organized** and the good things that happen when you apply the tools of a professional salesperson.

Chapter Highlight 4.3: Understanding Why It is Risky to Wait for the Tender to Come Out

Make Time Your Advantage: Four Good Reasons to Start Before It's Too Late

In the customer's project management process, the evaluation of options phase is separate from the procurement phase. In the evaluation of options phase, emphasis is on being involved with the customer prior to receiving a request for proposal. In the procurement phase, emphasis is on the actual contracting process. Here are some good reasons why these two phases are distinct and important:

1. In many companies, only minimum discussion between the supplier and buying center personnel is permitted during the procurement phase. Such discussion is usually restricted to tender clarification questions. Customers set this restriction to maintain the integrity of the tendering process and to minimize interference in the evaluation process. Because of this, efforts to modify the tender or include exclusive products or services are usually not allowed or evaluated.

2. To establish your price, you must understand how the customer perceives value in your differentiation. In general, the procurement process does not provide sufficient time for you to fully develop and reach agreement on your differential value.

3. Sales representatives who wait to receive tender before beginning the sales process will be dealing withprocurement departments. The flowchart shows a typical account organization with managers of each department (e.g., exploration) reporting to a higher level. Respective boxes list some objectives these departments have. The flowchart illustrates the dilemma faced by sales representatives who initiate a sales strategy only once they recieve a tender in the procurement stage. The procurement department's objectives are very different from those of other departments. Typically, the procurement department receives technical requirements, bid specifications and a list of acceptable suppliers from the technical staff. If there are several acceptable suppliers, the procurement department's focus in evaluating proposals is on contract terms, conditions and price.

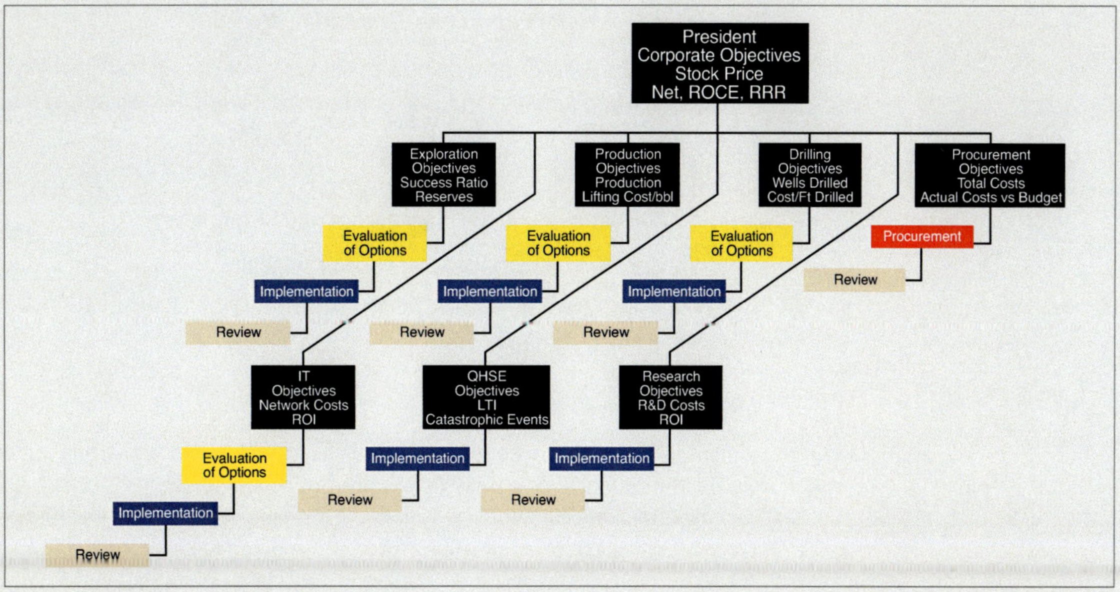

4. Most sales opportunities are repurchases from existing accounts. The customer may use a previous decision criteria that is not optimal for this purchase and may intentionally bypass the evaluation of options phase. The cycle may skip from implementation to the procurement phase when the current contract expires. In such situations, you must initiate an evaluation of options phase during the implementation phase by contacting buying center members, whether or not you are the current contract holder.

	Customer Action	Sales Objective
Stage 1: Identify Differentiators	Create decision criteria to differentiate alternatives	Uncover existing decision criteria Suggest other appropriate criteria
Stage 2: Establish Relative Importance	Assess relative importance of decision criteria and determine which are crucial explicit needs	Complete vulnerability analysis to identify your strengths and vulnerabilities
Stage 3: Evaluate	Customer compares alternatives to find "best fit" using evaluation model	Demonstrate how your product or service meets decision criteria using evaluation model better than competitors
Identification of Preferred Alternative		

Fig. 4.4
The three stages in the assessment of alternative choices.

Initial contact with buying center members will help you identify those members who can influence the supplier selection decision. You must also determine the issues involved in the decision, and the influencers' perception of you to devise your relationship strategy. In the Strategic Sales Plan chapter, relationship strategy is discussed in more detail. The predisposition of buying center members is a critical factor in deciding whether you can win.

Determine Decision Criteria and Evaluation Model

To establish the decision criteria, it is useful to review the basic stages of decision psychology. When a customer chooses between competing alternatives, the decision process normally advances through three stages:

- Identifying differentiators.
- Establishing the relative importance of differentiators.
- Judging alternatives using an evaluation model.

Figure 4.4 lists each decision-making stage with the customer action and corresponding sales objective.[4]

Identify Differentiators

When the evaluation of options phase begins, the customer establishes the criteria for the products and services required to complete the project and achieve the objectives. Most companies simplify this process by initially selecting providers who are capable of providing the required products or services. In some countries, the company or governmental authority dictates that a minimum number of qualified vendors be identified before proceeding to the procurement phase. In such cases, the most common differentiator is price, assuming that all other factors are comparable. The sales representative's objective in this stage is to educate the customer about aspects of your services that differentiate you from the competitors.

Chapter Highlight 4.4: Get Organized

Organization is Key

One Important Aspect is to Create a Toolbox Using an Organizer that Contains All the Tools for Every Skill Taught in Training.

-----Original Message-----
From: Shane
Sent: Friday, May 16, 2008 10:43 AM
To: JP Amlin Instructor
Subject: Re: SALES CLASS CERTIFICATION TEST NOW OPEN

JP,

I finally took both tests.

I wanted to take the time to thank you again **for the thoroughness and enthusiasm that you brought each day with the class. I truly think this was the best class I have attended.**

I am using the organizer and have slowly incorporated most of the worksheets. **It is a very easy way to stay organized and ensure you never see a client unprepared.**

I'm happy to also report that I was able to secure the work for the horizontal well project I presented in class. On top of that, we are close to securing another two wells on top of this. That is approximately $3M in revenue. **I guess the telltale, however, is a 15 well project (cementing) secured from a client that we have not worked for in over three years.**

Thanks again,

Shane

The author of this textbook delivers sales training programs of various lengths covering sales-related topics. One training is a two-week sales school covering most of the subjects in this book. The sales school objective is to provide the person new to sales with the skills sales professionals use to be successful. One take-away from the training was a leather folder called the organizer. The instructor was very emphatic that all the students use the organizer rather than blank pages of their diary when visiting customers.

This recommendation was based on the findings from a study conducted by a team of sales trainers for one company. When the trainers audited graduates of their sales training program, they observed that the graduates were not applying what they learned because of two factors. First, the sales training did not provide the specific tools to implement the concepts; second, the salespeople were not organized to implement the ideas effectively. As a result, the company launched a program called "Impact" to create a toolbox containing tools for every skill taught in the training.

The criteria for the toolbox were it had to include all the tools and be easy to use and updated by the salesperson. The result of the Impact project was the organizer, a professional-looking folder that could be taken to the customer's office by the salesperson with the forms needed for focused conversations at every phase of the opportunities management process. One student commented that this looked like too much work and would be too difficult. The instructor's comment was, "I never promised you shortcuts or tricks. What I promised was you would learn the theory, process, applications, and tools used by the professional salesperson to be successful in an ever-increasing competitive marketplace."

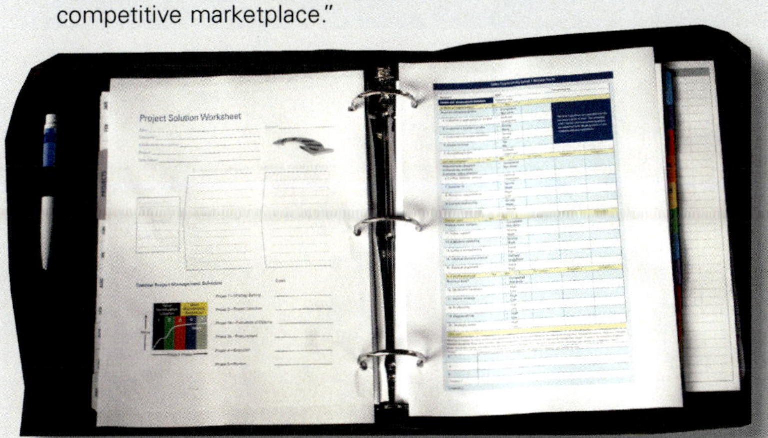

The instructor paused, looked at each student, and then said, "The only place where work comes before success is in the dictionary. If you like to win, then the results will justify the effort." One student, Shane, stood up and declared that he saw the benefit and was committed to using the tools of the sales professional. Above is the unsolicited email sent to the instructor.

Chapter Highlight 4.4: Get Organized (cont.)

Contents of the Organizer

The contents of the organizer include the standards for time management, such monthly pages for scheduling meetings, task record-keeping and business card holder. However, the heart of the organizer is the Projects tab, which provides space to organize the information on the salesperson's opportunities, plus key concept cards for sales skills that are frequently used by sales professionals. Below is a list of the organizer sales tools (and reference chapter).

1. Account Corporate Profile (Account Corporate Profile)
2. Project Summary (Opportunities Management)
3. Level 1 Review (Opportunities Management)
4. Sales Plan Worksheet (Opportunities Management)
5. Augmentation Analysis (Opportunities Management)
6. Request for Proposal Summary (Opportunities Management)
7. Strategic Sales Plan (Strategic Sales Plan)
8. Pricing Workbook (Pricing)
9. Bid Analysis Worksheet (Bid Evaluation)
10. Sales Call Preparation Worksheet (Sales Call Skills)
11. Sales Call Supporting Worksheet (Sales Call Skills)
12. Post Sales Call Analysis (Sales Call Skills)
13. Negotiation Analysis Worksheet (Collaborative Negotiations)
14. Negotiation Presentation Worksheet (Collaborative Negotiations)
15. Sales Call Skills Card
16. Collaborative Negotiations Skills Cards
17. Account Relationship Analysis (Account Relationship Analysis)
18. Account Plan (Account Management Plan)

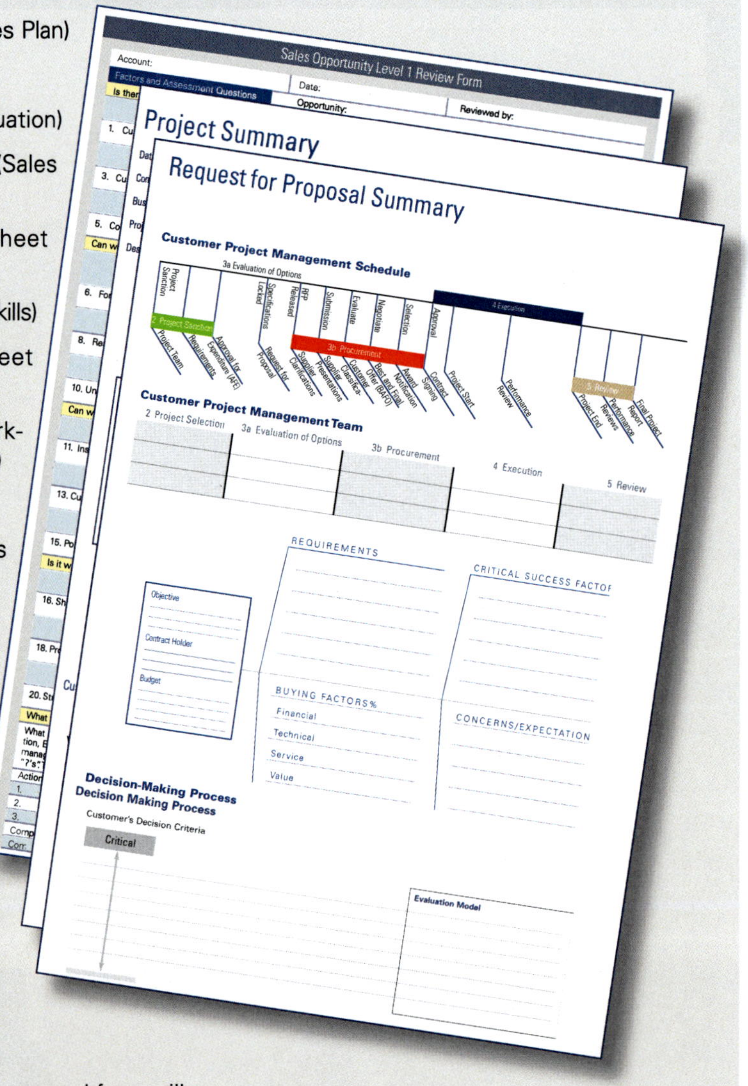

You have already seen the first three components listed above, and as you read the remainder of the textbook you will see the other tools. All the tools are available for download from http://www.b2bprofessionalsales.com

Shown to the right is the Request for Proposal Summary. This is an essential tool for having conversations with the people in the buying center in the early part of Phase 3a–Evaluation of Options.

A salesperson who uses the request for proposal form will not forget to ask for important factors about the opportunity they are trying to win. A full size copy of the Request for Proposal Summary is included in the appendix.

You can demonstrate differentiation from the competition in five main areas:

- Corporate capabilities
- Product or service features
- Service performance
- Company sales and support personnel
- Price

Corporate capabilities refer to the abilities of the company compared to those of the competitor. Your capabilities differentiate you from the competition only to the extent that the customer is aware of this advantage.

The customer may perceive that you have the financial strength and sufficient resources to overcome most catastrophic events. This factor—described as the "security of the offering"—differentiates companies such as IBM and Microsoft when they compete against smaller rivals. With this perception, your customers know that, no matter how cyclical the markets are, companies like you, IBM, and Microsoft will be there tomorrow.

The **product or service features** category is the most common differentiator after price. While specific capabilities of unique products and services are easy to demonstrate, you must convert the dollar amount of those capabilities to the added value the customer will gain by using the product or service. By clearly describing specific benefits that align with the customer's objectives, you are practicing customer focus.

Superior performance means applying superior technologies with competent staff and the advantage of experience. Performance criteria must be illustrated in terms of the customer's value drivers, such as reduced costs or improved production. The section to follow on phase 4 describes how you use service quality review meetings and the performance curve to demonstrate superior performance. **Chapter Highlight 4.5: Performance That Can't Be Beat (If you Report It!)** gives an example of using the performance curve to prove differential value.[5]

Company sales and support personnel staff also differentiate you from your competitors. Superior products and performance are even more valuable when supported by highly trained, experienced support personnel. In the evaluation of options phase, sales representatives should demonstrate the strength of your people in meetings arranged with the customer's buying center personnel.

Chapter Highlight 4.5: Performance That Can't Be Beat (If You Report It!)

What Does the Performance Curve Show? Differential Value (If You Plot It That Way!)

How do you leverage your excellent work as a differential value in the next opportunity? First, you find the metric the customer values and then plot it against an accepted standard of performance, such as an industry average or corporate average. The difference is then expressed in value dollars. This example for Venezuela illustrates the concept perfectly.

Added Value Calculation	
Prevented LTIs compared to international standard	85
Cost per LTI	$ 30,000
Added value for customer	$ 2,550,000
Other benefits	Goodwill Best practice
Payback compared to alternative competitive proposals	< 6 months

Supplier A was the incumbent and had very good performance on the current project for a major client in Lake Maracaibo. Because of the ongoing business relationship, Supplier A was able to develop best practices, thereby lowering the lost-time incidents (LTI) rate and reducing LTI costs while building goodwill by reducing LTI.The performance curve below for LTI clearly shows how Supplier A's service team significantly improved performance in a two-year project. However, the contract period for the current project ended, and the customer was required to request offers for another two-year contract period.

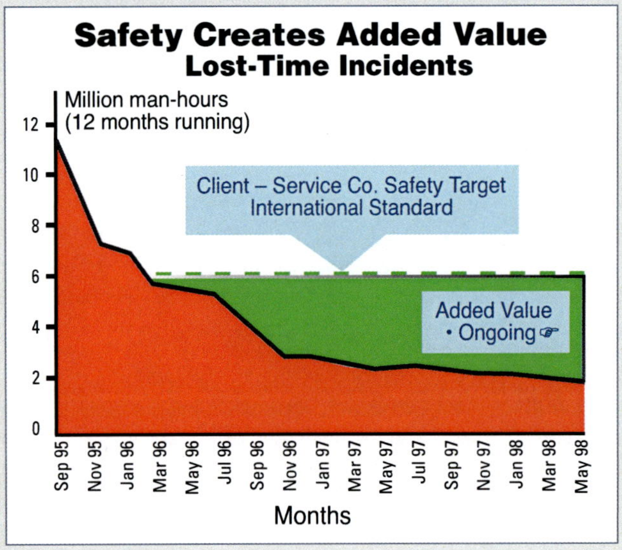

The strategy was to help the client understand that awarding the next contract to a competitor could mean losing the advantage gained over the last two years. The sales team showed the client an industry study reporting the average cost of a single LTI for injured personnel to be $30,000.

As shown in the Added Value Calculation table, the reduction of 85 LTIs resulted in $2,550,000 in reduced LTI costs. Supplier A's performance became the differential value to secure the project, even though the competitor's offer was $1 million lower. Collecting this type of information in your service quality review meetings with the customer is extremely useful in the opportunities management process.

Price is the most common differentiator. If the tendering process allows, you may use a two-tier pricing strategy to achieve pricing differentiation. With this strategy, you offer older technologies at a discount to secure the project, and then offer the customer value-added services at a premium price. However, if the customer buys only generic services, the sales representative must work with operations staff to offer a price-differentiated solution that provides the desired level of profitability.

Another approach to a price-differentiated solution is to develop a per unit low-cost solution that enables you to enter the market at a lower cost than competitors and still

▶ *Measuring Up?*

Evaluation models are used to determine whether you can compete. Below are examples of two evaluation models used by your customers.

MCP Evaluation Model

Criteria	Weight	Score	Total
Cost/value	25%	4	1.00
Technical	25%	3	0.75
Cultural fit	25%	2	0.50
Track record	10%	3	0.30
HSE	5%	3	0.15
Range of services	5%	3	0.15
Quality	5%	3	0.15
Total evaluation	100%		3.00

Rating: 5=excellent, 4=good, 3=average, 2=poor

Modified IPR

1 Bid price 60%
Bid price shall be determined from each bid. Each bidder's bid price shall be given points according to the following formula:

P = (60 x L): Be

Where P = points awarded for the bidder's bid price; L = lowest bid; and Be = bid being evaluated.

The lowest bid (L) necessarily gets the full 60 points possible. Example: L = \$30 million; B3 = \$3.5 million; P = (60 x 3.0): 3.5 = 51.43.

2 Qualifications of bidder's personnel and firm's experience 20%
At a minimum, personnel assigned to this contract should have prior experience in operating in similar conditions and should be qualified engineer(s); graduated engineer(s) or the equivalent, with three or more years' experience as a relevant engineer; and/or operator(s) skilled in these operations, with three or more years as a relevant operator. Bidders should include in the bidding documents a brief overview of the firm's experience in carrying out this type of service.

3 Bidder's work execution plan 20%
Bidders should submit a detailed mobilization plan with specific reference to timing per phase, support base(s), safety provisions, and quality control measures in accordance with a quality questionnaire.

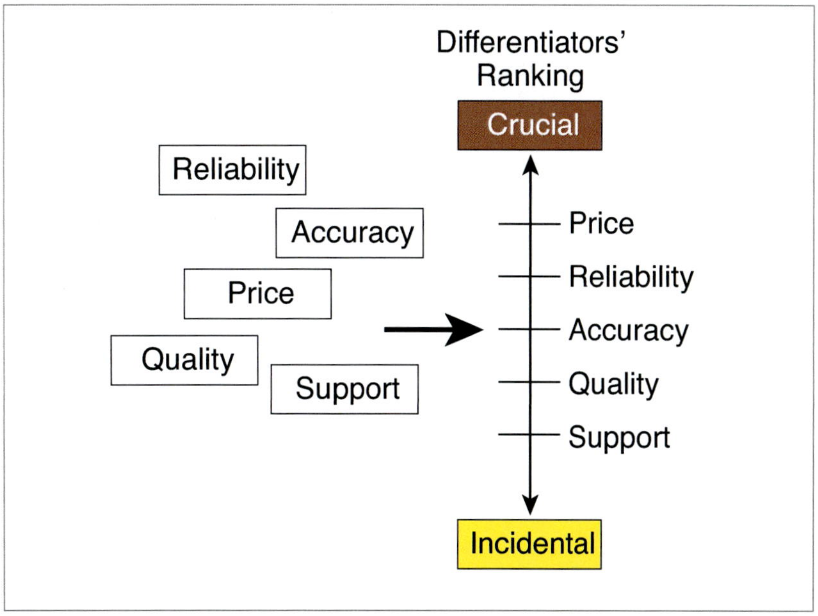

Fig. 4.5
Establishing the relative importance of differentiators.

meet profit targets by achieving operational efficiencies. A price-differentiated solution must be consistent with the pricing practices of the company and region.

Establish the Relative Importance of Differentiators

At this point in the decision-making process, the customer has identified the differentiators—or decision criteria—related to their needs and permits the analysis of alternative options. Then, the customer decides which of these potential differentiators are crucial in making the purchasing decision and which are incidental **(Fig. 4.5).**

Alternatives Using the Evaluation Model

In the final stage of the decision-making process, the customer uses an evaluation model to evaluate all proposals based on their perceived fit with the decision-making criteria. In many procurement processes, the customer has an evaluation model for assessing each proposal. Whenever possible, you want to know what the model is, how it works, and the customer's rating of you against the criteria. Some of the more common evaluation models are discussed below, and two examples from actual tenders are discussed in the "Measuring Up?"[6] sidebar.

Two-Envelope Technical and Financial (TETF)

In this evaluation model, bidders are requested to submit a technical proposal in one envelope and a separate commercial offer in another envelope. The technical evaluation is usually made on a point basis, followed by a ranking and selection of two or more proposals that meet the minimum technical specifications. Only the financial proposals of bidders that pass the technical requirements are opened. The financial proposals of the unsuccessful bidders are returned unopened. The financial proposal is usually evaluated by using a spreadsheet based on a certain activity model, including an economic evaluation of contract exceptions, logistics, and safety. The lowest bidder wins. This evaluation model is popular in countries where government review bodies are involved in the approval process.

Multiple Criterion Points (MCP)

This is perhaps the most widely used evaluation model. Companies such as Shell, BP, and Chevron commonly use this evaluation model because it can accommodate a multitude of criteria in the decision-making process. Each criterion is evaluated individually. Typical decision criteria—price, quality, technical requirements, and QHSE—vary with the kinds of services or products requested. For each decision criterion the bidder is evaluated and assigned a score, typically 1–5 or 1–10, and then each decision criterion is weighted so that the sum of the weights is 100. The winner is the bidder with the most points. In this model, the winning bidder does not necessarily have the lowest price. The winning bid price must be within a predetermined percentage of the lowest bid. If the winning bidder's price is more than the premium allowed, a negotiation will take place.

Inverse Proportional Rule (IPR)

Some customers and official bodies, such as the World Bank, use this evaluation system, which is a variation of the MCP system. Rather than rating each bidder against the criteria, each bidder is compared to how close they are to the best company in the specific criteria. The best company in each criterion gets the maximum number of points for that criterion. Other bidders are given points that are inversely proportional to how far they are from the winner. The winner is the bidder with the most points. As in the MCP model, the winning bid price must be within a predetermined percentage of the lowest bid. If the winning bidder's price is more than the premium allowed, a negotiation will take place.

Most Economically Advantageous (MEA)

In the MEA model, the customer is looking for the best solution. This model is very similar to the MCP, except the winning bidder is not confined to a percentage premium over the lowest bidder. In this model, as long as the winning bidder's solution is more economically advantageous to the customer than any other bidder, they win.

In addition to understanding the customer's evaluation model, you also want to know the stages of the customer's procurement phase. Depending on the account and country, procurement stages vary from simple to complex and informal to very formal. The procurement phase is discussed in detail later in this chapter.

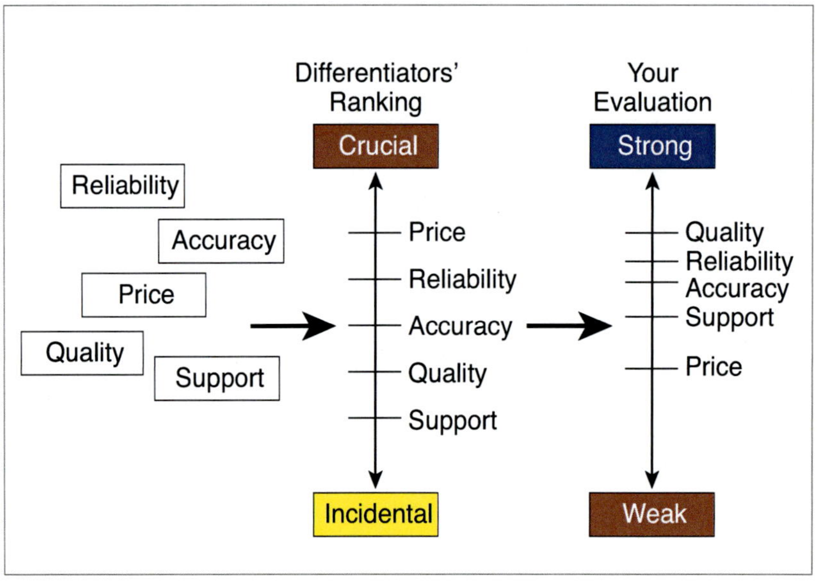

Fig. 4.6
Customer's perceived fit of the you offer compared to the decision criteria.

Formulate a Strategy That Maximizes Perceived Fit

Two analyses are used to formulate a strategy that maximizes perceived fit. The first determines how you will be evaluated against the customer's evaluation model **(Fig. 4.6).**

The second—called a vulnerability analysis—determines how each of the main competitors will be evaluated against the customer's evaluation model. In this analysis you try to ascertain whether a competitor is rated strong and you are rated weak in an area crucial to the customer.

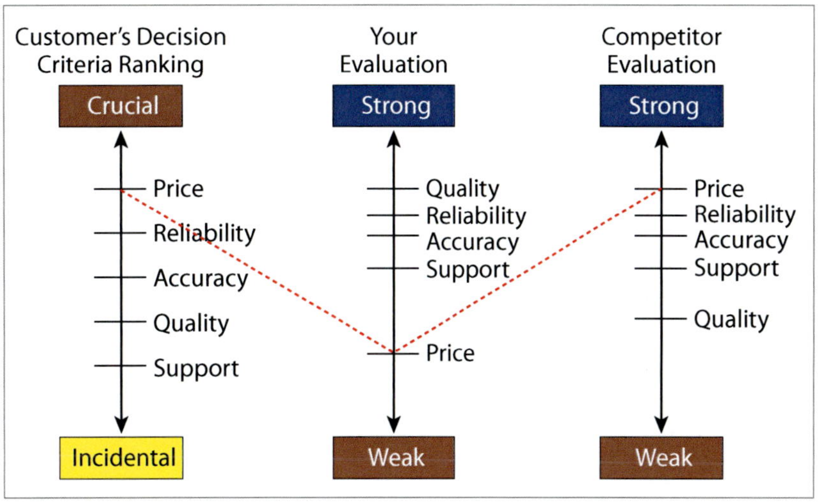

Fig. 4.7
Vulnerability analysis.

Figure 4.7 shows a completed vulnerability analysis. In this presentation, vulnerabilities are highlighted by the criteria that form a V shape (dotted line) when the competitor is rated strong and you weak in criteria crucial to the customer.[8]

This analysis helps you prepare a competitive strategy that takes into consideration the customer's needs and decision criteria, your evaluation, and your vulnerabilities with respect to the competition. In addition to other competitor companies, competition may come from the customer's own in-house services group. It may be a totally different type of solution or service, or it may be a do-nothing course of action. The best way to decide who you are competing against is to carefully analyze all the available options or solutions to the customer.

Figure 4.8 is a summary of the opportunities management activities discussed so far in this chapter. In time, the salesperson is at point A in Fig. 4.8. Now the professional salesperson must select their competitive sales strategy and determine how the sales team will spend the time remaining until they submit their proposal and enter the 3a–Procurement Phase. Up to this point, most of the energy is directed toward retrieving information and estimating the probability of winning the opportunity. From point A on, the sales strategy is set and the appropriate sales tactics are taken, as identified in the strategic sales plan. The creation of the strategic sales plan will be covered in detail in Chapter 9 "Strategic Sales Plan."

The goal of your competitive strategy, then, is to ensure that the buying center evaluates you as having the best-perceived fit for the customer's needs. To select your competitive strategy, you follow a decision process that focuses on the buying center and the customer's decision criteria.

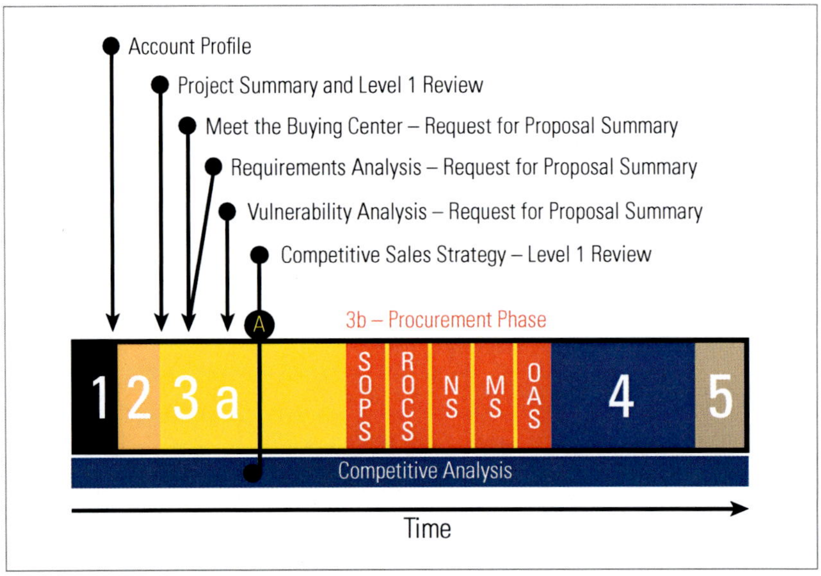

Fig. 4.8
Key activities during the opportunities management process that provide critical input into the selection of the competitive sales strategy. The phases in the opportunities management process are: 1. Account Corporate Profile, 2. Identification of the Compelling Event, 3a. Evaluation of Options, 3b. Procurement Phase, 4. Implementation, and 5. Project Review.

Point A on the chart represents the time when the pursuit decision is made and which competitive sales strategy will be followed for the remaining time in the evaluation of options and procurement phases.

Competitive Strategy Decision Process

From the vulnerability analysis, you determined whether you are in a strong or weak position. Next, you must determine if you can improve your ranking in the customer's evaluation given the customer's current specifications or whether you should change the scope of work in order to enhance your position. Another important consideration is the amount of time before the procurement process begins and what you can reasonably achieve during that period. In **Fig. 4.9**, the competitive strategy matrix highlights key factors in selecting the appropriate strategy. It shows four main competitive strategies—two variations for each strategy.[7] The next two sidebars discuss specifics for each tactic used with each strategy.

Frontal Competitive Strategy. If you are in a strong position and do not want to change the scope of work, consider using a frontal competitive strategy. A strong position indicates that you expect to be evaluated significantly better than the competition. Members in the buying center agree that you have a superior offering based on your solution or reputation. In a frontal competitive strategy, use tactics that:

- Influence decision criteria from needs uncovered earlier in the opportunities management process (see sidebar on "Influencing Decision Criteria");
- Reinforce crucial decision criteria that you can meet better than the competition;

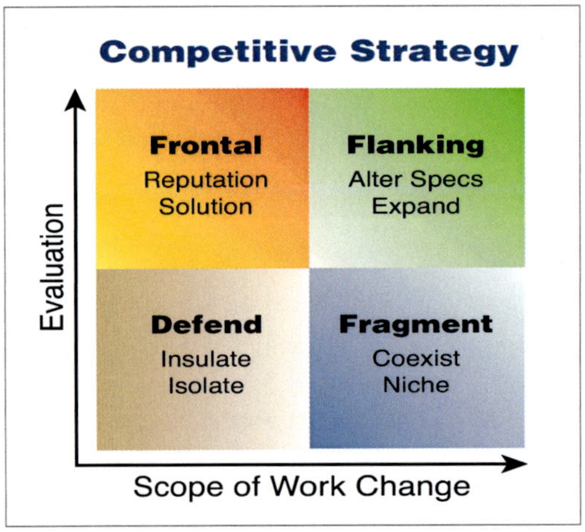

Fig. 4.9
Competitive strategy matrix.

▶ *Influencing Decision Criteria*

Four main tactics are used to influence decision-making criteria. Three are common to both strong and weak positions. The fourth is used in addition to the first three when you are in a weak position. Additional weak position tactics are discussed in the next sidebar.

1. Develop decision criteria from needs you uncovered in the opportunities management process. This is the easiest strategy to implement. Members of the buying center may not be aware of the needs you can satisfy with your products and services. This is particularly true for new products and services, which are developed in most cases to address customer needs not being satisfied by the current product offering. This is very effective when the benefits you offer are unique to you.

(cont. on pg. 86)

Chapter Highlight 4.6: Making Incidental Decision Criteria Crucial

Which Logging Company Should Pembina Choose for Their Lake Erie Project?

Pembina Exploration was in the process of selecting a logging company for their upcoming development program in Lake Erie. The project consisted of drilling, evaluating, and completing 30 shallow gas wells. Buying center members were an area manager (approver), operations manager (evaluator/decision-maker), and chief geologist (user/evaluator/decision-maker).

In previous years, competitors were awarded the work based on low bid. This time, Company A had a year of experience with another operator on the lake who drilled similar types of wells in a nearby area. The bid specification called for logging services for saline muds. In the previous drilling program, Company A logged the wells in half the time compared to competitors. The graph and benefit analysis to the right were presented to the buying center during the evaluation of options phase.

Company A	Salt Mud Wells	Competitor
5	Logging Time	16
$634	Rig Cost/Hr	$634
$3,170	Total	$10,144
30	No. of Wells	30
$95,100	Rig Costs	$304,320
$450,000	Logging Cost	$300,000
$545,100	Total Cost	$604,320
150	Total Hours	480
13.75	Days Saved	

Logging times were at an incidental level in Pembina's decision criteria. They had only asked the suppliers for estimated logging times to determine drilling curves. The drilling season was short because during winter months the lake was too rough to drill safely from barges; meanwhile during the drilling season, days lost due to bad weather could be significant, which often resulted in fewer wells being drilled than planned. The sales representative knew Pembina needed to be as efficient as possible during the short drilling season and was convinced that the faster logging times would provide Pembina with significant savings. Days saved would mean Pembina could complete the entire project in one season.

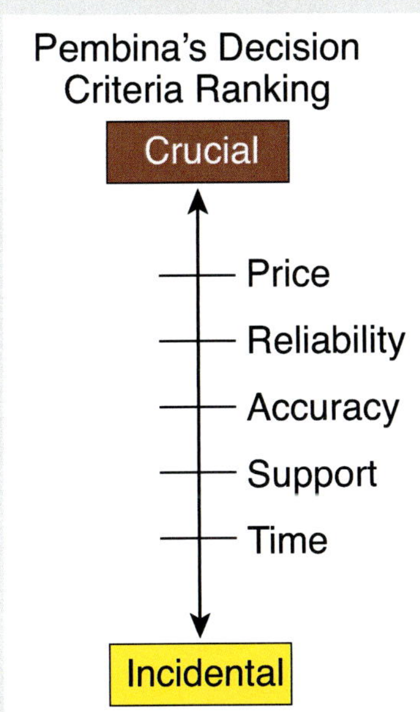

When the logging time comparison chart was shown to the area manager, he commented, "Is that so?" References were given from the other operator, who validated the logging times. In the procurement phase of the project, Pembina evaluated Company A as less expensive based on total costs, and the company was awarded the entire contract.

In subsequent discussions with the area manager, he stated that Pembina never realized there was a significant difference between service company logging, so they had always awarded the work based on price.

"We never realized there was a significant difference between logging companies for the time they take to log a well. We thought both companies were the same. You showed us that our total costs were higher if we use them even if they were cheaper. We had always awarded the work based on price. You guys actually save us 10 percent on our drilling costs and minimized the risk that we might not get all our budgeted wells drilled this season. Thanks—now go do it!"

Pembina Lake Erie Area Manager

▶ ***Influencing Decision Criteria (cont.)***

2. Reinforce that you can meet crucial decision criteria better than the competition. You can reinforce the importance of crucial decision criteria by providing the customer with case histories that demonstrate how you satisfied the crucial decision criteria in similar situations. This is a good opportunity to leverage the company's organization to provide the customer with examples and references where you have successfully satisfied similar crucial decision criteria.

3. Build up incidental decision criteria in areas where you are strong. Many times, the customer believes all competitors are equivalent in their ability to satisfy incidental decision criteria.

When you demonstrate that your offer is better than the competition in the incidental decision criteria and show how this differentiation provides benefits to the customer, the incidental decision criteria become more important. One technique used to your advantage and the customer's benefit is to have a recognized expert explain and demonstrate how important the incidental criteria really are.

In Fig. 4.5, reliability, accuracy, quality, and support are all rated below price in importance. You must show the customer the dollar benefit of the incidental criteria and overcome the apparent problem of having a higher price. See Chapter Highlight 4.3 for more about incidental decision criteria.

- Build up incidental decision criteria in areas where you are strong (see **Chapter Highlight 4.6**); and
- Ensure that supporters are prepared to minimize competitor attempts to reduce the strong position of your offer.

Defend Competitive Strategy. If you are in a weak position and do not want to change the scope of work, use a defend strategy. In this strategy, you either insulate your position from competitor attacks or isolate the competition. The defend strategy is more likely to succeed where you have a current contract and can use the implementation phase to build your defenses and relationships. With a defend strategy, you use tactics that:

- Reduce the importance of crucial decision criteria where you are perceived as weak[10] (see sidebar on the next page, "Weak Evaluation Tactics");
- Build dependencies via barriers to entry;
- Improve and expand relationships;
- Develop decision criteria from needs uncovered in the opportunities management process;
- Reinforce crucial decision criteria that you can meet better than the competition; and
- Build up incidental decision criteria in areas where your offer is better.

Flanking Competitive Strategy. When your offer is perceived to be in a strong position, use a flanking competitive strategy to expand the scope of work or alter the bid specifications to reinforce your position against competitors and their supporters in the buying center. With the flanking strategy, you use tactics that:

- Develop decision criteria from needs uncovered in the opportunities management process;
- Find buying center supporters for the flanking strategy;
- Demonstrate the benefits of the flanking solution;
- Review with supporter(s) to sell the concept of the flanking solution to other buying center members in your absence;
- Reinforce crucial decision criteria that you can meet better than the competition; and
- Build up incidental decision criteria in areas where your offer is strong.

Fragment Competitive Strategy. If you are in a weak position and your chances of improving that position are not great, you can use a fragment strategy, commonly called a "split the work" strategy. Variations to the fragment strategy are peaceful coexistence and niche.

In peaceful coexistence, you identify either a department or location that supports the fragment strategy. For this strategy to be successful, the customer must not perceive any complications with the split solution.

The fragment niche strategy is followed when you are considered stronger than the competition for a portion of the work and it is feasible to split this portion of the services from the main bid specification. With the fragment strategy, use the following tactics:

- Develop decision criteria from needs uncovered in the opportunities management process.
- Find buying center supporters for the fragment strategy.

> ▶ ***Weak Evaluation Tactics Reduce the Importance of Crucial Decision Criteria—Subtactics***
>
> Sales representatives commonly deal with customers who perceive their position as weak in the crucial price criteria. Four proven subtactics that can be used to improve your evaluation include:
>
> **Handling a drawback.** Build up the strength of other important criteria. This technique reinforces the danger of challenging crucial criteria and concentrates on building up the importance of other criteria. Key evidence of a drawback is when the customer says, "We would like to use you but you're too expensive" or "You don't have this feature." Faced with drawbacks, you must demonstrate or review the accepted benefits to make the drawback acceptable. The surest way to successfully implement this strategy is to determine the dollar value of the drawback and offset this with the dollar benefits to the customer of using your solution.
>
> **Redefining.** This tactic alters the way the buyer defines the criterion so that it becomes easier for you to meet. The crucial criterion remains important to the customer, but its definition is altered so that you can meet or exceed it. This tactic is used when the customer objects to the cost of your product or service without taking into account the reduction in other costs such as rig time, support, and installation. To implement this strategy, you must understand the bigger picture to demonstrate that your solution impacts total cost.
>
> **Trading off.** This technique balances decision criteria where you are weak or that you cannot meet against the limitations, penalties, or disadvantages of using the competitor. Trading off accepts the importance of a criterion but shows that there are other factors to be balanced against it. This strategy requires that you have a thorough understanding of the competitor's capabilities.
>
> All these techniques are discussed further in Chapter 8 "Handling Customer Objections."

- Demonstrate the benefits of multiple suppliers as the optimum solution.
- Rehearse with supporter(s) to sell the concept to split the work to other buying center members in your absence.
- Reduce the importance of crucial decision criteria where your offer is perceived as weak.
- Reinforce crucial decision criteria that you can meet better than the competition.
- Build up incidental decision criteria in areas where your offer is strong.

Alternative Competitive Strategies

When the above strategies are not appropriate, two alternative strategies can be used: the develop competitive strategy and the disengage strategy. The develop competitive strategy applies when there is no sales opportunity now, but there will be in the future. The disengage strategy is used when none of the four main strategies already discussed will put you in a position to compete, for either strategic or logistical reasons. It is also used when you are in a weak position and the competition has significantly better relationships with key members of the buying center.

Develop Competitive Strategy. The develop competitive strategy has two variations: invest and delay. When a compelling event has not been established, but you are reasonably certain it will in the future, you may choose to invest resources for the future opportunity to put you in a competitive position. You may invest in trials, on-site demonstrations, planning support, etc. With the develop invest strategy, you use the following tactics:

- Develop decision criteria from needs uncovered in the opportunities management process.
- Find buying center supporters for the develop invest strategy.
- Rehearse with supporter(s) to sell the concept to other buying center members in your absence.
- Influence requirement specifications for a future opportunity.
- Develop and expand relationships.

The other variation of the develop strategy is to delay. This is appropriate when there is insufficient time to execute the primary strategies or you cannot win or compete. When using the delay tactic, you must address the reason for the delay so that you will be in a stronger position for future opportunities. With the develop delay strategy, you use the following tactics:

- Find buying center supporters for the develop delay strategy.
- Rehearse with supporter(s) to sell the concept to other buying center members in your absence.
- Reduce the importance of crucial decision criteria where your offer is perceived as weak.
- Improve and expand relationships.
- Reinforce crucial decision criteria that you can meet better than the competition.
- Build up incidental decision criteria in areas where your offer is strong.

Disengage Competitive Strategy. When you do not want to win the project because of a lack of resources, a lack of financial attractiveness, or unacceptable risk, you follow a disengage strategy. With this strategy you disengage only from the current opportunity and in a way that ensures that you will be considered for future opportunities. Then you use the opportunity to improve the competitive environment for the next opportunity.

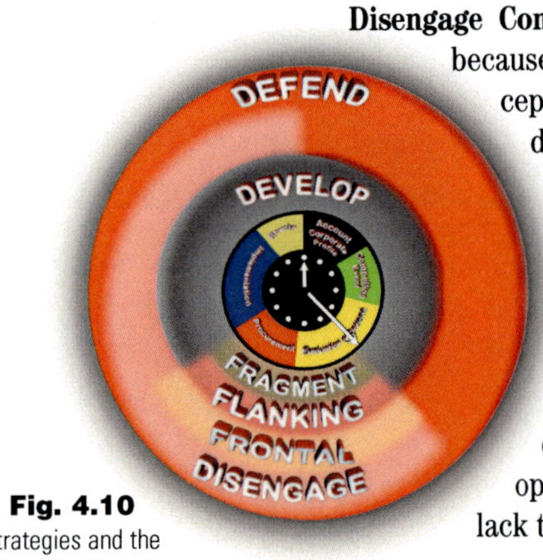

Fig. 4.10
Competitive strategies and the opportunities management clock.

In special cases, the disengage strategy can be used as part of an extended defend strategy, where you concede an opportunity to the competition to create a diversion so their resources are committed to the lesser opportunity. When the more important opportunity enters the procurement phase, the competition will lack the resources to secure the opportunity.

When following a disengage strategy, you can disengage at any time during the opportunity management process, but only after you have a complete understanding of the needs and requirements of the opportunity—usually early in the evaluation of options phase. When you disengage late in the evaluation of options phase or once the procurement process has started, you follow frontal strategy tactics except you price your proposal sufficiently above the strongest competitor to lose the work but not so high as to create the impression you are not serious about the opportunity. In a disengage strategy, you use the following tactics:

- Develop decision criteria from needs uncovered in the opportunities management process.
- Reinforce crucial decision criteria that you can meet better than the competition.
- Build up incidental decision criteria in areas where your offer is strong.
- Demonstrate justification of premium pricing.
- Rehearse with supporters to justify the premium pricing.

Figure 4.10 illustrates the timing for strategy selection and the use for each phase in the opportunities management process. At the beginning of the opportunities management process you are in a defend or develop competitive strategy, depending on whether it is a new project or account (develop) or an existing account or contract (defend). As you pass through the evaluation of options phase, you select a competitive sales strategy for the evaluation of options and procurement phases once you determine how the buying center will evaluate your offering. The earlier in the evaluation of options phase you select your competitive sales strategy, the more time you have to influence the decision criteria. Timing is essential if you plan to recommend an alternative solution, as in the flanking alter strategy, or expand or shrink the work scope, as in the flanking expand and fragment strategies. Once the work is awarded, you return to a defend position (won the contract), develop position (lost but want to position for a future opportunity), or do nothing and wait position (disengage).

To determine whether the project is worth winning, you must also answer the following questions:

- What is your expected short-term revenue?
- What are the prospects for future sales?
- What level of profitability can you expect?
- What is the degree of risk for the project?
- Is there any strategic value associated with winning the project?

Depending on the types of projects and contractual models used, answers to the revenue questions may be straightforward and easy to calculate. In projects with advanced contractual models or uncertain scope, considerable effort must be given to evaluating the value of the project early in the opportunities management process. Joint value and IPM reservoir optimization are examples of projects whose evaluation may be time-consuming and complicated.

The most difficult question to answer concerns the strategic value of the project. Here, sales representatives must engage upper management for guidance in comparing all potential opportunities, both current and in the foreseeable future. A project that is considered strategic at the location level may not be strategic at the HQ level. Sales representatives are responsible for capturing as much of the market share as possible at the required profit level. Before profit margins are sacrificed in the pursuit of a strategic opportunity, the strategic value must be sufficient to pass the strategic value test at higher levels in the organization.

To win an opportunity you must be in a strong position when you submit your proposal. This requires you to have focused conversations with the buying center members early in the evaluation of options phase before you select your sales strategy. Not having sufficient information can lead to bad decisions and disappointments when you discover you lost the sure bet. The professional salesperson uses the request for proposal worksheet to have these conversations. See Chapter Highlight 4.4: Get Organized and understand the good things that happen when you apply the tools of a professional salesperson.

Phase 3b: Procurement Phase

The procurement phase begins when the customer sends a request for services document. The procurement phase consists of five stages, as shown in Fig. 4.2:

- Submission of proposal
- Resolution of concerns
- Negotiations
- Monitor
- Outcome analysis

The procurement phase is also called "bidding" or "tendering" or one of any several terms. For a more detailed list of some of the procurement documents you may receive, see **Chapter Highlight 4.7: Procurement 101, Part 1.**[8] Many procurement departments follow these five stages. As discussed earlier, one objective of the evaluations of options phase is to understand the customer's evaluation model and the procurement stages used in the procurement phase. The complexity of the procurement usually increases with time.

1. **Early stage:** At this stage, bidding is relatively informal, communication is open, and negotiations are allowed. This stage takes place before the award. The client has no formal obligation to justify the choice.
2. **Mature stage:** This stage includes formal bidding, controlled communication, and a formal opening. There is an "opening price" followed by an evaluation process that results in an "evaluation price," which may differ from the opening price. Negotiation occurs with the "successful" bidder.
3. **Ultra-mature stage:** This stage is very formal, and the service company has only one opportunity to bid. The opening price is the final price, and this price is the value of the contract without negotiation.

When you understand the buying center's procurement stages, you have time to complete many of the standard requirements early in the process. By doing so, you can concentrate on more critical issues, analyze all the information gathered in the opportunities management process, and still have time to support ongoing business.

Usually, more people are involved in the procurement phase than in other phases, particularly during submission of the proposal. Often in the procurement phase a tender coordinator is assigned to oversee the process.

Phase 3b: Procurement—Submission of Proposal Stage

The submission of proposal stage consists of three substages:

- Receipt of the invitation to tender
- Bid documents and proposal review
- Submission of the proposal

This is one of the more rigorous stages of the opportunities management process. At the end of this stage, you submit a proposal that is the basis for a legal contract. In this contract, all services, pricing structure, liabilities, indemnities, etc., are fully and clearly documented.

Receipt of Invitation to Tender

When you receive an invitation to tender, the decision to bid or decline is made by management, with recommendations from marketing, sales, and operations staff. If management decides to bid, the tender acknowledgement form, included

Chapter Highlight 4.7: Procurement 101, Part 1

What's the Difference Between an EOI, RFP, RFT and RFQ?

If you're confused by the plethora of terms around bid management, tender consulting, proposals, and the equally confusing list of acronyms related to procurement, you're not alone. The various acronyms used in the procurement process have a lot to do with the buyer's readiness to purchase.

For example, an EOI (Expression of Interest)—often done in the early stages of the procurement process—may be released if the buyer is just looking, or is seeking industry input into scoping requirements that will then go back out to market later on. An RFP (Request for Proposal) is often the next stage, where the buyer goes to the market for solutions-oriented approaches to service or product delivery.

The RFT (Request for Tender) is a request to really get a proposal on the table around how you would design a solution or deliver a product or service, but usually delves further into what you are like to do business with, such as seeking information about organizational capability and resources, financial viability, sustainability principles, and value adding. An RFT may not seek pricing initially and may involve several phases of short-listing. An RFQ is a request to provide pricing on a product or service, which is generally not asked for in the early stages of procurement, such as with a Request for Information.

For simplicity, I have summarized the key differences below:

RFI – Request (or Registration) for Information

EOI – Expression of Interest

RFP – Request for Proposals

RFO – Request for Offer

RFT / RFQ – Request for Tender, Request for Quotation

RFT differences

In summary, EOIs are useful when the number of players, market size, or approach to solving a problem is largely unknown. RFTs are often used in the major infrastructure and construction industry where solutions to problems are high value, high risk, and very specific.

When to Use an EOI versus RFP and RFT.

In most cases EOIs and RFTs have been pre-designed and specified as a result of a significant amount of consultation, engagement, and preliminary design work. RFPs, on the other hand, provide for greater flexibility. This format is often used in the professional services sector (such as technology, recruitment, environmental consulting, and creative industries sectors), where there are many options and a variety of possible solutions.

in the invitation to tender, is returned to notify the client of your intention to submit a tender. The acknowledgement form must be reviewed to make sure it does not bind you to bid under the customer's terms and conditions.

If strict adherence to tender documents is a condition, and these documents contain requirements contrary to your company's contracts policy, the tender leader confers with the Contracts Department before responding to the customer. The acknowledgement must show the correct legal entity and signature, and the Contracts Department ensures that the tender details are logged into the contracts management database.

Bid Documents and Proposal Review

Once the decision has been made to proceed with a tender, the sales representative and contracts groups inform the Tax and Contracts Departments and the QHSE risk manager to ensure that all relevant parties receive a copy of the tender as early as possible.

The review process is conducted twice. First, the invitation to tender documents are reviewed to ensure that there is a complete understanding of the scope of work and the operational, technical, financial, and contractual requirements. This review process will be discussed in more depth in Chapter 10 "Competitive Bidding." The second review takes place once the proposal has been completed to be sure it follows the requests set forth in the invitation to tender and complies with your company's contracts policy.

Every proposal preparation involves a team composed of staff from sales and marketing, operations, contracts, finance, tax, and risk management. In most cases the contracts group participates on the tender team and coordinates with the finance, tax, and risk management groups. Each review process is discussed below. For larger bids or companies that have dedicated groups to prepare proposals, there can be people with dedicated roles, as described in **Chapter Highlight 4.8: Procurement 101, Part 2.**[9]

Operations and marketing. Operations and marketing groups study the commercial and operational/technical aspects of the bid. The tender submission generally incorporates a technical section, which can range from solutions to a series of technical questions and answers. These sections must be reviewed and qualified through consultation with appropriate experts.

The tender leader develops a bid strategy, which should complement the overall competitive sales and account strategy. The final bid package is tailored to meet the bid requirements to include the scope of work, pricing structure, and project objectives.

The final proposal is reviewed to ensure that all concerned parties understand the operational commitments and price structure, including any price escalations and incentive mechanisms, work logistics, and overall bid strategy.

Contracts. The Contracts Department examines the bid documents from a legal and commercial perspective. This department attempts to promote your standard terms (or refer to a master contract, if it exists) and examines the customer's terms and conditions, including insurance provisions.

The Contracts Department calls on support from the Tax and Finance Departments regarding the legal entity, tax/finance provisions (including terms of payment, taxes, customs, duties, and import/re-export formalities), local insurance provisions, structure of price, bid bond, and performance bond. The objective of the Contracts Department is to ensure that a clear understanding of the rights and obligations of all parties exist.

▶ ***Just Sign Here . . . What Contract Do You Use?***

An important step when, or prior to, entering the procurement phase is to determine if a master contract exists. Check with the Contracts Department to see if a master contract has been previously negotiated with the client in question, covering the type of equipment or service required. If not, then . . .

Can a standard form contract be used?

Standard form contracts should be used, whenever possible, in response to client bids and tenders. As you are the contractor, the experts performing the services every day, it is reasonable that your form of contract be used. A conscious effort must be made to propose standard contracts to clients, or they will rarely be used and you will be constantly in a defensive mode, having to make amendments to client contracts. Standard form contracts currently exist for use for many types of products and services. Copies of these standard form contracts can be obtained from your company's Contracts Department or website.

Chapter Highlight 4.8: Procurement 101, Part 2

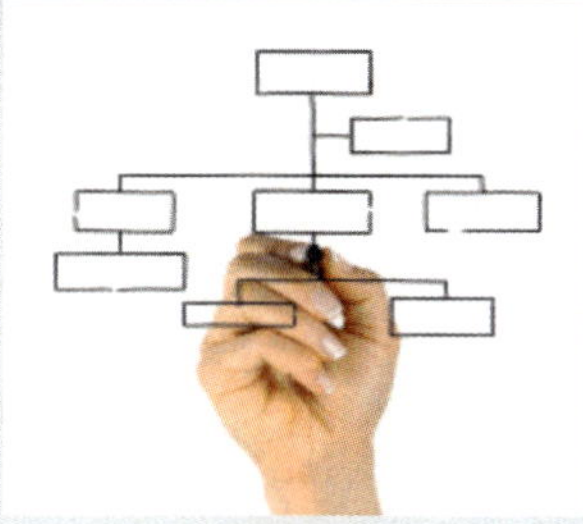

Are you resourcing a tender or bid team? Need a proposal writer? A bid manager... no, maybe a tender manager? If you are confused with the mix of terminology used by procurement and business development professionals, you are not alone. Here we explain the difference between bids, tenders, and proposals with a straightforward list of definitions every company needs. The first thing to realize is that terms vary from organization to organization and country to country. They also depend to some extent on the background and skill set of the person involved.

Bid: A bid is an approach to a client in order to gain significant new or repeat business. Bids, by their nature, involve staff from across the whole breadth of one or more organizations. The bid manager needs to be able to interact with many types of specialists, from technical to legal, finance, HR, and senior management, and will need to know their roles, responsibilities, and what they can and cannot be asked to deliver. The term bid or bidding can also relate to the documented offer submitted in response to a request or invitation to tender. The bid will then be evaluated against a set of criteria that are described in the request or invitation to tender.

Tender: The term tender is often used interchangeably with the term bid. However, bid is increasingly being used by the offerer (the supply side) while tender is used on the procurement side (the buyer).

Bid Manager: The bid manager takes full ownership of entire bid program. Sometimes, this may involve a period of research, information gathering, and strategic messaging prior to the bid being released. Responsibilities include overseeing best practice processes and procedures, and managing multiple resources —sometimes cross-functional, cross-jurisdictional and even across companies or the supply chain. As a leadership position, the bid manager—who must feel at ease working with executives and the board—requires strong people management skills as well as the ability to deal with complex business relationships, manage competing priorities, and drive the delivery of a strong winning business case to the client in a high stress environment within tight timeframes.

Tender Manager: The title is often used interchangeably with the bid manager title, although bids, by their nature, are project-based with a beginning and end point. The tender manager, on the other hand, has traditionally been charged with overseeing the capture lifecycle—from identifying and converting significant business opportunities to supervising and delivering tender responses and continually reviewing the bid management process. A tender manager can also be hired on the procurement side to manage tender requirements, oversee the Request for Tender process, and negotiate contracts (sometimes referred to as tender and contracts manager).

Project Manager: To some extent all bid managers act as project managers. A bid shares many characteristics of a project due to its defined beginning and end point, objectives, roles, responsibilities, milestones, and deliverables. For this reason some organizations assign project managers to bid management roles.

Business Profile or Corporate Credentials: A business profile (or corporate credentials) is a promotional or marketing tool that presents a snapshot of your company. It essentially serves as a resume for your business.

Capability Statement: Similar to the business profile, the capability statement is usually tailored to the audience or the contract requirements and describes the company's capabilities and experience, including who you are, what you do, and how you are different from your competitors.

Proposal: The proposal is a written offer from a seller to a prospective buyer. It is a critical step in the complex sales process—i.e., whenever a buyer considers more than price in a purchase—and serves as a persuasive business case for a product, service, or business opportunity. Proposals are client-centric selling documents that are highly tailored and solutions-oriented to the buyer's requirements.

Proposal Writer: Proposal writers are usually tasked with pulling together pre-existing information or creating custom content and tailoring it to the client's needs. Generally, a proposal includes a summary, identifies the problem or business opportunity, and defines the solution and how it will work (the methodology or project plan together with performance criteria), budget/pricing and organizational details, including names and description of credentials (past performance) and expertise of the individuals who will be responsible for managing and performing the work.

Technical Specialist: Also referred to as 'subject matter experts', technical specialists are usually industry specific and are central to developing the client's solution. Their focus is on design and functionality rather than the sale. In the IT space they might be systems programmers or network designers; for major infrastructure they may be civil engineers.

Technical Writer: Technical writers are usually professional communicators who are skilled at translating technical language into plain English instructions for the everyday user of a product or service. The technical writer and bid manager work closely with technical specialists to scope their information requirements and ensure they contribute positively to the bid.

The Contracts Department also reviews the bid for possible exposure risks that could affect the profitability of the project. The expected profitability is more certain when you can minimize your liability for both foreseen (e.g., cost of transportation) and unforeseen costs (e.g., liability for equipment lost or damaged downhole or for pollution damage).

Finally, the Contracts Department reviews the entire proposal as a complete package to ensure that changes inserted for commercial reasons do not pose legal difficulties, such as variations of warranties or penalties or the application of certain concepts (exclusive or call-out nature of the work, incentive mechanism, etc.). The review carried out by the Contracts Department is not confined to a scrutiny of the legal terms but extends to all facets of the bid that might have a bearing on your exposure and, consequently, on the profitability of the project.

Tax. The Contracts Department usually sends a copy of the pro forma contract to the tax advisor for review. The tax advisor's modifications and comments must be included in the tender submission. The Contracts Department reviews changes made for tax or commercial reasons to ensure that the changes will not have inadvertent legal ramifications.

Financial. The Finance Department reviews the tender in depth with regard to all financial issues, including payment terms, bonds and guarantees, currencies and credit checks.

Risk and insurance. The Contracts Department normally reviews the risk and insurance provisions and, where necessary, seeks advice from the Risk Management Department. Catastrophic risks are classified as such at the corporate level. The tender leader, in consultation with the Contracts Department (and, if appropriate, the Risk Management Department), must ensure that you do not accept any liability for catastrophic risks according to your company's contracts policy.

Proposal Submission

The formal proposal should have a professional look, present easy-to-find information, please the client, and make a good impression for your company. In addition to complying with all your contracting policies, the proposal should communicate a value proposition that compels the buying center to engage your company for the work.

The proposal must be prepared and delivered with strict confidentiality. Proposal documents must be closely controlled so that proposal information does not leak to your competitors or their allies. Final pricing details and significant contract terms should be the last information to be printed and inserted into the proposal package.

"The Customer's Point of View" sidebar (next page) features comments from clients about the do's and don'ts for submitting proposals.

Customization. Each proposal should be tailored to the specific customer and the invitation to tender so that it meets the customer's requirements. Your proposal should leave the buying center with the impression that you are addressing an important client issue. When several needs have been identified, they should be treated separately. The customization should also take into account that several buying center members may use the document for their part of the decision-making process. Each buying center role has different information requirements that you should accommodate in your proposal. **Figure 4.11** (page 94) lists the different types of information each role requires for input into the decision-making process.

▶ *Best Practice* Contracts Policy

Companies accept responsibility for reasonable risks associated with their activities. However, it has always been, and continues to be, a best practice not to accept any potentially catastrophic liability related to the performance of their services.

Clearly, the first rule is that you will not provide any services or perform any work without a properly signed service order or contract.

A contract or service order under which you will provide services to a client should be based on the mutual-harmless principle. That is, your company is responsible for its people and property, and the client is responsible for its people and property.

In addition, the contract or service order should stipulate that you will not be responsible for and will be expressly indemnified by the client for the following liabilities, except in cases of your intentional misconduct:

- Loss or damage to the well, the formation, or the reservoir
- Cost of controlling a wild well and cost of redrilling
- Damage or injury resulting from pollution originating below the surface or radioactive contamination related to operations, including the cost of cleanup and disposal
- Inaccuracy of any data, or incorrect interpretation or recommendation

For a complete list of your company's contracts policy, contact your contracts manager.

▶ ***The Customer's Point of View***

Below are comments made by customers regarding suppliers' proposal submissions.

Don'ts

- Do not change the rules of the game.
- Do not make pricing and discounts too complicated.
- No big packages.
- Do not impose the rules of the game.
- Complication comes from suppliers, not us.

Do's

- Fast and easy evaluation of bids.
- Simple to understand.
- Total Quality Management.
- One price list per project.
- One invoice per operation.
- Track record of delivering, as promised.
- Customers like flexibility.
- Answer as requested.
- Customers like fit-for-purpose services.

Advice from Customers

- Know personal priorities of evaluators.
- Know main priorities of the project.
- Presentation is important.
- Personalized and researched.
- Purchasing agents want to understand what they are buying.
- Purchasing agents like attention.
- Company policy is to ensure value for money.
- Win–win contracts are achieved through discussion with contractors in an open and cooperative atmosphere.
- Minimize duplication of contractor services.
- Streamline the in-house organization.

Your proposal should include executive summaries, strong value propositions, comparative tables, and detailed information to facilitate the decision-making process for each buying center role. Members in the buying center should be able to efficiently use your proposal to make decisions. When buying centers are large, you must identify the powerful members so you can meet their individual information needs for the decision-making process. Chapter 7 "Sales Call Skills" discusses how to tailor support documents to the specific customer profile of the buying center members.

When referring to the customer's operations in the proposal, you should use their terminology for referring to business units and functional groups. You should also refer to locations, reservoirs, rigs, etc., as they are called within the account.

Organization

Every proposal submitted should have at minimum the following sections:

- Cover letter with executive summary
- Technical proposal
  - Organization
  - Experience
  - Products and services
  - Customer support
  - Quality, Health, Safety, and Environment (QHSE)
- Commercial proposal
  - Pricing
  - Contractual issues
- Appendix

Cover Letter. As this may be the only portion of the document the decision-maker reads, the cover letter is an important part of the proposal. It should state on one page the value proposition and the differential value of the proposal as agreed upon in the evaluation of options phase. The cover letter should leave customers with a strong message about why they should choose you, and it should be placed at the beginning of the technical and commercial proposal when these parts are in separate envelopes.

Technical Proposal. The technical proposal is addressed to the users and technical evaluators in the buying center, who are typically the end users of the products and services called for in the tender to bid. Sometimes the technical evaluators also evaluate the commercial offering, but usually this task is carried out by the Procurement Department. The technical proposal comprises the following sections:

- **Organization.** A description of the you organizations supporting the project inside the region and other individuals or groups such as company headquarters, R&D, and technology centers. If appropriate, include any other support groups within your organization, such as your IT services, that will contribute indirectly to servicing the project and will differentiate you from the competition. Professional qualifications and work experience of the project service delivery team should also be included in this section.
- **Products and services.** This section contains a description of the products and services as requested in the invitation to tender and, if agreed upon by the buying center, any alternative products and services offered as part of a flanking strategy.
- **Customer support.** This is a brief description of the capabilities and resources available to provide direct support to the customer for the project.

> **▶ *I Do This, You Pay Me This—Simple, Right?***
>
> Below is a checklist for commercial terms in a contract. You should always have your operations manager and contracts manager review the commercial and legal terms and conditions of a contract before submitting your offer. This will keep pricing disputes to a minimum.
>
> **Checklist for Commercial Terms**
>
> Check what is included in your price, for example:
>
> - Mobilization/demobilization/stand-by charges
> - Personnel costs associated with delays/stopovers (especially for remote locations)
> - Back-up (at location or on rig)
> - Support services/special reports
> - Number of copies (unlimited?) distribution of copies to partners (worldwide?)
> - Safety equipment and regulations (costs of compliance?)
> - Third-party costs, including consumables and any administrative/handling charges.
>
> Check what items/services the client is prepared to provide at its expense (e.g., land/offshore transportation, accommodations and meals, medical aid, diesel, fuel, water, communications, etc.). Usually all other items/services are at your expense.
>
> If you agree to install your equipment, check the location of the rig at the time installation is due to take place.
>
> If you accept liability for a delay in start-up or completion of services, make sure it is limited "to delays attributable to your sole negligence" or "to the extent of you negligence." Consider a fixed financial limit.
>
> Does the client reserve the right to make you modify your equipment to its safety and other specifications at your cost? Make sure the right is limited to requirements specified in the tender and does not extend to future changes. Are there penalties for non-compliance?
>
> Who is to provide visas, permits, special certifications, etc., and at whose cost?
>
> Does the client only accept to pay depreciated value for lost/damaged equipment? If you accepts depreciated value, make sure there is a minimum residual value of 50% of landed replacement value. Is there a proviso that the client will not pay for loss or damage if your company insures equipment?
>
> Are you required to provide a bank guarantee, performance bond, or parent company guarantee? Is there a risk of the client defaulting on payment?
>
> Are you being asked to run the equipment of another supplier?
>
> Clarify safety/technical objections.
>
> Does the bid/contract specify that your company is to provide nominated personnel?

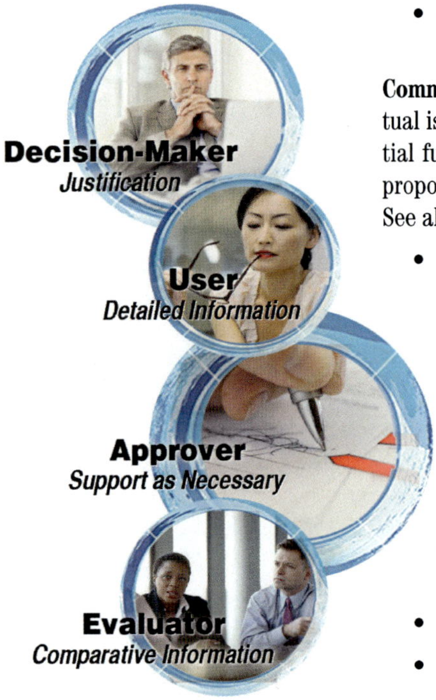

Fig. 4.11
Buying center members and required information.

- **QHSE.** This section calls for a description of your QHSE organization, program, policies, and QHSE records.

Commercial Proposal. This section contains your pricing proposal and contractual issues. The commercial proposal must be carefully completed to avoid potential future conflict between the customer and you. Those who draft commercial proposals must be familiar with commercial considerations in client contracts. See also the checklist in the "I Do This, You Pay Me This—Simple, Right?" sidebar.

- **Pricing proposal.** The pricing proposal should reference an attached price list and clearly explain any discounts and incentive pricing. It should be simple, clear, and easy to evaluate. It is a good practice to generate a sample invoice to make sure the customer understands the services offered and the associated costs.
- **Contractual issues.** This section should include any qualifications and exceptions to the proposed contract and any other legal issues.

Attachments. Attachments to the proposal include the following:

- Registrations with various organizations and government offices, such as taxes and commercial register.
- Business licenses for explosives, radioactive material, pressure, etc.
- Insurance certificates
- Curriculum vitae of operations personnel
- Reference letters
- Technical support documents, drawings, etc.

The actual process of delivering the contract varies from company to company and country to country. Instructions for submission range from very informal (no stamping or receipt of delivery) to very formal, where submissions have to be made by an authorized company representative and the packages with individual proposals must be sealed with wax and stamped. Late submission is usually cause for disqualification from the tendering process. Typically, requests for extensions must be made in advance of the due date, and usually an extension is granted to all companies if granted at all.

Opening of the tenders is as varied as the submission procedures. Some companies are very informal, and an assigned company representative opens the tender without a witness. In others, a very formal procedure is followed where the proposals are opened and authorized representatives from your company and competitors submitting proposals as well as a representative from the customer's legal department initial every page at the time of opening. Occasionally, submissions will be opened, read, and recorded in public.

After the bid has been submitted and opened, the next stage of the procurement phase—resolution of concerns—begins.

Phase 3b: Procurement – Resolution of Concerns Stage

Once the account has completed an initial evaluation of the proposals, the sale moves into the resolution of concerns stage. In this stage, fears, uncertainties, and doubts may block the decision or cause customers to reopen discussions with the competing bidders. Sometimes this phase is uneventful because the customer considers you to have an excellent reputation for delivering the products and services offered; other times, this is not the case—or the evaluation may be close between you and the other competitors. Resolution of concerns is very characteristic of large sales. This stage must be planned for and managed well.

In this stage, you must understand the risks and consequences for the buying center and work to resolve these issues. See the "What Causes Consequence Issues?" sidebar on the next page. Resolution of concerns includes the following tasks:

- Answering any questions
- Addressing any concerns
- Addressing any perceived consequences

Expecting Customer Concerns. You can prepare to handle the buying center's concerns by predicting those concerns as the decision point approaches. You make this prediction by using the information you gathered during the early phases of the opportunities management process or from the implementation phase of previous projects. For example, you might expect that a price-sensitive buyer, as discussed in the "What Causes Consequence Issues?" sidebar, would return to the pricing issue late in the procurement stage, the value buyer might come back with doubts regarding the value proposition, and the relationship buyer might have concerns about your level of corporate commitment.

Your relationship with the customer is also a good indicator of how likely you are to encounter concerns during the procurement stage. If you are regarded as a vendor, you are likely to have many more concerns to deal with than if you are regarded as a problem solver or stakeholder.

The customer's new technology adoption profile is also a very good indicator of possible concerns. If buying center members are unfamiliar with the technology or solution and they are mostly pragmatists, conservatives, or laggards, you should expect concerns as the decision point comes closer.

Your competitive sales strategy—especially a flanking strategy—may create concerns for the customer. If your flanking strategy suggests alternatives to their requested services, this may also cause concern regarding your capabilities.

> ### ▶ *What Causes Consequence Issues?*
>
> Based on their research, Neil Rackham and his colleagues at Huthwiate, found that consequences are the penalties or risks the customer believes could result from making a decision to select your company's products or services. But what causes consequences?[9]
>
> The researchers were able to gain some insights into the nature of consequences and their causes from a study they conducted about customer concern with price and how it changes during the selling cycle. They found price concerns to be high during the early stages of a sale. Often the customer's very first question is "What does it cost?" One of the reasons for this early concern with price is that the customer hasn't yet fully considered all their needs. As a result, the seller's product or service can't be judged in terms of the problems it solves; therefore, it must be judged on cost, not on value.
>
> As the exhibit below shows, price concern tends to drop as the sale progresses, usually reaching its lowest point in the middle of the cycle. In its place comes an increased interest in applications—in the capabilities, which the product or service provides. Finally, just before the decision, there's often a sharp increase in price concern, with cost issues frequently becoming the central issue on which the whole decision seems to rest. What accounts for this sudden increase in price concern?
>
> 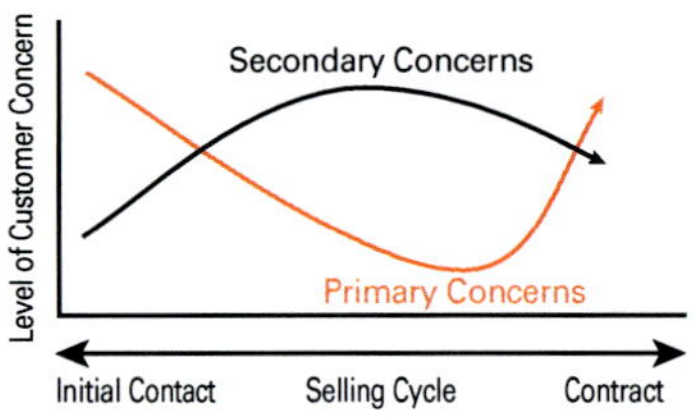
>
>
> One explanation is that the seller's efforts earlier in the cycle try to influence the value equation by developing solutions, savings, and benefits. However, as the decision approaches, the customer naturally looks at the other side of the equation and begins to assess what all these things will cost.
>
> Costs aren't just a question of purchase price. Part of what the customer must pay is measured in less tangible terms: The decision has costs in terms of risks, implementation problems, political dangers, and other things that could go wrong. These form the basis for the consequence issues, which often lie under the surface.

Concerns may also arise because the customer may not remember information that was presented during the evaluation of options phase. This is especially true when there have not been opportunities to reinforce the message throughout the procurement phase. See the "I Told Them That Over a Month Ago. How Could They Forget?" sidebar for a resolution of concerns example and a discussion on retention issues as they apply to a sales environment.[10, 11, 12]

Other Indicators. Buying centers may also develop concerns when large financial amounts are at stake in the decision. As the decision grows in gross dollar size, so do buyers' concerns about risks—especially those related to making an expensive mistake and disrupting business. Senior management may be actively involved or very much interested in the buying decision; consequently, buying center members may be under increased pressure to make the right decision.

When there are many buying center members participating in the decision, there may be political concerns—such as risks of upsetting influential individuals or functions.

Finally, the more competitors involved in the tender, the more alternatives on the table in the buying decision. Here, issues of vendor credibility and competence become important customer concerns. If the competitor is the incumbent and has given good service or is better known, buying center members may worry about the risk of changing service providers.

Discovering Concerns. Once you understand when to expect buyer concerns, you must take action to uncover them if they exist. The most direct way to do this is to ask the customer whether there are any concerns or consequences that you need to address. Be alert for signs of concerns that suggest there may be unresolved consequences.

Often, signs of concern are evident in discrepancies between what should be happening and what actually is. For instance, signs may come in the form of unusual events, such as previously resolved issues coming back as an issue, unjustified postponements, contacts who were willing to meet earlier but are now elusive, and information being passed selectively to competitors but not to you. Unrealistic price concerns are often amplified by unresolved consequences.

▶ *I Told Them That Over a Month Ago. How Could They Forget?*

You were able to get the key buying center members to gather all at the same time early in the evaluation of options phase and let you make your presentation on the great proposal you were able to put together for their project. It was a great presentation, there were a lot of questions, and everyone thanked you. You then submitted your tender feeling confident you would be awarded the work based on the earlier presentation.

Then you discovered they awarded the work to the competition. In the debrief with one of the evaluators, the customer revealed they were not comfortable that you would be able to make the mobilization in time for the advanced technology. You were shocked, because in the presentation you told them you had another project in the country demobilizing in the next six weeks. How could they forget?

The fact is, they probably forgot 90% of what you told them in your two-hour presentation. The graph above demonstrates why.

In his book based on his research, Tony Buzan suggests adults can listen and understand for 90 minutes, but they can only listen with retention for 20 minutes.

Based on Buzan's research, to ensure that customers retain information over time, the message must be reinforced as shown in the graphic above.

Exhibit 1: Retention versus Reinforcement

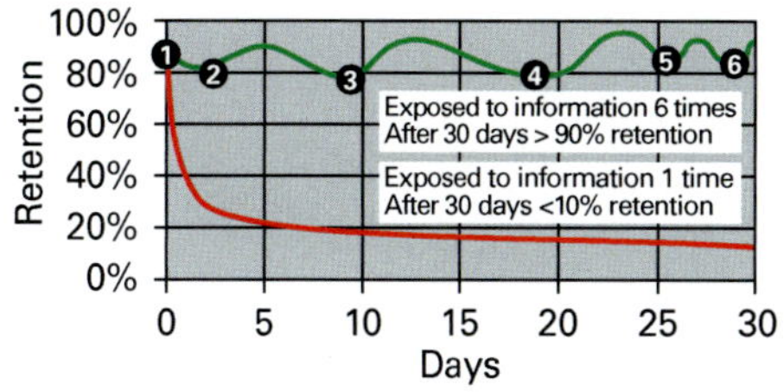

Robert Pike, a leading trainer of trainers, in his book *Creative Training Techniques*, suggests using the 90/20/8 rule for the highest level of retention. Present for no more than 90 minutes on any one topic, have a change of pace every 20 minutes, and try to involve the people in the content every eight minutes.

Handling Concerns and Consequences. Concerns and consequences fall into five categories, as follows:

- Indifference
- Skepticism
- Misunderstanding
- Technical drawback
- Financial drawback

Use these guidelines when handling concerns and consequences:

- Don't ignore them; they will not go away.
- Minimizing the issue will not resolve the issue. In fact, this may cause the customer to avoid any further discussion about the concerns or consequences.
- Help the customer resolve the issue rather than prescribe a solution.
- Avoid pressuring the customer to close the sale. This technique works for small sales but is often counterproductive in large sales. If the customer seems indecisive, probe to understand why and address those issues.

The "Sales Call Skills" and "Handling Customer Rejection" chapters discuss specific steps for dealing with each type of customer concern and consequence.

The next stage in the procurement phase is negotiations. Most customers in the evaluations of options phase identify possible products or solutions and suppliers who can provide those products or solutions. In the procurement process, the customer narrows this list to two or three preferred suppliers. The final selection comes after negotiating with each potential supplier to get the best offer. Sometimes, the negotiations stage comes after the customer has made a final selection based on the tendering process. The award, however, is conditional upon reaching an agreement.

Phase 3b: Procurement—Negotiations Stage

Competitive battles are fought in the evaluation of options phase, but the rewards for winning are decided in the negotiations. The following conditions must be met before negotiations can take place:

- A package of work has been tendered, an offer made, and the value of that package determined.
- All concerns and consequences have been resolved.
- Both parties can still vary the terms.
- Both parties have something the other party needs and can trade items of value.

The negotiations stage must fulfill the following objectives:

- Both parties come to an agreement where the value of the final deal is close to the value of the deal going into the negotiation.
- Both parties consider the final deal a win–win agreement.
- The negotiation process strengthens the relationship between you and the account.

Negotiations are a structured process that improves with preparation. To negotiate effectively, you must leverage all the information and value developed in earlier phases of the opportunities management process, such as information regarding the needs and priorities of the account, importance of the opportunity to the account, account and project value drivers, your differential value, and profiles of buying center members and their alignment.

Because of the importance of having this information, a key strategy is to negotiate as late as possible in the buying cycle. This strategy provides more time to gather information in the buying cycle and strengthen your position in the evaluation process. Negotiating too early is a common strategic error. See the "Can I Negotiate Now? No, Later!" sidebar for research on negotiating too early.[13]

The opportunities management process clearly illustrates that each phase of the sales cycle has specific objectives and strategies. By achieving the objectives of the early stages, sales representatives are in the best position to negotiate successfully. The negotiations process and required preparation are discussed in detail in Chapter 12 "Collaborative Negotiations."

Next in the procurement phase is the monitor stage, which is the waiting mode of the sales process. Negotiations are finished, best offers and trades have been made, and the final decision is very near. Did you win or lose? What do you do in the monitor stage is described next.

> ***▶ Can I Negotiate Now? No, Later!***
>
> Many studies have demonstrated that when salespeople are given the authority to offer discounts to help secure business, they usually give the maximum discount they are allowed to give, and the customer requests still further discounts before awarding the work.
>
> In one study, sales representatives were given authority to give up to a 10% discount in order to win the work. In 93% of the cases, all the sales representatives offered the maximum discount and requested additional discounts later in the selling cycle. How could this be? Their pricing authority was to be used as a negotiation tool, so why did they ask for additional pricing decreases to win the work?
>
> These sales representatives made the mistake of offering a discretionary discount early in the sales cycle, during the evaluation of options phase. They used the discount as a sales tool before the evaluations of options phase was completed. When they started the negotiations phase, they had nothing to trade.
>
> In the above study, management thought the discount would produce an increase in market share and possibly a 3% to 5% change in pricing. What ultimately happened was no change in market share and a 9% drop in prices.

Phase 3b: Procurement—Monitor Stage

In the monitor stage, the customer's decision-maker in the buying center has made the decision and is in the process of passing the recommendation for final approval. In this stage your mission is to:

- Defend your position from competitor tactics;
- Prepare your attack strategy; and
- Prepare for customer negotiation tactics.

Defending From Competitor Tactics

Once competitors discover they have lost the work, they may attempt to interject at higher approval levels to delay, block, or overturn the decision in their favor.

They can also work to have your selection rejected or can attempt to have the entire procurement process canceled and restarted.

This defense highlights the importance of the question "Can you win?" You may never know such maneuvers are taking place if there is no one in the buying center who is aligned with you, and upper management may be susceptible to competitor tactics if you have no alignment at that level. This is the stage where any enemies in the customer's organization may attempt to intervene. Therefore, it is critical you have mentors and supporters in the buying center who can alert you and defend your position.

Here are some actions you can take to combat such events:

- **Alert mentors and supporters in the buying center that this may happen.** If in the past the competition has tried to block an award being made to you, the probability for this is high.
- **Meet with mentors and supporters.** Shortly after negotiations have ended, rehearse with mentors and supporters the benefits of awarding the work to you.
- **Provide mentors with the most recent and succinct support and justification for using you.** Assist mentors by providing support materials so they are ready to quickly address any concerns or consequences the competition or internal enemies may try to create.
- **Meet with the approver to review the decision.** In this meeting your representative reinforces the benefits and addresses any concerns and consequences. In most cases, a high-level manager from your organization who has been thoroughly briefed attends this meeting. This visit should be scheduled ahead of time based on a best estimate of when the procurement process will enter this stage. By waiting until there is a problem to schedule this meeting, the approver may be called on by many suppliers, or the meeting may be blocked.

Your Attack Strategy

In an attack strategy, a last-minute, high-level attempt is made to block the award to the competition. Because of the sensitivity of this strategy, you must determine very early the conditions under which you would use this strategy. You must also consider the consequences of such a maneuver. If you decide to proceed, you must decide who will make the contact and with whom. Should you directly approach the approval level, or should you contact a person who would support your efforts and who has a direct relationship with the approver? Your earlier analysis of the buying center will help you make this decision and really pays off when executing an attack strategy.

Your intervention must be based on your belief that the customer will not benefit from the decision not to choose you. As such, you must have specific reasons for this belief. Prior to launching an attack strategy, it is a good practice to alert your mentors that you plan to take such action and to get their feedback and recommendations.

Preparing for a Customer Negotiation Tactic

Now it is time to rehearse. You thought the negotiations were finished, but the customer has come back to you asking for a concession before they award you the work. You must be prepared to deal effectively with this negotiation tactic. See the "I Can't Believe What Has Happened" sidebar on the next page for an example of last-minute negotiations.

You can be flexible provided the customer is as well. When asked for a last-minute concession, you must be prepared to explain what you are willing to do and what you want the customer to do for you. You must brainstorm internally to develop a list of inexpensive, yet valuable trade-offs that you can suggest in response to such a request. Chapter 12 "Collaborative Negotiations" discusses this topic in more detail.

Once you receive notice that the procurement process is over, you perform an outcome analysis.

Phase 3b: Procurement—Outcome Analysis Stage

Once the customer has made a final decision, you analyze the results of the opportunities management phase to determine how these contributed to your success or failure. The analysis should be done from three perspectives: the customer's point of view, what you achieved, and what the competitors did.

Customer's Point of View

- **Reasons why you won or lost.** You analyze the customer's point of view to determine their reasons for the final decision. You ask the customer how you and your competition scored in the evaluation. You also ask the customer what you did well and what you could have done better.
- **Reasons why your competitor won or lost.** What did the competitors do better than you?
- **Final amount of differential value the customer gave you.** Did the customer discount your differential value more than you expected? Why didn't the customer give you the full amount you expected?

What Did You Achieve

How did you do in each phase of the opportunities management process up to this point? Starting from the beginning, you should evaluate how effective you were in each phase of the opportunities management process by answering the following questions:

- Did you correctly identify the account and project value drivers?
- Did you correctly analyze the buying center? You should update buying center information in your CRM system so it reflects more accurately what happened. Who was the most influential? What were the alignments? Were there

▶ *I Can't Believe What Has Happened . . .*

It is 4:00 on Friday afternoon. It has been a long and difficult battle to win this project, but things are looking good. The decision-maker has recommended using you, and mobilization takes place next week.

Then you get a phone call from your friend in the Procurement Department. Your friend describes a desperate situation. They can't believe what just happened. To everyone's surprise, the competitors increased their discount when their operations vice president visited with the asset manager. The asset manager asked your friend to call to see if you can close the gap, and they want an immediate answer. Otherwise, you will lose the work.

What do you do?

The sales representative in this situation acknowledged the telephone call and thanked the client for making the effort to give him a chance to respond. The sales representative reconfirmed his commitment to the project and, as always, wanted to remain flexible and accommodating. The sales representative asked how big the competitor moved and learned the competitor had discounted an additional 10%. After a long pause, the sales representative suggested he could move 3%, provided the customer paid for transportation charges of the equipment from their place of mobilization. The sales representative explained how the customer was going to be shipping parts of the rig from the same location and could include his equipment in their shipment. In the call for tender, suppliers were to pay for all mobilization and demobilization. The customer didn't commit, but said that he would discuss with the manager and get back to the sales representative Monday morning.

The sales representative's weekend was ruined as he waited anxiously, but on Monday morning the reward came when he received word that the customer had decided to go with his company.

people in the organization you should have tried to motivate or neutralize? Were there buying center members you did not know until it was too late?

- What did you learn from the negotiations? Who carried out the negotiations, and what was their style? What were the key negotiating issues?

What Did the Competitor Do?

To determine what your competitor did, you should answer the following questions:

- What was the offer made by the competitor? Answer with as much detail as possible and include pricing, incentives, discounts, etc.
- Did the competitor have mentors in the buying center?
- What was the competitor's sales strategy, and when did they actively start to pursue this opportunity?
- Did the competitor use any significant tactics such as engineering center visits or last-minute contacts to upper levels in the customer's organization? Did they make any last-minute concessions? Did they bring corporate-level executives to make contacts regarding this opportunity?
- What was the competitor's reaction after notification of the result?

Despite its importance, the outcome analysis stage is often overlooked, or the analysis is not carried out in a factual and methodical manner. "You lost on price" is not an outcome analysis; it is merely an assumption. Outcome analysis helps you prepare for the next opportunity by gaining a better understanding of the customer's final decision. It helps you better analyze the buying center and improve your next competitive sales strategy.

If the opportunity is part of an ongoing operation that is tendered regularly every year or two, the perfect time to formulate the strategy for the next tender is immediately after the outcome analysis with the same sales team, regardless of whether you won or lost the work.

Chapter 9 "Strategic Sales Plan" demonstrates how to conduct an effective sales plan review process, which is a key input when completing the outcome analysis.

If you were awarded the work, the opportunity passes on to operations. In most companies, the sales staff are responsible for providing some level of support during the implementation phase. The next section discusses the reasons for this.

Phase 4: Implementation

The customer has awarded the work to you and begins to implement the project. The sales representative's objectives are to:

- Deliver on the promises made in the evaluation of options and procurement phases; and
- Use the implementation stage as part of the account development process.

Deliver on the Promises Made in the Evaluation of Options and Procurement Phases

To deliver on your promises, the sales representative and operations team join together in the implementation phase to form the service delivery team. The sales representative is responsible for ensuring that operations understands the promises made (this happens before the bid) and delivers the product or services as expected.

This is a good time to review Chapter 1 on T. Levitt's concepts of "looking through a mirror not a window" (discussed in his paper called "Marketing Myopia"[14]) and the total product concept (discussed in *Marketing Success Through Differentiation—of Anything*[15]).

Service Quality Review Meeting

The service quality review meeting is held to determine how well your company is performing; and it is also a good time to understand how well the customer is performing compared to their objectives. You need to know the customer's metrics for success, which were discovered in the identifying the compelling event phase. In this meeting, you report any major operating failures to ascertain what happened and define how you can prevent the failure from occurring again. You also review any major operating successes to ensure that you can repeat them. These two events should be captured as part of your total quality management program.

As Levitt's total product concept suggests, you must look for ways to augment the product during the implementation phase so that you can better meet the customer's needs and impact future decision-making. Once you discover ways to augment the product, you have to decide whether to introduce the augmentations at the service quality review meeting or at some other time.

If you know the project will be tendered again, perhaps as part of the contract renewal process, or if there will be upcoming similar projects, you might want to wait to formally introduce the augmentation in the next evaluation of options phase as part of a flanking alter the rules competitive strategy. Several reasons may compel you to wait. For instance, if the augmentation is easy for the competition to copy, you could lose your advantage in the next opportunity. If the competitor has mentors or you have enemies in the customer's organization, you may want to be protective of improvements that give you a competitive advantage, as the competitor's mentors and your enemies will assist the competitors in duplicating your improvement. It is a very beneficial process for the sales and operations team to take the time to complete an augmentation exercise in the middle of a project implementation. See **Chapter Highlight 4.9: "This is as Good as it Gets?"** about how one sales and operations team impressed their customer and made more revenue.

Strategies for Success in the Implementation Phase

To ensure success throughout the implementation stage, it is useful to review how the customer's learning, efforts, and motivation evolve during the life of the implementation. **Fig. 4.12** on page 106 splits implementation time into three phases. The early phase, called exploring, is where something happens with very little effort. Motivation in this stage is high, but enthusiasm may wane as the implementation moves into the learning stage. Great effort must be expended in the learning stage as the customer uses the new product or services. Motivation continues to drop as efforts are high and results are low. In the next stage—the effectiveness stage—the customer gets the results and motivation goes back up.

The challenge for the sales representative and operations is to anticipate factors that would lead to the effectiveness stage and take action to keep the learning stage as short as possible. In fact, this graph can be shown to the customer when you explain what you can do to shorten the learning stage to keep their personnel motivated throughout the implementation.

To do this, the service delivery team must develop a strategy to address any critical issues the customer may have regarding the implementation. This is best done during the evaluation of options phase as you tailor your products and services to fit the customer's needs and practices. This step will ensure a smooth implementation.

Chapter Highlight 4.9: This is as Good as it Gets?

Mid-Project Augmentation Exercise. Taking Time to Look for Improvements in the Middle of a Project

Product augmentation refers to the total product concept and involves adapting, expanding, or modifying the product or service so it delivers more value to the customer. This process is only successful with a thorough understanding how the current product is being used or its limited utilization in the client's decision-making process. Product augmentation opportunities are typically specific to one client, and the associated costs are not significant for the seller. In fact, there may be no extra cost at all; however, the opportunity may disappear if the seller does not fulfill the client's need or if a competitor does. Sales teams and operations often get together to figure out how to add value to the product offering for the customer and to further differentiate the seller's company from a competitor. One example of such collaboration was the creation shown below.

Mid-Project – Product/Services Augmentation Workshop

Account Department Project	Supplier/Product Line(s) Contact	Issue Red-Problem Green-Opportunity	Profile Innovator Visionary Pragmatist Conservative	Current Level Generic Augmented Potential	What Is Required? Describe the offering. What is required? Are there other product lines required?	Cost Incremental Cost to Develop Augmented Offering	Value $ Financial Benefit to Customer of Offering	Global? Yes/No	Ability to Cope Easy Difficult Impossible	Introduction As Soon As Possible/ Next Tender	Marketing Name Be Creative
Drilling	Wireline Cased Hole	Customer's workover costs are increasing at 25% per year. Workovers do not seem effective.	Pragmatist	Generic -> Augmented	1. Need close coordination between wireline and cementing groups to generate cement evaluation report and recommendations. 2. Need dedicated log analysts in computing center to generate and deliver report within 24 hours.	No more than $1k/report. Already have equipment and people. Just need assigned log analysts.		Yes		ASAP	Cement advisor costs $10k/report
Drilling	Cement Advisor	Lessons learned from previous WO campaigns are not captured and easily shared, causing repeated mistakes.	Pragmatist	Augmented -> Potential	3. Create database of Cement Advisor searchable by issue and location. Put on drilling floor in a computer kiosk touchscreen.	Programmer-$5k one time Hardware-$10k Maintenance contract $1k/month	Making Cement Advisor available easily for Drilling. Engineers would be beneficial and can be used as a training tool.	Yes	Kiosk-easy Cement Advisor-Difficult	Next tender	Cement Advisor plus costs $2k/report

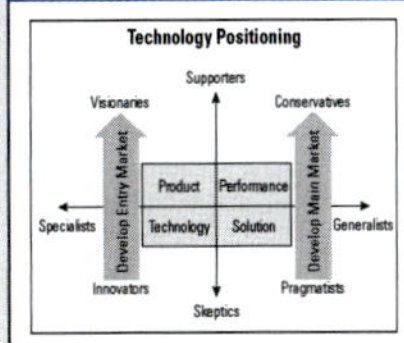

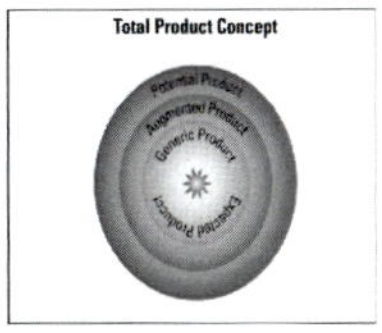

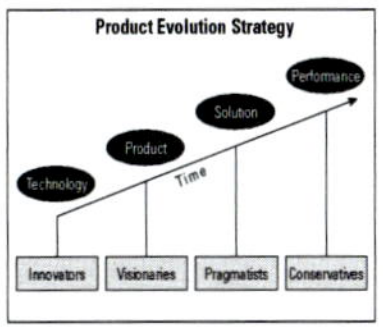

The workshop began with a brainstorming session of the most pressing issues or opportunities that the client was experiencing. Then the team discussed and selected two items from the list to develop ideas on what they could propose to address their assigned issue. The poster shown above is what one team proposed to address the issue of rising workover costs for their customer. The first idea to create the Cement Advisor, a coordinated effort between two of the supplier's divisions working for the customer in their oilfield on the North Slope of Alaska. This augmentation took the generic product cement evaluation and improved the product delivered to the customer; rather than simple data, it became an interpretation and recommendation report. The customer bought the Cement Advisor and installed the "Cement Advisor Plus" in the next contract. This improvement of making a cement advisor database accessible from a kiosk on the drilling department floor is considered to be at the potential level because of the customer's positive reaction and the competition having nothing comparable. The drilling manager indicated that he was impressed with the Cement Advisor and considered it a significant improvement. Now the drilling engineers were given the cement evaluation results in a much more useful format and, consequently, their workover costs had finally dropped year-on-year for the first time in a long time. In addition, the Cement Advisor Plus, from his perspective was state-of-the-art and his team was using it to train their new drilling engineers in workover operations and capturing best practice. His final comment was, "For cement evaluation, this is as good as it gets."

A copy of the augmentation workshop poster is included in the appendix.

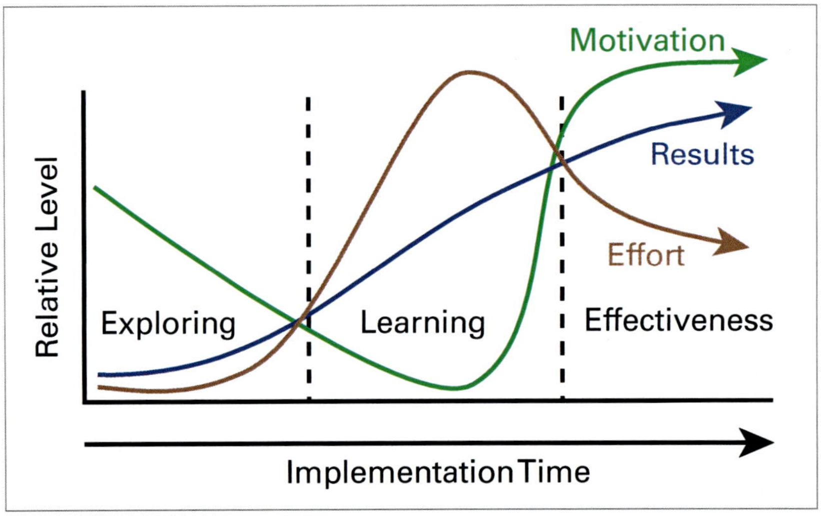

Fig. 4.12 Phases of an implementation.

A good implementation plan must be technically sound and include participation and commitment from key stakeholders. The easiest way to gain participation and commitment is to involve the customer with the service delivery team when the final implementation plans are developed.

The earlier you start to monitor the customer's reactions to your delivery of the product or service, the better. This is where you can use the exploration stage to your advantage. You must examine how the implementation is going and anticipate anything that would prevent your ability to shorten the learning stage once the real work begins. Sometimes you have to create the exploration stage.

Use the Implementation Stage as Part of the Account Development Process

A study by F. Reichheld[16] shows that improving customer retention can significantly improve a company's profitability. Reichheld emphasizes the importance of total customer satisfaction as measured by customer loyalty and that relationship management is critical to achieving total customer satisfaction—the key requirement in retaining customers and improving relationships. There is no better time to develop relationships than when you have the work—when you are on the inside and the competition is on the outside. You can use this opportunity to improve your relationship in several areas:

- **Improve your relationships with contacts in the account.** You do this by developing the relationship rather than just maintaining contact. For example, you can hold lunch-and-learn events or give training courses that include time for both lecturing and entertainment, such as holding a new technology seminar targeted at a customer-specific need combined with a golf outing. Such interactions help create awareness of products and services that may help your customers meet their objectives, and they set the stage for a customer solutions selling environment. You use a more relaxed atmosphere to gain a better understanding of the contacts' objectives and opinions and get to know them better on a personal level. This technique will be discussed in more detail in Chapter 7 "Sales Call Skills."

  Have you improved your status with members in the buying center who were neutral and non-supporters? The best way is to ask buying center members how they perceive your product and services and how you could improve. By contacting neutral and non-supporters, you demonstrate a concern for whether the customer's requirements are being met.

You can also improve your position by contacting your enemies to look for ways to improve the relationship. Having the work is a good reason to visit with them.

- **Improve your understanding of buying center dynamics.** When you ask questions about how the approval process flows, you can better understand and observe exchanges between contacts in the account. This will help in identifying the powerful, influential buying center members.
- **Generate leads and references.** Assuming the implementation is going smoothly, ask those who are involved if you can use them as a reference for another department or location where you could offer the same products or services.
- **Reassess your understanding of the value drivers for the account, project, and contacts.** You must confirm the assumptions made initially in the identifying the compelling event phase to ensure that they have not changed or been added to.
- **Look for ways to improve future projects.** You always want to make suggestions on how things could be done better in the future and on changes or additions to the work scope that would enable you to provide more value. Then you can track and report on factors that should be included in future decision criteria. As in the Pembina example in Chapter Highlight 4.6, during the implementation of the drilling program the sales representative began to report on logging times and improvements made to reinforce the value and importance this should have in future decision-making processes.
- **Key factors to track.** During the implementation you want to monitor the relationship between you and the project team. You should determine whether your role is improving or becoming less important to the account. A good measure of how the relationship is developing is to gauge whether you are taking on more responsibility, participating more in the customer's internal meetings, or providing more products and services to the account as the implementation proceeds. Each opportunity presented in the implementation phase should be incorporated into the long-term account strategy. Have you been able to achieve your account management objectives for this opportunity for this account? This is discussed in more detail in Chapter 15 "Planning."

Earlier in this section the role of the service quality review meeting and its importance in the implementation phase were discussed. The performance review at the end of the project provides the same benefits. Sometimes, the nature of the project does not allow for multiple service quality review meetings, and only a performance review is held at the end of the project.

Phase 5: Performance Review

At the end of the project or contract period, most customers conduct an end-of-project review to compare planned versus actual activities. Some companies, such as BP, call these After Action Reviews, which are considered part of their knowledge management initiative.[17] The objective of these reviews is to capture best practices and lessons learned. From your perspective you want to use this time to:

- **Check for customer satisfaction.**
- **Ask the customer whether everything was delivered as promised.**
- **Document lessons learned.** What major actions would you do again, and what you would do differently next time? This is an indirect approach to reinitializing the sales process.
- **Summarize the project performance.** This should be done in terms of the customer's key performance metrics, major operating successes, major operating failures, and appropriate actions for each.

- **Confirm that everything has been completed.**
- **Ask when the next opportunity will come.** This approach reinitiates the sales process if the customer does not offer the information. You should also select the buying center members from whom you want ask for a reference.
- **Review with all key buying center members not present at the performance review meeting.** You should contact key buying center members who were not present at the performance review meeting and go over meeting highlights with them individually. Typically, initiators and approvers do not attend the meeting.

Key activities in the performance review phase are:

- **Plan and conduct the performance review meeting.** Going to a performance review unprepared sends a worse message than failing to conduct one. The performance review meeting is a considerable opportunity to ensure customer satisfaction and reinitiate the sales process.
- **Report Major Operating Successes (MOSs) and Major Operating Failures (MOFs).** Many studies have shown that if you only talk about problems, the customer remembers the problems. If you constructively talk about both successes and failures, the customer remembers the successes.
- **Document the performance review.** Adults typically remember only 10% of what was presented at a meeting in 30 days if there is no reinforcement effort. The documented performance review becomes a sales aid for the next evaluation of options phase, so take the time to make a professional report.
- **Document lessons learned and propose next steps for future projects.** A detailed list of what happened during the project is not a performance review. The purpose of the performance review is to determine what you can do better next time and leverage the knowledge gained from the completed project. Include a section specifically titled "Lessons Learned and Recommendations." This is another indirect way to influence the decision criteria for the next project.
- **Always check for customer satisfaction.** If you believe the customer may not be fully satisfied, you have time at this point to resolve any outstanding issues. Otherwise, you create a customer that doubts your abilities and may not give you another opportunity to do the work. This is a critical part of successful account management.

This concludes this chapter on the opportunities management process, a tool used by professional salespeople to use time to their advantage over their competition. In this chapter, many activities were recommended for the life of an opportunity to assist the sales professional in prioritizing their actions.

In addition to prioritizing activities, it is also important to recognize the critical factors in each phase of the opportunities management process. **Chapter Highlight 4.10: Opportunity Management Stages: Description, Objectives, and Issues** provides a summary of every stage of the opportunities management process.

Many of the activities involve customers, and being successful requires the salesperson to have excellent communication skills. Communication skills are the foundation for successful sales call skills and handling customer rejection. These three skills are addressed in the next chapters in the Consultative Selling section of the textbook.

Chapter Highlight 4.10: Opportunity Management Stages: Description, Objectives, and Issues

Customer Project Management Schedule

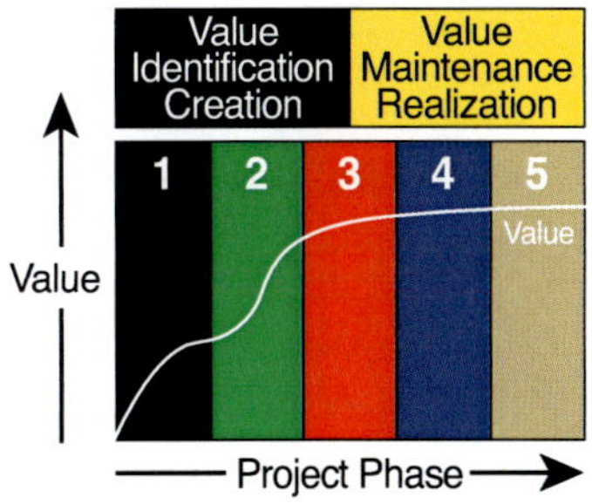

Phase 1—Strategy Setting

Phase 2—Project Selection

Phase 3a—Evaluation of Options

Phase 3b—Procurement

Phase 4—Implementation

Phase 5—Review

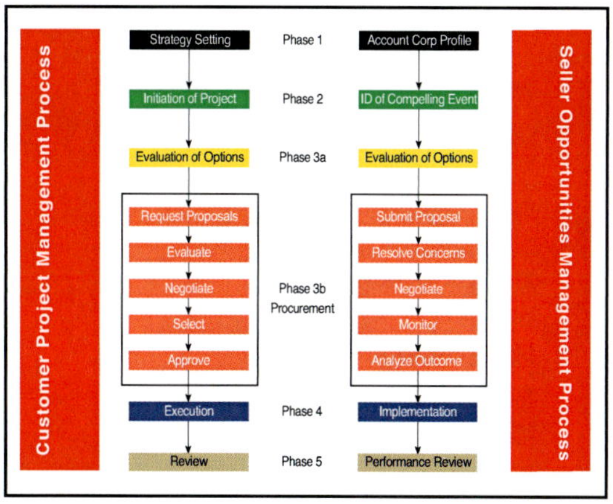

Phase 1: Account Corporate Profile

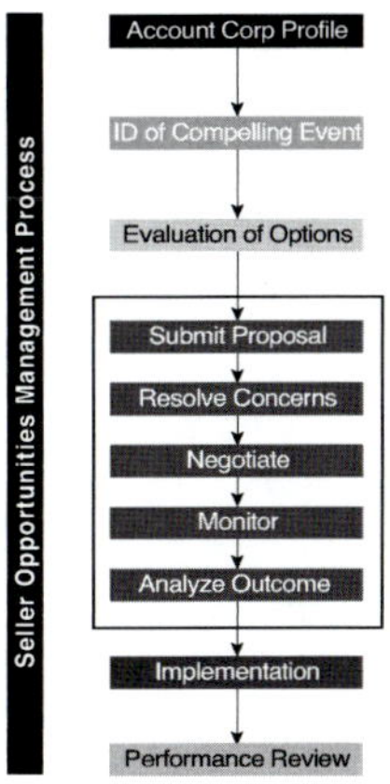

Description

- Have complete understanding of customer's high-level business drivers.

Objectives

- Uncover key metrics and strategies.
- Identify areas of focus for customer.
- Define opportunities to align.

Issues

- Must happen as a regularly scheduled event, ideally after budgeting or planning process.
- Must be documented and shared with Account Team.
- Not recognized as part of the sales cycle.

Phase 2: Identify Compelling Event

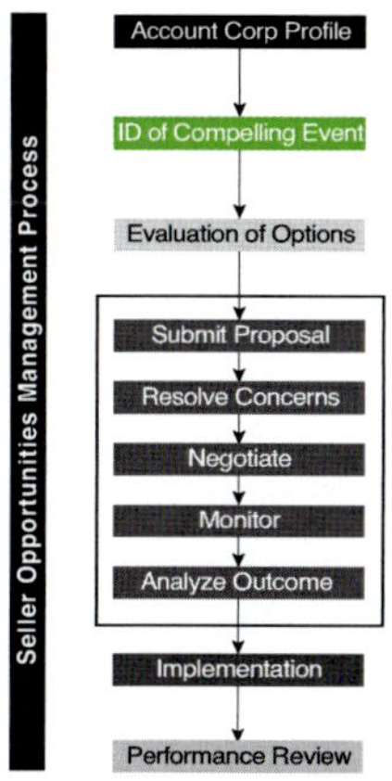

Description

- Account approves project, allocates budget, and assigns project team.

Objectives

- Qualify the compelling event.
- Understand project factors, timeline, and who managers are in the decision-making process.

Issues

- Must be at the executive sponsor level.

Phase 3a: Evaluation of Options

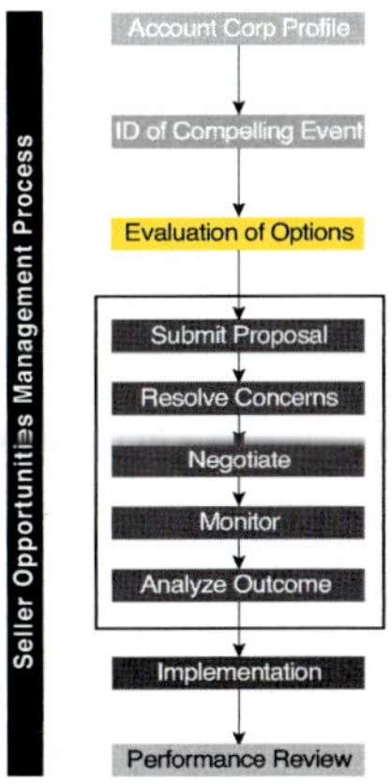

Description

- Account makes choices between competing alternatives.

Objectives

- Can we win? Can we compete? Is it worth winning?
  - Meet the buying center's needs.
  - Uncover decision criteria.
  - Influence decision criteria.
  - Maximize perceived fit.

Issues

- Don't know all the buying center members.
- Account may set criteria before needs are fully established.
- Our offering may not be superior for all decision criteria.
- Importance of soft and hard differentiators.

Phase 3b: Procurement Phase

Submission of Proposal Stage

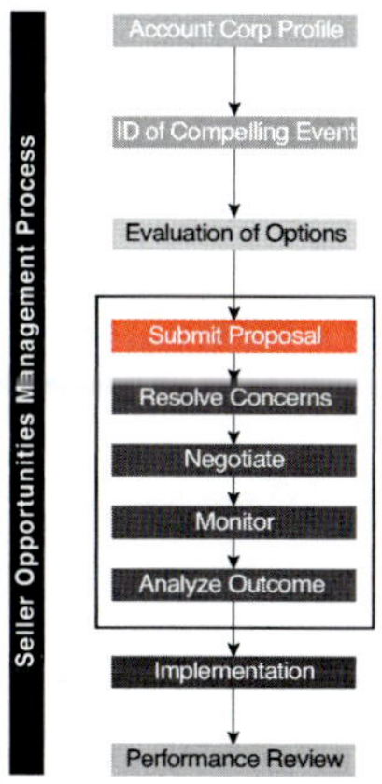

Description

- Official submission of final proposal.

Objectives

- Clear communication of value, technical, QHS&E, and pricing considerations.
- All legal and contractual considerations presented and complete.

Issues

- No statements of value.
- Pricing proposals not clear.
- Accurate assessment of risks/review not completed.

Chapter Highlight 4.10: Opportunity Management Stages: Description, Objectives, and Issues cont.

Phase 3b: Procurement Phase
Resolution of Concerns Stage

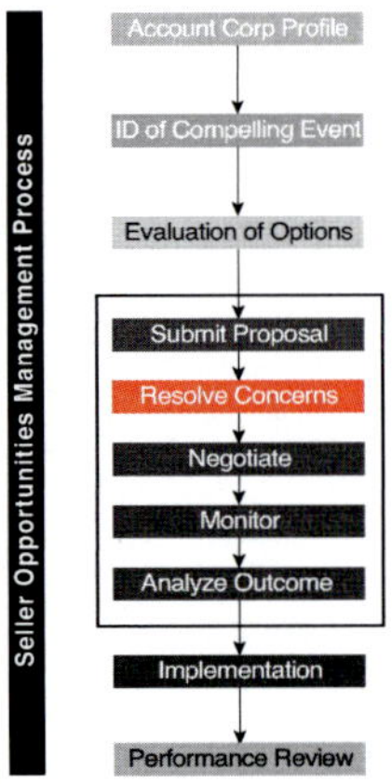

Description
- Fears, uncertainties, and doubts that are barriers to final purchasing decision in your favor.

Objectives
- Answer any questions.
- Answer concerns.
- Answer consequences.

Issues
- Ignore sensitive risks.
- Price is not the real issue.
- Lack of reinforcement.

Phase 3b: Procurement Phase
Negotiations Stage

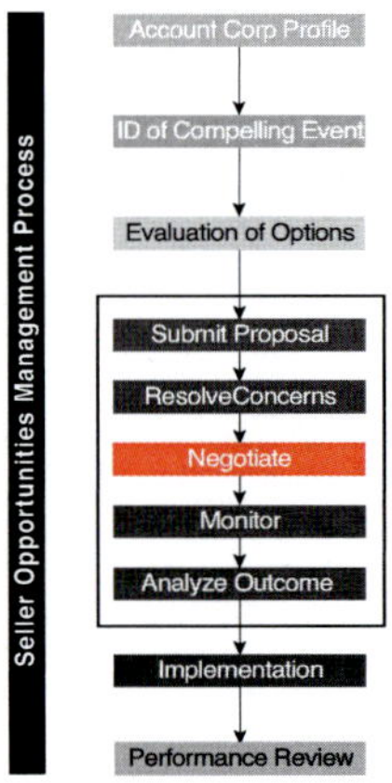

Description
- A process for reaching agreement.

Objectives
- Prepare.
- Know how to negotiate collaboratively.
- Know your alternatives.
- Have trades.
- Know how to deal with competitive negotiators and their tactics.

Issues
- Not prepared.
- Not leveraging information.
- Negotiating too soon.

Phase 3b: Procurement Phase
Monitor Stage

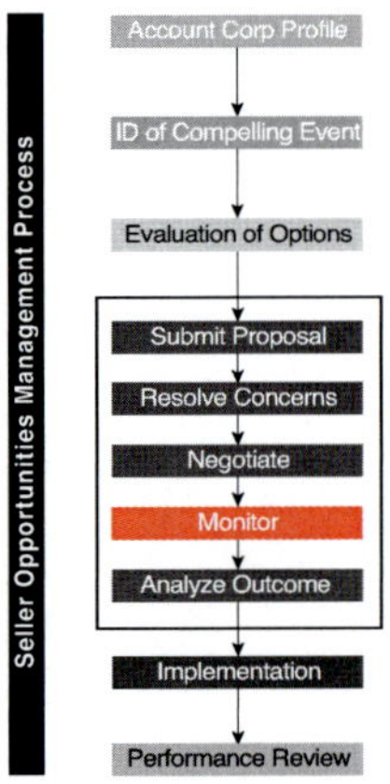

Description
- Monitor progress of decision through to the final approval process and contract signature.

Objectives
- Defend against competitor's desperation attempts.
- Prepare for your attack strategies.
- Prepare for any customer demands prior to award notification.

Issues
- Monitoring responsibilities.
- No preparation or monitoring at approval levels.

Phase 3b: Procurement Phase
Outcome Analysis Stage

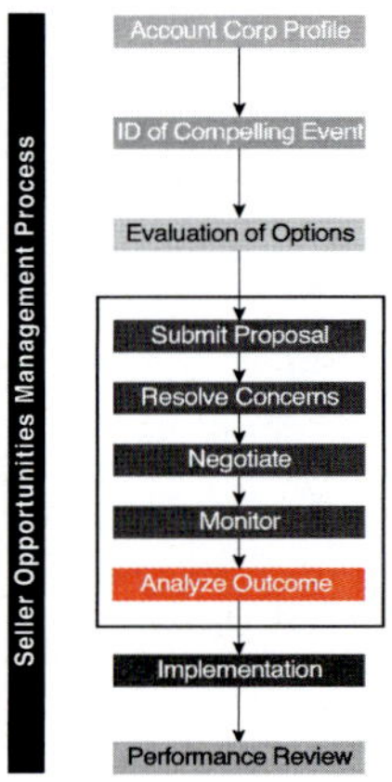

Description
- Outcome analysis of opportunity management process up to end of award decision.

Objectives
- Understand decision from
  - Customer's point of view.
  - What we achieved.
  - What competitors did.
- Analyze sales strategy effectiveness.

Issues
- Not done.
- Not done in a factual manner.
- Not documented.
- Not input into CRM.

Phase 4: Implementation

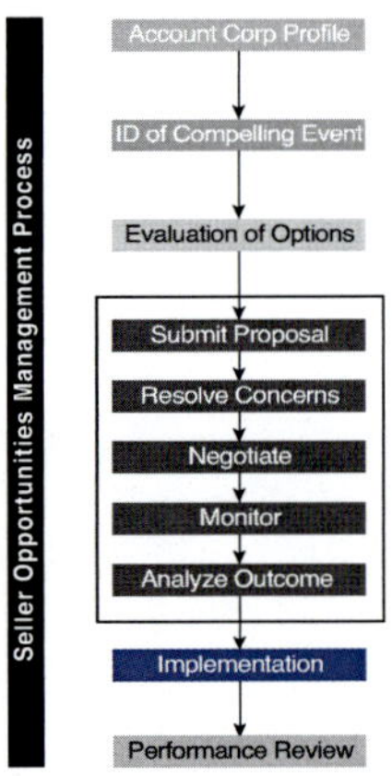

Description
- Account starts project.

Objectives
- Deliver on promises made during early part of sales cycle.
- Use as part of account development.
- Complete augmentation workshop.

Issues
- Address the stages of implementation.
- Handle problems and successes.
- Fail to check for satisfaction.
- Reinitiate the sales cycle.

Phase 5: Performance Review

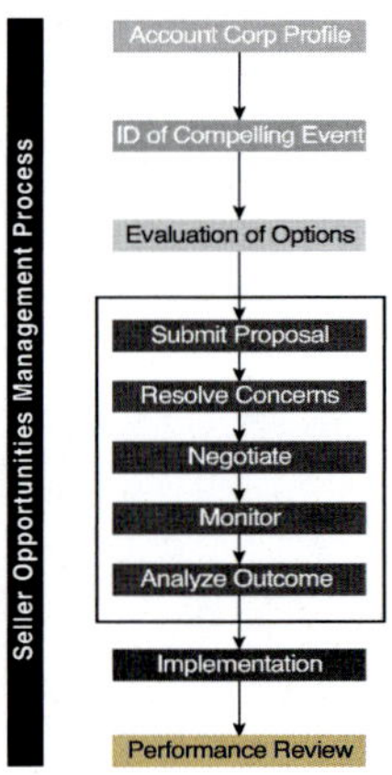

Description
- Customer has completed project or conducts scheduled review.

Objectives
- Check for satisfaction.
- Was everything delivered as promised?
- Document lessons learned and what we would do differently next time.
- Confirm that everything is complete.

Issues
- Not doing the review! (Failure to check for satisfaction).
- Not reporting major failures and successes.
- Not proposing next steps for next project lessons learned.

Summary of Chapter Objectives

Opportunities management is the key to strategic sales planning. It breaks the sales process into logical milestones with objectives focused on customer needs that can be satisfied with your offer. The process is used by sales representatives to prepare a strategy that clearly communicates and justifies the additional resources needed from others involved in the opportunity. The process helps you balance opportunities and priorities with day-to-day account servicing responsibilities. Following this process allows you to use time to your advantage.

1. **The opportunities management process has five phases.**

The first phase is the **account corporate profile**. The objective is to build an account corporate profile that describes the account's business environment, goals, objectives, strategies, and value drivers. This phase should be completed once for all opportunities and updated on a regular basis after the account's corporate planning process. This is an important step in the sales process.

The next phase is to **identify the compelling event**. This phase starts once the customer has sanctioned a new project or repurchase. In this phase your objective is to develop an understanding of the project objectives, expected outcomes, the decision-making process and milestones, the buying center members, and whether the project is worth winning. It is also your objective in this phase to get access or introductions to the buying center, if needed. It is important in this phase not to start the selling process too soon; do not make presentations and product demonstrations, or discuss pricing before you fully understand the compelling event and have determined the decision-making process and buying center members.

The next phase is the **evaluation of options**. This phase starts when the account begins a search for the best method and supplier. This is the most critical phase of the opportunities management process, as you begin your competitive battle against the competition to present your company, products, and services as the best option for their project. In this phase you answer two very important questions: "Can you win?" and "Can you compete?" The first question focuses on your relationship with the buying center; in other words, will buying center members assist you or try to prevent you from winning? The answer to the second question is based on whether you have a solution or product that fits into the account's requirements. To answer these questions, you contact the buying center members to build a buying center profile, determine the decision criteria and level of importance of each factor, estimate how you will be evaluated against the criteria using the customer's evaluation model, and compare your evaluation against the competition. With this information you determine if you are in a position of strength or weakness relative to the competition and select your best competitive sales strategy to use from this point to the procurement phase. Failure in this phase happens when you do not exploit the customer's project management process and miss an opportunity to improve your sales strategy. When this happens, the decision criterion is likely to be price comparison with the low bid. Customers in some repurchase scenarios bypass this phase and go straight from implementation (end of one contract period) into procurement, using previously established decision criteria. In such situations, you should initiate an evaluation of options phase in advance of the procurement phase. To answer "Is it worth winning?", you must consider: costs to service the project, the timing of expected revenues, and any risks associated with the project. Other factors to be considered are future revenues and strategic factors. Answering the strategic question requires input from your company's executives.

The next phase is the **procurement phase**, which is made up of five stages: submission of proposal, resolution of concerns, negotiations, monitor, and outcome analysis. In this phase the customer begins the official tendering process. This process is usually very formal, with restricted discussions and involvement with buying center members. The sales effort is joined by a large number of other support staff both for your company and for the account. Legal, contracts, tax, finance, QHSE, and operations have input on the supplier side when completing a proposal. Objectives are set for each procurement stage.

In the **submission of proposal stage** the objectives are to prepare a complete proposal that provides the customer with all the information needed to make the buying decision. The proposal should be easy to read, with your value proposition clearly communicated. All aspects of proper contract preparation have to be followed in order to assess your risks and ensure that all you contracting policies are followed.

The objective of the **resolution of concerns stage** is to ensure that you discover and address any customer questions and concerns that were not addressed by your proposal. You also want to build a win–win agreement that strengthens your relationship with the account.

The outcome of the **negotiations stage** benefits from all the information collected in early phases by allowing you to know the significant issues for the customer, to understand your differential value, and to pinpoint inexpensive yet valuable items that can be used for trades. You must be well prepared to negotiate and have a well-planned strategy for negotiation. While the competitive battle is fought in the evaluation of options phase, the rewards come in the negotiations stage.

After negotiations, you enter into the **monitor stage**, where you watch for and are prepared for last-minute attempts by the competition to interfere in the decision-making process. You do the same, however, only after carefully considering the benefits and risks of doing so. In this stage you must also be prepared if the customer tries to change your proposal in their favor by using last-minute negotiating tactics.

Finally, the decision is made and you complete an **outcome analysis**. The objective is to fully understand why the decision was made either in your favor or against you. What did you learn about the account and the competition that will help you do a better job in your next opportunities management process?

If you win the project, you move to the **implementation phase** as part of the customer's implementation team. The objectives in this phase are to deliver on promises made earlier in the sales process and to use the opportunity to develop the account relationship and reinitiate the sales process. In this phase, you must take care to anticipate implementation problems, measure your progress in delivering on your promises, and capture significant successes as well as lessons learned.

With the project completed, you enter the **performance review phase**, when the customer has completed the project or contract period and determines what the project achieved. Your objectives are to check for satisfaction, ask if everything was delivered as promised, document lessons learned, summarize the project performance, review with all key buying center members not present at the performance review meeting, and ask when the next opportunity will be. The review is an essential part of the overall opportunities management process.

2. A useful tool for applying the concepts discussed is the opportunities spreadsheet.

This is a logical step-by-step process for laying out the information you know regarding the opportunity and then selecting the competitive sales strategy and appropriate tactics. This tool is used in preparation for completing a strategic sales plan.

Applying the Concepts

1. For an opportunity that you recently closed, complete the Project and Request for Proposal Summaries and a Level 1 Review form. How much of the information do you know? The forms are in the appendix and can be downloaded from http://www.b2bprofessionalsales.com.

2. Which of the five phases in the opportunities management process do you think is managed best by your team and which phase is the weakest? Give specific examples of why you think this is the case.

3. Which phase do you spend most of your time addressing? Would you like to spend more time on another phase?

4. By applying the opportunities management process, do you think you will be a more effective salesperson? If so, how will this help you?

References

1. Rackham, Neil: *Major Account Sales Strategy,* London, England, McGraw-Hill, Inc. (1989).
2. Bonoma, T.V.: "Major Sales: Who Really Does the Buying?" *Harvard Business Review* (May–June 1982) 3–11.
3. Jones, T. and Sasser, Jr., W.E.: "Why Satisfied Customers Defect," *Harvard Business Review* (November–December 1995).
4. *Ibid.,* Rackham, N.
5. All examples used in this chapter were selected due to the powerful message and lesson learned for the sales professionals directly involved in the project, with which the author had a role or interviewed.
6. *Ibid.*
7. *Ibid.,* Rackham, N.
8. McKenzie, N. (2013, September 17). "What's the Difference Between an EOI, RFP, RFT and RFQ?" Retrieved December 27, 2014, from http://thoughtbubble.com.au/the-hook/whats-the-difference-between-an-eoi-rfp-rft-and-rfq/
9. McKenzie, N. (2013, September 18). "The Difference Between Bids, Tenders and Proposals." Retrieved December 28, 2014, from http://thoughtbubble.com.au/the-hook/the-difference-between-bids-tenders-and-proposals/
10. Pike, R.: *Creative Training Techniques Handbook, 2nd Edition*, Lakewood Books (1994).
11. Graph of retention and reinforcement taken from Mehrabian, A., *Silent Messages*, Lakewood Books (1990).
12. Buzan, T.: *Using Both Sides of Your Brain,* 3rd Edition, New York, NY: E.P. Dutton (1991).
13. *Ibid.,* Rackham, N.
14. Levitt, T.: "Marketing Myopia," *Harvard Business Review* (July–August 1960) 45–56.
15. Levitt, T.: "Marketing Success Through Differentiation—of Anything," *Harvard Business Review* (January–February 1980) 1-9.
16. Reichheld, F.: *The Loyalty Effect: The Hidden Force Behind Growth, Profits, and Lasting Value* (Boston, MA: Harvard Business School Press 1996).
17. Taken from a presentation at the BP Knowledge Management Forum, Milan, Italy (1998).

Appendix A

Project Solution Worksheet

Date: ______________________ Contact: ______________________

Company: ______________________

Business/service unit(s): ______________________

Project: ______________________

Description: ______________________

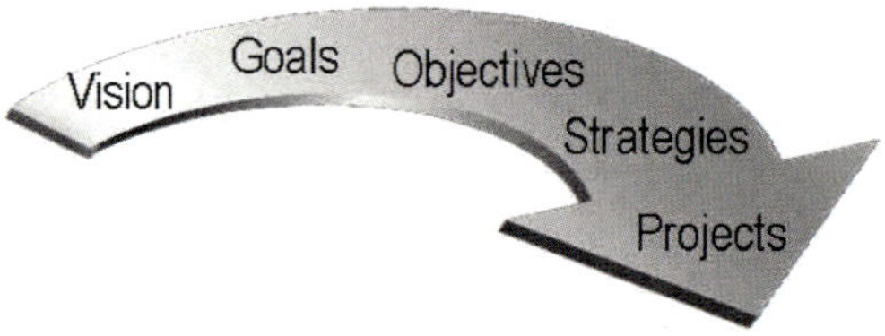

BUSINESS DRIVERS

CRITICAL SUCCESS FACTORS

Project Objectives

Project Manager

Budget

MANAGEMENT TEAM

Operations

Technical

Finance

Procurement

Partners

Government

CONCERNS/EXPECTATIONS

Customer Project Management Schedule

Dates

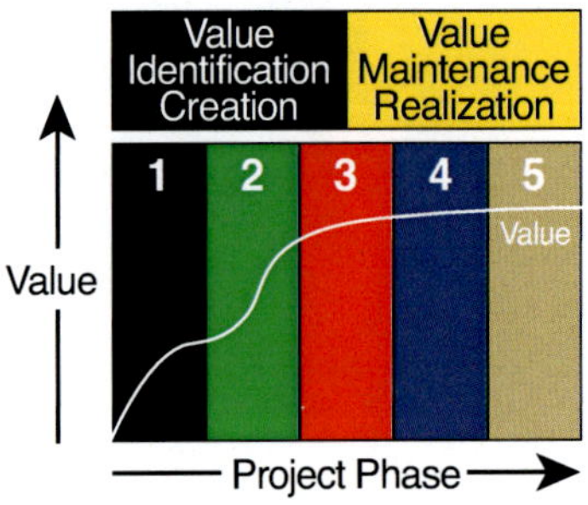

	Dates
Phase 1—Strategy Setting	______
Phase 2—Project Selection	______
Phase 3a—Evaluation of Options	______
Phase 3b—Procurement	______
Phase 4—Implementation	______
Phase 5—Review	______

Appendix B

Sales Opportunity Level 1 Review Form

Account:	Date:	Reviewed by:
Factors and Assessment Questions	Opportunity:	

Is there an opportunity? ❑ Yes	❑ No ❑ ?	Account		
Account corporate profile	+ Completed – Not done		The first four questions are assessed from the customer's point of view. The remaining level 1 factors and assessment questions are answered from the perspective of your company and your competitors.	
1. Customer's appl. or project	+ Defined – Undefined			
2. Customer's business profile	+ Strong – Weak			
3. Customer's financial condition	+ Strong – Weak			
4. Access to funds	+ Yes – No			
Can we compete? ❑ Yes	❑ No ❑ ?	**Our Company**	**Competitor 1**	**Competitor 2**
Requirements diagram Vulnerability analysis Customer value analysis	+ Completed – Not done			
5. Compelling event	+ Defined – Undefined			
6. Formal decision criteria	+ Defined – Undefined			
7. Solution fit	+ Strong – Weak			
8. Resource requirements	+ Low – High			
9. Current relationship	+ Strong – Weak			
10. Unique business value	+ Strong – Weak			
Can we win? ❑ Yes	❑ No ❑ ?	**Our Company**	**Competitor 1**	**Competitor 2**
Buying center analysis	+ Completed – Not done			
11. Inside support	+ Strong – Weak			
12. Executive credibility	+ Strong – Weak			
13. Cultural compatibility	+ Good – Poor			
14. Informal decision criteria	+ Defined – Undefined			
15. Political alignment	+ Good – Poor			
Is it worth winning? ❑ Yes	❑ No ❑ ?	**Our Company**	**Competitor 1**	**Competitor 2**
Business case?	+ Completed – Not done			
16. Short-term revenues	+ High – Low			
17. Future revenue	+ High – Low			
18. Profitability	+ High – Low			
19. Degree of risk	+ Low – High			
20. Strategic value	+ High – Low			

What next?

What has to happen for you to win this sales opportunity? The Action field identifies the sales tactic being used (e.g., retrieve information, emphasize strengths, minimize weakness, prove value, insultate against competition). Make sure to consider all opportunity management stages. If early in the evaluation of options phase, you should retrieve information from any level 1 factors that have "?'s". The last two actions are the most important actions for Competitor 1 and 2.

Action	Description of action, name of customer, contact from your company, and completion date.
1.	
2.	
3.	
Competitor 1	
Competitor 2	

Request for Proposal Summary

Description:

Date: ______________________

Contact: ______________________

Customer Project Management Schedule

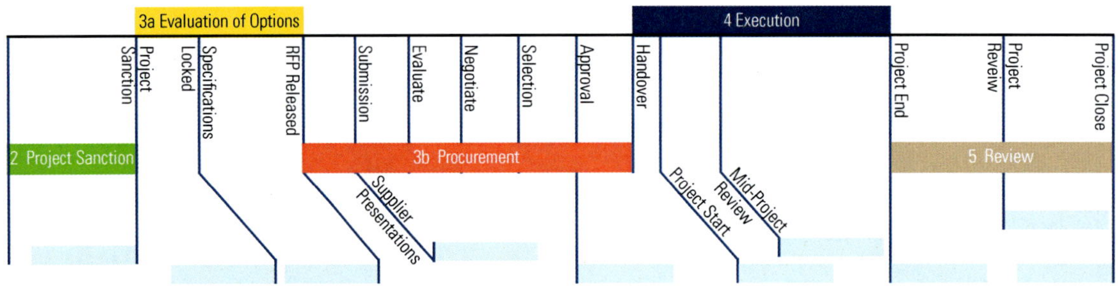

Customer Project Management Team

2 Project Selection	3a Evaluation of Options	3b Procurement	4 Execution	5 Review

Objective

Contract Holder

Budget

REQUIREMENTS

CRITICAL SUCCESS FACTORS

BUYING FACTORS %

Financial

Technical

Service

Value

Other

CONCERNS/EXPECTATIONS

Decision-Making Process

Customer's Decision Criteria

Critical	Strong	Strong	Strong
Incidental	Weak	Weak	Weak

Evaluation Model

Appendix D

Mid-Project – Product/Services Augmentation Workshop

Account Department Project	Supplier/Product Line(s) Contact	Issue Red-Problem Green-Opportunity Pragmatist	Profile Innovator Visionary Potential Conservative	Current Level Generic Augmented	What Is Required? Describe the offering. What is required? Are there other product lines required?

Mid-Project – Product/Services Augmentation Workshop cont.

Cost Incremental Cost to Develop Augmented Offering	Value $ Financial Benefit to Customer of Offering	Global? Yes/No	Ability to Cope Easy Difficult Impossible	Introduction As Soon As Possible/ Next Tender	Marketing Name Be Creative

Technology Positioning

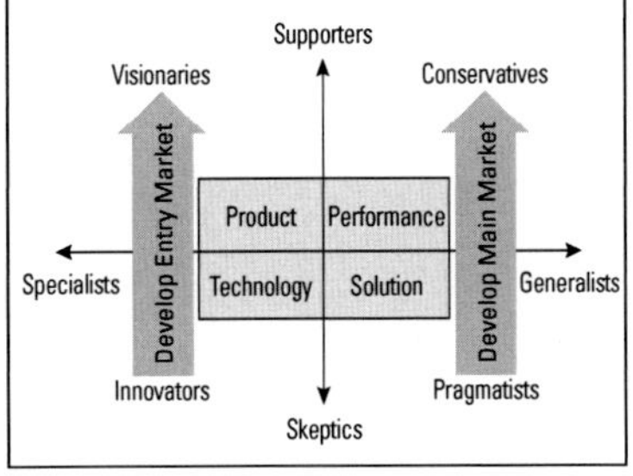

Total Product Concept

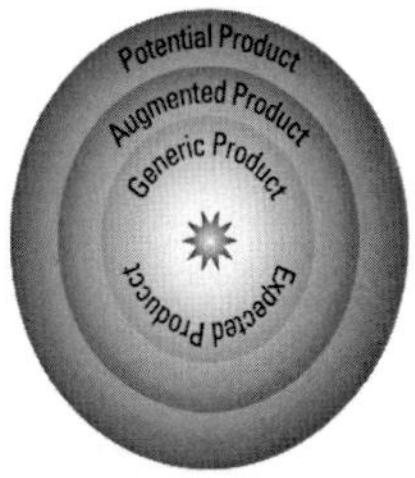

Product Evolution Strategy

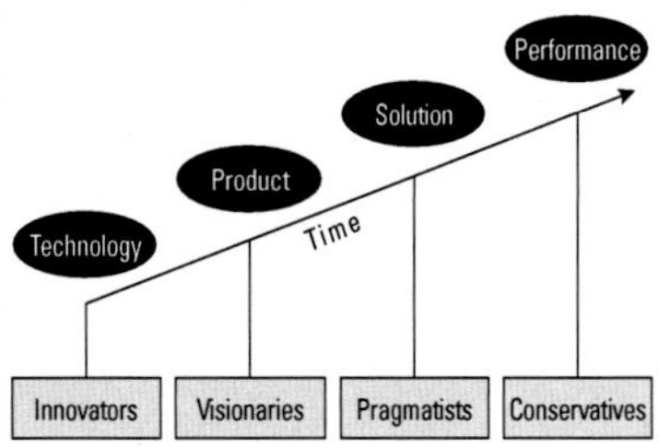

Communication Skills

The Most Important Tool

The most important skill for a salesperson is effective communication skills. Communication is a complex activity that requires the exchange of information, ideas, and feelings with minimal distortion. The meanings of words and thoughts conveyed to and from your customers must be received exactly as conceived.[1]

This chapter describes the basic communication process and discussion skills that are fundamental to conducting effective and efficient communications with the customer. This chapter is organized in two parts. The first part presents the basic communication process for any exchange between two parties. The second part examines communication skills that are fundamental to effective and efficient communications with the customer.

Chapter Objectives

After reading this chapter, you will be able to:

- Describe and apply the communication process and understand the key factors for successful communication.
- Apply discussion skills in your everyday communications with the customer.
- Prepare effective aligning strategies for individual customers based on their social profile.

Communication Skills

Effective communication is a critical part of the sales representative's job. Your ability to communicate defines your ability to give and get information, evaluate and explore ideas and opinions, and persuade others. This section covers the following:

- Basic communication process
- Discussion skills
- Social profiling

Figure 5.1 illustrates how sales communication skills are at the center of each common sales situation.

Each communication skill is used every day in your position as a sales representative. Such skills apply whether you are selling a solution, providing after-service support, negotiating, or handling client dissatisfaction or successes. Good communication skills and understanding of the basic communication process are essential to all of the above interactions.

Fig. 5.1
Communication skills and common sales situations.

▶ *Popular Myth: "Communication Is Simple. I Never Think About It."*

Or so you think! Many transactions are processed in every communication. The illustration to the right shows the elements in the communication process. Definitions of these elements follow and apply to a conversation between a sales representative and customer.

Sender: The person sending the message to another person—the customer.

Encoding: The process of putting thought into symbolic form—customer shows engineer a sketch of a well.

Message: The set of symbols the sender transmits—customer explains the need for products or services.

Media: The communication channels through which the message moves from sender to receiver—in this case, the specific conversation and diagram the customer has with the sales representative.

Decoding: The process by which the receiver assigns meaning to the symbols encoded by the sender—the sales representative listens to the customer and interprets the words and diagram.

Receiver: The person receiving the message sent by another person—the sales representative.

Response: The reactions of the receiver after being exposed to the message—clarification question from the sales representative.

Feedback: The part of the receiver's response communicated back to the sender—what the customer hears the sales representative ask.

Noise: The unplanned static or distortion during the communication process, which results in the receiver getting a different message than the one the sender sent—for example, the telephone rings.

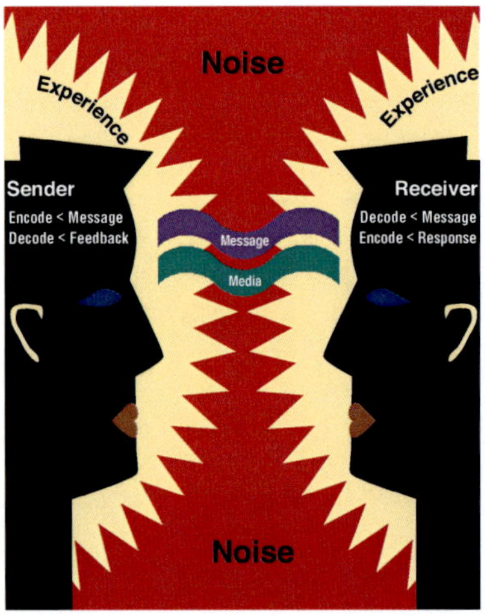

Communication Process

The foundation of effective communications is an understanding of the basic communication process that occurs between you and the customer. This is an aspect that many of us have never thought about. There are nine elements that make up the communication process, as shown in the above diagram in "Popular Myth."[1]

Two of these elements are the major parties in any communication: the sender (the person doing the talking) and the receiver (the person doing the listening). Two other elements are the major communication tools: the message and the media. Four more elements are major communication functions: encoding, decoding, response, and feedback. The last element is noise in the environment.

For a message to be successful, there are two factors that must be considered. First, the sender's encoding process must mesh with the receiver's decoding process. The most effective messages consist of words and other symbols that are familiar to the receiver. The more the sender's field of experience overlaps with the receiver's, the more effective the message is likely to be. The second factor is that the message should be memorable, and results in achieving the objective of the communication. Making a message memorable is dependent not only on the words and symbols used to deliver the message, but also on the delivery of the message. **Chapter Highlight 5.1** lists several techniques to use to make messages more memorable.

Salespeople might not always share their customers' field of experience or their situation. For example, when dealing with a person from the customer's procurement or legal department, the sales representative might not fully understand the procurement or legal issues that are important to the customer. However, to communicate effectively in these situations, the sales representative must make an effort to understand the customer's situation.

This model points out several key factors in good communication:

- Senders need to know the customer and the responses the customer wants.
- Senders must be good at encoding messages that take into account how the customer decodes them.

- Senders must send messages through media that are efficient and be ready to receive feedback.
- Senders must be ready to receive feedback and have an efficient feedback mechanism in place.

One of the most important tasks a sales representative has in the communication process is receiving feedback. To be efficient at receiving feedback in the sales communication process, it is essential that the sales representative be a good listener.

Listening

It's been said that listening is the most important of all sales behaviors. In fact, research shows that it is the most used and underdeveloped communication behavior! See the "Is Anyone Listening?" sidebar.[1] We all listen to each other at varying levels of effectiveness and attentiveness, depending on the value we place on the conversation and our level of comfort in that situation. There are three basic levels of listening:

- Level 1: Listener is completely attentive, focused, and "tuned in." Listener is concentrating on and absorbing what is being said. Listener effectively decodes all the feedback from the sender and encodes relevant messages.
- Level 2: Listener's attention is intermittent, is divided, or "wanders." Concentration is less intense and often variable. Listener "tunes in and out" of the conversation. Listener starts to miss feedback or messages being sent.
- Level 3: Listener has "tuned out" the speaker. Concentration and attention are weak or distracted. Listener is, practically speaking, not listening, encoding messages, or decoding feedback.

No one can be expected to listen at level 1 all the time. A good indication of level 1 listening is the level of retention you have of the messages and feedback from the communication. As discussed earlier, an adult's retention after 90 minutes in a presentation would fall dramatically to less than 10% unless multiple reinforcements are made. The ability to stay at level 1 for more than 90 minutes is difficult. There are many sources of noise or barriers to effective listening. Some are completely outside the listener's control. For example:

- External or environmental distractions (noise, interruptions),
- Speaker-related problems (accents, speech, and gesture mannerisms),
- Unfamiliar or unexpected content,
- A desire to put one's own viewpoint first, and
- Lack of readiness to listen (fatigue, anxiety).

To overcome the effects of noise on listening, it is essential that sales representatives practice active listening and help the customer hear through the noise.

▶ *Is Anyone Listening?*

In Enshrood Atwater's book *I Hear You,* he shares his research, which found that adults, when communicating, spend 45% of their time listening. This seems odd when you consider that in the formal education system we teach reading, writing, and speaking, but not listening.

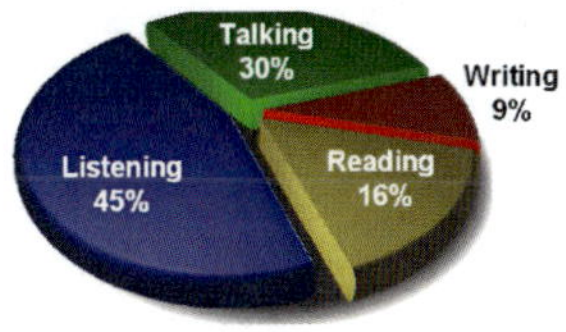

Distribution of Communication Activities

Active Listening

Even sales representatives and customers whose behavior indicates level 1 listening don't always get the most from every conversation. The average person can process ideas three times faster than anyone can speak. It is a behavior that fast-moving television and radio ads use to their advantage. Therefore, two-thirds of your listening time is "free" when someone else is speaking. Effective listening is an interactive process that requires feedback and involvement. That's why it is also important to make sure that you are fully prepared to ensure that messages are heard and feedback is given when communicating with the customer. If you don't consciously manage the communication process, then the level of retention for both you and the customer will be low.

Chapter Highlight 5.1: They Did Not Remember What I Said! No, They Did Not Remember You!

In the sidebar "Communication is Simple. I Never Think About It," the point made is that there are a lot of unconscious activities that are going on using several of the senses and processes in the brain for a successful communication. It is also important to realize that, as a salesperson, not only do you want to have a successful communication with your customer, but you also want to make it memorable and action-oriented.

For this aspect, it is the salesperson's responsibility to plan their communications to make the communication more memorable. Combining neuroscience and cognitive psychology gives us clues about where attention is processed in the brain, how memories form, and how decisions are made. This information is applied to practical applications, such as making content memorable and actionable.[2] One of the main contributors to forgetfulness is the concept in cognitive psychology called "interference." If your communication isn't distinctive enough, if it looks too much like other content; people forget it and—possibly even worse—attribute it to somebody else. Most researchers agree that people typically forget 90% of the content to which they are exposed. This premise is true for any content presented in a finite amount of time, such as sales calls, presentations, web content, and marketing content. It doesn't apply to training that must be 100% learned and remembered to perform a job, such as the skills needed to pilot an airplane or make a successful sales call. Extensive training and repetition increase retention beyond the 10%.

For content with limited exposure to an audience, your goal is to make a strong impression: to take control over the 10% of the information we want the customer to remember. Therefore, there are two important questions:

- What do you want your customer to remember? (three or four points)
- What do you want the customer to do? (call to action)

You can measure success by how closely customers' memories and actions match what you wanted them to remember and do. People forget things for a variety of reasons. By understanding why people forget, you can craft your content to increase what is remembered.

There are entire books on this topic, but here are six tips to make your message more memorable:[3]

- **Recency and Primacy:** Reserve the first and last parts of your discussion for the most important topics. This is part of the 10% of what the customer will remember. These effects are known as the recency and primacy effects. Customers will better remember what you say at the start and end of your conversation.

  In Chapter 7 "Sales Call Skills," these very important parts are called the value proposition (first) and next steps (last).

- **Visualization:** Describe a picture of what you are discussing. This will help the customer visualize what you are discussing by using drawings, metaphors, analogies, or a prop like a physical object to demonstrate the concept you are talking about.

- **100% Market Share:** If you have a relevant story related to your discussion, tell it to the customer. An effective story should be efficient and told in a couple of minutes. This is a very powerful technique for connecting with the customer so they better remember your

Chapter Highlight 5.1: They Did Not Remember What I Said! No, They Did Not Remember You! (cont.)

discussion. A proven effective way to make stories stick is to tell them using the "Hero Model" in five steps: Step 1: Everything is normal. Step 2: Something changes. Step 3: The Hero pushes back. Step 4: Enter the mentor, who makes a recommendation to the Hero. Step 5: The Hero decides and saves the day.[4]

- **Exercise:** Not all people learn or absorb information in the same way. Some people learn and remember better if the information is presented orally, allowing them to discuss more; others are more kinesthetic learners and remember better by physically interacting with a hands-on approach. Still others learn better when they can visualize, as highlighted in tip No. 3.

- **Read and Record:** Use all the customers' senses by having a handout or summary of your discussion that allows them to read supporting information and make notes on the handout as your message is delivered.

Ensure that your handouts provide ample white space for the customer to take notes. The way the message is delivered has as much to do with retaining the message as the message itself. In a very good book titled *Conversations that Win the Complex Sale,* the authors again draw on neuro research to identify the critical do's and don't's of successful conversations. Their top three "deadly sins" of messaging are the following:

1. Information overload
2. Not from the customer's point of view
3. Not telling what is different between you and the competition

Commit any of these sins and the conversation is dead. In fact according to research completed by Miller (1978),[5] information overload or any combination of these sins will cause the customer to become irritated, confused, and unable to make a decision—not a good state for a salesperson to put their customers in. The do's are based on the fact that in decision-making three parts of the brain play a significant role. These are the cortex, responsible for logic and complex thought; the limbic system, responsible for many functions including emotion; and finally, the brain stem, the oldest part of the brain, responsible for survival, the startle response, and the basic functions that keep you alive. Think of them as the three main parts of a buying center in each customer's head. Based on these facts, the author recommends using one or more of the following factors in your conversations with the customer to improve retention and facilitate decision-making: use emotion, make it personal, contrast, provide concrete examples, keep it simple, and use stories.

When dealing with customers, try to communicate with emotion. A landmark study conducted by Professor Albert Mehrabian at the University of California, Los Angeles concluded that, when communicating messages with emotion (feelings and attitudes):

- 7% of meaning comes from the words that are spoken;
- 33% of meaning is paralinguistic (comes from the way the words are said: tone, pitch, pace, and volume); and
- 55% of meaning is in the facial expression (body language).

The take-away from this chapter highlight is you have a lot to do with whether or not your message is remembered, and if the customer doesn't remember you they probably won't remember your sales call.

One last critical point: You only get one chance to make a first impression—make a good one. Be on time, be dressed appropriately, and be prepared. All these factors demonstrate you care, and most of us will remember people who we think care.

Practice active listening skills with others in your day-to-day activities outside the customer's office. This can help you identify the barriers that are distracting and habits that interfere with effective listening. **Chapter Highlight 5.2: Active Listening Best Practices** lists techniques to help identify at what level of listening both you and the customer are and suggests aids that can help keep the other person and yourself at level 1.[6] **Chapter Highlight 5.3: "12 Reasons Why You Might Hear 'You Are Not Listening To Me!'"** discusses common traps that people can fall into when having a conversation. The way to improve is to be aware this might be happening and then, in your next discussion, be mindful. If you sense you are making one of the twelve mistakes, force yourself to give the other person your full attention.[7]

Discussion Skills

▶ ***Opening a Discussion***

- Begin with preliminaries.
- Make a general reference to the topic(s).
- Use a neutral tone.
- Do not share your opinion.
- Check for feedback from the customer.

Many communication interactions with the customer will be in the form of discussions. An effective discussion is easier to have once you recognize it as an activity that has these three main components:

- Opening the discussion
- Delivering the message
- Closing the discussion

Later chapters covering common sales situations customize each of these components and processes to make them more effective for a specific situation.

Opening the Discussion

When holding a discussion with one or more customers, you have a responsibility for the outcome of that discussion. You need to participate to be sure the customer understands the purpose and focus of the discussion and you both leave with a common understanding of what has been explored, accomplished, or agreed to.

At the beginning of any discussion, there is always a degree of tension between you and the customer. The degree of tension can vary from very high to almost non-existent, depending on the circumstances. One of your most important jobs in opening the discussion is to initiate conversation in a manner that reduces the level of tension to one that is productive before proceeding.

Figure 5.2 shows the level of tension throughout a discussion. It is your job to look for signs when the level of tension is too high or too low, and try to manage the level to stay in the productive green zone.

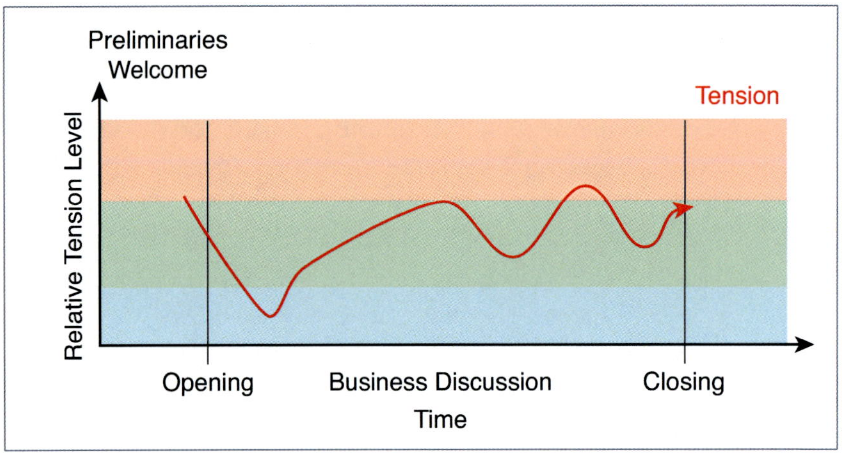

Fig. 5.2
Level of tension in a business discussion. The level of tension is plotted as the time during which the business discussion progresses. Typically, tension at the beginning is high (red zone) and does not facilitate holding a discussion. In this phase of the discussion, you use preliminaries at the opening to reduce tension to a productive level (green zone). There are also times when tension might become too low (blue zone) and discussion can easily be stalled and unproductive, perhaps distracting from the main purpose for the discussion. Our responsibility during the discussion is to be alert to signs that indicate tension is getting too high or too low and try to manage tensions back to the productive green zone. This characteristic of a discussion is probably most important in the different sales situations you will encounter.

Chapter Highlight 5.2: Active Listening Best Practices

Who is Listening to Whom?

Review these active listening best practices before your next value presentation for the upcoming multimillion-dollar contract. They can make the meeting more memorable.

Level 1

THEY

- Make eye contact.
- Sit straight/lean forward.
- Nod in agreement.
- Use gestures.
- Ask questions.
- Take notes.

YOU

- You are completely "tuned in" to the person.
- You have no difficulty concentrating.
- You easily absorb what you hear.

Level 2

THEY

- Make intermittent eye contact.
- Slouch/lean back.
- Maintain noncommittal facial expression.
- Fidget.
- Say very little.
- Do other simple activities.

YOU

- You are tuning in and out.
- Your attention is divided between the speaker and other thoughts.
- Your concentration varies from weak to intense as your mind wanders and returns to the speaker.

Level 3

THEY

- Have a fixed and glazed stare.
- Slouch/lean away from speaker.
- Project a look like you are not there.
- Remain immobile and silent.

YOU

- You are pretty well tuned out.
- Your attention is mostly elsewhere, and your concentration is weak.
- For all practical purposes, you have stopped listening.

Tips for Keeping Them and You at Level 1

THEY

- Vary the tone of voice from time to time.
- Emphasize critical points. Speak lower when asking a question.
- Make sketches or use a white board for drawing to illustrate points periodically.
- Ask for confirmation and understanding.
- Ask their opinion.
- Move closer or lean in to move closer to the other person.
- Take a break during a long meeting.
- Make eye contact.
- Keep the presentations interactive.

YOU

- Organize the information as you hear it.
- Classify what you hear.
- Separate main ideas from supporting ideas.
- Put the facts in chronological order.
- If a single focal point fails to keep you at level 1, apply 2 or 3 at once.
- Identify the emotions behind the words by monitoring body language, facial expression, and tone of voice.
- Before you start the conversation, tell yourself to be at level 1.
- Prepare questions that are stimulating.

Chapter Highlight 5.3: 12 Reasons Why You Might Hear "You Are Not Listening to Me!"

Blocks to Listening

There are twelve blocks to listening. You will find that some are old favorites that you use over and over, while others are held in reserve for certain types of people or situations. Everyone uses listening blocks, so you should not worry if a lot of blocks are familiar. This is an opportunity to become more aware of your blocks at the time you actually use them.

1. Comparing: Comparing makes it hard to listen because you are always trying to assess who is smarter, more competent, and more emotionally healthy: you or the other person. Some people focus on who has suffered more or who is a bigger victim. While someone is talking, you think to yourself: "Could I do it that well?" You cannot let much in because you are too busy seeing if you measure up.

2. Mind Reading: The mind reader does not pay much attention to what people say. In fact, he often distrusts it. He is trying to figure out what the other person is really thinking and feeling. The mind reader pays less attention to words than to intonations and subtle cues in an effort to see through to the truth.

If you are a mind reader, you probably make assumptions about how people react to you. These notions are born of intuition, hunches, and vague misgivings, but have little to do with what the person actually says to you.

3. Rehearsing: You do not have time to listen when you are rehearsing what to say. Your whole attention is on the preparation and crafting of your next comment. You have to look interested, but your mind is going a mile a minute because you have got a story to tell, or a point to make. Some people rehearse whole chains of responses: "First I will say, then he will say, then I will say," and so on.

4. Filtering: When you filter, you listen to some things but not to others. You pay only enough attention to see if somebody's angry or unhappy or if you are in emotional danger. Once assured that the communication contains none of those things, you let your mind wander.

Another way people filter is simply by avoiding hearing certain things—particularly anything threatening, negative, critical, or unpleasant. It is as if the words were never said: You simply have no memory of them.

5. Judging: Negative labels have enormous power. If you prejudge someone as unqualified, you do not pay much attention to what they say. You have already written them off. Hastily judging a statement means you have ceased to listen and have begun a "knee-jerk" reaction. A basic rule of listening is that judgments should only be made after you have heard and evaluated the content of the message.

6. Dreaming: You are half-listening, and something the person says suddenly triggers a chain of private associations. You are more prone to dreaming when you feel bored or anxious. Everyone dreams—and you sometimes need to make Herculean efforts to stay tuned in. But if you dream a lot with certain people, it could indicate a lack of commitment to knowing or appreciating them. At the very least, it is a statement that you do not value what they have to say very much.

Chapter Highlight 5.3: 12 Reasons Why You Might Hear "You Are Not Listening to Me!" (cont.)

7. Identifying: In this block, you take everything a person tells you and refer it back to your own experience. They want to tell you about a difficult operation, but that reminds you of the time you had a worse situation in another country. You launch into your story before they can finish theirs. Everything you hear reminds you of something that you have felt, done, or suffered. You are so busy with these exciting tales of your life that there is no time to really hear or get to know the other person.

8. Advising: You are the great problem-solver, ready with help and suggestions. You do not have to hear more than a few sentences before you begin searching for the right advice. However, while you are thinking of suggestions and convincing someone to "just try it," you might miss what is most important. You did not hear the feelings, and you did not acknowledge the person's pain. He or she still feels basically alone because you could not listen and just be there.

9. Sparring: This block has you arguing and debating with people. The other person never feels heard because you're so quick to disagree. In fact, a lot of your focus is on finding things to disagree with. You take strong stands and are very clear about your beliefs and preferences. The way to avoid sparring is to repeat back and acknowledge what you have heard. Look for one thing you might agree with. One subtype of sparring is the put-down. You use acerbic or sarcastic remarks to dismiss the other person's point of view.

A second type of sparring is discounting. Discounting is for people who cannot stand compliments. The basic technique of discounting is to run yourself down when you get a compliment. The other person never feels satisfied that you really heard his appreciation. And he is right: You did not.

10. Being Right: Being right means you will go to any lengths to avoid being wrong. You cannot listen to criticism, you cannot be corrected, and you cannot take suggestions to change. Your convictions are unshakable. And since you will not acknowledge that your mistakes are mistakes, you just keep making them.

11. Derailing: This listening block is accomplished by suddenly changing the subject. You derail the train of conversation when you get bored or uncomfortable with a topic. Another way of derailing is by laughing something off. This means that you continually respond to whatever is said with a joke or quip in order to avoid the discomfort or anxiety in seriously listening to the other person.

12. Placating: "Right, right ... Absolutely ... I know ... Of course, you are ... Incredible ... Yes ... Really?" You want to be nice, pleasant, and supportive. You want people to like you, so you agree with everything. You might half-listen, just enough to get the drift, but you are not really involved. You are accommodating rather than tuning in and examining what is actually being said.

To open a discussion, begin with preliminaries, such as referring to events in which both you and the customer perhaps have an interest or asking general questions about the customer to get to know the person's field of experience or situation. These preliminaries help reduce tension to a comfortable level. You then begin the business discussion with a general reference to the topic(s). By doing this, you achieve two goals: You introduce the purpose of the discussion, and you prepare the other person for participation.

By using a neutral tone, you do not impose your personality on the discussion. By withholding your opinion when opening the conversation, you do not influence the other person's opinions. It is important to maintain a neutral, non-judgmental tone and avoid offering your opinion on the subject. A judgmental tone or expression of opinion often gives the impression that you have already made up your mind about what has happened or what should be done.

Once you have completed communicating the purpose of the discussion, you then ask for feedback from the customer. If you are the receiver, you want to be sure the sender (the customer) has clearly given an opening before you begin the discussion so you are clear on the customer's purpose for the discussion. If the person doesn't offer an opening, then ask for the reason and objective of the meeting before beginning the discussion. With this clear understanding, the level of tension for the discussion should be very much in the green zone. We now begin to deliver or receive the message.

Delivering the Message

The message can be a variety of subjects you want to communicate to the customer. It can be delivering a proposal for a project or making a presentation on features/benefits/value, providing after-sale support, handling customer dissatisfaction, negotiating, or communicating a success. Each of these messages is specific to a sales situation. Each message must be clear, concise, and appropriate for the targeted customer or audience.

During the delivery of the message, you want to make good use of these discussion skills:

- Probing
- Clarifying and confirming

These skills allow you to test for understanding and acceptance as the message is being delivered. You will often be required to use one or several other discussion skills, such as the following:

- Exploring ideas
- Triangulating the topic being discussed
- Using constructive criticism
- Managing differences of opinion
- Giving credit

Each of these skills is discussed below, along with examples of how they are used in typical sales situations.

Probing

During delivery of your message, use open and closed probes to keep the communication interactive and the participant's level of listening high. Depending on the sales situation, you might even begin the conversation after opening with probing.

For you and a customer to make an informed, mutually beneficial decision, the two of you must share an understanding of the customer's needs, concerns, issues, and circumstances. Use open and closed probes to collect information and improve your understanding. Probing is the means by which you gather information to achieve that understanding.

After listening, probing is one of the most important skills any sales representative can develop. The ability to ask questions that logically and efficiently uncover important information about a customer's needs is a distinguishing characteristic of the sales communication skills process.

Your goal in probing is to build a clear, complete, mutual understanding of a customer's needs, concerns, issues, and circumstances. A clear understanding means that, for each client topic being discussed, you learn:

- Specifically *what* the customer wants, and
- *Why* it is important.

A complete understanding means that, for the particular decision the customer is making, you learn each of the client's needs, concerns, and issues as well as the priority of each. A mutual understanding means you and the customer share the same understanding—that the clear, complete picture you have of the customer's needs is the same picture the customer has. A clear, complete, mutual understanding ensures that the recommendations and actions you take to address those needs contribute to the customer's satisfaction in the most effective way possible.

Probe when you want to get information from a customer. The signal to probe comes from you. Probe whenever you feel you need more information to achieve a clear, complete, mutual understanding of a customer's needs. How much or how long you probe depends on the complexity of the topic being discussed and the clarity with which the customer describes it. The more complex the topic or the more difficulty the customer has explaining it, the more you have to probe.

The more you know about problems and challenges before a meeting, the better prepared you are to explore them. Of course, understanding problems and challenges involves more than understanding the facts. You must also understand the customer's perception of the facts.

Customers' perceptions of problems and challenges are necessarily "filtered" through their own viewpoints. Customers' viewpoints are shaped by:

- Their jobs;
- The function or department they work in;
- The organization or company they work for; and
- The project they are working on or thinking about.

Therefore, it is necessary to know something about most or all of these layers. To do so, learn as much as you can about a customer's circumstances, problems, and challenges before meeting face to face. When there are gaps in your understanding, fill in the gaps by probing.

Open and Closed Probes

A probe is a question or other request for information. There are two general types of probes: open probes and closed probes. Open probes encourage customers to respond freely. In general, it's a good idea to keep your probing as open as possible. For example:

- What are the key factors for success in this project?
- What are the costs associated with the failure?
- How can you leverage this technique to other operations?

Open probes encourage customers to open up and allow them to share information they think will be useful to you. Open probes in sales situations are used to gather information about a customer's field of experience, situation, and circumstances.

Closed probes limit a customer's response to yes or no, a choice among alternatives that you supply, or a single, often quantifiable fact. For example, you might ask:

"Have you selected a company?"

"Have you considered this kind of approach before?"

"Do you believe my company is responsible for the failure?"

Closed probes bring focus or closure to a discussion and make efficient use of time. But if you rely too heavily on closed probes, customers may feel as if they are being interrogated and become unwilling to share information. Two frequent uses of open and closed probes are to confirm and clarify the message, and to prompt feedback exchange.

Confirming and Clarifying

> ▶ ***When and How to Confirm***
>
> - Confirm when you think you understand, but you're not 100% sure or you want to reject, ignore, or disagree.
> - State your understanding of *what* and *why*.
> - Ask if you understand correctly.

Confirming and clarifying are basic skills in all sales communication processes. When used properly, they make certain you have a complete and accurate understanding of what the other person is saying and the person also clearly understands what you are saying. Partial understanding or misunderstanding wastes time, causes confusion, and weakens mutual confidence.

Confirming. Confirm your understanding whenever you think you understand, but you're not 100% sure, or you want to reject, ignore, or disagree with what you've heard. When you state your understanding of *what* and *why*, you let the other person know exactly what you understand. This helps the other person tell you whether your understanding is correct.

For example: "In other words, you want to focus on the Baku project *(what)* in order to meet your mobilization date for that project first?" *(why)* Then, ask a closed probe to find out whether or not your understanding is correct. For example: "Is that right?"

At times, you will confirm your understanding simply to reassure the other that you understand. For example: "Yes, I see why the issue of on-site support is critical. It will allow you to keep your specialist on the other project." When you confirm to reassure, it is especially important to state both the *what* and the *why*.

Clarifying. Clarify when you don't understand the *what* or the *why* of what you've heard. To clarify, you simply ask for information to complete your understanding. For example: "What did you mean by 'extreme conditions' *(what)* and why did you bring it up at that point in the discussion?" *(why)* Or, "Tell me more. Where do you see a conflict in the Bintang information?"

Clarifying and confirming are important and easy to do. The trick is remembering to use the skills. Sometimes it is easier to assume that you understand or just guess at the meaning. However, for effective communications, it is always important to confirm and clarify. Despite your best efforts to listen and communicate effectively, there is always the possibility that you have missed or misunderstood something the customer says. One way to be sure you and the customer achieve a mutual understanding of what is being discussed is to confirm and clarify.

Another good use of probing skills is when you are exploring ideas with the customer. Perhaps you are looking for alternative approaches to a project, remedies to a problem, or ideas about what each has to trade in a negotiation.

▶ *Exploring Ideas*

When you invite a suggestion:

- Give a reaction.

When you make a suggestion:

- Invite a reaction.

When you use or build on the ideas of others:

- Acknowledge the connection.

When you need to be innovative or imaginative:

- Temporarily alter restrictions.

When you need to triangulate:

- Use a neutral tone.
- Do not express your opinion.
- Refer to the problem as an "it."

Exploring Ideas

When exploring ideas, your intent is to promote a free exchange of information or suggestions. You want to make sure that everyone's ideas—including your own—are listened to, understood, and responded to. Often, while exploring ideas, you might wish to encourage the customer to respond creatively or to view the issue from another perspective. At other times, your own ideas will build upon those of your customer.

The discussion skills of exploring ideas will help you encourage the free exchange of information, while retaining responsibility for the outcome of the discussion. However, it is not appropriate to explore ideas when you have already decided what you are going to do. When you explore ideas, you are inviting the customer to participate in the free exchange of alternative ideas and suggestions. If you are unwilling to consider alternatives, you should not extend such an invitation. For the same reason, you should never present your decision in the form of a suggestion or try to lead others into coming up with your decision. These practices can damage your credibility and cause the other person to feel manipulated.

Inviting Suggestions

To arrive at a mutually acceptable decision, both parties should participate in the exploration of ideas. However, as customers are more likely to be committed to ideas they've developed, it is often helpful to begin by inviting a suggestion. Since you have invited a suggestion, it is important that you give a reaction to the customer's idea. If your reaction is negative, it should be given as balanced feedback—even if you have to clarify to find merit.

Ignoring others' ideas is the equivalent of rejecting them. This can make others less willing to offer ideas again. By inviting reactions to your own suggestions, you demonstrate that you are willing to consider alternative ideas. You also show that you are interested in finding a course of action acceptable to the customer. This increases the probability that the customer will be committed to implementing the final decision. For example:

"I think you should... How does that sound?"

"What do you think about...?"

"I'd like to try... Would that work for you?"

As with the other interpersonal skills you've learned, your intent in using these is to encourage others to continue to seek mutually satisfactory outcomes and solutions. Often, the suggestions you make are based upon the ideas of your customer. When this happens, it is important to acknowledge the connection to the original idea, which recognizes the customer who contributed the idea by giving proper credit. It also promotes continued cooperation and teamwork. For example:

"Your suggestion for manning the project might be even more workable if you changed it this way. Let's add..."

"What you said about... has given me another idea. I think you might be able to..."

"Lonnie's approach will also help solve another problem you've had with..."

Remember, this skill is an alternative way of making a suggestion. As you know, whenever you make a suggestion, it is important to invite a reaction. For example:

"What do you think?"

"Does that support your original idea?"

When you explore ideas, you can sometimes find solutions or alternatives quickly. At other times, it can be difficult to find workable ideas. In such cases, you might need to explore ideas in greater depth. A good way to do this is to temporarily alter restrictions—to enter the world of "suppose" and "what if."

Alter Restrictions Temporarily

Why alter real-world restrictions? Sometimes the best way to find a realistic, practical alternative is to start with one that is fanciful or impractical and then make it workable. Innovative solutions require imagination, and too much concern for real-world requirements can chain down anyone's imagination. By temporarily altering restrictions, you can break the mold of conventional thinking.

In addition, some customers have trouble stating—or even recognizing—their real needs and concerns. By temporarily altering restrictions, you can often encourage customers to discover or express what is really important to them. When temporarily altering restrictions, either remove restrictions or impose additional ones. For example:

"Suppose price weren't an issue?" *(restriction removed)*

"What if you got the equipment now?" *(restriction removed)*

"What if the meeting were tomorrow?" *(restriction imposed)*

"How would you do it if you were us?" *(restriction imposed)*

"Suppose you had to do both wells in the same day?" *(restriction imposed)*

By changing real-world requirements, you stimulate creative thinking.

Triangulating the Topic

During your discussions with customers, you might have concerns, issues, or problems that must be discussed. It could be an operational problem, sales issue, or concern you have about their ideas and suggestions. When you discuss these types of topics, it is important that you disassociate the topic being discussed from the person. You can do this by turning the topic into an "it" instead of linking it to the actions or statements of the customer. This process, known as triangulating the topic, removes responsibility for the topic being discussed from the people discussing it and places the topic on neutral ground, where both parties can participate equally in solving it, looking for solutions from both parties' perspectives. **Figure 5.3** represents the process of triangulating the topic.

For example, you would not respond to an idea by saying:

"You know, the last time you tried that, your people never gave us the 24-hour notice you agreed to." Instead, you would triangulate the concern "off" the customer by saying: "That might present the additional logistics for the operation and make 'it' difficult for them to administer."

Sometimes your discussion will address an existing concern. It could be a formal problem-solving session, a post-mortem, or an informal attempt to find useful answers. This technique is used extensively in handling client dissatisfaction and negotiations. In these sales situations, introduce the discussion by triangulating the concern. As always, use a neutral tone and withhold your own opinion when you open the discussion. In addition, refer to the problem as an "it" instead of linking the subject to the actions or statements of any group or individual.

At times when dealing with concerns and exploring for ideas, you might want to discuss alternative ways of handling the issue without acknowledging the customer's ideas. To do this, you use the discussion skill of constructive criticism.

Fig. 5.3
Triangulating a topic. Treat the issue, concern or problem as a challenge for both parties. Look for solutions from both parties' perspectives. Refer to the topic being discussed as "it."

▶ ***To Give Constructive Criticism, You...***

1. Introduce the subject.
2. Give balanced feedback.
3. Specify what you want to see retained.
4. Specify what you want changed.
5. Explore the next steps:
   a. Invite ideas; offer responses
   b. Offer ideas; invite responses
6. Summarize the next steps you've agreed to.

Constructive Criticism

Constructive criticism is a powerful tool for retaining the positive points of a discussion while addressing the weaker points. In various sales situations, the customer's constructive criticism will help you develop the best solution for the topic being discussed. It helps you earn the customer's commitment to the next steps and strengthens your relationship, because the criticism is applied in a positive fashion.

The first step in constructive criticism is making sure you understand what you've seen or heard—accurately and completely. Constructive criticism based on incorrect or incomplete understanding often does more harm than good. As always, you want complete, accurate understanding by clarifying and confirming.

Begin by letting the customer know what you plan to talk about. It is just that simple, and it is important because many of us have a tendency to start talking with no introduction. If the customer is sending the message and you are unsure of it, clarify what is going to be discussed in order to avoid confusion. To make sure your intent and message are clear, begin your constructive criticism by stating what you intend to discuss (as appropriate) and why. For example:

"Sheila, I want to talk about our last job on the Z Pad well *(what)* so you can evaluate what went wrong and come up with ideas of doing it better" *(why)*. Or, "I think you should review wellsite procedures *(what)* so you can find ways of eliminating the confusion you experienced on the last well" *(why)*.

The next step is to give balanced feedback by discussing what you want to see retained and what you want to see changed. Balanced feedback builds the customer's confidence in your objectivity and fairness. It shows you are as interested in what is right as what is wrong—that your feedback is intended to offer an improved option.

Equally important, by focusing on the positive, you capture the customer's interest and set the stage for serious consideration of what needs to be improved.

To complete the constructive criticism, identify the positive aspects of what is being discussed and how this relates to the aspects you want to change. The more closely these "retain" and "change" aspects are related, the more natural and persuasive the balanced feedback will be.

Sometimes you won't find much that you want to see retained, in which case, never try to fake it. Instead, refer to the customer's good intentions (to improve, do things right, please the customer, etc.). Then make the connection between what you want to see retained and what you want to see changed. When you do so, avoid using "watch out" words such as "but," "however," "unfortunately," and "nevertheless." These words might suggest that stating the positive aspects has been a set-up for negative aspects, which defeats the purpose of specifying what you want to see retained. Instead, use phrases like:

"And you'll do even better if...,"

"It's also important to...,"

"I'd also like to discuss...,"

"In addition, I noticed...,"

"And to improve the overall performance even further..."

Phrases like these unite both parts of the balanced feedback in a natural, believable way. Once you've made the connection, describe what you want the customer to change and why. For example, assume that you want the customer to change the terms of a contract. You might start your constructive criticism this way:

"I really like the incentive clauses you've included in the contract terms. I think this will have everybody aligned to achieve the project objectives *(positive aspects of what you want retained in the contract)*. I'd like to discuss the term of the contract. One year is not going to get the resources you need dedicated to this project to make your deadline" *(aspects of the contract you want to see changed)*.

Once you've described what should be retained and what needs to change, discuss the next steps for achieving change and retaining desirable aspects. As always, you want the customer to contribute ideas. Explore the next steps by:

- Inviting ideas and responding to them.
- Offering ideas and inviting responses.

The most important part of this skill step is maintaining the two-way flow. When you respond to the customer's ideas, you show you are interested and really listening. Of course, when your response involves honest criticism of the customer's ideas, that criticism should take the form of balanced feedback.

When you invite responses to your ideas, you show you care about the customer's viewpoint. When you listen to the customer's response, be sure that your expression and body language convey focus and concentration. By showing you take the customer's ideas seriously, you strengthen the customer's perception that you've developed the next steps together. This encourages commitment to whatever next steps emerge from the discussion.

Following from the example above, you might invite suggestions from the customer like this:

Sales representative: "Would there be any other contract period you could consider?" *(invite suggestion)*

Customer: "We could make it three years." *(feedback)*

Sales representative: "Great. That would justify dedicating the required resources." *(respond to feedback)*

You could choose to offer ideas. In this case, the conversation might proceed like this:

Sales representative: "I would like to suggest a three-year term that would justify dedicating the required resources for the project. *(make a suggestion)* Do you think that would be acceptable?" *(invite feedback)*

Customer: "The three-year term would be okay as long as you have a termination clause." *(feedback)*

Finally, summarize the next steps on which you've agreed. This ensures that your next steps are mutually understood and sets the stage for predictable, accountable follow-through.

At times, customers will resist your ideas. When this happens, use the communication skill of managing differences.

▶ ***Managing Differences***

1. Defining the difference:
   - You're not sure that a difference exists.
   - You don't fully understand the difference.

   How:
   - State what's important to you (what and why).
   - Clarify what's important to the customer (what and why).
2. Discussing the difference:
   - You fully understand the difference.
   - You can honestly consider alternatives.

   How:
   - Invite and respond to the customer's ideas.
   - Offer ideas and invite the customer's responses.

Managing Differences

A difference of opinion occurs when you want one thing to happen but the customer prefers something else. More often than not, these disagreements reflect opinions about what has already happened. Typical differences can involve these situations:

- Resolution of problems
- Interpretation of contract terms
- Fair pricing conditions
- Operating procedures that are not in accordance with your company's standard procedures

When differences like these arise, you can handle them in several ways, depending on the difference and the situation.

- When you're not 100% certain that a difference exists or what the difference is, define the difference.
- You understand the difference and are willing to consider alternatives. You discuss the difference.
- You cannot (or will not) consider an alternative. You conclude the discussion.

Defining the Difference

When you're not sure a difference exists or what the difference really is, the first step is to make sure that you and the customer have a clear, mutual understanding of the situation. To do so, state what is important to you *(what you want to happen and why)* and clarify or confirm what's important to the other person *(what the customer wants to happen and why)*. For example:

"I'd like to be sure I understand what you want. What you want is for my company to mobilize the equipment before your president has signed the contract, because if you don't start now, it could jeopardize getting the well drilled before monsoon season *(important to customer)*. I fully understand your reasons. The reason my company does not start any job before the contract is signed is because, if anything catastrophic happens before the contract is signed, the potential risks are huge" *(important to you)*.

It is essential to define the difference when you have any doubts at all about the nature of the difference. This way you eliminate confusion on both sides and resolve many differences by identifying what is really important to both parties. Sometimes, the real difference is smaller than the imagined difference and can be resolved immediately. For example, the customer might say: "Well, you might be able to get a work order signed for the mobilization." By defining the difference, you learn that the customer really wants to start the mobilization, and there can be possible alternatives to cover the risks to your company by having a work order signed.

As this example shows, the difference is more easily resolved than what you might have first thought. What the customer really needs to know is what you need in writing to start to mobilize for the project. Before the sales representative defined the difference, the sales representative thought the customer didn't care and didn't take his concerns seriously.

Once the difference is defined, decide whether you will discuss it in order to find mutually acceptable alternatives.

Discussing the Difference

You cannot discuss every difference in the same way. For example, the difference might involve legal, policy, or safety issues that leave no opportunity for discussion. A difference might be the result of a management decision you cannot modify. Occasionally, you may simply have no time for a real discussion. However, when you can discuss the difference, invite ideas and responses to the customer's feedback or offer ideas and invite feedback to your ideas. In the previous example, if the customer had not suggested the work order, the conversation could have gone as follows:

Sales representative: "I would like to suggest that our region manager meet with your president to explain the importance of having the signed contract before you mobilize, and at the same time, if your president has any questions, our region manager can answer them. *(make a suggestion)* Do you think that would be acceptable?" *(invite feedback)*

Customer: "Okay. That might help expedite the situation. Does your region manager know our president?" *(feedback)*

Another approach could be:

Sales representative: "What would it take to have your president sign the contract in the next couple of days?" *(inviting ideas)*

Customer: "If you had your region manager contact our president and discuss any issues he has, it might get him to sign it faster." *(responding)*

Sales representative: "Good idea. I can arrange that today." *(feedback)*

Once again, the key is to maintain the two-way flow of conversation. Even if you cannot find an alternative that completely satisfies both parties, the respect you show by discussing the difference will help the customer accept an unwelcome decision.

Concluding the Conversation

When you've reached an agreement and are ready to conclude the discussion, summarize what has been discussed and the agreed-upon actions to follow the discussion, and then check for feedback from the customer.

As mentioned earlier, you won't always be able to search for or find mutually acceptable alternatives. Sometimes, after trying, you cannot find any. In either event, conclude the conversation in a way that safeguards your relationship with the customer and eliminates any possible confusion about what you've decided. To conclude the conversation when you cannot find an acceptable solution, acknowledge the customer's right to differ and explain what you've decided and why.

▶ ***Concluding the Conversation***

1. When you have found an agreeable solution or follow-up action.

How:

- Summarize the discussion.
- List the action items to be done.

2. Check for feedback from the customer.
3. When there is a difference of opinion and you cannot honestly consider alternatives or you cannot find mutual agreement.

How:

- Acknowledge the customer's right to differ.
- Explain what you've decided and why.

Acknowledging the customer's right to differ demonstrates your respect for the individual. As appropriate, you may want to thank the customer for that input. For example:

"Jim, you've made a clear, logical case and I appreciate your position. What's more, I hope you'll always feel free to state your case this way, even when you have a fundamental disagreement."

Explaining what you've decided and why also demonstrates respect by showing you believe the customer deserves a full explanation of your decision and the logic behind it. For example:

"As far as this project goes, I'm going to ask you to try to do whatever you can to have the contract signed, because my company cannot mobilize without it."

Handling differences is always a difficult situation. However, if you take the approach described above, you will be able to have a difference of opinion and still maintain the relationship between you and the customer. If you apply this process, you may find that you end up with fewer differences.

The last discussion skill—giving credit—is easier and more pleasant for most people to do.

Crediting

As an effective sales representative, use positive events and efforts as building blocks for continuous improvement in your relationships and in your delivery of your services and products.

One way of supporting this effort is to reinforce the desired aspects and behavior that inspire further efforts. Often, the desire to improve is contagious. When your team and customer demonstrate their desire to do better, an "improvement ethic" tends to affect all aspects of the relationship. Crediting is a powerful tool for motivating individuals (and the team) to improve. Unlike some conventional rewards and incentives, crediting costs nothing, strengthens team spirit, and makes you feel good, too.

When to Credit

Give credit when the customer or other colleague:

- Performs better than expected (e.g., customer sends you a complete project overview in addition to the bid specifications);
- Performs consistently to expectations (e.g., customer always keeps you totally informed of the operations and needs); and/or
- Meets expectations the customer usually does not meet (e.g., customer is able to arrange a field visit with key buying center members on your behalf).

These three steps create a powerful impact that influences behavior by giving the customer positive feedback and an emotional incentive to maintain and improve performance.

▶ *Crediting*

Give credit when the customer or colleague:

- Performs better than expected (e.g., customer sends you a complete project overview in addition to the bid specifications).
- Performs consistently to expectations (e.g., customer always keeps you totally informed of the operations and needs).
- Meets expectations that the customer usually does not meet (e.g., customer is able to arrange a field visit with key buying center members on your behalf).

To give complete credit, follow these steps:

1. Give a specific example of performance.
2. Mention personal qualities that contributed to performance.
3. Mention resulting benefits to:
   - The customer.
   - You, your team, or both.
   - Your company.

Begin the crediting process by mentioning the behavior or activities that make the customer's performance worth crediting. This makes the credit believable, gives the customer useful information about what you see as valuable, and provides recognition of the aspects that will improve the topic being discussed. For example:

"I'm impressed by the coordination between the operations team and the stimulation group."

Next, mention the personal qualities that contributed to the performance. Mentioning personal qualities gives your credit emotional power. This part of the credit ties the valued performance to something even deeper and more essential: the individual's personality. It says something positive about the customer as an individual and shows you have focused seriously on the credit and that you really mean it.

To complete this step, relate the behavior you've identified to a talent, quality, or other virtue you associate with the valued performance. For example:

"Your thorough, point-by-point planning made the operation very efficient."

Always, provide only honest feedback. Never fall into exaggeration or flattery, which weakens the credit, your overall credibility, and your ongoing coaching effort. It is often helpful to think about the customer's self-image. If you can truthfully refer to qualities you know the customer considers especially important (e.g., intelligence, creativity, and determination), make an effort to spotlight those qualities as part of the credit.

Next, mention resulting benefits. By addressing the outcome of the customer's performance, you give that behavior added importance in the customer's mind. The value of the behavior increases with every good result you mention. Therefore, the more results you can honestly describe, the better. For example:

"I estimate that the advanced planning you proposed made the job 20% more efficient, reducing rig costs for the stimulation by 4 hours, or $40,000."

Crediting can have an extraordinary effect on just about any individual. All of us respond to a credit that 1) focuses on a specific contribution; 2) praises a quality, talent, or virtue in ourselves; and 3) demonstrates the importance of what you've done by describing its impact on other people. When you deliver a sincere, well-deserved credit, the customer will:

- Think about it often;
- Discuss it with pride; and
- Feel a strong impulse to justify the compliment.

Be alert to situations that warrant giving credit to the customer. The gesture will be appreciated and contributes to improving the relationship and aspects of the operation.

The skills discussed up to this point make up the core sales communication skills. These skills are used in all sales situations commonly encountered. In the communication process model discussed at the beginning of this chapter, it was stated that it is important to know the customer's field of experience to relate better to situations and prepare effective messages in your communications. As one of the most successful sales training companies, Richardson has identified what it considers to be the critical skills for sales conversations, shown in **Chapter Highlight 5.4 "Six Critical Skills for Successful Sales Conversations."**[8] Another important skill you can use to help communicate effectively is to determine the customer's behavioral style. The technique for doing so, called social profiling, is discussed in the next section.

Chapter Highlight 5.4: Six Critical Skills for Successful Sales Conversations

There are numerous factors and variables that go into a sale or selling situation. Many of those are beyond the sales representative's control or influence, but the one aspect that is in the representative's control and can make or break the sale is the conversation. Richardson has identified six critical skills used in dialogue with buyers needed for sales excellence. They are critical because you cannot be highly effective in sales without mastering all of them.

These skills provide the flexibility to be client-focused. If you are weak in any one of the areas, it will reduce your overall effectiveness. Your objective in using these skills is to maintain a 50/50 client-to-salesperson dialogue.

1. Presence. Projecting interest, conviction, energy, professional appearance, and confidence. What image do you portray as you stand before your potential clients? Too immature (and therefore unseasoned) to understand the complexities of business? Too old (and therefore too seasoned) to connect with the way things work today? Do you come off as smug and overconfident or too humble and possibly desperate?

To be effective, you need the right combination of each of these traits to make your prospect to want to work with you.

2. Relating. Connecting with the client includes three levels of relating: rapport, acknowledgment, and empathy. One you've established the right presence with your audience, you then need to show that you can relate to your client and their needs and interests.

- Rapport: You don't need to become best friends, but you also have little chance of a successful relationship if you rub each other the wrong way. Building rapport requires feeding off of their verbal and nonverbal cues to know how best to communicate with your prospects on an interpersonal level.

Finding things in common to bond over helps, but it isn't absolutely critical as long as comfort and trust are enabled.

- Acknowledgment: It's not about you; it's about your client and their needs or wants. It's also about their personal stake in the successful outcome of what you're selling them to make their company better. Share with them your sincere understanding of why you're there and of the client's situation.

You could also share what you hope to achieve, but this is in very broad terms at this point—don't launch off into a presentation, but rather, set expectations for the discussion.

- Empathy: Beyond acknowledgment, you need to demonstrate that you not only understand the issue, but that you also realize the impact it has on their business and the importance of rectifying it. A key factor in conveying empathy is to effectively restrain and hide any critical opinions or judgments beyond stating the obvious.

3. Questioning. Probing to understand the prospect's needs or wants. This can be tricky and might take longer than you'd like, so be patient. You know where you want to lead your prospect, but how you get there can vary depending upon the prospect's degree of understanding and acceptance of the issue and solution. The best outcome is for the buyer to feel as though they had an equal part in leading the way or that it was their idea all along.

Chapter Highlight 5.4: Six Critical Skills for Successful Sales Conversations (cont.)

Imagine getting directions to a destination. As the seller of the solution, you can see the clearest, shortest path from point A to point B. However, if you rush to get there without the consent or understanding of the buyer, you could lose them (literally). Realize that in questioning, you might be better off taking a more circuitous route that satisfies their concerns and expectations before arriving at the destination. Of course, you also need to collect any relevant information that explains how they got where they are and where they want to go, key stakeholders, timing, etc.

4. Listening. Listening in an effective way (versus efficient listening) is one of the most critical skills to master in sales. You have your own agenda for the conversation, but don't forget that so does your prospect. You can't half listen if you're going to engage your customer and respond to what they're saying or asking instead of simply preparing to barrel forward with what you want to say.

If you're not actively listening, then several things could happen (none of which are good). You could miss an important piece of information that, while you can inquire about later, makes you look distracted and inattentive for not hearing it the first time around. You could miss an opportunity to cross- or upsell your prospect. Or, you could be seen as what you are: someone with their own agenda regardless of what is of interest to the client.

5. Positioning. Being persuasive (versus only exchanging information). Although it's important to maintain focus on what the buyer wants and says during the conversation, don't lose sight of why you're there, too. You want to be actively engaged. The buyer might already be sold on you and your services, which should make your job easier. But when you're up against competitors, you're facing an uncertain buyer, or the buyer has objections, you'll need to be able to respond accordingly and persuasively. There is an art to doing this effectively without coming off as arrogant or defensive.

6. Checking. Remember that this is a conversation, not a presentation. As such, you must get into the habit of asking for feedback on what you have said. This is important because it lets you know how the client is reacting and lets you adjust your presentation. It also keeps the client involved. Checking is a key aspect of Questioning, (see #3). You want to confirm that everyone's tracking on the same page before you find yourselves in drastically different places.

Of course, you don't want to stop after every sentence, which gets tedious and annoying very quickly. Rather, think in terms of bits and chunks of information to discuss and validate before moving on to the next point.

These six critical skills will allow you to create a dialogue; understand the client's needs, priorities, and perspective; and close profitable business.

To reiterate what was said at the beginning of this post, being weak in any of the skills will reduce your overall effectiveness. Your objective in using these skills is to maintain a 50/50 client-to-salesperson dialogue.

You can also use the six critical skills as shorthand to prepare for and critique your calls and give yourself and your teammates feedback.

Social Profiling

Social profiling is a model developed from the Jungian concept of personality types. The social profile model is based on two dimensions of human behavior: assertiveness and responsiveness.

Assertiveness is the degree to which a person is perceived as attempting to influence the thoughts and actions of others. Responsiveness is the degree to which a person is perceived as expressing feelings when relating to others. **Figure 5.4** lists characteristics people display for behaviors of assertiveness and responsiveness.

Social Style Matrix

When you combine the behaviors shown in Fig. 5.4, you can describe the following four broad social profiles:

- Analytical
- Amiable
- Driver
- Expressive

From the person's social style, you can infer a number of inherent tendencies. For example, Drivers and Analyticals tend to be more task- or people-oriented than Amiables or Expressives. Each social style is shown in **Fig. 5.5**.

Analytical Style

A person who behaves in an analytical style tends to be more Ask Assertive and Control Responsive. In a sales situation, the analytical person is perceived as detail-oriented, deliberate, and well organized. This type of person listens and studies information carefully before weighing all alternatives, with reference to established policies, criteria, and objectives. An Analytical tends to avoid personal involvement with salespeople and lets others take the social initiative. In general, this type of person prefers an efficient, businesslike sales approach.

▶ ***How Would You Describe an Analytical?***

- Conservative and practical in business decisions.
- Detail-oriented; relies on a structured approach and factual evidence.
- Tends to avoid uncomfortable situations by changing the topic or withdrawing.
- Prefers a systematic, thorough approach to data-gathering and presentation of recommendations.

The strengths commonly attributed to analytical buyers include the following:

- Ensures that company's needs are met
- Is careful about committing company resources
- Analyzes facts and evidence before deciding
- Makes practical, cost- effective buying decisions

Assertiveness

Ask Assertive	**Tell Assertive**
Observes and listens	Directs and tells
Acts deliberately	Acts quickly
Minimizes risks	Takes risks
Wants appreciation	Wants visibility
Suggests	Requires
Responds	Initiates

Responsiveness

Control Responsive	**Emote Responsive**
Responds carefully	Responds spontaneously
Wants response	Wants collaboration
Controls expression	Expresses freely
Protects feelings	Shares feelings
Relies on facts	Uses intuition
Thinks	Feels

Fig. 5.4
Perceptions of assertive and responsive behaviors.

The analytical person wants to understand how things work in detail, as opposed to being given an overview. An Analytical's needs are best met when information is gathered in a systematic, efficient manner; sufficient information about the company, product, and service is provided; and time for processing recommendations is allowed.

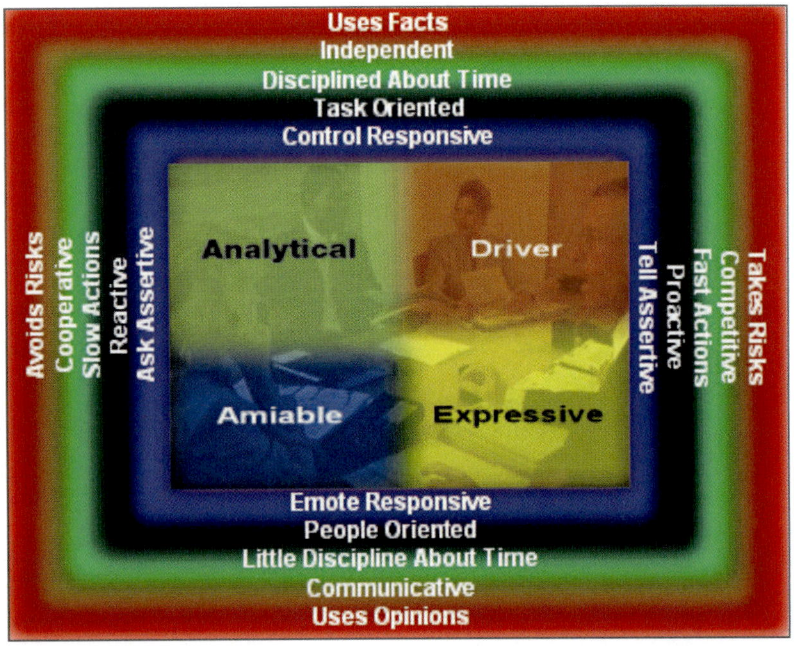

Fig. 5.5
Social profile matrix and common behaviors.

Amiable Style

The amiable person tends to be more Ask Assertive and Emote Responsive. An amiable person is seen as warm, cooperative, and deliberate. This type of person generally gathers information and processes it with others before making a decision.

An Amiable wants to establish a strong, trusting relationship with a salesperson prior to considering a purchase. This type of person wants to be assured that others will support buying decisions and that the salesperson will keep commitments. The amiable customer wants to feel confident that the product or service will be accepted. An Amiable's needs are best met when a trusting relationship is established, and the salesperson takes the time to understand the needs of the person and the organization and is responsive to requests and problems.

Driver Style

The driver person tends to be more Tell Assertive and Control Responsive. A Driver is seen as controlling, forceful, and results-oriented. This type of person usually has clear objectives and responds to those who can demonstrate that their product or service can efficiently and effectively achieve results. A Driver tends to have a high sense of urgency and little need for establishing relationships with salespeople.

This type of person wants to know options and their probabilities of success. The Driver wants a salesperson to listen carefully before recommending products and services. A Driver's needs are best met when information is gathered in an organized manner and the salesperson listens willingly and avoids becoming defensive. Follow-up on requests is timely; case histories, references, and factual support are provided; and time for considering options is allowed.

Expressive Style

The expressive person tends to be more Tell Assertive and Emote Responsive. An Expressive is perceived as fast-paced, outgoing, and enthusiastic. This type of person often has a vision of the future and is responsive to products, services, and people that help achieve that vision. An Expressive will take the time to establish open, trusting relationships with those who can make it easier to achieve goals.

This type of person wants a salesperson to collaborate in finding and implementing quality solutions to meet their needs. The expressive person wants to see the "big picture" before probing the details. An Expressive's needs are best met when the salesperson questions and listens well, can demonstrate competence, allows

▶ *How Would You Describe an Amiable?*

- Careful but cooperative in business situations.
- People-oriented; relies on the support of others and shared decision-making.
- Tends to avoid uncomfortable situations by withdrawing or changing the topic.
- Prefers an interactive approach to problem-solving.

The strengths commonly attributed to amiable buyers are as follows:

- Ensures that others will accept buying decisions
- Carefully determines whether commitments will be honored
- Processes recommendations with others before deciding
- Is sensitive to the needs of others in the discussion
- Establishes trusting relationships with others

▶ *How Would You Describe a Driver?*

- Knowledgeable and controlling in business decisions.
- Goal-oriented; relies on information that supports results.
- Tends to act quickly and confront issues directly.
- Expects people to listen carefully and respond in a timely manner.

The strengths commonly attributed to driver buyers include the following:

- Keeps discussions focused on objectives
- Explains situations so that the salesperson can recommend appropriate solutions
- Makes expectations clear
- Acts quickly, after careful consideration of options
- Attempts to balance quality and cost considerations when making decisions

▶ *How Would You Describe an Expressive?*

- Futuristic, holistic in thinking.
- Motivating; attempts to make others enthusiastic about visions and ideas.
- Tends to be direct and open, even in uncomfortable situations.
- Prefers a collaborative, team approach to problem-solving.

The strengths commonly attributed to expressive buyers include the following:

- Openly offers information to help the salesperson meet needs
- Collaborates on the proposal to make it effective within the organization
- Is concerned about the quality of solutions and their implementation
- Adapts to the needs of others
- Is innovative and willing to take risks

the other person's input to the proposal, helps the person obtain internal support for the proposal, and stays on top of the implementation.

In a sales environment, the Social Style Summary table shown in **Fig. 5.6** on pg. 142 lists some strategies to apply when dealing with customers with the respective social profile.

Sixteen Sub-Quadrants

Studies have shown that people rarely display only one type of social profile. Actually, less than 5% of the people studied showed the behavior of only one social style. What is typically seen are people who have a dominant or main profile and a secondary, less dominant profile. When combined, you get a matrix of 16 sub-quadrants that describe people's behavior. This information is used to determine how your customers like to make decisions and how you can better align with them in different sales situations. The model or profiles you use are shown in **Fig. 5.7.**

When describing a customer's social profile, you use one of the 16 quadrants (e.g., B1 Analytical Driver). B1 is the cell and abbreviated reference to the social profile. In this case, the dominant style is Driver and the secondary style is Analytical. You use this information to help you better align with your customers in different sales situations.

This information is entered into the CRM database, along with other information specific to the individual customer.

Managing Tension

Each social profile type reacts differently when experiencing tension, stress, conflict, or disagreement or dealing with an incompatible personality type. As sales representatives, you must be aware of the type of behavior that indicates when the customer is experiencing tension and what the fallback behavior is. You should manage and avoid creating tension when dealing with the customer. When planning interactions with the customer, align with the customer's preferred way of doing business that best fits with the customer's social style.

In some situations, such as negotiations and when handling customer dissatisfaction, the customer could resort quickly to, or already be in, a fallback behavior when you arrive. In such situations, it is important that your responses be appropriate for the customer's personality type in order to resolve the issue quickly. The typical fallback behaviors for each type of personality are shown in **Fig. 5.8.**

	Driver	Expressive	Amiable	Analytical
Likes	Control	Social	Supportive	Detailed
Measures personal value by	Power Results	Applause Support	Approval Attention	Respect Activity
Needs environment	Responds	Inspires to their goals	Suggests	Provides details
Support their	Conclusions and actions	Dreams and intuitions	Relationships and intuitions	Principles
Give benefits that answer	What	Who	Why	How
For decision give them	Options and probabilities	Testimony Incentives	Guarantees and assurances	Evidence and service
Take time to be	Efficient	Stimulating	Agreeable	Accurate
Let them save	Time	Effort	Relationship	Reputation
Backup style	Autocratic	Attacker	Acquiesces	Avoider

Fig. 5.6 Communication strategies for specific social styles.

The most effective strategy for managing tension when dealing with the customer is to take a proactive approach. Try to deal with the person in a way that best fits with the individual's social style. This is called aligning with the customer's personality type. People with conflicting personality types are frequently uncomfortable with each other. In sales situations, this conflict or tension can impede communication. Depending on the extent of the disparity between personalities, types of awareness and adaptation become prerequisites for a successful or satisfactory outcome.

D1 Analytical Analytical	C1 Driver Analytical	B1 Analytical Driver	A1 Driver Driver
D2 Amiable Analytical	C2 Expressive Analytical	B2 Amiable Driver	A2 Expressive Driver
D3 Analytical Amiable	C3 Driver Amiable	B3 Analytical Expressive	A3 Driver Expressive
D4 Amiable Amiable	C4 Expressive Amiable	B4 Amiable Expressive	A4 Expressive Expressive

Fig. 5.7 Social profile matrix with 16 quadrants.

Aligning with the Customer's Personality Type

To ensure effective and efficient communications with customers, learn to align by adapting your behavior so that it is compatible with the customer's social style and makes the person feel at ease. Compatibility does not require you to give up or change your own natural personality type. It simply means that you must be versatile: You must be willing and able to adjust and modulate your own behavior so the client finds it neither disagreeable nor threatening in any way.

The first step in the process of aligning is to be sure you understand your own personality type. Review the previous figures and see where you fit in. Which social style best describes you? Then ask your manager and peers how they would describe your social style. Self-image is often an erroneous indicator of personality type, as it can vary depending on the situation and with whom you are dealing.

To practice identifying social styles, discuss the social profile model and apply those criteria to colleagues and customers you know well. This allows you to share perceptions and correct misunderstandings or misinterpretations about behaviors common to each personality type. To further assist you in determining your social style, see **Chapter Highlight 5.5: You Got Style? Let's Find Out** on the next page.

All sales situations require that you align and follow the specific sales situation process simultaneously. Before an important meeting, plan your strategy for aligning with a particular client at every stage of a specific sales situation.

First, identify the customer's personality type and describe the behavior patterns or characteristics that support your conclusion. Then, develop specific plans for adapting the tone and content of remarks at each stage to the customer's personality type. In each sales situation discussed in the next chapter, you will recommend ways for tailoring each stage of the sales situation to each of the personality types and recommend ways to respond to fallback behaviors to help get a customer back on track.

When planning the details of a particular call in advance, focus on exactly how to anticipate the specific customer exhibiting "typical behaviors" and how that individual will respond. Role-playing is often a good technique for getting personalities out on the table, allowing you to improve your aligning skills in a safe environment.

Analytical	Driver
• Avoiding • Expresses disappointment in terms of the solution rather than the person • Draws attention away from issue by focusing attention on detail • Becomes defensive when pressed for a response	• Autocratic • Expresses disappointment in terms of results • Remains focused on the results and calculates new strategies to achieve them • Changes the rules
Amiable	**Expressive**
• Acquiescing • Tends not to express disappointment; instead, plays through, then refuses to do business • Appears impatient and inattentive • Justifies refusal to buy by referring to other's dissatisfaction	• Attacking • Expresses disappointment personally • Verbalizes judgmental feelings • Detaches or moves away from situation to avoid loss of self-esteem

Fig. 5.8
Fallback behavior for each social style when experiencing tension.

By concentrating on the social profiling skill, you maximize your effectiveness with your customers. The establishment of rapport is an important factor for building successful relationships with your customers. Unless you and your customer can understand each other and work harmoniously toward a single goal, your sales efforts won't have much positive impact. **Chapter Highlight 5.6: That's Funny, the Last Customer Liked My Presentation** discusses some strategies for aligning with the different types of social styles.

The concepts of personality type and aligning techniques apply internally at your company. As part of an effective team, you should apply these techniques in all aspects of your job. In the next chapter, you will examine specific sales situations regularly encountered and the processes to follow as a sales representative.

Chapter Highlight 5.5: You Got Style? Let's Find Out

A Test to Figure Out Your Style

You can download a simple test to determine your style. To complete the test, answer questions in an Excel spreadsheet identifying in a group of four words which word is least like you and which word is most like you. There are 27 groups of words for you to repeat the same selection process. After completing the survey, you are presented with your social style analysis, a summary of your style, and what might be some of your tendencies and growth opportunities with tasks and people.

To learn more about other social styles, you can browse the social style database, which has descriptions of the majority of social types described in the social profile matrix in Fig. 5.7.

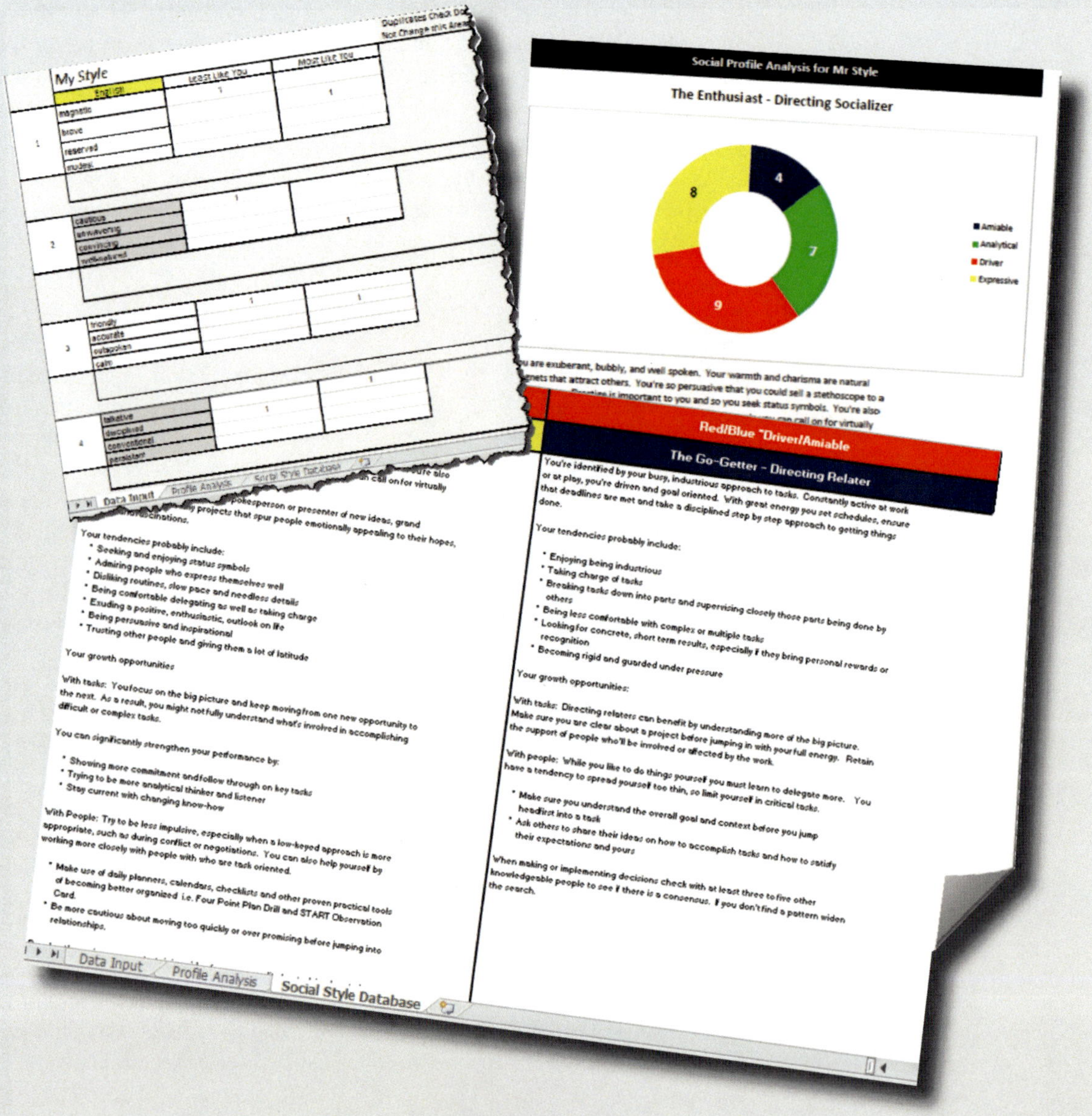

Chapter Highlight 5.6: That's Funny, the Last Customer Liked My Presentation

How Does the Customer Prefer to Do Business?

Aligning with the customer is one of the most powerful skills you can use to improve the chances of successful communication. Below are the aligning strategies for the four main social profile classifications. One of the best ways to discover how the customer prefers to do business is to ask the person what type of information is needed, how much detail, options, etc., the customer would like to have to make a decision.

Analytical

- Is highly detailed → Talk in specific terms about client needs and product features and benefits.
- Thinks and works deliberately → Present information, feedback, and ideas in a logical, orderly way, clarifying and confirming frequently.
- Relies on facts and structure → Solicit information so that your understanding of situations is complete and accurate.
- Avoids personal involvement → Keep conversation on a business level.
- Focuses on immediate details → Avoid idealistic long-range projections.
- Withdraws from uncomfortable situations → Focus on aligning; concentrate on immediate situations, actions, and short-term results.
- Respects professionalism → Approach situations factually rather than emotionally.
- Dislikes surprises → Review action plans and other agreements in writing, and provide advance notice of changes.
- Values efficiency → Respect the customer's time.

Amiable

- Is friendly → Establish a casual, informal atmosphere.
- Values strong relationships → Demonstrate personal interest based on trust in the customer, by sharing personal information.
- Likes to hear about people as well as facts → Mention co-workers and clients when discussing ideas and solutions.
- Enjoys give-and-take → Share information freely, be open to questions, and solicit ideas and input.
- Engages the help of others in making decisions → Provide feedback and ideas, acting as a resource for making decisions.
- Avoids conflict by agreeing and backing out later → Raise difficult topics gradually, clarifying and confirming frequently and establishing commitment in stages.

Driver

- Values time → Make concise points, avoid digressions and interruptions, and respond quickly to requests for information or assistance.
- Expects their input to be taken into account → Solicit the customer's input into your recommendations and respond to them directly.
- Has little need for on-the-job relationships → Maintain a business relationship, avoid personal questions, and start business discussions quickly.
- Is forceful and controlling → Be forthright but brief, remaining open-minded and flexible to avoid conflict; make recommendations to issues for their consideration.
- Is results-oriented → Inquire about the customer's project and personal objectives.
- Acts based on a high probability of success → Share information on previous success; present a range of possibilities, action steps, and ideas.
- Requires factual support → Provide evidence, examples, and testimonials supporting your proposals.

Expressive

- Focuses on the big picture more than details → Discuss concepts and provide details when requested.
- Appreciates people/information as well as technical facts → Discuss the individuals involved in the situation.
- Is fast paced, outgoing, and enthusiastic → Maintain a brisk pace and express enthusiasm for the customer's ideas.
- Visualizes ideal outcomes → Inquire about the customer's goals, ideas, and expectations.
- Appreciates support → Offer to participate in implementing action plans.
- Enjoys give-and-take; provides information willingly → Listen attentively, provide information, and solicit ideas and input.
- Prefers an open, direct approach → Address difficult issues straightforwardly.
- Wants input into solutions recognized → Use crediting.
- Appreciates creative incentives → Suggest innovative approaches with recognition.
- Is innovative and willing to take risks → Offer bold, imaginative solutions.

Summary of Chapter Objectives

This chapter set the foundation for applying the specific sales processes you can expect to encounter in day-to-day sales activities. The majority of your time will be spent communicating with the customer. Doing so successfully requires that you have an understanding of the communication process and basic communication skills.

1. Describe the process and key factors for successful communication.

The communication process consists of two or more individuals exchanging a message and giving feedback. The message is encoded by the sender and delivered using a medium that is appropriate for the situation. The receiver decodes and interprets the message and encodes any feedback to give to the sender. The sender has to consider the receiver's field of experience and abilities to decode the message. The sender has to be prepared to decode any feedback the receiver might exchange as a result of the communication. Sometimes external noise can make it difficult for the receiver to get the message clearly. Examples include physical noise or noise in the medium used, such as inappropriate words and images, that the receiver cannot decode as expected by the sender.

In your day-to-day activities, it is important to check the quality of your communications. The key factors for successful communication require the message to be clearly prepared by the sales representative and received by the customer. Ask yourself: Are you relating to the customer's field of experience and does your message medium and symbols have relevant meaning for them? Do you have a system in place to make it easy for the customer to send you feedback, and do you respond quickly to the feedback?

At the center of good communication skills are good listening skills. The most effective way to ensure good listening practices is to use active listening. This requires that you use free time during communications to process what the other person is sending and to keep focused at level 1 listening.

2. Apply discussion skills in everyday communications with the customer.

Discussion skills consist of opening the discussion, delivering the message, clarifying and confirming, and closing the discussion. When opening the discussion, the main objectives are to make certain the tension level is at an acceptable level to facilitate the discussion, inform the customer what you are going to discuss, and ask for any feedback regarding what you want to discuss.

With this done, you then deliver or receive the message. Proceed by using the appropriate medium for the message in a specific sales situation. Each message must be clear, concise, and appropriate for the targeted customer or audience. During the delivery of the message, make good use of the discussion skills of probing, clarifying, and confirming. These allow you to test for understanding and acceptance as the message is delivered. At times you will also be required to explore for ideas and triangulate topics being discussed to find agreeable solutions or follow-up actions to the discussion.

Frequently, the discussion skills of constructive criticism, managing differences, and crediting must be used. These skills are particularly useful when dealing in sales situations where there might be a strong difference of opinion, such as when handling customer dissatisfaction and negotiations. In constructive criticism and managing differences, try to modify behavior so the project or task can be successful. Crediting is used to maintain the type of actions and behavior people have exhibited to help you be successful.

Once the discussion is finished, conclude by summarizing what was discussed and agreed to, and check for feedback from the customer. On some occasions, you will not be able to agree on what needs to be done. In these situations it is important that you safeguard the relationship by concluding the conversation in an appropriate manner. Do this by acknowledging the customer's right to disagree and explain what you've decided and why.

3. Prepare effective aligning strategies for individual customers based on their social profile.

Each customer differs in terms of how they like to conduct business and discuss information, the manner in which it is presented, and how the person interacts with others. A skill you use to tailor your communications is social profiling. To do so, ask how the customer likes to conduct business, observe the person's behavior, and ask others. Our perception of the customer's social profile is biased by our own social profile, so it is important that you know what your social profile is. Once you feel comfortable knowing what the customer's social profile is, you can then modify and align your approach so the customer can be efficient in making decisions. Each customer's social profile exhibits typical behavior when experiencing tension. Be alert to these signals when you see these actions and make every attempt to reduce tension.

Applying the Concepts

On your next meeting with the customer, prepare the following precall sales sheet. Then, analyze the call using the analysis column to rate your call as to how well you applied the sales communications skills. Use the form below.

Date: ____________ Account: ____________ Opportunity: ____________

Customer: ________________________ Social Style: ____________

Your Social Style: ____________ Purpose of meeting: ____________

Opening statement: ________________________________

What is your main message? ________________________________

What percentage of the call where you at: Level 1___% Level 2___% Level 3___%

How did you align with the client? ________________________________

What communications skills did you use during the meeting? ____________

____

Give a brief description of how you used the skill. ________________________

Probing Description: ________________________________

Clarifying and Confirming Description: ________________________

Explore Ideas: ________________________________

Triangulating the Topic: ________________________________

Constructive Criticism: ________________________________

Managing Differences: ________________________________

Crediting: ________________________________

What was your concluding statement? ________________________

How would you describe the tension as the meeting progressed?

Always green level ☐ Sometimes blue, mostly green ☐

Sometimes red, mostly green ☐ Mostly blue ☐ Mostly red ☐

Which communication skills do you feel comfortable with?

____

Which communication skills do you need to practice?

____

____

____

D1 Analytical Analytical	C1 Driver Analytical	B1 Analytical Driver	A1 Driver Driver
D2 Amiable Analytical	C2 Expressive Analytical	B2 Amiable Driver	A2 Expressive Driver
D3 Analytical Amiable	C3 Driver Amiable	B3 Analytical Expressive	A3 Driver Expressive
D4 Amiable Amiable	C4 Expressive Amiable	B4 Amiable Expressive	A4 Expressive Expressive

Purpose of the call?
☐ Yes ☐ No

Checked for feedback?
☐ Yes ☐ No

Aligned?
☐ Yes ☐ No

Probed?
☐ Yes ☐ No

Clarified/Confirmed?
☐ Yes ☐ No

Explored ideas?
☐ Yes ☐ No

Triangulated?
☐ Yes ☐ No

Constructive criticism?
☐ Yes ☐ No

Managed differences?
☐ Yes ☐ No

Credited?
☐ Yes ☐ No

Concluding statement?
☐ Yes ☐ No

Meeting a success?
☐ Yes ☐ No

References

1. Atwater, E.: *I Hear You*, New York, New York, Walker and Company (1992).
2. Ronning-Hall, K., & Simon, C.: (2015, March 5). "The Science of Creating Memorable Content." Retrieved May 15, 2015, from http://www.intelligentcontentconference.com/science-creating-memorable-content/
3. Pike, R.: *Creative Training Techniques Handbook: Tips, Tactics, and How-To's for Delivering Effective Training* (2nd ed.), Minneapolis, MN, Lakewood Books (1994).
4. Peterson, E., & Riesterer, T.: *The Hero Model: Play the Right Part. In Conversations That Win the Complex Sale: Using Power Messaging to Create More Opportunities, Differentiate Your Solutions, and Close More Deals* (1st ed., p. 84). New York, McGraw-Hill (2011).
5. Miller, J. G.: *Living Systems,* New York, McGraw-Hill (1978), 147–167.
6. Kirrane, D.: "Listening to Learn: Learning to Listen," ASTD Info-Line (1997).
7. Germain, P.J.: (March 6, 2011). "The 12 Blocks to Listening," Retrieved November 11, 2006 from EzineArticles.com.
8. Priolo, D.: (April 23, 2014). "Six Critical Skills for Successful Sales Conversations". Retrieved May 21, 2015 from http://blogsrichardson.com/2014/04/23/six-critical-skills-successful-sales-conversations/

Sales Activities

The Steps to Success

The sales activities are used throughout the opportunity management process and in the broader responsibilities of successful pipeline, account, and territory management. The definition of each management process is shown in the sidebar "I'm not Management, I'm Sales". There are five main sales activities as shown in **Fig. 6.1** with the core skill of relationship management being a part of each sales activity.

In this chapter each of the main sales activities will be discussed in detail and pipeline management will be briefly introduced. Later in the textbook there will be a dedicated chapter discussing pipeline, account, and territory management.

Chapter Objectives

After reading this chapter, you will be able to:

- Understand the key sales activities to manage a sales pipeline.
- Make relationship-building a specific and continuous process.
- Choose which components of prospecting to include in your prospecting plan.
- Apply a structured approach for building proposals.
- Know how to manage key follow-up activities.

Relationship Management

Many things go into winning a sale—the fit of your solution, your value proposition, pricing, track record, responsiveness, and so on. Although all these factors impact your customers' decisions to buy, Aberdeen, an independent research firm, in its September 2009 study with 500 best-in-class companies, identified the relationship between the customer and salesperson as the #1 reason why a customer buys from a salesperson. It boils down to how the customer feels about (i.e., trusts and relates to) the salesperson or sales team. Successful salespeople have known this for a long time, and hard data affirms it.[1]

In another study published in the *Journal of Marketing,* the authors concluded that salespeople involved in the marketing of complex services often perform the role of "relationship manager." It is, in part, the quality of the relationship between the salesperson and the customer that determines the probability of contin-

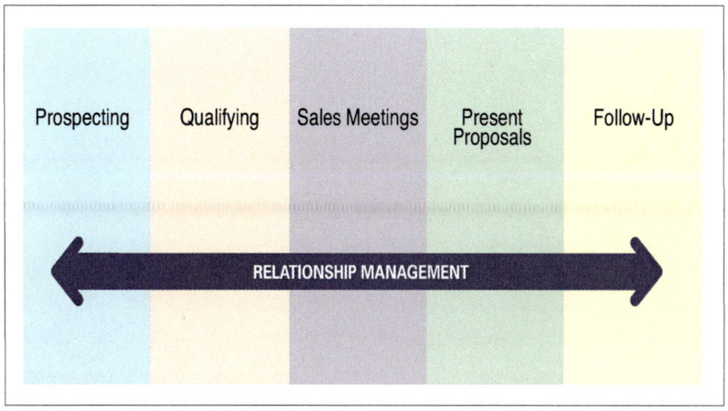

Fig. 6.1
Sales activities critical to a salesperson's success.

ued interchange between those parties in the future. The findings suggest that future sales opportunities depend mostly on relationship quality (i.e., trust and satisfaction), whereas the ability to convert those opportunities into sales hinges more on conventional source characteristics of similarity and expertise. Relational selling behaviors such as cooperative intentions, mutual disclosure, and intensive follow-up contact generally produce a strong buyer–seller bond.[2]

In the context of a salesperson, there are very specific skills and activities that lead to stronger customer relationships, as follows:

- Communication skills
- Customer profiling
- Trust building
- Application of the sales activities in a professional productive manner for both the customer and salesperson

Building Strong Relationships

It is very important for the salesperson to recognize the value of building relationships and getting to know and understand their customers. The success and satisfaction that result from having ongoing business relationships with satisfied customers are what professional salespeople strive to achieve. Up to this point in the textbook, you have already read about the communication skills you will use in the sales activities and two very important customer profiling factors: technology adoption and social style. These factors provide insights into how to better align with the customer to assist them in making a business decision.

However, what does building relationships mean? One of the best references for building relationships is the book entitled *The Trusted Advisor*[3] in which the authors are experts in the professional services and consulting industry. The authors share their real-life experiences coming from their fifty years of professional services and consulting industry experience. The basic premise of their book is to build stronger relationships with your clients. What you are trying to do is have them trust you more. Trust or stronger relationships can be measured by the level of the customer's perception of four key elements that make up the trust equation:

- Salesperson's credibility
- Salesperson's reliability
- Level of intimacy
- Salesperson's self-orientation

For more description of the trust equation, see **Chapter Highlight 6.1 "Tipping the Scales."** The major take away from the trust equation for salespeople is that you can develop relationships by strengthening the elements making up the trust equation. For salespeople, the rewards of stronger relationships with your customers are many. A few of the more significant benefits are as follows:

- Earlier notification of customer projects, giving the salesperson more time to prepare a winning proposal
- Willingness from the customer to act as a reference or provide leads to help the salesperson gain access to decision makers of future business
- More productive and efficient negotiations that are conducted in a collaborative spirit, resulting in the best deal for both sides
- Honest feedback regarding proposals and levels of service and satisfaction with the salesperson's organization and performance

▶ "I'm Not Management, I'm Sales"

You may not be in management, but sales staff are expected to effectively manage their assigned area of responsibility, which most commonly in B2B sales is either a territory or one or more accounts. To determine the value of your business, you need to have an opportunity pipeline.

Specific definitions for each are:

Opportunity Management
Strategically managing a single opportunity in a competitive marketplace.

Pipeline Management
A pipeline is a database consisting of all identified opportunities for the area of responsibility of the salesperson. Each opportunity falls in one of the ten stages of the opportunity management process. To maximize revenue from a pipeline, the salesperson must prioritize sales activities based on opportunity stage, revenue, competitive threats, and strategic importance of the opportunity.

Account Management
Develop strong relationships with all of a client's executives and decision-makers; understand the account's business drivers and how the account prefers to do business with it's suppliers. The goal of account management is to maximize the long-term value for both the supplier and the account. For large key or strategic accounts, there can be a dedicated Account Manager who is a resource for salepeople selling to the account.

(cont. on opposite page)

Territory Management

The salesperson's responsibility is an assigned a territory. Within the assigned territory, the salesperson must prioritize how they spend their time with the goal of maximizing revenue from the territory. The most common territory assignments are as follows:

- By Country, Region, City, or Zip Code
- By Vertical Market: Examples of vertical markets include manufacturing, health care, and energy. Large vertical markets such as energy may be divided into sub-markets, such as conventional and unconventional
- By Named Account: Several accounts are assigned by company name. Large accounts may be further subdivided by geography, division, business unit, etc.

Each of these benefits are significant for a salesperson working in a competitive marketplace. Receiving the benefits requires the professional salesperson to invest time and resources into building stronger relationships with their customers. The salesperson should ask themselves in which situations they have to demonstrate credibility and reliability to get to know the customer better (intimacy) and show the customer they care about their success.

Some of the opportunities for professional salespeople to positively impact each of the trust factors are listed below. This is not meant to be an exhaustive list, but a start to which you can add your ideas of things you can do for each factor.

Credibility

- Do your research into your target markets and accounts. Understand the customer's needs.
- Prepare: Have proof of the benefits your customer will receive if they use your company's product and services.
- Understand your products and services. Know what your strengths and weaknesses are for the major issues and successes.
- Take time to become familiar with the competitors' products and services.
- Share industry reports of interest and share insights.
- If you cannot answer a question, tell the customer you do not know, but will try to find out and get back to them.

Reliability

- Be early for appointments.
- Use appointment requests to formalize and have meetings posted on personal calendars.
- Check with operations or manufacturing to ensure availability and deliverability of products and services before making commitments to the customer.
- Keep the customer up to date on progress and changes. Be the first to call before they call you.
- Always check timing at the start of meetings and stay on schedule.
- Be predictable in a professional sense. Use checklists, forms, and procedures to ensure that important information is discovered and critical factors are always considered.

Chapter Highlight 6.1: Tipping the Scales

The Trust Equation

We hear a lot of conversations these days about building relationships, but just exactly what does that mean? For most of us, a better relationship means a relationship where the level of trust between the individuals is increasing. So how do you increase the level of trust? According to the authors of *The Trusted Advisor,* trustworthiness revolves around words, actions, emotions, and motives.

- Trustworthiness.
- Credibility revolves around words and is high when the other person believes they can believe what you say.
- Reliability is more action oriented and increases when the other person believes you will do what you committed to.
- Intimacy is more about emotion and increases when the other person feels comfortable around you.
- Self-Orientation is about motives and decreases when the other person trusts that you care about their success as well as your own.

The relationship between these factors and how each affects your ability to build trust is described by the Trust Equation, as shown below:

$$T = \frac{C + R + I}{S}$$

Where:

T = Trustworthiness.

C = Credibility. This factor revolves around words and is high when the other person believes they can believe what you say.

R = Reliability. This is more action oriented and increases when the other persons believes you will do what you committed to.

I = Intimacy. Intimacy is about emotion and increases when the other person feels comfortable around you.

S = Self-Orientation. This factor is about motives and decreases when the other person believes that you care about their success as well as your own.

To estimate trustworthiness, the authors assigned values to each factor on a 10-point scale, with 1 being low and 10 being the best for the C, R, and I factors. For the S factor, a rating of 1 indicates very low self-orientation, meaning you care much more about the customer than yourself, and a rating of 10 indicates that you do not care about the customer, but only yourself. Based on this measurement, the authors then estimate a typical level of trustworthiness for a new client and a successful existing client relationship as:

New client: $T = (C+R+I)/S = (5+3+2)/8 = 10/8 = 1.25$

Existing client: $T = (C+R+I)/S = (7+8+5)/4 = 20/4 = 5$

Chapter Highlight 6.1: Tipping the Scales (cont.)

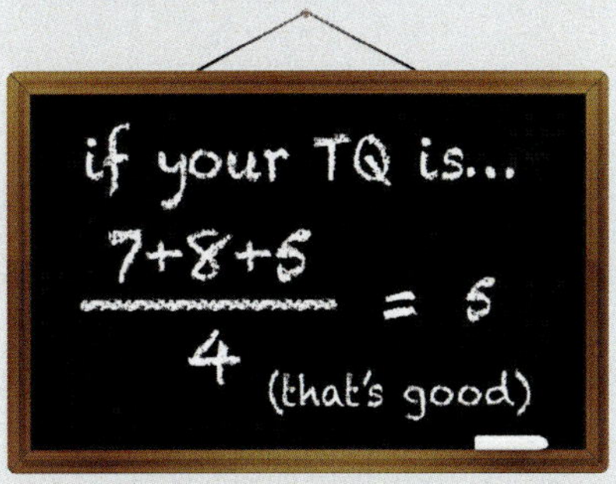

For salespeople, this is very helpful as the equation gives you specific factors to focus on to build relationships with your customers. What is evident from how the equation is calculated is that self-orientation is the most critical factor.

Not all relationships are going to develop without some issues. What the trust equation suggests is if you have a problem with the factors in the numerator (top part of the equation) you can recover the relationship but having a problem with the self-orientation is much more serious. It will be very difficult to recover the relationship, and it will take much longer than recovering from problems with the factors in the numerator. For example, if you recommend something to your customer and it does not work, you can apologize. State you were convinced this should have worked and your reasons why, and commit to investigating why the problem happened and try to find a remedy. In this scenario, your credibility has decreased, but with proper handling of the problem you will recover. The same can be expected for reliability and intimacy. However, if your actions demonstrate your motives are for you and not the customer, this will be very difficult to recover from. For example: To make your assigned quota for selling a new product or service, you sell this to the customer and they pay for it. However, they do not need this and they do not use it. If the customer realizes this, it will be very difficult for you to recover from this type of action. The customer will not trust you next time you try to sell them something they have not asked for. In most cases this will result in you not being considered for the next purchase or only involving your company when they send out the request for proposals.

In today's competitive marketplace, relationship is more important than ever. If in an evaluation for the award of work is close, the relationship between the supplier's salespeople and the customer's buying center members can be the deciding factor.

Tip the scales in your favor—show that you are a trusted advisor!

Level of Intimacy

- Take time to build rapport at the beginning of conversations.
- Extend invites to social events and other activities not directly connected to business.
- Ask about your customers and their family, as appropriate. First meetings in most cultures expect and allow for these types of conversations.
- Send holiday gifts, as appropriate.
- Take an interest in your customers—make note of special dates and anniversaries.
- Take customers and their spouses out for lunch or dinner or to other types of sporting or entertainment events outside of normal working hours.
- Share common hobbies or interests and charitable group activities.

Self-Orientation

- Understand the customer's needs fully before you start to sell. The opportunity management process is designed to help sell in this manner.
- At the start of sales meetings, begin with the value proposition.
- When presenting proposals, start with the customer's need or benefit.
- Check to ensure that the customer understands and whether they have any other issues or concerns.

- Prepare questions you think the customer may have of you when meeting for the first time or making recommendations.
- Always ensure that you deliver on your promises made during the pursuit phase of an opportunity in the implementation stage. Ask whether the customer used and benefited from what you sold them.

In the later sections of the textbook, you will see:

- There are steps included in the sales call skills to ensure that you keep focused on relationship building during sales meetings and presentations of proposals.
- The level of relationships will be considered when building a strategic sales plan for a specific opportunity. Special attention is given to relationship factors to answer the question "can you win?" Do you have strong enough relationships with key members in the buying center who want you to win and who will defend choosing you over your competitors?
- In account plans, there are relationship assignments. People from the supplier team are required in an ongoing business relationship for their assigned contacts and to become a resource for others who want advice or information about contacting the person for the first time.

Pipeline Management

Pipeline management (also referred to as sales funnel management) enables the salesperson to prioritize their sales activities. One of the key factors for prioritizing is opportunity sales stages. **Figure 6.2** below shows the relationship between sales activities, the sales pipeline and the opportunity sales stage. Leads, sometimes referred to as potential opportunities, are added to the pipeline as the result of successful prospecting. Once the salesperson completes the qualification process, the less attractive leads will be dropped from the funnel and the sales stage is set to closed withdrawn and the remaining opportunities are now in the sales stage as confirmed leads.

The salesperson will make additional customer contacts and decide if this is a sales opportunity their company can win. At this point in time, the confirmed lead sales stage becomes a sales opportunity for which additional sales calls will be made with the buying center members and a proposal or bid will be prepared and submitted. At the time the proposal is submitted or in the more formal tendering process when the request for proposal is received from the customer, the sales

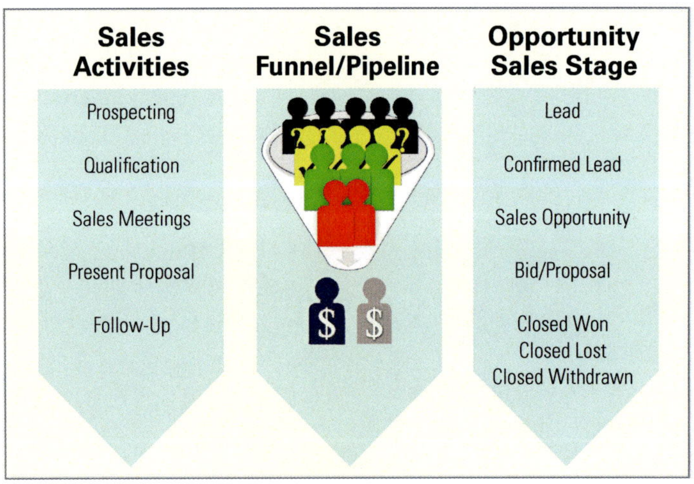

Fig. 6.2 Shows the relationship between sales activities, sales pipeline and opportunity sales stage.

stage is changed to bid/proposal. Once the customer decides the winner, the sales stage is changed either closed won or closed lost and either you or your competitor will make revenue from the sale.

At any time after a lead is added to the pipeline, the opportunity sales stage can be changed to closed withdrawn for reasons such as the customer cancels the project or it was discovered after the lead was entered into the funnel that in fact there was no real opportunity and it is not pursued, effectively taking it out of the pipeline. The reason for tracking such types of opportunities will be discussed later in Chapter 13 "Pipeline Management."

The follow-up sales activities vary depending on the type of award. Some awards are for the single purchase of products and the follow-up activity can be as simple as ensuring that the products are received on time and in good condition before checking for any other needs of the client and agreeing to a follow-up contact. In other types of awards, there may be an ongoing contract that can last from months to years and requires a significant portion of the salesperson's time to follow up with the customer over the life of the contract. These types of follow-up activities were discussed in detail as part of the opportunities management process in Chapter 4.

In the next section, each of the key sales activities will be discussed in more detail, starting with prospecting.

Prospecting

Prospecting can be considered successful if it results in an opportunity being added to your sales pipeline. To add an opportunity to your pipeline, there must be a qualification decision. Qualification will be discussed in a separate section. Unfortunately, a lot of salespeople have a negative perception of prospecting because it is often associated with a popular or unpopular prospecting technique called "cold calling." See the sidebar "Making a Cold Call Warm." However, a good prospecting plan includes several prospecting activities, as illustrated in **Fig. 6.3** and listed below:

- Corporate Marketing Communications Plan (MCP)
- Research
- Current Accounts
- Referrals
- References
- Networking
- Conferences
- Cold Calling
- E-mail Marketing
- Tracking

Fig. 6.3
Prospecting activities.

Corporate MCP

In Chapter 1, marketing communication plans were discussed and when done well result in a significant number of leads (request for further information or follow-up by company representative). In some companies that have industry brand recognition, the salespeople never use any other prospecting techniques. These lucky salespeople have access to more leads than they will ever have time to qualify. What makes most corporate MCPs successful is the variety of techniques

▶ *Making a Cold Call Warm*

Salespeople dread the thought of making a cold call to set up a meeting with someone they do not know and potentially for a company they have never worked for before—maybe in a city where they have no business that is i n a country where they have no business. Help! I think I'd rather go to the dentist.

Well it does not have to be stressful. Warm up your cold calls by doing some up-front preparation, as listed below:

- Check your internal CRM system to see if the prospect is in your CRM system and whether anyone has contacted the person recently. If so, contact that person and ask for some insider information on how to deal with this person
- If there are no recent contacts but the person is in your system, then check to see who entered the person into the system and contact them
- Hold a marketing event (lunch and learn, breakfast briefing, webinar, etc.) for the targeted company or territory and specifically invite the list of people you considered cold calls. If they attend now, you have the opportunity to meet them and thank them for attending, and now they are no longer a cold call
- Send out an email to generate awareness by addressing a challenge or issue you believe the cold contacts have. Include two levels of requesting information: a link they can go for additional information and a second link to be contacted with your email link

- Check with your suppliers to see if they know the people on your cold call list and ask if they could act as a referral
- Check with your current customer base; if someone knows the people on your cold call list, ask them to act as a referral
- Check one or several of the social media sites for insights about the person. This may lead to a common point of interest or you may discover someone who knows them and may be agreeable to introducing you or providing some insights about the person
- If you cannot find any information or anyone who knows the people on your cold call list, research their company and use your experience with similar companies as your common ground

Chances are, with a minimum amount of preparation before you pick up that phone, making a cold call could turn out to be a walk on the beach!

that are used to target the early stages of the buyer awareness stages of awareness, liking, knowledge, and preference. The techniques or components of successful corporate MCPs are as follows:

- Internet presence (web and social media) that is easy to find with high rankings on Internet searches
- Website with high quality content, white papers, success stories, and other publications available to the general public, with easy request for information or contact facilities as well as visitor statistics to help manage and improve the website
- Subscription services for regular updates via e-mail or regular mail
- Participation in industry conferences and events (speakers, booths and sponsorships of events)
- Advertising
- Public relations such as participation in national and local charities, corporate-sponsored charities, or donations of either money or employees' time
- Industry-sponsored training sessions can be either for a fee or by invitation

In some companies, it is that salesforce who must source some or all of their own leads if they are to achieve their sales targets. However, in this situation they should be aware of what the corporate MCP consists of (content, schedules, other support resources, etc.) so they can leverage when possible the corporate MCP assets in their prospecting plan.

Research – Account Specific

Prospecting is more successful when it is focused on specific requirements of a target market segment that your product and services can provide. For account-specific research, the main tool is the Account Profile described in Chapter 3. From the account research, the salesperson then develops an account plan identifying a pipeline of opportunities for which a sales plan is created. The specifics of what an account plan consists of will be covered in Chapter 13 "Pipeline Management."

Research – Territory Specific

To support your selling efforts in a territory, you need to identify the following:

- Territory size in terms of market expenditures and number of customers
- Type of customers (profit/non-profit, government, international, national, large, medium, small, very small)
- Segmentation of market by customer needs or industry
- Number of competitors, market share, value proposition, call patterns
- Customer buying behavior (formal/informal, buying frequency, process). A best practice when entering new territories is to hold interviews with target customers to learn about their needs prior to committing resources to the territory. A good source for this type of information is customer procurement departments or financial managerss
- Existing territory pipeline
- Significant industry events or conferences
- Professional organizations and local chapters

From the territory research, the territory salesperson, revenue objectives, or quotas are allocated. Quotas are then used to set call patterns, which includes the allocation of the salesperson's time with target customers or segments. The biggest challenge is to ensure that the salesperson's time is optimally allocated across a large group of multiple customers.[4] Important outcomes from the territory research include any additional demand generation efforts, such as resources or support needed beyond the corporate MCP, and the amount and type of prospecting the salesperson will commit to as part of the territory plan.

Current Accounts

Too often, salespeople do not allocate a portion of their prospecting time to their current accounts, which are accounts they are currently selling to. This happens when the salesperson becomes confident that the account will continue to buy from them or has a fear of changing anything when they are being successful. Prospecting in current accounts must be done tactfully and is most effective when the salesperson goes:

- Deeper into departments for which they are selling to, getting to know more people who are in the department. Rather than depending on a single point of contact, for example, in procurement, also make contact with operations and finance, etc.
- Vertical, to contact higher levels in the customer organization and more end users. When contacting different levels in an organization, it may not result in adding more opportunities directly into your pipeline, but can provide you with a better understanding of the company's needs and decision-making process. This will assist you in preparing better proposals to defend against the competition trying to win work from your account. This better understanding can help you discover additional

> **▶ *The Amazing Dozen Donuts***
>
> If there was a Prospecting Hall of Fame, this story would be hanging proudly on display. A sales manager of a city sales group was brainstorming with his sales team for innovative ways to capture more business. In many of the accounts, customers were splitting the work between his company and several competitors. In one sales meeting, a salesperson got an idea that every Friday the sales team should deliver donuts to a select group of accounts. His logic was that there was a chance these clients would need a supplier over the weekend and their operations team would often simply assign the work to the last salesperson they saw before the weekend. The idea was if the clients became confident that they would see the salesperson in the office every Friday morning, the customer would assign the weekend jobs to that salesperson. Therefore, as part of the company's client appreciation initiative, they would bring one to three dozen freshly baked donuts—chocolate covered, frosted, jelly filled—every Friday depending on the size of the account. The result was amazing! Salespeople identified up to $100,000 of additional work being secured. As expected, when the salesperson stopped by to drop off the donuts and have coffee, operations staff started to ask the salesperson to come by their office before they left so they could brief them on upcoming work on the weekend. In this case, the convenience buyer behavior was resulting in the salesperson's company being assigned the work.
>
> 

needs from the current account that enables you to sell more products and services within the same opportunity. This can be additional sales of similar or complementary products or selling up to higher levels of products or services.

- Wider, to contact other departments or locations within the same account or partners of the account. These departments may have similar needs and provide new opportunities for you to sell to them.This type of prospecting in current accounts is referred to as cross-selling. This will be discussed in more detail in the account development strategies in the "Account Management Plan" chapter later in the textbook. Current account prospecting leverages your current customers to act as reference or referral to gain access to new contacts. The access can be in several forms:
- Assisting you in setting up an internal marketing event, such as a lunch and learn presentation. For example, they assist you with identifying who should be on the invitation list.
- Introducing you to other people who may be interested in your products or services or have similar needs. This can be in person or through a telephone call or e-mail.
- Giving permission to use their name or reference your experiences with them.
- Providing a letter of reference that can be used internally and possibly externally.
- Co-authoring industry or white papers or success stories that can be used as sales collateral in future sales calls or marketing programs.

In the opportunities management process, this activity is recommended as part of the implementation stage for generating leads and references. In Chapter 1, referrals are classified as word-of-mouth marketing, which was identified as the number one influence for B2B purchasing decisions. Every salesperson needs to make securing referrals part of their prospecting activities in their current accounts.

Walking the Halls

When you have customers that you visit on a regular basis, always try to either arrive early or stay after finishing a meeting to give yourself time to walk the halls to say hello to contacts that you may not have spoken to recently. You should also have a list of customers who you have not met but would like to meet and give them your business. A great example of another version of walking the halls is in the sidebar "The Amazing Dozen Donuts."

Multiple Visits

When visiting an existing customer, you should always try to schedule at least one more visit in addition to your primary visit. If the visit requires you to travel to another country, city, or location, try to schedule additional visits to fill the open time before or after your primary visit. As mentioned earlier, in current accounts you always want to establish more relationships. When you are already in the customer's building, you can ask your primary contact if they could introduce to another contact who they think may be interested in talking with you.

Referrals

Why are referrals so powerful? Part of the answer is contained in the first part of this chapter. It has to do with relationship and trust. According to one article on referrals, when you ask for and get a referral from an existing customer or business associate, there's more than simple familiarity working in your favor.[5] You're tapping into existing relationships, which accelerate your ability to obtain new business. In typical selling situations, trust is the first and foremost issue in the mind of your prospects. The prospect asks himself or herself, "how do I know I can trust this person and this company?" Brian Tracy, author and sales training professional, cites building the trust bond as the critical first step in the selling process. He says building trust with customers is 40% of the process, followed by uncovering needs, presenting solutions, and asking for the decision. The value of the referral in this sense is illustrated below in **Fig. 6.4.**

Some salespeople feel it is not professional to ask for referrals and that good service is not something that should be rewarded, but expected. This is not why you ask for a referral. A referral is for your future customers. What you are trying to do is make it easy for them to believe and decide to have the first meeting with you. Getting referrals becomes more natural and easier when you use referrals as part of your sales call processes. Once you begin to make the use of referrals as part of your sales call processes, then you can refer back to your earlier meetings and have a conversation similar to this:

Salesperson: "Mr. Customer, how do you perceive the performance of our products for your operation?"

Customer: "So far excellent. Your products have done what you said they would."

Salesperson: "Thank you. I really do appreciate your comments. Do you remember when I called you the first time and I mentioned that your colleague, Mrs. Jones, recommended that I contact you?"

Customer: "Yes, I remember that very well."

Salesperson: "May I ask why you agreed to meet with me?"

Customer: "I respect Mrs. Jones and if she was satisfied, then I was pretty sure it would work for us."

Salesperson: "That is what I thought and now I would like to ask you, based on your experience, do you know anyone with similar needs as yours that could benefit from similar products? Calling someone new to ask for a meeting is a rela-

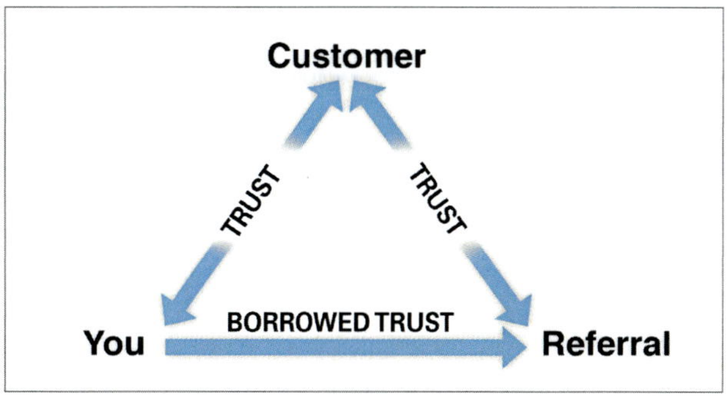

Fig. 6.4
Trust bonds already exist between you and the customer and between the customer and the referral. The referral process creates a level of borrowed trust between you and the referral, a great advantage for starting the selling process.

	tively easy decision for the customer if someone they know and trust recommends the meeting."
Customer:	"Well yes, I do know of someone. Would you like me to introduce you?"

References

Salespeople should handle references the same as referrals. References are sales aids that can be used as proof when selling, specifically when supporting and handling customers' negative reactions. Both supporting and handling customers' negative reactions will be discussed in the next two chapters. References, like referrals, come from existing customers. The most compelling references are when the references are on the customer's company letterhead and signed by the customer. There is an excellent example of a reference letter on page 208 in **Chapter Highlight 7-2: The $200,000 Makeover.**

The conversation the salesperson may have asking the customer for a letter of reference might go like this:

Salesperson:	"Mr. Customer, how do you perceive the performance of our products for your operation?"
Customer:	"So far, excellent. Your products have done what you said they would."
Salesperson:	"Thank you. I really do appreciate your comments. Do you remember when we first met and, when I was explaining how our products would benefit your operation, I showed you a letter from Mrs. Jones stating that our products helped them reduce their rejection rates by 13%, reducing their production costs by 18%?"
Customer:	"Yes, I remember that very well. In fact, for us the improvement may be even greater."
Salesperson:	"What is your estimate of your savings?"
Customer:	"Closer to 20%. Our parts are more expensive than Mrs. Jones' department."
Salesperson:	"Mr. Customer, can you give me a similar letter like what I showed you from Mrs. Jones? For my future customers, it is more compelling when someone like yourself, who is known in the industry, shares your success by using our products. If you want, I can write a draft for you and send it to for your consideration."
Customer:	"Perfect. Send that to me and I will put the final version on our letterhead, sign it, and give it to you the next time we meet."
Salesperson:	"Excellent, I really appreciate it."

As outlined in **Fig. 6.5,** some customers will provide references of different levels or restrictions:

- Give a letter of reference, but only for use inside their company or with their partners.
- Use their example, but remove specifics about their particular situation.
- No released documents, but will allow you to use their name and have interested customers call them.

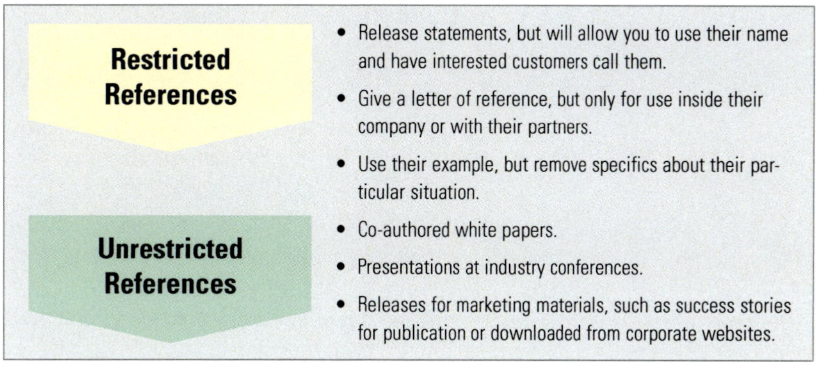

Fig. 6.5
Restricted and unrestricted versions of references.

All releases are good, and by using referrals and references during your initial contacting and sales processes, you are clearly demonstrating to the customer the purpose of the referrals and references. Other versions of references are:

- Co-authored white papers,
- Presentations at industry conferences, and
- Releases for marketing materials, such as success stories for publication or downloaded from corporate websites.

Whenever you use a referral or reference, you must take the time to do several things:

- When you use the referral or reference for the first time, let the customer that gave you the referral or reference know that you used it and thank them for their help. Show them your appreciation by inviting them to lunch or a social event or giving them something of interest, such as an industry report.
- When a customer gives you a referral, make it a habit to call upon the referral as soon as possible.
- When you use a reference and there is a chance the prospect may contact the customer, you must immediately follow up with the customer giving you the reference after the meeting in which you used the reference. If the prospect does contact the customer in regard to the reference, they may not remember what it is that you would like them to emphasize. Make it easy for them to help you and alert them they may be contacted. Review what you would like for them to communicate to the prospect.
- Always offer to write the letter of reference or have an example that you can leave with them.

A very good health check for any business is how many references, referrals, and other marketing materials are generated from current accounts on a monthly basis.

Networking

The salesperson should be looking for ways to increase the number of people you know. In a business context, there are many ways available for the sales professional to do this, such as the following:

- Professional societies
- Conferences and industry exhibitions
- Training
- Social events
- Social media
- Community activities

Professional Societies

These types of groups are perhaps the best form of business networking. If the audience of the professional society is your target market then there are many opportunities for you to meet new potential customers and competitors and to market or build your brand awareness. For example, if your company is selling upstream products and services to the oil and gas industry, there are many professional societies, such as the Society of Petroleum Engineers (SPE). The SPE has 143,962 members in 147 countries with 199 sub-sections or special interest groups. If your company sells computer parts and services, a great professional society to join is the Association of Computing Machinery (ACM). ACM has over 100,000 members globally with 37 special interest groups, holds 170 conferences each year, and provides more than 50 publications annually.

Each society offers networking opportunities, such as the following:

- Participating at annual conferences at which you have opportunities for presenting, exhibiting, and socializing
- Most professional societies are non-profit; as such, there are many opportunities for volunteers to work at conferences and social events
- Marketing opportunities such as advertising, training to sponsoring local chapter meetings, and lunches. Advertising can be done in printed materials and online websites
- Perhaps the best networking opportunity is becoming an active committee member

Be very selective when deciding which professional communities to join. Consider membership benefits such as access to papers, research and conferences as well as the number of networking opportunities in your area.

Conferences

Conferences are a great way to network and provide another opportunity for active participation. Planning is the key to getting the most from a conference as most conferences will have keynote speakers at breakfast and lunch. There are typically several sessions running concurrently during the day, so you have to choose which ones to attend. Some conferences will have several social events during the evenings. These are great opportunities to have your spouse join, adding another dimension to your networking efforts. For the major conferences, which can have literally thousands of attendees with many concurrent sessions, it is a best practice to plan as a sales team and ensure that targeted sessions and social events have a representative from your company. To ensure this happens, it takes a coordinated team effort. At the end of each day, the team should meet back together to debrief on the day's events and share contacts made during the day. It is also a good idea when there are multiple conferences relevant for your company create a conference calendar and assign specific people to attend, while others remain on duty and take calls for those attending the conference.

Training

Continued professional development and education are a great way to rejuvenate your processional drive and another great opportunity for networking. Training can be considered from two scenarios:

- Publicly available training
- Training as a marketing tool

▶ **World Wide Webinars**

By carefully selecting which publicly available trainings you register for, you can find yourself sitting with potential customers during the training and working in teams. Most publicly advertised training will state which companies attend and provide a roster at the training. Coffee breaks and lunches are great times to introduce yourself to people you have not met and trade business cards.

Training as a marketing tool is a very powerful networking tool. In this scenario your company can send invitations to targeted companies and individuals you would like to meet. There are a variety of options for training, varying from:

- Lunch and learns (popular in most industries), where guests arrive at 10:30 am, listen to a 45-minute presentation followed by question-and-air session and then eat a buffet lunch.
- After-hours cocktails or dinners, following a similar format as the lunch and learn.
- ½ day training sessions, which start at 9:00 a.m. and finish at noon, followed by lunch.
- Multiple-day sessions.
- Webinars. Online training can be both live and on-demand. Webinars are one of the growing techniques companies are using today to create brand awareness and prospecting without many of the limitations of the traditional techniques discussed, and the number of webinar service providers are increasing every day. For some interesting webinar facts, see the sidebar "World Wide Webinars."[6]

Do some research before your training to determine if your training session qualifies for continued educational units or credits and include this information in your invites. As in all marketing events, make it easy for your customers to request additional information or contact and collect feedback. Follow up after the training event to say thank you for attending and offer any further assistance.

Social Events

These types of events can take on many forms, such as entertainment, sporting, holiday activities. As with the conferences, there are many types of social events available, and planning and careful selection will ensure that you are rewarded for your time spent at the event. It is also a good idea to create a social event calendar and assign sales team members to specific events to ensure the best coverage of the events while maintaining people available to cover for those attending. Some social events have costs, so proper planning is critical to ensure the best return on the investment. Social events can also be a good opportunity to invite current customers and potentially new customers as part of your prospecting efforts.

Social Media

For a lot of people the Internet changed the way they think, work, and discover. Today online social media has created another option for networking. Some of the more popular social media online sites are LinkedIn, Twitter, and Facebook. Sites such as LinkedIn offer professional level accounts that are designed to make on-line networking more organized and effective. **Figure 6.6** on the next page is an example of the LinkedIn Premium subscription benefits as related to on-line networking and prospecting. Consider social media to build your personal brand. Create interesting posts, while allowing your audience to feel a personal connection to you. Leverage your core group to retweet items of interest, identify things you like, and follow others with similar interests as you. Give back to your groups by adding comments when you have insights to share.

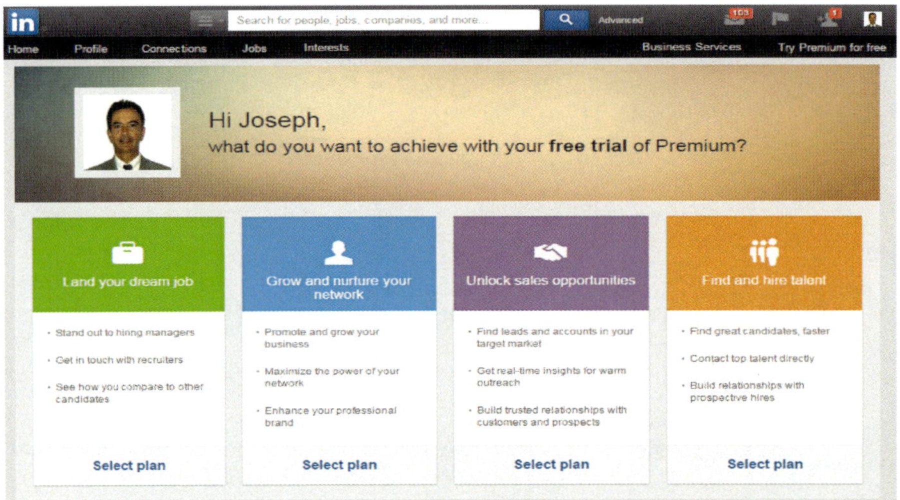

Fig. 6.6
LinkedIn Premium service targeted for online networking and prospecting.

There are many options for learning how to use social media effectively for prospecting, including on-line and instructor-led training and even entire conferences dedicated to the topic of social media. In addition, on-line social media offers an easy way for you to research contacts in preparation for your first meetings.

Community Activities

There is a saying that people prefer to buy from friends rather than strangers and, as one survey showed, people will consider recommendations from people they know the most. See the sidebar "Who Would You Trust?"[7] Your participation in community activities is a great way to network and give back something to the neighborhoods where you live and work. As discussed in Chapter 1, in the buyer readiness section, buyers prefer to buy from companies and people with whom they have a favorable impression. There is no better way to build that favorable impression than by participating in local charitable events. If your company does not have a specific community or charity they sponsor, then ask your customers which community events or charitable groups and associations they support and do the same. The favorable impression and the good personal feeling you get from participating in these activities make this type of networking very rewarding.

Elevator Speech

The purpose of all forms of networking is to come into contact with people who may need or benefit from your products or services. At a networking event, you are not going to have a sales meeting. When you meet someone at a networking event, you want to follow these steps:

- Exchange pleasantries (introductions, including why you are attending or who invited you to this event).
- Ask questions about the other person (where are they from, is their family with them, etc.).
- Ask what line of business are they in.
- Inquire which company they work for.
- Find out what they do.
- Tell who you work for and what you do. Develop a thoughtful and engaging statement that describes you and your company. Describe what you or your

▶ *Who Would You Trust?*

Recommendations from personal acquaintances or opinions posted by consumers online are the most trusted forms of advertising, according to the latest Nielsen Global Online Consumer Survey of over 25,000 Internet consumers from 50 countries.

Ninety percent of consumers surveyed noted that they trust recommendations from people they know, while 70% trusted consumer opinions posted online.

"The explosion in Consumer Generated Media over the last couple of years means consumers' reliance on word of mouth in the decision-making process, either from people they know or online consumers they don't, has increased significantly," says Jonathan Carson, President of Online, International, for the Nielsen Company.

However, in this new age of consumer control, advertisers will be encouraged by the fact that brand websites are trusted at that same 70% level as online consumer opinions.

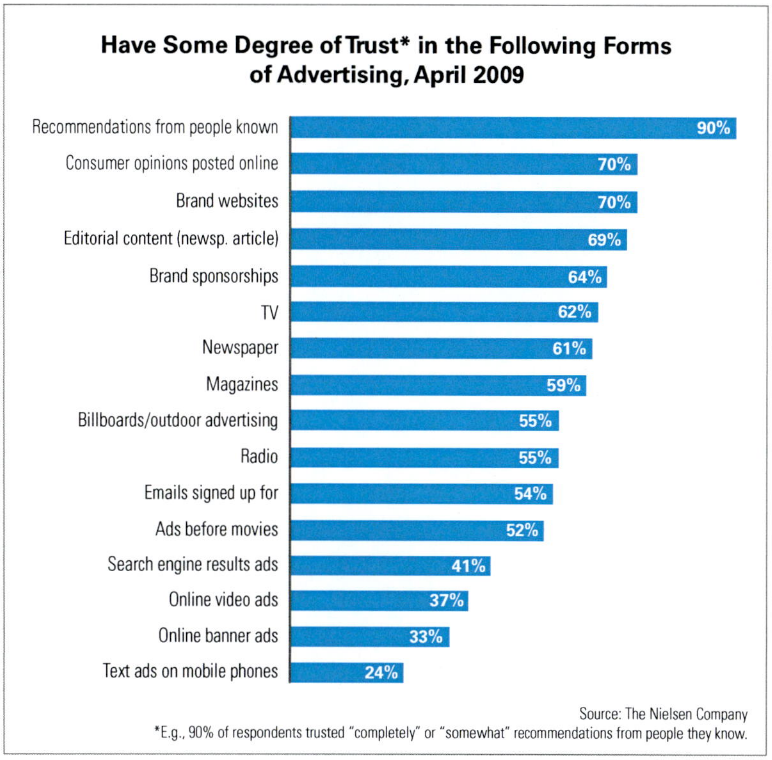

company does in terms of benefits your customers receive or what you help your customers do. Make sure it is not a selling statement. Networking isn't about the sale. It is about the relationship.

- Listen to their response, and if it appears there is a business connection or other connection, exchange business cards or contact information. It is okay not to exchange business cards if giving the business card does not have value. If you do decide to give your business card but they do not offer you their card, it is acceptable to ask them for a business card. If they do not have one, then write their contact information on the back of your card.
- Ask if it would be okay for you to follow up with them appropriately, for example, to set a time for a meeting or send some additional information.
- Comment that it was nice meeting them and you look forward to meeting them in the future.
- If you are going to follow up with them, make a couple of notes on the back of their card to remind you where you met.

There are different versions of the elevator speech for different occasions. As the name suggests, the elevator speech is short with one purpose: create interest in you and your company and agree to a follow-up action. If you are in the reception area of your customer's office waiting to go into a meeting and someone walks in who does not know you (or you them), this is a perfect time for an elevator speech. In this case, after you have determined who they are and what they do, rather than describing what your company does generically, describe the intended benefit of the meeting or presentation you are waiting for. Depending on their response, decide if a follow-up action is required. A very effective follow-up action for a senior executive is to ask them who would they suggest you talk to. In most cases, they will recommend a gatekeeper or manager responsible for the relevant area and now you have a referral—perfect.

For your elevator speech to be effective, you have to think, plan, and say your elevator speech before arriving at the event. Think about the different types of people you might meet and what an appropriate follow-up action would be depending on the person's job, department, position, etc.

Cold Calling

As stated at the start of this section, prospecting and cold calling are what some people envision when people talk about sales. Unfortunately, most people have a negative opinion of this type of activity and would prefer not to do this, even though in many cases the person has never tried cold calling. As described in the sidebar "Making Cold Calls Warmer," a cold call is calling someone you do not know but you want get their agreement to meet. At this meeting, there will be a sharing of information. The objective of the meeting is for you and your customer to agree that there is potential for your company to work for the prospect. In today's world, there are very few occasions when you should make a cold call. There are, however, times that you will want to meet people for the first time and set a time for that meeting. As with all prospecting activities, prior to making the call, do your research. You should have a reason for calling someone, as follows:

- A referral
- In your research you discovered their company has a program or project that is planned that will require your company's products and services
- They purchased from your company in the past and you are following up
- You or someone from your company submitted a proposal or quote in the past and you are following up
- They made an on-line request for more information
- You will be in their office or building, or city visiting with another customer and would like to visit with them
- Competitors of their company are benefiting from your products and services
- You are following up on an earlier correspondence you sent (e-mail, mail, etc.)
- Your company is holding a promotion, running trials, giving away samples, etc.

Once you have your reason for calling clearly established, then think about the call. A best practice is, in advance of the call, send an e-mail letting the person know:

- The reason you are calling them.
- Your value proposition.
- Time and day you will call. Also, give them an option to suggest another time and day for the call if what you suggested is not convenient.
- If they are not the correct person to contact, ask them to suggest the correct person to contact.

When you make the call, follow this flow:

- Introduce yourself and remind them you are following up on an earlier e-mail that you sent them.
- Exchange pleasantries.
- Explain the reason for the call and your value proposition.
- Ask a qualifying question.

- Ask to set a time or define the next steps.
- Check if they will invite anyone else to the meeting.
- Ask if there is anything else they want you to be prepared to discuss.
- Thank them for their time and tell them you are looking forward to the meeting.

An example conversation is below:

Customer: "Hello, this is Mrs. Jan."

Salesperson: "Good morning, Mrs. Jan. This is Mr. Salesperson from Company X. I hope you are enjoying the break in the weather this week."

Customer: "I'm not, but I hope I can this weekend."

Salesperson: "Yes, let's hope it stays. Mrs. Jan, I'm following up on an earlier e-mail that I sent on Monday. Did you receive that?"

Customer: "Yes, I did."

Salesperson: "Great. As I stated in my e-mail, Mr. Partner recommended that I contact you as he said that you have a very similar project coming up in the next 12 months and he felt your project would be as difficult as his. Is this still in your plans?"

Customer: "Yes, it is and it will be very similar."

Salesperson: "In Mr. Partner's project, he was dealing with some very tough deadlines. He decided to use our FAST service, which he estimated reduced his project days by 10%, which allowed him to meet his project time-line. Is that something that you would be interested in?"

Customer: "Yes, indeed."

Salesperson: "What I recommend is for us to meet and discuss your project so I can understand your objectives and your critical success factors. Then I can make some recommendations as to what type of products and services would best help you. Do you have time for a 30-minute meeting next Monday at 10:00 am?"

Customer: "That works for me, and I will have a couple of other team members in the meeting."

Salesperson: "Oh thank you. And may I know their names?"

Customer: "Yes, my operations manager, Mr. Smith, and my procurement manager, Ms. Putu."

Salesperson: "I'm looking forward to the meeting. Is there anything else you want me to come prepared for?"

Customer: "No, but thank you for asking. See you next week."

The cold calling practice is not only for new clients. It can be done with customers you are currently working for. As mentioned earlier, during the implementation stage of a customer's project, you should leverage your existing relationships to meet more people in the customer's organization. Follow the same format for a cold call when calling new contacts in existing customers' organizations.

E-mail Marketing

E-mail is a nice complement to cold calling. It is also an important part of the corporate MCP program that can be leveraged by the salesperson. The idea is the salesperson registers on their company e-mail subscription list. When there is an e-mail update sent from the corporate MCP that the salesperson believes is relevant for target customers, the salesperson forwards the e-mail to his or her customers to build awareness and the customer's reply for further information will be sent back to the local representative. For this to be used as a prospecting technique, the salesperson must have an e-mail list of potential customers. This same list can also be used to send out local success stories and announcements.

The purpose of a prospecting e-mail is to create awareness and generate interest so the recipient can request further information or follow-up. Below are some guidelines for creating e-mails as a prospecting tool. They need to be created with the purpose of generating interest. As such, an effective format for a marketing e-mail is:

- **Interest-generating subject line.** The most important element of effective e-mail marketing is the subject line, which can be thought of as the headline, according to Linda Pophal, author of *Direct Mail in the Digital Age.*[8] The headline should provide a short, immediate, and specific benefit to the audience, she says, and must also avoid including words likely to get caught up in spam filters because they sound like "advertising talk"—a word like "free," for instance.
- **Personalized.** Use the name of the receiver and send it to one person at a time. This is simple to do with the mail-merge option in most e-mail software packages, such as Outlook. The salutation you choose immediately indicates if you cared enough to figure out who should really receive your e-mail, or you just picked a name out of a list. It also communicates respect, professionalism and friendliness.
- **Body of the message.** Be brief and to the point. You want your prospects to be so compelled by your e-mail that they'll act now. To make that happen, you must include key pieces of information: the prospect's specific need, expected benefits, demonstration of capabilities, and call to action. Best practice is keep the message in the body to 75-125 words. Keep paragraphs brief and vary the length. Draft the e-mail and send it to yourself. How does it look in your in-box? See if it grabs your attention when you open it and begin reading. Leverage your work. Use the same e-mail for prospects that have similar needs.

▶ ***E-mail—Could Get You $16,000—A $16,000 Fine That Is!***[9]

Compiling an e-mail list of people who have opted in to receive information about products and services is a no-cost, high-performance means of connecting with target prospects through e-mail. Giving consumers the opportunity to opt in keeps e-mail marketers in compliance with the Federal Trade Commission Controlling the Assault of Non-Solicited Pornography And Marketing Act of 2003 (FTC's CAN-SPAM) regulations, guidelines that say what e-mail marketers can and cannot do. Failure to comply may result in fines as high as $16,000—per e-mail—according to the FTC. The main requirements include not using false or misleading header information or deceptive subject lines, clearly identifying messages as advertising, and including contact information and business location. In addition, the sender needs to include information about how recipients can opt out of receiving future mailings.

- **Call to action.** Make it easy for your reader to ask for more information or request a contact. It should be one click and require a minimum amount of information before clicking send.
- **Lead-generating signatures.** Your signature is not just the opportunity to provide all your contact information. Use it to hook your prospects into learning more about you and your company with a simple click.
- **Opt-out option.** The reader with one click should be able to be taken off your mailing list. (See "E-mail–Could Get You $16,000–A $16,000 Fine That Is!").

Tracking

One of the most critical factors of a successful prospecting plan is persistence because the results from prospecting may take time to materialize. Like all programs, to understand how effective you are, you must track the results, such as which prospecting efforts return results as measured by new business, repeat business, generating more leads, and size of orders. Also, once a prospect has been contacted but does not have an immediate need, it is very good practice to keep in regular contact, possibly through marketing programs and periodic follow-up via telephone, web, social media, sms, or e-mail.

If your prospecting efforts do not get a response from the prospect the first time you make contact, then set a reminder to follow up. The customer's silence may not be due to a lack of interest but bad timing. Your follow up may very well be appreciated when they have more time to talk to you.

After a successful prospecting effort, you have potential buyers and opportunities that are in the sales stage-lead. The next activity is to qualify the lead and determine if there is a real opportunity for which the customer will spend money and purchase products or services from you or your competitor. This sales activity is called qualification.

Qualification

To qualify a lead, you complete an opportunity level 1 opportunity assessment as discussed in Chapter 4 "Opportunities Management," Stage 2 Identification of the Compelling Event.

The level 1 assessment, as described earlier, contains four categories of questions:

- Is there an opportunity?
- Can you compete? Do you have a competitive offering?
- Can you win? Do we have sufficient buying center support?
- Is it worth winning? Will it earn your required profits or is the opportunity strategic?

To change an opportunity from lead to confirmed lead sales stage, the salesperson must, at a minimum, answer the first category of questions: "Is there an opportunity?" To facilitate this discussion with the customer, the salesperson should use the Project Solution worksheet, as described in Chapter 4.

The earlier and faster the qualification activity can be completed, the sooner the salesperson can decide if they should spend more of their time trying to win the opportunity. However, as with all of the sales activities, there are no shortcuts and the salesperson must complete the qualification by talking with the customer. See the sidebar "Let Me Try Mental Telepathy First. I Hear It Works." The other common issue with the qualification activity is the qualification is not done or the qualification is done too late. The qualification activity needs to be as soon as

▶ Let Me Try Mental Telepathy First. I Hear It Works.

"Scientists claim 'telepathy' success after sending mental message from one person to another 4,000 miles away."[10]

They connected one person in Mumbai, India, to a wireless headset linked to the Internet and another person to a similar device in Paris. When the first person merely thought of a greeting such as *ciao* (Italian for "hello"), the recipient in France was aware of the thought occurring, according to a report in the journal: The subject receiving the message could not comprehend the word itself, but could report flashes of light in their brain that corresponded to the exact moment when the word *ciao* was being thought.

Well, this has some way to go before salespeople can sit in their offices and rub their temples to have a conversation with their customers. Too often, when salespeople are asked who told you that, there is a moment of silence that means "no one, it is what I assumed." This is not good enough in the qualification activity. When completing an assessment, if the information has not come from a conversation with the customer done by the conventional means, then the assessment for that factor is ?.

In sales, if you do not know or have not asked the customer, don't guess. It is very dangerous to make strategies from assumptions when the customer is only a conversation away.

possible so the salesperson removes low probability opportunities and focuses their time on the confirmed opportunities. During the qualification activity the salesperson is retrieving information about the opportunity and the people involved in the customer's decision-making team.

The qualification assessment is conducted by answering the following questions and assessing a negative –, question mark ?, or, positive + depending on the answer to the question. The questions below are more detailed than originally discussed in Chapter 4 "Opportunities Management."

Question 1: Customer's Application of Project

- What is the objective of the customer's project?
- Do you understand the connection between the company's vision, goals, and objectives and requirements for the project?
- If you can answer these questions, evaluate this as + to indicate it has been defined by the customer.
- If the customer has not defined the requirements, select – for undefined. If you do not know or understand the requirements, select the ?.

Question 2: Customer's Business Profile

- What is the account condition, as described in the account corporate profile?
- If the account is in a strong position, select the + for strong. If not, select – for weak. If the business profile is unknown, select the ?.

Question 3: Customer's Financial Condition

- Customers in a strong financial condition are evaluated as +.
- For lesser known accounts, you should check with your controller for input on the customer's financial condition and payment practices. Your financial department will use credit ratings and other financial reports to determine the account's financial condition. If the financial condition is weak, select the – option; if it is unknown, select the ?.

Question 4: Access to Funds

- Have funds been allocated to this project, and if they have, what is the budget?
- If not, what is the approval process, and what are the chances of approval for this project?
- Are other competing projects more likely to be selected before this project for the current fiscal year?
- If funds have been approved and you know the budgeted amount, select the +. If not, select – , and if you do not know the answer, select the ?.

Question 5: Compelling Event

- Why does the customer have to do the project and when will the customer do it?
- What are the expected outcomes and paybacks?
- What are the consequences if the project is delayed or accelerated?
- Who has the objective for implementing the project?
- Who is the sponsor of the project?
- If you can answer these questions, the compelling event is defined as a +. If not defined, select the – , and if you do not know the answer, select the ?.

Chapter Highlight 6.2: "I Got Questions. You Got Questions"[11]

Meet Ben Duffy

This is an old story, but vitally important in understanding the power of empathy and questions.

Ben Duffy (1902–1970) was a high school dropout from Manhattan's Hell's Kitchen neighborhood who eventually became an icon in the advertising world.

Literally going from the mailroom to the presidency of BBDO, a worldwide advertising agency headquartered in New York, he had a stellar career that advertising people still talk about today. BBDO currently has over 15,000 employees and is the most awarded agency network in the world. Many would argue that much of that success is the result of Duffy's work.

How Duffy Discovered the Power of Empathy

Many years ago at American Tobacco, the largest tobacco company at that time, an ad account was available and every advertising agency in the country was aggressively pursuing it. At that time, Duffy owned a small advertising agency and was eager to obtain an account of this size.

Among his competitors were several very large agencies with more money, more resources, and more staff. Duffy had an appointment with the president of the tobacco company coming up soon. He thought to himself, "How can I possibly compete with these large agencies? What can I offer this company that the big boys can't?" The more he tried to prepare, the more frustrating the situation became. He just could not see how his little company could compete.

After some time, he realized that "How can my small company compete with the big companies?" was the wrong question. He had been approaching the situation from the point of view of a salesperson, not from the client's point of view.

Key to Successful Selling

On that day, Duffy discovered the key to successful selling: empathy through questions. He thought, "I'm going to put myself in this guy's shoes. I'll think of all the concerns and questions that I would have if I were him." He wrote down fifty questions, then honed them down to the ten he thought would be most important to his prospect.

When the day of the appointment arrived, he sat down with his potential client and said, "In preparing for today's meeting, I put myself in your position and thought there were probably some things that you would like to know about me, my company, how we do business, and what's in it for both of us. So I have prepared a list of ten of those questions."

The tobacco company president looked surprised and said, "Well, that's interesting, I wrote down ten questions for you, too." They swapped lists, and six of the questions were exactly the same.

Based on Duffy's preparation and the similarity of the lists, the president of the tobacco company decided that maybe the two companies did have something to talk about.

Guess who got the account?

Another key point to remember when in the qualification activity is you not only need to qualify the opportunity, but the customer also needs to assess and qualify you and your company as an acceptable supplier. There is a very famous story about how one salesperson was able to secure the biggest opportunity of his life by not only preparing his questions for his first meeting but also preparing a list of questions he thought the customer may have of him. See **Chapter Highlight 6.2: "I Got Questions. You Got Questions"** for the rest of the story.

When having sales-related discussions with the customer, you apply a consultative and customer-focused selling approach following what is called the need-satisfaction selling process. The professional selling processes have developed over many years. In their literature search on B2B selling, authors Terry Bacon and David Pugh read books written as early as 1894.[12] Since that time, professional selling has gone through a continuous evolution, becoming more relationship based, customer focused, and value driven. A brief history of the professional sales development is provided in **Chapter Highlight 6.3: From the Sea to Sales: The Evolution of a Profession.**

The consultative selling approach used in conjunction with the need-satisfaction process are two of the guiding principles for professional salespeople today. These concepts will be used throughout the sales activities for both large and small sales. Chapter 7 will provide a detailed look at sales call skills used to execute the need-satisfaction process.

The next activity after qualifying an opportunity to confirmed lead is sales meetings.

Sales Meetings

In the opportunities management process described in Chapter 4, sales meetings are the core activity in Stage 3a Evaluation of Options. Once an opportunity has been confirmed (assessment question "Is there an opportunity?" is answered yes), then the next three questions of the opportunity assessment are evaluated. Answering these questions will determine if the opportunity is a sales opportunity that you want and you can win. There are many times when there is a confirmed opportunity, but a company competing for the work will never win because of one or more reasons in the assessment. To answer the next three questions in the assessment, the salesperson uses the request for proposal interview form (described earlier in Chapter 4) to hold further conversations with people in the buying center from the customer's organization. By using the request for proposal interview form, the salesperson should be able to answer the following questions.

Can You Compete?

Question 6: Formal Decision Criteria

- A fully defined formal decision criterion meets the requirements described in the vulnerability analysis described in Chapter 4. The customer must have a defined set of criteria ranked from critical to incidental and have an evaluation model by which to evaluate the competing offers. You should know who has created the decision criteria. If approval comes from depart-

Chapter Highlight 6.3: From Sea to Sales: The Evolution of a Profession

The selling presentation has changed over the years. The changes are a reflection of the nature of the economy and underlying theories of how people buy. The following periods witnessed different approaches to selling:

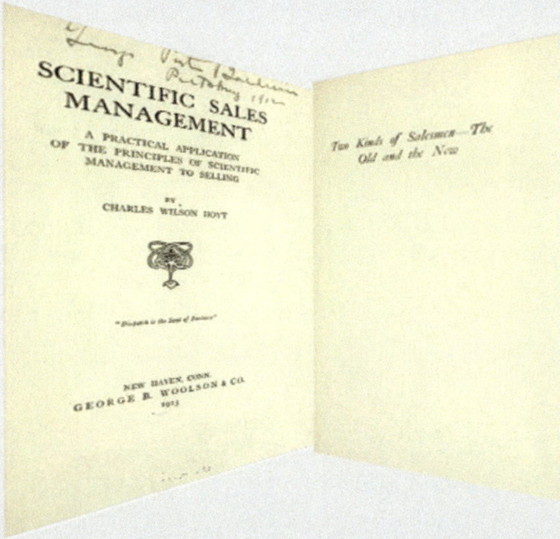

Agrarian Age. 1850 and earlier. Selling was based on self-learned skills of salespeople. There were no major efforts to study the art of selling.

Early Industrial Age. 1850–1920. The economy of the United States began to shift from an agrarian economy to industrial. With the rise of manufacturing, salespeople became of increasing importance to the economy. During this period, owners of factories began to shape the army of salespeople from a loose network of "peddlers" to a more organized selling force. For example, around 1850, Cyrus McCormick (the inventor of the wheat reaper and thresher) organized a national network of selling agents who operated on stricter selling controls than the peddlers of the past. As time went on, manufacturers such as Gillette, Eli Lilly, Scovill, and others began to hire salespeople specifically to represent one company. This was a dramatic change from the past. In 1894, William Miller wrote *The Art of Canvassing: How to Sell Insurance.*[13]

From 1910 to 1920, there was a growing interest in improving the selling process. Psychologists, notably Freud and Jung, essentially founded the discipline during this period as many of the new psychologists began to study the buying process. They were interested in discovering the mental states that buyers went through so that salespeople could better influence the buying process. Chicago-based System Company published *How to Increase Your Sales: 126 Selling Plans Used & Proven by 54 Salesmen & Salesmanagers* in 1908. Fredrick Taylor published one of the most influential management books ever written, *The Principles of Scientific Management.*[14] In 1913, C Hoyt. influenced by Taylor wrote *Scientific Sales Management; a Practical Application of Principles of Scientific Management to Selling.*[15] (pictured above).

As early as 1911, psychologists were studying and describing the mental states that customers would exhibit as they proceeded through various phases of making a purchase. At this time, the buyer action theory was developed, consisting of five stages: (a) favorable attention, (b) interest, (c) desire, (d) action, and (e) permanent satisfaction.

Mature Industrial Age. 1920 to 1950. Building upon earlier psychological observations, in 1922, Edward K. Strong's first book, *The Psychology of Selling Life Insurance,* became the first academic book on selling.[16] Strong attempted to translate the abstract psychological customer descriptions and observations into concrete techniques that could be used by salespeople. In the section "The Tactics of Selling," (pp. 351–465), Strong talked about tactical selling techniques as a series of five steps. He prescribed presentation techniques that salespeople could use to cause the potential customer to enter each of the psychologically described buying mental states, thereby leading them to buy. This approach is still being taught today and is prevalent in traditional "transactional selling."

Post Industrial Age. 1950 1980. Selling and marketing made a tremendous leap forward. Led by marketing researchers, the marketing concept was introduced to industry by academicians. The concept began its journey of wide acceptance in sales and marketing theory. The marketing concept uses a customer focus as opposed to a seller or product focus. Essentially, the selling practices as advocated by Strong in the 1920s were "seller-centric"—that is, they were focused on the various techniques that could be applied to the customer to induce or make them enter mental states that would lead to buying. The marketing concept advocated that sellers start

Chapter Highlight 6.3: From Sea to Sales: The Evolution of a Profession (cont.)

with customer needs and then try to satisfy these needs. The marketing concept led to a new theory of buying called the need-satisfaction buying theory is shown to the right and will be discussed in detail in Chapter 7"Sales Call Skills."

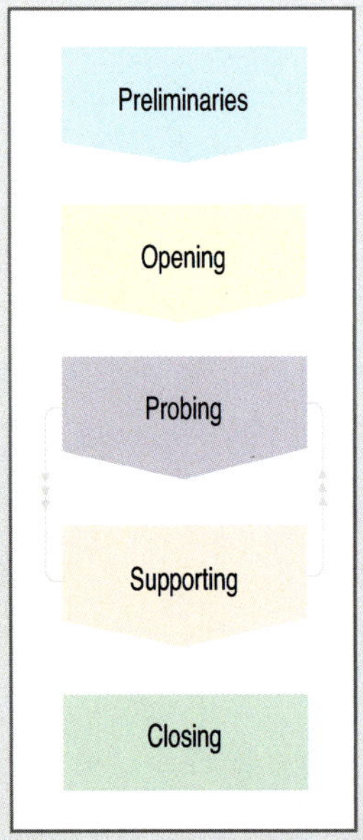

The Need-Satisfaction Buying Theory

The need-satisfaction buying theory is the basis for "consultative selling." Essentially, sellers adopt the philosophy that they are consultants to help potential customers solve need problems; the customer has a problem to be solved, and the product/service has the potential benefits to solve the problem. This approach to selling is "customer-centric." The seller adds-value and is important to the buyer throughout the buying process. The theory states that the buyer goes through the discrete steps to make a buying decision, especially a decision on complex and expensive products/service. The consultative selling approach consists of five steps:

1. Recognition of Needs: The value that a salesperson can add in this stage is the help customers recognize and the definition of problems and needs in a new or different way.
2. Evaluation of Options (Alternative products): The value that a salesperson can add here is showing superior solutions, options, and approaches that customers may not have understood or considered.
3. Resolution of Concerns (Decide on one of the alternative products): Value here is created by the salesperson helping customers to overcome and remove obstacles to acquisition.
4. Purchase (Logistics of acquisition): The value a salesperson can contribute here is making the purchase painless, convenient, and hassle-free.
5. Implementation: The salesperson adds value by showing customers how to install and use the product/service.

Information Age. 1980–present. The United States was "on the ropes" economically as it fought increasing global competition. The "Toyota Phenomena" and the quality movement invaded the US economy. The country responded by copying the Japanese and other competing global companies. With a proliferation of look-alike quality products, competition for customers began to shift to more abstract nuances to differentiate one product from another. The salesperson, as well as his or her supporting company, became an important component of the product or service that the customer considered as value. In addition, the growing proliferation and availability of information (the Internet and web) developed a generation of increasingly informed buyers.

In the past, salespeople were primarily providers of product/service information. However, the increased availability of information to buyers began to shift the salesperson's primary roles. Salespeople now had to reexamine who they were and why they existed. While their traditional role of providing the means to make "transactional" sales was still important (there are still many products/services today requiring this approach), the legacy of the marketing concept and adding value within the need-satisfaction buying theory of the buying process became increasingly important.

Thus, for many commoditized (standardized and look-alike) products/services, potential customers are relatively sophisticated and have access to information. They do not need salespeople to make a buying decision. "Transactional selling" is also taking place electronically. However, for complex, customized products and services, salespeople need to add value during the buyer's need-satisfaction buying process. This consultative selling approach has its roots back to the 1920s and was documented by W. F. Hypes who wrote a chapter titled "The Salesman as the Customer's Partner" in the System Company publication *How to Increase Your Sales* mentioned earlier.[17] In modern times, the first book published on this topic was Marck Hanan, James Cribbin and Herman Heiser's *Consultative Selling,* published in 1970.[18]

The remainder of this book will leverage these pioneers' thinking and contributions to the professional selling community. In addition, many more of the modern thought leaders' works will be referenced to build actionable sales processes for today's competitive world of sales.

ments outside the account (such as partners and government agencies), you must meet with them and determine whether they have the same decision criteria.

- Do you know the process for approval in such situations? If you believe the customer (including external approvers) has well-defined decision criteria, select +. If not, choose –, and if you do not know, evaluate the question as ?.

Question 7: Solution Fit

- Will you be evaluated as strong or weak against the customer's decision criteria when compared to competitors?
- Can you do anything to improve your evaluation, such as redefining the decision criteria or addressing the customer's negative reactions, such as misunderstandings, skepticism, or drawbacks?
- How do the most influential buying center members rank our solution? If you believe you will be evaluated as strong, select + . If weak, choose – . If you do not know or have not validated your expected ranking with someone in the buying center, select ?.

Question 8: Resource Requirements

- For you to secure and implement the project, will it require additional resources and investment?
- Are there other projects that could use the resources if you do not do the project?
- Must you make significant modifications to your solution to qualify?
- Must you invest significant time and effort to sufficiently analyze the risk and build a complete proposal that makes a strong business case? Input from the business managers should be provided for large projects. If the resources required are low, select + . If high, select – , and if you do not know, select ?.

Question 9: Current Relationship

- What is the status of your current relationship?
- Do you have an ongoing business relationship, and are you working with the customer on other projects?
- How well do you know the key buying center members?
- When completing this question, compare your relationship relative to the competitors. To answer this question, only one company should be evaluated positively to reflect their competitive advantage. The company with a + will most likely have information in advance of their competitors and could also be the company the customer will speak to last before making their final decision. For the company with the strongest relationship, select + . For companies with weaker relationships, select – , and if you do not know, select ?.

Question 10: Unique Business Value

- What differential value does your solution bring to the customer's project? To answer this question, you should complete the customer value analysis and validate your differential value with appropriate buying center members.
- In which of the five common differentiating factors (product or services, service quality, company capabilities, service and support personnel, and price) do you provide differentiated value? Will your value be evaluated in the decision criteria?

- If you have significant differential value that will give you a competitive advantage, select +. If you do not have differential value, select – , and if your differential value has not been validated, select ?.

Can You Win?

Question 11: Inside Buying Center Support

- Do you have mentors and supporters inside the buying center?
- Can they influence the purchase decision, and will they act on your behalf?
- Do the competitors have more inside support?
- You should be able to reference specific actions of the mentors or supporters to prove their support. If you believe you have significant inside support that improves your chances of securing the opportunity over the competitor, select + for strong, – for weak, and ? if you do not know.

Question 12: Executive Credibility

- Do you know which executives have an interest in the project? Do your executives have on-going business relationships with them?
- How do they know you if they are not a current account?
- Do the customer's executives consider you a vendor, problem-solver, or trusted advisor?
- Can your executive make contact with the account executives easily during the resolution of concerns and monitoring stages of the procurement phase? These factors were explained in Chapter 4 "Opportunities Management" in the procurement phase section. If you have an active account management program, you should be in a good position relative to your competitors. If you are in a strong position, select + ; if in a weaker position than the competitors, select – ; and if you do not know, select ?.

Question 13: Cultural Compatibility

- Does your account relationship profile indicate a good match between what the account wants from its suppliers and what you provide? (This is discussed in Chapter 13 "Account Management Plan.")
- Does your company have executive-to-executive level ongoing business relationships?
- Does the account consider you the best company to work on this project?
- If you are not well positioned, what would you have to do to gain a better position? Is there time? If corporate compatibility is good, select + ; if it is poor, select – ; if you do not know, select ?.

Question 14: Informal Decision Process

- What will be considered beyond the formal decision criteria, and who will contribute to the final purchase decision? If external departments or government agencies have to give final approval, do you understand their informal decision process?
- Do you have previous experience knowing what it takes to get approval beyond having a best-evaluated solution?
- Have you had a previous experience with the account where an award or loss was turned around in the late stages?

- What issues can be negotiated? If you are confident you understand the informal decision process and have a plan to manage it, select + ; if you are not capable or do not have the right contacts and supporters, select – ; if you do not know, select ?.

Question 15: Political Alignment

- How well aligned are you with the high-influence buying center members? Are they supporters of your company?
- Do you know their business and personal agendas? Can they change the decision criteria after the evaluator or decision-maker submits a recommendation?
- Will they act on your behalf?
- Do you have more influential supporters than the competitors?
- Who has the most powerful buying center member as their supporter?
- If external departments or government agencies have to give final approval, are you in alignment with their powerful approvers? If you believe you have a stronger political alignment than your competitors, select + ; if you are weaker, select – ; if you do not know, select ?.

Is It Worth Winning?

Question 16: Short-Term Revenue

- Is the short-term revenue for this calendar year high or low?
- Once the contract is awarded, can you sell additional services or expand the work scope?
- Will there be other projects coming in the short term that would enable you to leverage the resources allocated to this project?
- Will your equipment and staff be utilized at full capacity, or can you generate other revenue with the same resources from other projects unrelated to this opportunity?
- Is there anything you could do to improve short-term revenue? If the resources for this project have a reasonable probability of generating high short-term revenue, select + ; if low, select – ; and if you do not know, select ?.

Question 17: Future Revenue

- Ask the same questions as the short-term revenue questions but now from the long-term perspective.
- What kind of year-on-year growth might you expect in future revenue streams?
- If long-term revenue-generating prospects are high, select + ; if low, select – ; and if you do not know, select ?.

Question 18: Profitability

- Is the expected profitability high or low?
- What would have to happen to increase profitability?
- Could you negotiate items that would improve profitability or lower your costs?
- Does the level of expected profitability warrant the resources, or are there more profitable projects that could use the resources?

- Do you have contractual protection for the resources requested, but not used? If profitability prospects are good, select + ; if they are not or are low, select – ; if you do not know, select ?.

Question 19: Degree of Risk

- What are the levels of technical, financial, and other risks associated with the project?
- What are the risks of the customer not fulfilling the work scope, ending the project early, or canceling the project? How could you cause your solution to fail?
- What are the critical dependencies in delivering value to your customer?
- How could the customer cause your solution to fail?
- What is the impact on your business if the solution fails?
- How much investment do you need to make to start the project?
- How much of this investment is at risk? If the risk profile of the opportunity is low, select + ; if it is high, select – ; if you do not know, select ?. If the risk factor is high, what could you or the customer do to reduce it?

Question 20: Strategic Value

- To determine whether a project is strategic, you must determine whether the project is more profitable than other projects of the same time period that use the same resources. If so, why?
- Do long-term account factors such as product development or competitive issues make winning this project strategic? To answer this question when resources are limited, it is advisable to obtain upper management input. The strategic value of a project is best answered by upper management. If the strategic value is high, select + ; if it is low, select – ; if you do not know, select ?.

With the assessment completed, the salesperson then decides on the appropriate sales strategy for this opportunity. The opportunity sales strategies were described in detail in Chapter 4. The options are:

- **Disengage.** This strategy is chosen when the salesperson decides this is not a sales opportunity their company can win. This can be the result of too many negatives in the assessment analysis and or they do not have enough time to try and improve their position or the opportunity is not attractive. The sales stage will be set as disengage and as per guidelines described in Chapter 4. Once the outcome of the opportunity is known the salesperson sets the sales stage to closed lost and record in their CRM system which competitor won and the estimated value of the deal.
- **Attack.** The salesperson believes they can win this opportunity and selects one of the competitive sales strategies as described in the opportunities management process. The sales stage will be set frontal, flanking, defend, or fragment. In the attack mode, the salesperson executes their sales strategy as described in Chapter 4, focusing on building buying center support for their proposal.
- **Develop.** The sales proposal will not be presented in the current calendar year. The salesperson will stay engaged with the customer to improve their position and use the develop sales strategy tactics as described in Chapter 4. Most companies have well-defined guidelines for reviewing sales opportunities before making the final decision to disengage or pursue and which competitive sales strategy to select. This process will be reviewed in Chapter 7 "Strategic Sales Plan."

During the sales meetings activities, the salesperson will use their probing skills to retrieve more information about the needs and concerns the people in the buying center have about the opportunity. Once they have a good understanding of the customer's needs, the salesperson is then ready to present their proposal, which is the next step in the sales activities.

Present Proposals

In this sales activity, the salesperson uses the skill of supporting in the need-satisfaction process. The skill of supporting will discussed in detail in Chapter 7 "Sales Call Skills." When the salesperson begins to present their proposal or, in a more formal bidding process, receives the request for proposal from the customer, the opportunity sales stage is set to bid/proposal.

The effective creation and presentation of proposals requires a number of sales skills as shown in **Fig 6.8.** The need-satisfaction process skills of opening, probing, supporting, and closing will be discussed in the next chapter. Handling objections, and negotiations have dedicated chapters later in the textbook. Communication skills were discussed earlier. Proposal writing skills will only be touched upon for a couple of critical aspects of the proposal, and there is a dedicated chapter for competitive tendering that includes a discussion of factors to be covered in tender submissions.

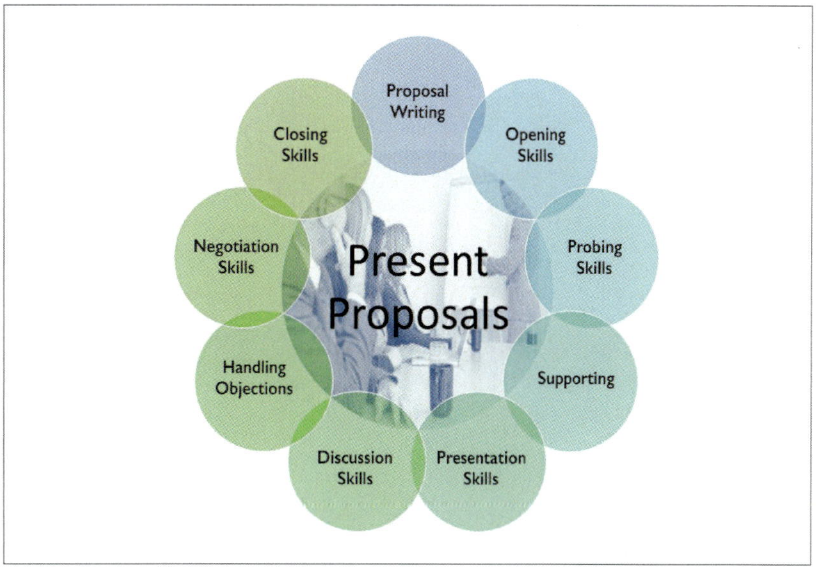

Fig. 6.8
Presenting proposals is a multifaceted sales activity.

Writing proposals is a process that starts early in the opportunity management process and leverages the outcomes of each of the sales activities. A four-step process shown in **Fig 6.9** is followed to create a powerful customer-centric proposal. Each of the steps will be described in more detail next.

Step 1: Determine Content

The best tool to collect your proposal content is the client interview form and, in particular, the request for proposal form. These forms help the salesperson to have customer-focused conversations with people in the customer's buying center.

Fig. 6.9
Four-step process for creating a powerful customer-centric proposal.

Step 2: Organize

To organize the content, use the Sales Call Preparation Support Worksheet, which will be discussed in detail in the next chapter. In general, for each one of the customer's stated requirements, you will identify which products or services you have that will be used to satisfy that need. In advance of presenting the proposal, consider the buyer's profile information and determine how to best present this information. Also at this time consider what negative reactions you may encounter while supporting this need and include in your proposal a demonstration of capabilities to make it easy for the customer to believe. Organize your proposal around three to five main components that are important to the customer. A fatal mistake for some salespeople is to discuss only what they do better than the competition and not, without talking about where they are the same or weaker. This will be discussed in more detail in the next chapter.

Step 3: Draft Proposal

There are many ways to write a proposal. One way is to organize the proposal components of a customer-centric proposal as shown in **Fig. 6.10.** This format is very common and has been proven to be effective.

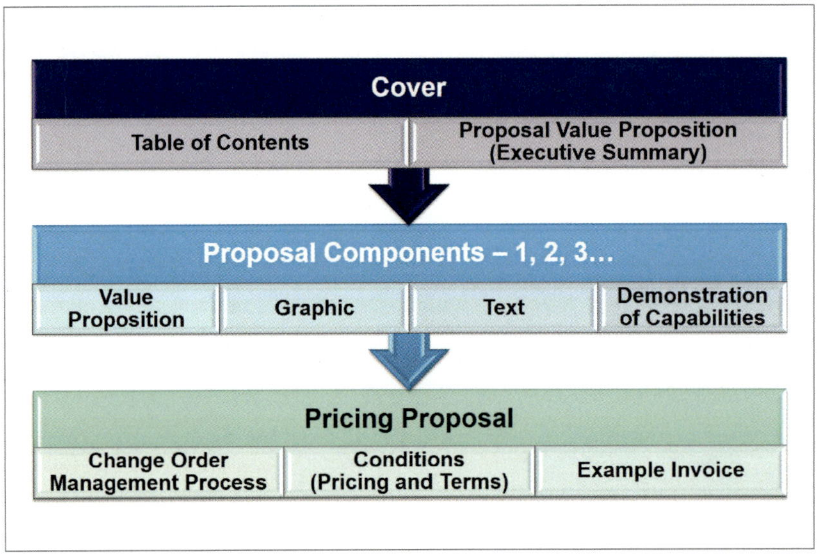

Fig. 6.10
Components of a customer-centric proposal.

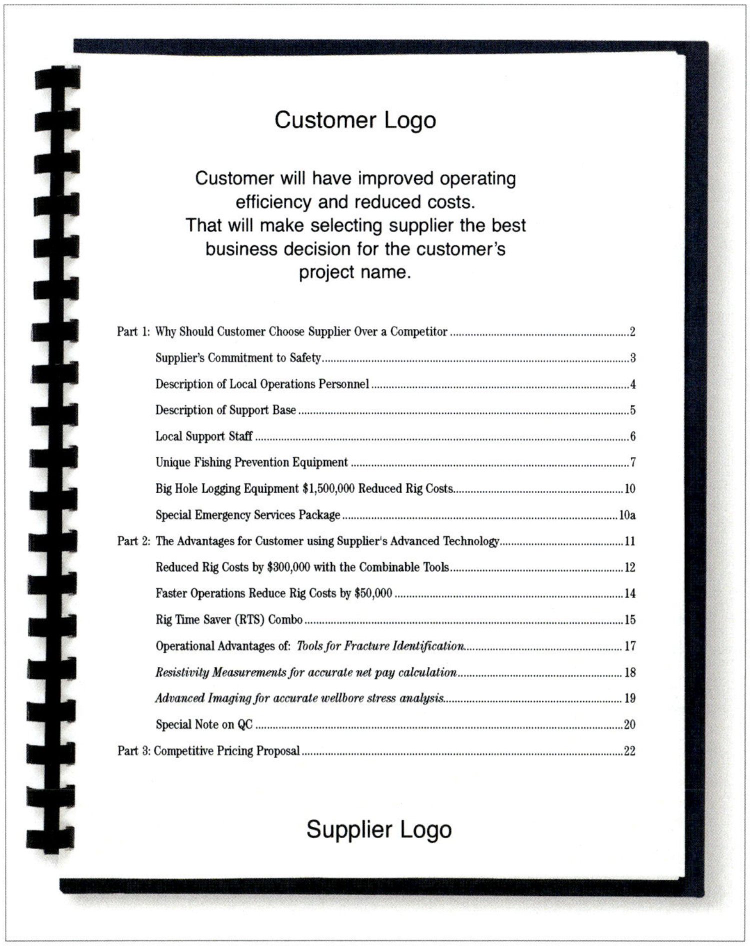

Customer Logo

Customer will have improved operating efficiency and reduced costs.
That will make selecting supplier the best business decision for the customer's project name.

Part 1: Why Should Customer Choose Supplier Over a Competitor 2
Supplier's Commitment to Safety 3
Description of Local Operations Personnel 4
Description of Support Base 5
Local Support Staff 6
Unique Fishing Prevention Equipment 7
Big Hole Logging Equipment $1,500,000 Reduced Rig Costs 10
Special Emergency Services Package 10a
Part 2: The Advantages for Customer using Supplier's Advanced Technology 11
Reduced Rig Costs by $300,000 with the Combinable Tools 12
Faster Operations Reduce Rig Costs by $50,000 14
Rig Time Saver (RTS) Combo 15
Operational Advantages of: *Tools for Fracture Identification* 17
Resistivity Measurements for accurate net pay calculation 18
Advanced Imaging for accurate wellbore stress analysis 19
Special Note on QC 20
Part 3: Competitive Pricing Proposal 22

Supplier Logo

Fig. 6.11
Table of contents to facilitate proposal presentations.

Cover

Place the customer's logo on top of the pages and your company's logo on the bottom. Include a simple title, date, prepared for who, and prepared by. There should also be a back cover, again with the customer's logo on top and your logo on bottom. The covers add a professional look to your proposal.

Table of Contents

The table of contents is more than headers and page numbers. Not to minimize the importance of having a simple way to navigate the proposal, but the table of contents also adds a professional touch to the proposal. A clever way to write the table of contents is to indicate the proposal component name and the benefit. This is another way to emphasize the added value of your proposal. The table of contents is also a useful tool for your supporters to easily find the key points they will use to defend the selection of your company. Shown in **Fig. 6.11** is an example of an effective table of contents for a real proposal.

Proposal Value Proposition

This is an executive summary, meaning it is less than one page. The executive summary should be from the customer's perspective; start with the customer's name, restate the customer's objectives, and then define what it means to the customer when they choose your products or services. A customer-centric way to think about value for the customer is the value stairs, shown in **Fig. 6.12.** At the base of the stairs is the way salespeople think about their products and services—feature, benefit, and value. On the steps of the stairs is the way it should be explained to the customer in terms of what it is, does, and means for the customer both for their project and them personally, when applicable. This will be discussed in more detail in the supporting section in Chapter 7 "Sales Call Skills." **Fig. 6.13** is an example of a value proposition written using the structure of the value stairs.

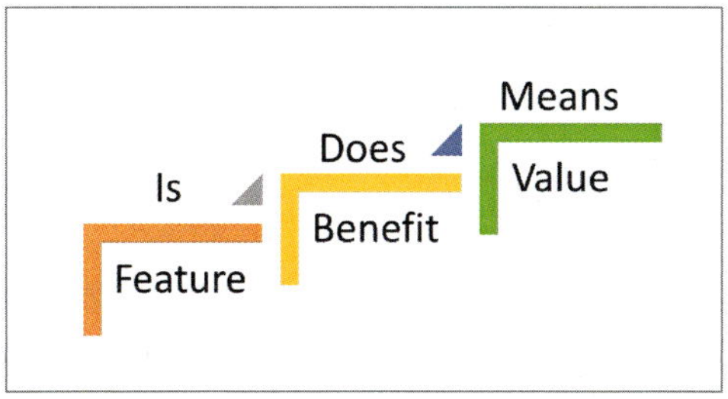

Fig. 6.12
The value stairs.

Proposal Components

There can be as few as one proposal components or as many as required. A good writing guide is to keep the proposal components linked to the customer's key needs and have no more than three to five components. There can be multiple elements to each component. The objective of writing your proposal this way is that it facilitates your conversation with the customer during the presentation.

It is important to remember that your objective is to convince the customer you have the best product or solution for their needs. As discussed in the communications chapter, the customer does not need to remember all the details, just that for the three to five proposal components they were convinced you had the best proposal for their needs. If they want the details that made up each proposal component, they can go back to the proposal.

In the table of contents section in Fig. 6.11, there are three proposal components. The first proposal component is presented as a question to the customer: "Why should customer choose supplier over a competitor?" The second proposal component is "The advantages for Customer using Supplier's Advanced Technology," and the third proposal component is "Competitive Pricing Proposal." These were the three proposal components for this opportunity that the salesperson wanted the customer to remember after the presentation of his proposal. As you can see in the table of contents in Fig. 6.11, there are many more details for each component. This level of detail was added to the component because for this client these were all important factors for customers in the buying center who were going to make the buying decision. If you follow these guidelines you will win the opportunity and stay out of sales jail. See the "Staying out of Sales Jail" sidebar for some good sales tips.

There are many excellent books on writing powerful proposals. One of the best books on the topic is called *Powerful Proposals: How to Give Your Business the Winning Edge.*[19] *Powerful Proposals* gives businesses proven strategies for creating customer-centered documents that outshine the competition. *Powerful Proposals* goes beyond "this is what we do" documents and takes the reader step by step through designing customer-focused proposals that highlight the firm's tangible benefits to the client. This book contains invaluable information on creating effective executive summaries, writing themes, and generating the text, plus how to maximize graphics, call-outs, and other visual elements.

Applying the advice from the authors of *Powerful Proposals* to the Star Oil proposal for which the executive summary was shown in Fig. 6.13, the proposal

▶ *Stay Out of Sales Jail*

There are three sales laws that, when followed, will lead to sales call success. For each sales law, there is a specific sales tactic that is selected when setting your sales call objective.

Sales Call Law No. 1

People prefer to buy from friends rather than strangers.

Sales call tactic: Retrieve information about the company and person.

Sales Call Law No. 2

Understand before you sell.

Sales call tactic: Retrieve information about the project and specifically what it is the customer needs to ensure that their project objectives are achieved.

Sales Call Law No. 3

Talk to the customer about three things.

Short version

What is important to the customer.

What is important to the customer.

What is important to the customer.

Expanded version

What is important to the customer and why you are better than the competition.

Sales call tactic: Prove value

What is important to the customer and why you are the same as the competition.

Sales call tactic: Emphasize strengths

What is important to the customer when you are not better than the competition.

Sales call tactic: Minimize weaknesses

Ensure that every sales plan uses the above sales tactics for generally retrieving information in the early part of an opportunity. This is done by having conversations with people in the buying center using the project solution and request for proposal worksheets. The next tactics are to prove value, emphasize strengths, and minimize weaknesses.

By following a plan constructed in this way when it comes time for the customer or buying center members to select their supplier, you will be insulated from the competition. This is very important because in most B2B large sales, when the purchase decision is made, you will not be in that meeting with the customer.

Star Oil Production Team

Your Production Team can achieve increased production rates of 20% from the Block M production wells by stimulating with Company's New System*. This estimate is based on calculations using Block M wells data and results from the current practice of using standard acid clean-up operations for Block M wells and from similar carbonate reservoirs in near by areas that switched to New System. A 20% increase in production will result in a return of $2,037,158 for an investment of $250,000 per well.

When Star Oil is prepared to stimulate the Block M production wells Company is ready to pump New System with 5-days notice.

Sales Engineer
Sales Engineer

Fig. 6.13
Executive summary written using value stairs model.

Themes Skimmers

Block M Stimulation Program

Star Oil can achieve maximum production rates from each Block M well by stimulating with Company's New System*. In similar carbonate reservoirs the New System stimulation has achieved production rate increases of 238% as shown on the next page.

Visuals Skimmers & Scanners

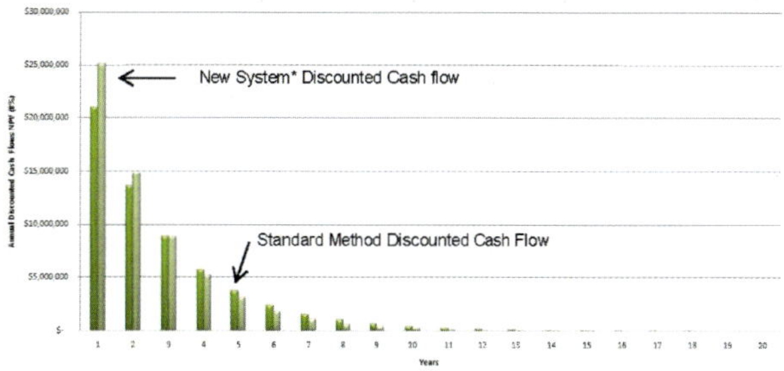

Figure 3.1: New System stimulation achieves $2,037,158 (NPV 8%) return on an investment of $250,000.

Text Scanners

In matrix stimulation of oil and gas carbonate formations, the objective is total zonal coverage. While the use of diverters has been well proven, most diverter methods use particulates that, post-treatment, can damage the formation. For cost effectiveness and ease of operation, the ideal system is one that can be bullheaded, is self-diverting and leaves no residual damage.

Unique properties for extended application
Existing technology for self-diverting systems relies on polymer-based fluids in which post-treatment can result in residual damage and are limited to bottomhole conditions of approximately 200°F. The New System has unique properties based on Company viscoelastic surfactant technology capable of covering a wide temperature range to 300°F. The use of viscoelastic surfactant technology eliminates the damage associated with solids and polymers in matrix treatment. The New System may be used as the sole treating fluid or for diversion when used in conjunction with other treating acids.

In the Net Present Value (NPV) calculation for the example above the accelerated production scenario was used calculating net annual cash flows after royalties and tax. The assumptions were:

Block M Calculation Recoverable oil volume 6,000,000 bbl/well Price of oil $40/bbl
Royalty of rate - 25%
Corporate tax rate - 50%

HCL Treatment
Initial production of 5,000 bbl/d
Decline rate - 30%
Production period 20-years

New System case
Production Increase - 20% or 6,000 bbl/d
Decline rate - 36%
Production period 17-years
Additional cost for New System - $250,000

The net benefit of using New System for the above example is $2,037,158 with a payout period of less than 1 year and an ROI of 715%. Included in the appendix of this proposal is the spreadsheet analysis, and sensitivity analysis for several factors.

4/17/2013 *Page 1*

Fig. 6.14
Proposal component page following layout recommended in *Powerful Proposals.*

component for the "Block M Stimulation Program" is shown in **Fig. 6.14.** As discussed in the communication chapter, each person has their own communication style as influenced by their technology adoption, social style, learning channels and the buying factors such as their role, objectives, and concerns. To ensure that each page of your proposal is effective and appeals to as many customers as possible, each page should have a theme, visuals, and text. This layout will satisfy the way most people review information for the first time, such as when you are presenting your proposal. As described in *Powerful Proposals*, some people are skimmers. Skimmers will flip through a magazine to find what is interesting. Having themes accommodates this type of customer. Some people are scanners. Scanners want to see the details, like when you scan a page into text. Having text accommodates this type of customer. Visuals appeal to both. A best practice when adding captions for figures in a proposal is include the "what it means to the customer".

The additional benefit of applying this writing style for responding to customers RFP's is it demonstrates compliance and responsiveness. As pointed out in *Powerful Proposals*, in the customer's first phase of evaluation, they are looking to eliminate non-compliant proposals. They do not want to waste their time evaluating proposals that are not compliant. This first review also affects their initial impression of how responsive the proposals are to their needs. Using themes that follow the customer's issues or requirements gives the proposal a more compliant appearance and the composition of the pages with themes, value propositions, visuals, and text make the proposal look responsive.

Another component of any page is white space. White space encourages and provides the customer with an area to make notes and add highlights as you present your proposal. It is a good practice when presenting your proposal to have a copy for yourself and each person you are talking to and encourage them to make notes on details specific for their purchase.

For smaller sales, when the salesperson is possibly qualifying and presenting a proposal in the same meeting, it is efficient to have a template with blanks for the customer to enter their specifics.

Step 4: Review and Rehearse

Review

The review at this stage is focused on proposal qualities. Before this review, the proposal must be edited, meaning the proposal has been checked for grammar and spelling and flow. The review of the proposal qualities include[20]:

- **Compliance.** There are two compliance considerations. Customer compliant: Is the proposal structured according to solicitation proposal instructions, evaluation factors, and other solicitation requirements such as licences, permits, and résumés? Company compliant: Has the proposal been reviewed as per your company requirements, such as signing authority, terms and conditions, operational commitments, and pricing.
- **Completeness.** For small sales, after the request for proposal interviews are completed, the salesperson (as described in Step 2: Organize) should use one or several supporting worksheets to identify which requirements will be discussed in the proposal. In larger sales, where the customer has provided a specific format and content of proposals, then in the review the reviewer should check if all the proposal sections are completed as per the customer's instruction.

- **Responsiveness.** Does the proposal respond to the factors identified during the client interviews? Are the customer's objectives and critical success factors as they stated in the proposal? Does your proposal express your understanding of the prospect's situation and strategic drivers? For each expressed want and need, have you minimized any gaps between your offer and the ideal solution? Does the proposal give the impression that the customer's business is important to the salesperson?
- **Appearance.** Does the proposal look good? Do the proposal components have the same style and color palette? Is the text consistent in terms of the message being communicated? Are the discussions logical and flowing? When required, are there examples to clarify how topics being discussed will work or be applied in the customer's environment?
- **Win Themes.** How well does your proposal express your culture, relationship capabilities, and technical offering as a natural fit for this prospect and their requirements? Do the three to five key proposal components resonate and create confidence in you as a provider? Does the proposal sell the company's proposed features/solutions by turning them into customer benefits and clearly explain what this means for the customer in their situation? Does your proposal differentiate your company from its competitors for considerations that are important to the customer? Differentiators are features that matter to your prospect and cannot be matched by your competitors. Differentiators can be unique products and services that your company has or unique capabilities to deliver the required products and services the customer requires. In tight situations, the winning margin often comes down to small advantages in differentiation.

In this stage, someone should complete the review who:

- Is not directly involved in the opportunity. There have been many studies done that prove we cannot proof our own work. See the sidebar "Get a Second Opinion."
- Understands the customer's perspective and will read the proposal like a customer. In small sales the proposal will normally be reviewed by one person. If a team of people will be evaluating the proposal, have two people review: one person as the evaluator and the other as the decision-maker.

The reviewer or reviewers will give feedback to the salesperson or sales team on the strong parts of the proposal and areas that could be improved. The list below includes some of the more common issues that can be fixed if caught in time:

- Failure to focus on your client's business problems.
- No persuasive structure: information dump.
- No clear differentiation from your competitors.
- No compelling value proposition.
- Buried key points: no impact, no highlighting.
- Too hard to read: overuse of jargon, abbreviations, too technical.
- Customer-to-seller's name ratio is less than recommended 3:1.

In larger more formal tender submissions, customers will insist that suppliers accept their terms and conditions and the opportunity can have complicated requirements. For these types of tenders, there will be a separate discussion in Chapter 10 "Competitive Bidding."

▶ *Get a Second Opinion*

You have finally finished writing your proposal. You've sweated over your choice of words and agonized about the best way to arrange them to effectively get your point across. You comb for errors, and by the time you publish you are absolutely certain it is perfect. But, the first thing your customer notices isn't your carefully crafted message, it's the confusing word choice in the executive summary. You want to slide off the chair and hide. Before you present your proposal, get a second opinion. A reviewer might see something you missed during proofing.

The reason these problems get through isn't because we're stupid or careless, it's because what we're doing is actually very smart, explained psychologist Tom Stafford, who studies at the University of Sheffield in the UK. "When you're writing, you're trying to convey meaning. It's a very high level task," he said.[21]

As with all high level tasks, your brain generalizes simple component parts (like turning letters into words and words into sentences) so it can focus on more complex tasks (like combining sentences into complex ideas). "We don't catch every detail, we're not like computers or NSA databases," said Stafford. "Rather, we take in sensory information and combine it with what we expect, and we extract meaning." When we're proofreading

our own work, we know the meaning we want to convey. Because we expect that meaning to be there, it's easier for us to miss when parts (or all) of it are absent. The reason we don't see our own mistakes is because what we see on the screen is competing with the version that exists in our heads.

This can be something as trivial as transposing the letters in "the" to "hte," or something as significant as omitting the core explanation of your article.

Generalization is the hallmark of all higher-level brain functions. We can become blind to details because our brain is operating on instinct. By the time you proofread your own work, your brain already knows the destination.

This explains why your readers are more likely to pick up on your errors. Even if you are using words and concepts that they are also familiar with, their brains are on this journey for the first time, so they are paying more attention to the details along the way and not anticipating the final destination.

When you're proofreading, you are trying to trick your brain into pretending that it's reading the thing for the first time. Stafford suggested that if you want to catch your own errors, you should try to make your work as unfamiliar as possible. Change the font or background color or print it out and edit by hand. "Once you've learned something in a particular way, it's hard to see the details without changing the visual form," he said.

Rehearse

There are two types of rehearsals:

- Presentations used when there will be a formal presentation of the proposal to the customer's team
- Role-plays used when the salesperson will reviewing the proposal with one or two people from the customer.

The salesperson should, whenever feasible, request to present their proposal in person and not simply send their proposal via e-mail or courier.

Professor Pentland of Living Labs at MIT conducted thousands of hours of studies examining how people communicate with one another. He published what he learned in an excellent book entitled *Honest Signals.*[22] One conclusion was there is an unconscious communication channel between people that reveals itself through nonverbal signals. Because these honest signals happen mostly at the unconscious level, they are very hard to fake. The signals are tied to your biology and are very difficult to suppress. In one of his studies that consisted of MBA students presenting their business plans for funding from venture capitalist, one group saw the presentations and another only received the printed proposals. The group seeing both the presentations and proposals choose a completely different set of proposals than the group only receiving the printed proposals.

One significant conclusion from Professor Pentland's study was the way you deliver your message has a direct impact on the perceived content of the message. The implication for salespeople is you are part of your company's value proposition and, when presenting your proposals, let your commitment, enthusiasm, and belief in what you are offering help convince the customer that your proposal is the best.

As being in front of your customer is so important when presenting your proposal, being your best requires rehearsing. You want to rehearse the delivery of your proposal in order to ensure all the mechanics of the delivery are smooth so you can focus on delivering the proposal with the biggest emotional impact.

For both the presentation and informal rehearsals, the salesperson briefs the person playing the customer on how they expect them to react to the proposal and possible negative reactions to the proposal. The person playing the customer gives feedback after the rehearsal. If possible, the presentation or role-play should be recorded. You cannot lose by doing a rehearsal for several reasons:

- If the actual delivery of the proposal goes as you described for the rehearsal, it is an indicator you have a good understanding of the customer.
- If the real presentation does not go as you described, it is an indicator you do not have a good understanding of the customer and it is much better to know this so you can improve on future proposals.

During the rehearsals, will discover your strengths, gaps in the proposal information, and how well the proposal flows while you and/or your team respond to customer questions and objections during the presentation. This type of feedback is invaluable and cannot be discovered by only having someone reviewing your proposal.

Going through the review and rehearsal steps gives you the insights to correct or improve your proposal before you take it to the customer. In the sales world, it is about the small things that can make a big difference. See the sidebar "I'm Not a Loser!"

There is a lot of work to be done after a proposal has been presented, as described in Chapter 4 "Opportunities Management," particularly in terms of the resolution of concerns, negotiations, and monitoring stages. All these actions keep you close to your customer, enabling you to react quickly to developments that may prevent you from winning the deal. The final sales stage after the results are known is closed won or closed lost. Now the salesperson will start follow-up activities.

Follow-Up

Follow-up activities, as described in the opportunity management chapter, consist of actions taken during the later stages of:

- Outcome analysis
- Implementation
- Project review

The actions listed in the opportunities management chapter were for closed won opportunities. These actions ensure that, by following up, the salesperson and their team communicate that the customer's business is important, deliver on the promises, strengthen the relationship, build trust, and use this time to develop more business with the account.

▶ *I'm Not a Loser!*

In my sales training seminars, I start off the seminar by first showing this flip chart to stress the point that in sales it's not okay to simply do a better proposal than your last proposal. It must be the best proposal for the customer. If it is not the best, it does not mean you are better or good: it means you are a loser. Some people, especially when they enter sales from a technical position, have come from a job where it is okay not to be the best provided you are trying to get better—and even if you are not trying to get better, as long as you are doing a good job that is acceptable.

In sales, good is not good enough. In sales, the salesperson must realize that your competitors' salespeople are talking with your customers every day and are trying to beat you—to make you a loser.

The second part of my introduction is to show the names of the people in the graphic and ask what these people do—are they politicians, golfers on the European tour, scientists, swimmers, or soldiers?

Very few people get the answer correct, but they do know Michael Phelps, the greatest swimmer of all time and the most decorated Olympian of all time. The names of the people on the list are swimmers Phelps beat. They all came in second. The biggest margin of victory in those victories was 0.025 seconds! In fact, in the 2008 Beijing Olympics, Phelps beat Cavic by .01 seconds to win his seventh gold medal and tie Mark Spitz's record.

The point is, in sales there is no silver or bronze medal. If you are not the best, you are a loser. Phelps was the best, but that never stopped him from relentlessly training and trying to improve. He was not looking for big improvements; he just wanted to be the best he could be.

In sales, when you think you have a great proposal ready to go, jump back in the pool and review and rehearse your proposal and then do one more lap. Getting just a little bit better might bring you the gold!

In this section, four additional key areas will be discussed:

- Handling problems or customer dissatisfaction
- Initiating a difficult message
- Handling successes
- Outcome analysis customer debrief

Once the customer starts to purchase your products or services or enters into the implementation stage of the project, it is critical for the salesperson to be sensitive to how the project is going from the customer's perspective. This was described in Chapter 1 "Understanding the Role of Marketing and Sales" as selling by looking through the customer's window and not looking in a mirror. Once in the closed won sales stage, some projects will go as planned or even better; these make for great references. Some do not go as planned and can result in significant problems; these make for great references depending on how the problem is handled.

Handling problems and successes are key follow-up activities, and both are built around the key concepts of total quality management (TQM) and 6 Sigma and solid communication skills. The important factors are gather the facts, analyze, act, and report. The continuous improvement process applies for both problems and successes.

Handling Problems and Customer Dissatisfaction[23]

When a customer raises a problem you were not prepared for or expecting:

- Encourage feedback from the customer, ask questions to understand, ask permission to take notes on key points, and mark points for clarification.
- Let the customer talk first and ask clarifying and confirming questions after the customer has finished. Try to develop a clear understanding of how the problem has impacted the customer, project, and company, if appropriate. When possible, ask for specifics about how this problem has affected them specifically, the project objectives, and the company.

- Be polite and sympathetic; show empathy with your words, body, and language, and lean toward the customer.
- Check with the customer for what they recommend for the next steps.
- Take ownership of trying to resolve the problems and communicate internally to the people who need to be involved from your company to deal with this issue.
- At this point it may be appropriate to take this information back to your office or discuss it with another person. If so, give the customer a time you will return to them with an update.
- Deal with complaints as quickly as possible and be available or arrange to have the best person available to discuss the problem with the customer in person, if feasible.
- Keep the customer aware of your progress and establish remedies for the problem.
- Address the underlying causes of the problems.
- Document the actions to be taken both to remedy the problem and to ensure that the problem will not happen in the future.
- Check for the customer's satisfaction.
- Thank the customer for taking the time to share and cooperate with you on this issue.

After Meetings—Relating to Handling Problems and Customer Dissatisfaction

- Follow up with a summary of the meeting that is suitable for distribution to the customer and internally and distribute it as soon as possible. Attach all correspondence to the company CRM system linked to the opportunity.
- Do not avoid the customer.
- Work to retain the relationship by making contact as soon as possible after the problem has been addressed. This contact is best if in person but can also be via e-mail, telephone, or social event. As required, fulfill expected servicing contacts.
- If appropriate, have your manager or other executive follow up with the customer management to acknowledge the situation and restate the importance of the customer's relationship.
- Be prepared to brief any other external customers who have contact with the customer.
- When the issue has been resolved, ask the customer for correspondence stating that the problem has been handled to their satisfaction. If the customer states they cannot, ask why. If the reason is due to unresolved issues, apply the problem-handling steps to resolve the open issues. If the customer states they do not want to for other reasons, ask if they can be a reference if other customers want to validate that the problem has been resolved.

Even though having a customer express their dissatisfaction is not pleasant, you want to ensure that you:

- Don't become defensive. When listening to the customer, listen, clarify, and confirm your understanding. In most cases, take the time to go back to your office and review the information with the other team members and determine what can be done.

- Don't pass the responsibility or cause of the problem to others. Use the skill of triangulation as discussed in the communications chapter.
- Don't make excuses. However, identify all contributing factors in your analysis and recommended actions.
- Don't accept abusive behavior or language from the customer. Tell them this is not constructive behavior and ask them to stop and continue on a more productive manner. If they do not stop, politely stop the meeting, tell the customer you will contact them later in the hopes that you can continue a more useful dialogue, and report the situation to your management.

If the customer does not accept your recommendation or solution, then handle it as a difference of opinion as discussed in Chapter 5 "Communication Skills." Be polite. Agree to disagree. Thank the customer for their time.

Initiating a Difficult Message

Sometimes you have to initiate a difficult message. This can be for such reasons as the project start-up has been delayed due to equipment or crews arriving late, equipment failure, or overdue invoices not being paid. When these types of situations happen, you need to take steps to inform the customer and correct the situation. In cases like these, before you engage with the customer, break the conversation into three parts: before, during, and after.

Before the Meeting

- Prepare. Be sure you have researched facts and options.
- Review the communication skills summary card.[24] The communication skills of constructive criticism will be used and, if needed, the skills of handling a difference of opinion and triangulation.
- Prepare the message considering the customer's social style. Review the "Managing Tensions" section in Chapter 3.
- Put yourself in the position of the customer. Identify the consequences, both positive and negative, to the customer whenever possible.

During the Meeting

- Open the meeting. Take time for pleasantries, rapport building, checking for how much time they can spend with you, and if there is anything they wanted to discuss while you're there. Then state the purpose of the meeting by positioning the message clearly, providing a rationale and a positive outcome. Be concise and carefully choose language not to incite. Do not state what you want the customer to do. That will be stated at the end of the discussion.
- Describe your preparation for this meeting and any efforts you have made on the customer's behalf.
- Avoid being defensive. Do not shift blame to the customer or someone in your organization. Use the skill of triangulation. Refer to the issue as "it."
- Explain the situation in a neutral tone.
- Explain your company's position and the reason why. Ensure that you stay committed and your support for your organization's position and express empathy for the customer's position.
- If the customer disagrees, then probe to understand why they have taken this position. If this is the situation, use the skill of handling a difference of opinion. Be prepared to offer and ask for alternatives or options to identify an alternative acceptable solution.

- If no alternatives or viable alternatives are identified, ask the customer to brainstorm, if appropriate.
- If a solution is agreed to, summarize the next steps.
- If no solution is agreed to, state your respect for the customer's position by acknowledging it and the and reasons why, as stated by the customer. Then state you and your company's position and the reasons why as well as the next steps.
- Reconfirm and express empathy again for the customer's position.
- Ask the customer for their support and explain that you value the relationship.
- Ask if there is anything you can do for them to help close this issue, such as contacting any of their colleagues or management.
- Thank them for taking the time to discuss this issue.

After the Meeting

- Follow up with a summary of the meeting that is suitable for distribution to the customer and internally and distribute it as soon as possible. Attach to the company CRM system linked to the opportunity.
- Do not avoid the customer.
- Work to retain the relationship by making contact as soon as possible. This contact is best if in person but can also be via e-mail, telephone, or social event.
- If appropriate have your manager or other executive follow up with the customer's management to acknowledge the situation and the, restate the importance of the customer's relationship.
- Be prepared to brief any other external customers who have contact with the customer.
- The next opportunity you have to discuss the same situation, ensure that you use the skill of crediting as discussed in Chapter 5 to demonstrate your appreciation for their efforts and the benefits resulting from this.

Handling Successes

Handling successes is a very important aspect of continuous improvement. Companies wanting to achieve their best performance make analyzing failures and successes equally important. In a recent performance study, it was concluded that soldiers who discussed both successes and failures learned at a higher rate than soldiers who only discussed failures.[25] In another more recent research, it was shown that in fact neurons retain successes better than failures.[26] This has significant implications for salespeople and helps us understand the results in a separate study, which concluded that customers who experienced problems and successes remembered the successes better (detail and recall one month later) than the failures. However, what the salesperson needs to ensure is that, when you have a success or you and your team beat expectations, don't just brag about it. You have to take the same TQM and 6 Sigma approaches as when handling a problem and apply it to the success to ensure that you can make it happen again. If you do not take the time to demonstrate to the customer that you understand why the success happened, then the customer may just think you got lucky. See the **Chapter Highlight 6.4: "How Did You Know?"**

Chapter Highlight 6.4: "How Did You Know?"

In a sales training session on the Nile River in Cairo, the instructor's recommendation was to report successes and failures and you will have a more satisfied client.

The instructor had just described a study where, in the first control group, when the parent came home, the other parent only told about all the good things their son had done. In another group, the returning parent was only told all the bad things their son had done. In the third group, the returning parent was told both the good and bad things their son had done. The impressions of each group were as follows:

- First group: the other parent was hiding something
- Second group: their kid was a problem
- Third group: we have a pretty good kid

The instructor stated the conclusion: Report both successes and failures and the customer will be left with the impression that you are a good supplier. At that time, Ahmed (one of the students) raised his hand and said that he understood what the instructor was suggesting, but it just does not work like that in Egypt. The instructor was puzzled and suggested, jokingly, that maybe it was the pyramids that had an effect. After a few chuckles, the instructor asked Ahmed to explain.

Ahmed explained his company had, one month earlier, set a world record for running their tool for thirteen years non-stop, with no failures. So he had sent a flyer to his customers announcing the success. Then, just last week, the same type of tool failed after just two weeks. The operations team collected the equipment and other operating information and sent the machine back to the factory in Singapore for analysis and inspection. And after all that, Ahmed delivered a two inch binder full of analyses, findings, and recommendations to eliminate this type of failure. The instructor acknowledged Ahmed's information and asked, "And what is your point?"

Ahmed paused and said, "I was just notified over break that we lost. So you see, it just doesn't work that way here." The instructor then said, "Okay, let me confirm. You had a success and you sent a flyer." Ahmed said, "Yes." The instructor then stated, "Then you had a failure and took the equipment back, did the analyses and tests in Singapore, and gave the customer a two inch report." To add effect, the instructor picked up the seminar training textbook, which was almost two inches thick and quite heavy, and let the textbook drop and slam onto the desk. "And you gave that to the customer." Ahmed said, "Yes." The instructor said the customer stated, "You got lucky." Ahmed was startled and said, "How did you know?"

The instructor said "The flier is bragging. Why did you not send that equipment that set the world record back to the factory and gather all the operating statistics possible and make a similar report like the failure, identifying what were the critical success factors and recommendations to achieve a similar performance as the equipment had run for thirteen years? Had you done that, the customer would be excited about the prospect of having more of that level of performance."

The instructor then shared another incident from his experience in Indonesia. His operations team held monthly service quality review meetings with the customer. Normally, the topics of discussion were a review of the previous month's operations and what was coming up in the next thirty to sixty days and report on any failures and successes following the TQM process. In this particular meeting, and after reviewing the expected activity, the operations manager reviewed a failure, the outcome of the root-cause analysis, and recommendations to ensure that the failure would not happen again. Then in the same month of operations, there was a significant success where a new service was run successfully, saving the customer significant costs. This was of particular interest because in earlier attempts the new service was not successful. The operations manager went through the same type of review for the success and presented the root-cause analysis and recommendations to ensure that this type of performance could be counted on in the future. After the service

Chapter Highlight 6.4: "How Did You Know" (cont.)

quality review meeting over lunch, the only topic of discussion was how soon the new service could be introduced across the customer's operations. The instructor said, "While I was at lunch after the meeting, I was thinking if we had not discussed the success, most likely the customer's staff would have had reasons why they could not attend lunch."

The instructor than asked, "Who has heard of Babe Ruth?" Ahmed again put up his hand and said "He was the homerun king in the US in the 1920s." The instructor was impressed he had the era correct. "Yes, and did you know he was also the strike-out king of all time? Not many people remember that." The instructor then said to the class, "People remember the successes... if you tell them."

Ahmed said, nodding his head, "I get your point. I wish I had taken this training a year ago."

Customer Recognizes Success

When the customer recognizes a success, you:

- Encourage feedback from the customer, ask questions to understand, ask permission to take notes on key points, and mark points for clarification.
- Let the customer talk first and ask clarifying and confirming questions after the customer has finished. Try to understand how this impacts the customer and project- and company-level objectives and value drivers. When possible, ask for specifics of how this success has specifically affected them, the project objectives, and the company.
- Be excited about the success, show enthusiasm with your words, body, and language, and lean towards the customer.
- Check with the customer for what they recommend for next steps.
- Take ownership to ensure that an analysis of the success is done and document the success to understand the contributing factors and communicate this information internally to the people who need to be involved in your company to agree on the actions.
- At this point it may be appropriate to take this information back to your office or discuss it with another person; if so, give the customer a time you will return to them with an update.
- Deal with success as quickly as possible and be available or arrange to have the best person available to discuss the success with the customer in person, if feasible.
- Keep the customer aware of your progress as you discuss and establish next steps.
- Document the actions to be taken and capture the best practice that resulted in the success.
- Address any underlying issues associated with the success that could be improved.
- Check for the customer's satisfaction.
- Thank the customer for taking the time to share and cooperate with you on this issue.

Chapter Highlight 6.5: Perfect!

Plato is credited for saying "beauty is in the eye of the beholder." Like beauty, success is subjective for the person looking at the performance. What you may consider standard or expected could make the customer ecstatic. Here is an excellent example from a quarterly service quality review meeting.

The operations manager had just presented a list of eight changes his crews had made, resulting in small efficiency improvements. When the eight items were looked at individually, none of the items alone would be significant; however, when added together, the eight items resulted in the customer being able to open an additional outlet in the same year. Rather than opening ten outlets as per the original plan, the customer was now able to open eleven in the same timeframe. The customer's reaction was, "That's perfect. This is just what we need." The customer's delight was due to the fact that he had become very concerned that his company was not going to be able make the objective of ten outlets and now, with the efficiency improvements, he was confident eleven was achievable. He would have some very good news to report to his management.

What the customer did not know was that this list the operations manager presented at the service quality review meeting did not exist just two days earlier. What happened during the preparation for the meeting? The salesperson for the account went to the location and asked the operations staff to share some of their successes since the project started. The room was silent. The salesperson's response was, "People, I know you are doing good things. There have not been any issues on this project. Tell me what improvements, big or small, have you made since you started." The salesperson asked the room to split into two groups and brainstorm a list of improvements they had made and an estimated benefit to the client as a result.

After twenty minutes, the groups had come up with fifteen items that they then grouped into six categories. They discussed the list, eliminating several of the items, leaving eight items that had quantifiable efficiency gains and when added together were something the salesperson was excited to share with the customer. However, one project manager asked, "Why are we reporting this? This is what they pay us to do." The salesperson's reply was, "You're correct—this is what they pay us to do, but it is not what they pay us for." The project manager was now looking confused and asked, "What do you mean?" The salesperson said, "Our customer pays us for the products and services they require to build these outlets. There are a lot of companies that can provide this for them."

"However, not every supplier is going to do what you have done. You are thinking about the customer's objectives and trying to eliminate waste and improve efficiencies. The customer knows what they pay for, but not necessarily what they can do better because of our efforts. It is up to us to ensure that they know about our efforts that result in them being more successful. If we do not, and for the next project, the customer chooses a cheaper supplier for their products and services and they can only open ten or fewer outlets rather than eleven, they made a bad decision. And as far as I'm concerned, that would be our fault for not letting them know what we do for them. It is like knowing you have a supplier that is watching out for you. Not all suppliers will do that."

This is a powerful example with two take-aways. First, you have to look for successes. Imagine a small child sitting in the back of a car going through the forest and seeing deer playing along the road. The child gets excited and asked her father, "Daddy, Daddy, do you see the deer?" The father, who is concentrating on driving the car, says, "No Sweety, I don't". To which the child answers, "Daddy, you have to be looking to see them." The same is true for successes: You have to make it a follow-up activity to be looking for successes.

Chapter Highlight 6.5: Perfect! (cont.)

Second, don't discount the small successes. As Robert Collier, a famous American, stated, "Success is the sum of small efforts—repeated day in and day out." A good way to find successes is to ask: Are there actions that your company has taken to enable the customer to:

- Improve operational efficiencies.
- Reduce risks and uncertainties.
- Make faster decisions.
- Reduce overall project costs.
- Earn a better return on investment.
- Increase more sales.
- Improve profitability.
- Improve logistics.
- Have access to limited resources or experts.
- Addressing customers-stated concerns and expectations.
- Achieving or beating stated objectives.
- Achieving customer objectives consistently.

The improvements in any of the above could be due to better supplier performance; new products or services; innovative processes; continuous improvement; better understanding of the customer's business goals and objectives; organization and processes; and transfers in staffing, with expertise in a given domain. Understanding what your company's contribution was to the better performance and knowing how to capture and report this to the customer are key actions in the follow-up activities for salespeople.

- As appropriate, ask the customer for a reference and release to use the reference with other customers as a demonstration of capabilities. Have an example or draft of what you would like the customer to provide.
- Follow up with a thank you note or small gift of appreciation, as appropriate, for sharing the success. Ensure that you use the skill of crediting, as discussed in Chapter 5 "Communications Skills."

Salesperson Recognizes Success

Before you initiate a discussion to confirm a success, you must first clearly define the success. This should be done as part of the process when discussing the customer's objectives, critical success factors, concerns, and expectations. These factors are captured during the qualification and sales call activities. In addition to these factors, once a project or sales is initiated, the customer may decide to purchase new products or services. For these sell-up sales, it is always important to understand what the customer will define as success as a result of buying new or additional products and services. There are also other scenarios that can be considered success; see **Chapter Highlight 6.5: Perfect!** for some other ideas for success. When you believe an event deserves being highlighted as a success, bring it to the customer's attention. In cases like these, before you engage with the customer, break the conversation into three parts: before, during, and after.

Before the Meeting

- Prepare. Be sure you have researched the facts and have completed the root-cause analysis for the success with the operations team and you have made an estimate to quantify the impact of the success.
- Prepare the report. Document the success and understand the contributing factors. Consider the customer's social style and the type of information they will need to validate the success.
- Determine what the best practice procedure will be to replicate the success again.
- Address any underlying issues associated with the success that could be improved.

During the Meeting

- Open the meeting. Take time for pleasantries, rapport building, checking for how much time they can spend with you, and if there is anything they wanted to discuss. Then state the purpose of the meeting by positioning the message clearly, providing a rationale and a positive outcome.
- Describe your preparation for this meeting and any efforts you have made on the customer's behalf.
- Let your enthusiasm show with your words, body, and language, leaning toward the customer.
- Review your report with the customer. Check often to ensure that the customer is in agreement.
- Check with the customer for what they recommend for the next steps.
- Take ownership to ensure that any follow-up activities are done and the people who need to be involved in your company agree on the actions.
- At this point it may be appropriate to take this information back to your office or discuss it with another person; if so, give the customer a time you will return to them with an update.
- As appropriate, ask the customer for a reference and release to use the reference with other customers as a demonstration of capabilities. Have an example or draft of what you would like the customer to provide.

After the Meeting

- Follow up with a summary of the meeting that is suitable for distribution to the customer and internally, and distribute it as soon as possible. Attach to the company CRM system linked to the opportunity.
- If appropriate, have your manager or other executive follow up with the customer management to acknowledge the success and then restate the importance of the customer's relationship and the opportunities to work collaboratively as in this success.
- Be prepared to brief any other external customers who have contact with the customer.
- Followup with a thank you note or small gift of appreciation, as appropriate, for sharing the success. Ensure that you use the skill of crediting as discussed in the communications chapter.

All the activities discussed up to this point in this chapter highlight two points:

- Focus on the customer after the sale.
- Employ excellent communication skills.

Without the focus on the customer and the ability to handle difficult conversations with the customer and to capture successes in a productive fashion, the salesperson's attention can all too often turn to the next sale. It is the follow-up activities that make for stronger relationships with the customer and provide the sales collateral to help make it easy for future customers to believe in your company's ability to deliver on your promises. The next follow-up activity is the outcome analysis customer debrief.

Outcome Analysis Customer Debrief

As described in Chapter 4 "Opportunities Management," the last stage of the procurement stage is outcome analysis. The outcome analysis customer debrief is done for all opportunities closed won, lost, and withdrawn. The outcome analysis customer debrief needs to be done as close to the customer decision and, if possible, with a minimum of two people in the buying center—ideally, the person who evaluated the proposals and the decision maker or other influential person in the buying center. The guidelines below are for each opportunity outcome won, lost, and withdrawn.

Closed Won Opportunity

- Express your excitement in winning their business and thank them for the award or order.
- Explain that the purpose of the interview is to learn as much as possible about the customer's perceptions and experience during the recent sales process so your organization can continually improve.
- Discuss confidentiality. State that you want to communicate feedback throughout your organization; if the customer/prospect feels there are certain aspects that are too sensitive, they should be identified during the conversation.

Feedback Regarding Your Proposal

Ask simple open questions regarding your proposal:

- Why did they make the award to you?
- What did they like best about your proposal?
- What could have been improved?
- Was there anything additional they would have liked to include?
- Do they have any recommendations for the next opportunity?
- Now that they have made the award, do they have any concerns or expectations?

Product- and Service-Specific Feedback

Ask more specific questions, if not answered previously by the customer:

- Overall, what do they think of your products or services?
- How well did your product capabilities meet their expectations?
- How would they characterize the completeness of your portfolio?
- Who were you competing against?
- How did you stack up against the competition?
- What did the customer view as your strengths and weaknesses?
- What did the customer view as your competitors' strengths and weaknesses?

Marketing

- What marketing messages resonated during the buying process?
- What marketing tools were most effective?
- Are there marketing tools that they would recommend be made available (web, social media, etc.)?

Sales Effort

- Did you focus and identify all their needs?
- How well did you explain your solution for their environment?
- Were all their questions or concerns addressed in the proposal?
- Is there anyone else they would like to talk with now?

Decision-Making

- Who was involved in the decision-making process?
- What was the primary driver in their decision?
- What were the contributing factors?
- Was there a model?
- What did they evaluate as the costs of your offer?
- Did they contact your references? If so, were they helpful?

About the Company

- What was the customer's perception of your organization before entering the buying cycle?
- Did their perception change?
- If so, how did it change?
- Were they aware of the company's roadmap and future product and service strategies?
- Did the company's future direction factor into their decision?

Open Feedback

- Does the customer have any additional comments or suggestions?
- Do they know of anyone else who has similar types of projects or needs they recommend you contact and could they give you an introduction?

After the Debrief

- Send a thank you note to the customer for taking the time to debrief with you.
- Have your manager or executive send a thank you note or make a telephone call to their executive thanking them for the opportunity and stating that your company is looking forward to working with them.
- Summarize in writing the notes from the interview and distribute them to appropriate internal personnel.
- Conduct a debriefing meeting internally and list any action items that came out of the meeting.

Some of the information above should have been discussed during the qualification and sales call activities, such feedback regarding your products and services and the decision-making process. However, that was before the customer had offers from the competition. It is good to compare the feedback you had before and after as this will indicate if there were any misunderstandings and how good of a job the competition did selling against you.

Closed Lost Opportunity

- Express your disappointment in not winning their business and how you really believed what you had submitted a winning proposal.
- Explain that the purpose of the interview is to learn as much as possible about the customer's or prospect's perceptions and experience during the recent sales process so your organization can continually improve.
- Discuss confidentiality. State that you want to communicate feedback throughout your organization; if the customer/prospect feels there are certain aspects that are too sensitive, they should be identified during the conversation.

Feedback Regarding Your Proposal

Ask simple open questions regarding your proposal:

- What did they like best about your proposal?
- What could have been improved?
- Was there anything they would have like to include?
- Any recommendations for the next opportunity?
- Now that they have made the award, do they have any concerns or expectations?

Product- and Service-Specific Feedback

Ask more specific questions if not answered previously by the customer:

- Overall, what do they think of your products or services?
- How well did your product capabilities meet their expectations?
- How would they characterize the completeness of your portfolio?
- What did the customer/prospect view as your strengths and weaknesses?
- What did the customer/prospect view as your competitors' strengths and weaknesses?

Marketing

- What marketing messages resonated during the buying process?
- What marketing tools were most effective?
- Are there marketing tools that they would recommend be made available (web, social media, etc.)?

Sales Effort

- Did the you focus and identify all their needs?
- How well did you explain your solution in their environment?
- Were all their questions answered?
- Is there anyone else they would like to talk with now?

Decision-Making

- What was the primary driver in their decision?
- What were the contributing factors?

About the Company

- What was the customer's perception of your organization before entering the buying cycle?
- Did their perception change?
- If so, how did it change?
- Are they aware of the company's roadmap and future product and service strategies?

Open Feedback

- Does the customer have any additional comments or suggestions?
- When will they next be making a purchase? Would it be ok for you to contact them for that opportunity?
- A best practice is to agree with the customer that you will contact them in three to six months unless they need to contact you before that. This can be via e-mail, telephone, social media, or in person.
- Do they know of anyone else who has similar types of projects or needs they recommend and could they give you an introduction?

After the Debrief

- Send a thank you note to the customer for taking the time to debrief with you.
- Ensure that they are on your contact list for future marketing campaigns.
- Summarize in writing the notes from the interview and distribute them to appropriate internal personnel.
- Conduct an internal debriefing meeting internally and list any action items that came out of the meeting.
- Have your manager or executive send a thank you note or telephone call to their executive thanking them for their team's time and disappointment in not winning their business. Let the customer executive know the sales team will do an review of the feedback from their team and your company is looking forward to having an opportunity to work with them in the future.

Closed Withdrawn Opportunity

Express your disappointment regarding the opportunity being canceled. If the opportunity was canceled after submitting your proposal and the customer evaluated it, follow the same debriefing as for a closed lost opportunity. Ask for more details to understand why the project was canceled and if there is a possibility the project or purchase could be done at a later date. If the customer did evaluate, ask them who would have won the opportunity.

If the opportunity was withdrawn before you submitted your proposal, you should still debrief the customer on the following topics, as appropriate.

- Explain that the purpose of the interview is to learn as much as possible about the customer's or prospect's perceptions and experience during the recent sales process so your organization can continually improve.

Feedback Regarding the Future Submission of a Proposal

Ask simple open questions regarding what they want to see in future proposals:

- What do they look for in a proposal?
- What are common aspects of proposals they think can be improved?
- Do they have any recommendations for the next opportunity?
- What are their concerns or expectations when evaluating proposals?

Product- and Service- Specific Feedback

Ask more specific questions if not answered previously by the customer:

- Overall, what do they think of your products or services?
- How well did your product capabilities meet their expectations?
- How would they characterize the completeness of your portfolio?
- What did the customer/prospect view as your strengths and weaknesses?
- What did the customer/prospect view as your competitors' strengths and weaknesses?

Marketing

- What marketing messages resonated during the buying process?
- What marketing tools were most effective?
- Are there marketing tools that they would recommend be made available (web, social media, etc.)?

Sales Effort

- Did the you focus and identify all their needs?
- How well did you explain your solution in their environment?
- Was there anyone else they would like to talk with now?

Decision-Making

- What was the primary driver in their decision for canceling the project?
- What were the contributing factors?

About the Company

- What was the customer's/prospect's perception of your organization before entering the buying cycle?
- Did the perception change?
- If so, how did it change?
- Did future directions factor into your decision?
- Were you aware of the company's roadmap and future product and service strategies?

Open Feedback

- Does the customer have any additional comments or suggestions?

After the Debrief

- Do they know of anyone else who has similar types of project or needs they recommend and could they give you an introduction?
- When is the next time they will be purchasing and would be okay for you to contact them for that opportunity?
- Send a thank you note to the customer/prospect for taking the time to debrief with you.
- Ensure that they are on your contact list for future marketing campaigns.
- Summarize in writing the notes from the interview and distribute them to appropriate internal personnel.
- Conduct the debriefing meeting and list any action items that came out of the meeting.
- Have your manager or executive send a thank you note to their executive thanking them for their time and expressing disappointment that the opportunity was canceled. Also state that your company is looking forward to having an opportunity to work with them in the future.

This concludes the discussion on the sales activities. All the activities are scalable and should be adopted to fit the sales environment of the salesperson. The sales activities need to be adjusted to fit the salesperson's assignments. For example, a salesperson who has been assigned a new territory will need to dedicate more of their time to prospecting initially and, as they secure more business, their time will be divided more evenly among all the sales activities. A salesperson who is assigned one or two accounts or a large account with ongoing business will do less prospecting and spend more time building relationships and conducting sales meetings, proposals, and follow-up.

Conversations and meetings with customers are a reality of the sales profession. All the sales activities require that the salesperson have conversations and meetings with the customers. This contact can be in person, via telephone, or via e-mail. It is essential that the salesperson be very good at having successful conversations and meetings with their customers. The skills for successful sales-related conversations and meetings are called sales call skills and are based on the needs-satisfaction process discussed earlier in this chapter. The next chapter will discuss in detail the sales call skills and tools for having successful sales-related conversations and meetings.

Summary of Chapter Objectives

1. Make relationship building a specific and continuous process.

Relationship building is about making a positive impact on the level of trustworthiness between you and your customers and prospects. The more trustworthy you are, the easier it is be successful with your clients and make your sales objectives. There are many possible opportunities for a salesperson to build trust with their customers. Different situations can be used to strengthen or improve the customer's perceptions of your credibility, believe what you say, build reliability, have confidence in your ability to deliver on specifics and results especially for promises made during the pursuit of an opportunity, create intimate and comfortable feelings with you, and orient your customer so they know that you have considered their best interests and objectives before you try selling to them.

2. Understand the key sales activities to manage a sales pipeline.

To maximize the value of a pipeline, the salesperson must pro actively manage the pipeline. The active management of a pipeline starts first with new opportunities being continuously added to ensure that there is a continuous revenue stream, with new sales replacing opportunities that are closed. Leads that have been qualified become either confirmed leads or closed withdrawn. A confirmed lead passes the qualification questions in the opportunity assessment for **"Is there an opportunity?"** and it is confirmed that the customer will make a purchase of the products and services you provide. A closed withdrawn lead is something that does not pass the assessment questions and will not result in the customer spending money to purchase the products and services from your company. In the opportunity management process, the qualification activities occur during the identification of the compelling event. The main tool for holding the customer qualification conversation is the Customer Project Solution Worksheet.

Once an opportunity is in the confirmed lead sales stage, the salesperson uses sales meeting activities to learn more about the customer's needs from different people in the buying center by completing the assessment questions for "Can We Compete" (do you have a technically acceptable offering), "Can We Win" (do you have enough people in the buying center who want you to win) and **"Is it worth winning?"** (financial and strategic questions). At this point, the salesperson will select their competitive sales strategy and ask the fifth question of the opportunity assessment: What are they and the sales team going to do next? At this time, the salesperson will have their strategy reviewed and set the sales stage to closed withdrawn if the assessment questions indicate there is no real opportunity. In the sales opportunity-disengage stage, the sales team is not going to pursue the opportunity and will let the competition win the opportunity for a number of reasons. The sales opportunity-attack stage includes four competitive sales strategies of frontal, flanking, defend, or fragment. The competitive sales strategy selected will guide the salesperson on what they will do going forward to win this opportunity. The other option the salesperson can choose for the sales stage is sales opportunity-develop. In this sales stage, the opportunity will not be closed in a calendar year, but the sales team will stay engaged with the customer to better improve their chances of winning the opportunity in the future. The opportunity management process stage evaluation provides a significant level of detail and the tools used during confirmed lead and sales opportunity stages. Later in the textbook, there is a dedicated chapter focusing on deciding and creating a strategic sales plan built to execute a competitive sales strategy. The strategic sales plan review process is also described at the end of that chapter.

The next key sales stage is bid/proposal, which is when the salesperson will present their proposals; in larger more formal opportunities following a customer's tendering process, the bid/proposal sales stage is set once the RFP is received. The key sales activity in this stage is present proposals. A proposal is not a quote. A proposal is a sales document that is a tool for both the salesperson and supporters inside the customer's buying center. The opportunity management process is a very important resource for the salesperson during this stage. Later in the textbook for formal tendering processes, there are three chapters dedicated to these activities: bid evaluation, pricing, and negotiations.

Once the outcome is known and the winner is announced, the sales stage is set to closed won, closed lost, or closed withdrawn.

3. Choose which components of prospecting to include in your prospecting plan.

Many people have a negative perception of prospecting, mostly due to using prospecting incorrectly. By understanding the purpose of prospecting and how to create a buying environment for your customers, prospecting becomes rewarding by creating opportunities to talk to many new potential customers. Prospecting involves finding the customers in your target markets or accounts that can benefit from your products and services. The objective of prospecting is to have the customer agree to talk to you about their business. Too many salespeople try to take shortcuts and try to sell while prospecting, which is not effective. An effective prospecting plan has a variety of components used together to keep a continuous source of leads flowing into your pipeline. The prospecting components are: corporate marketing communications Plan (MCP), research, current accounts, referrals, references, networking, conferences, cold calling, e-mail marketing, and tracking. Prospecting should include each of these components, with the amount of time and frequency allocated to each dependent on the salesperson's area of responsibility territory versus account assignments and the level of brand recognition the salesperson's company has in their marketplace and their position compared to their competitors.

4. Apply a structured approach for building proposals.

The proposal is a tool to convince the customer you have the best option for them. The creation of the proposal starts with the early research completed as part of the prospecting stage and the information collected during the sales meetings earlier in the sales activities. This information is then classified as to the important points that must be discussed in the proposal, organized into three to five proposal components, each with a well-defined and written value proposition that explains to the customer what you will provide as part of your proposal, what the features and benefits do for the customer, and what this means for the customer for their specific application. Many people from the buying center can use your proposal to make their decision. To ensure that your proposal appeals to as many people as possible, the proposal must be written with pages consisting of themes (headings and value propositions), visuals (graphics), and text (details). The opportunity management process procurement stages identify all the critical customer milestones that a proposal must go through before being selected.

5. Know how to manage key follow-up activities.

For each of the outcomes there are specific follow-up activities that need to be done, including debriefing with the customer tailored for each outcome and the other activities as described in the opportunity management process. In addition, there are three activities the salesperson must be very good at to be successful at managing the follow-up activities: handling customer problems or dissatisfaction, initiating a difficult message, and handling successes. The salesperson's ability to handle these different customer scenarios will have a direct impact on the customer's perception of how well and what level of service they received from their supplier. The opportunity management process stages included in the follow-up activities are outcome analysis, implementation, and project review. Each of these stages has several additional activities the sales team should complete as part of the follow-up activities.

Most of the activities a salesperson will spend their time on involves sales-related conversations with the customer following a consultative selling approach using the need satisfaction process. The consultative selling approach is made up of all the factors discussed and recommended in the textbook up to this point, and the approach will continue to be followed for the remaining sections, with added emphasis during the bidding and negotiations. The needs-satisfaction process at the heart of the consultative selling approach includes the most critical selling skills: sales call skills and handling customer negative reactions. These skills will be presented in detail in the next two chapters.

Applying the Concepts

1. List your top five opportunities you are working on now down the left side of an Excel worksheet, as shown below. Identify the sales stage for each opportunity, your last contact date and objective (what you wanted the customer to agree to at the end of the meeting), and when your next contact is planned for and the objective of the meeting. The purpose of this exercise is to have you think about your activities and apply the terminology used in the chapter. This is also a very basic pipeline.

Opportunity Name and ID	Sales Stage	Last Contact Date	Activity	Objective	Planned Contact Date	Activity	Objective
Star Oil New Installation X09-TGE	Confirmed Lead	May 6	Sales Meeting	Have our company included on bidder's list	May 30	Sales Meeting	Key people from customer's buying center to visit our base emphasize what this means to the customer. Have customer agree the local facilities are a factor that should be considered in their evaluation model.
Shell Single Well Peforating Proposal	Sales Opportunity - Frontal	May 7	Sales Meeting	Support customer's need of deep penetrating through tubing perforating system. Have customer acknowledge what this would mean for them on their project.	Jun 1	Present proposal	Have customer award perforating to us.

2. From the list of prospecting components below, how many of these are you doing now and, if you are not doing them now, what could you do for this component? Refer back to the prospecting section of this chapter for a description of each.
   - Corporate Marketing Communications Plan (MCP)
   - Research
   - Current Accounts
   - Referrals
   - References
   - Networking
   - Conferences
   - Cold Calling
   - E-mail Marketing
   - Tracking

3. From the customers you know, pick which customer would rate you highest (on a scale of 1 to 10, where 1 is low or bad and 10 is high or excellent) for credibility, reliability, and intimacy. What did you do to deserve that rating? Considering self-orientation, where 1 is great and 10 is very bad (you only think of yourself), which customer would give you the best self-orientation rating and why? Once this is done, think of your customer base again and which customers would rate you the lowest on each factor and why. An example is shown on the next page. Can you think of some things you can do to improve the relationship with the people in your worst list? Of the trust factors overall, which do you think is your strongest and weakest? Can you think of how you can leverage your strengths and address your weaknesses?

Factor	Best	Rating	Why
Credibility	Thomas	7	Co-authored SPE paper.
Reliability	Sarojini	8	Last project everything went like clockwork.
Intimacy	Michelle	7	Have played squash a lot and have gone to dinner with spouses.
Self-Orientation	Yingtai	3	Let Yingtai present the paper at SPE even though I did most of the work.

Factor	Worst	Rating	Why
Credibility	Ben	3	Could not deliver on promise made on new technolgy on last project.
Reliability	Artur	3	Missed our last two planning sessions for community football team.
Intimacy	Ahmed	3	New engineer for custom drilling team arrived 6 months ago and we have not met.
Self-Orientation	Gulgzel	8	Current project:she believes I was not clear about charges for equipment ordered but not used.

4. Following the format for a proposal component page, as shown in Fig. 6.13, think about an upcoming proposal you will present and make a rough draft of your page. Include a theme (heading), a value proposition under the heading, a graphic with the caption stating what this means for the customer, and what would be in your text for a more detailed explanation.

5. Follow-up activities: Make a list showing your last follow-up activity. Now knowing what you know about how to complete the activity, would you have done anything differently? What would you add to the list of actions based on your personal best practice?

Activity	What would you do differently?	Add–based on your best practice
A. Outcome Analysis Customer Debrief		
B. Handling Problems or Dissatisfaction		
C. Initiating a Difficult Message		
D. Handling Success Customer Recognized		
E. Handling Success Salesperson Recognized		

References

1. Richardson, L.: *New Decade–New Focus on Relationships.* Retrieved May 22, 2015, from https://www.richardson.com/PageFiles/346/NewDecade-NewFocusonRelationships_012710RC_FINAL.pdf (2010).
2. Crosby, L., Evans, K., and Cowles, D.: "Relationship Quality in Services Selling: An Interpersonal Influence Perspective," *Journal of Marketing* 54 no. 3 (1990), 68–81. Retrieved May 22, 2015, from http://www.jstor.org/stable/1251817?
3. Maister, D., Green, C., and Galford, R.: *The Trusted Advisor,* New York, Free Press (2000).
4. Jordan, J., and Vazzana, M.: *Cracking the Sales Management Code: The Secrets to Measuring and Managing Sales Performance* (p. 167), New York, McGraw-Hill (2012).
5. Caroll, J.: (2004, October 1): *Referrals: A Sales Professional's Best Friend.* Retrieved May 25, 2015, from http://www.eyesonsales.com/content/article/referrals_a_sales_professionals_best_friend/
6. Arthur, I., (2012, August 10). *Top 7 Webinar Statistics You Should Know. Retrieved June 13, 2015, from http://e3webcasting.com/top-7-webinar-statistics-you-should-know/*
7. Newswire: (2009, July 7) Retrieved May 26, 2015, from http://www.nielsen.com/us/en/insights/news/2009/global-advertising-consumers-trust-real-friends-and-virtual-strangers-the-most.html.
8. Pophal, L.: *Direct Mail in the Digital Age*, North Vancouver, B.C., Self-Counsel Press. (2011).
9. Richards, L.: *Email Marketing Techniques.* Retrieved May 26, 2015, from http://smallbusiness.chron.com/email-marketing-techniques-3581.html (2015).
10. Norton, J., (2014, September 6). *Scientists claim 'telepathy' success after sending mental message from one person to another 4,000 miles away.* Retrieved June 13, 2015, from http://www.dailymail.co.uk/news/article-2745797/Scientists-claim-telepathy-success-sending-mental-message-one-person-4-000-miles-away.html
11. Korisko, G., (n.d.). *The Amazing Power Of Empathy.* Retrieved June 1, 2015, from http://rebootauthentic.com/power-of-empathy/
12. Bacon, T., and Pugh, D.: *The Behavioral Advantage: What the Smartest, Most Successful Companies Do Differently to Win in the B2B Arena.* New York: AMACOM (2004).
13. Miller, W.: *The Art of Canvassing: How to Sell Insurance.* (1st ed.), New York, Spectator (1894).
14. Taylor, F.: *The Principles of Scientific Management.* New York, Harper (1919).
15. Hoyt, C.: *Scientific Males Management: A Practical Application of the Principles of Scientific Management to Selling.* New Haven, Conn., G.B. Woolson (1913).
16. Strong, E. K.: *The Psychology of Selling Life Insurance.* New York, Harper & Brothers Publishers, (1922).
17. Hypes, W. F.: "The Sales Man as the Customer's Partner," in *How to Increase Your Sales: 126 Selling Plans Used and Proved by 54 Salesmen and Sales Managers* (7th rev. ed.) Chicago, System Company (1910).
18. Hanan, M., Cribbin, J., and Heiser, H.: *Consultative Selling.* New York, American Management Association (1970).
19. Pugh, D., and Bacon, T.: *Powerful Proposals: How to Give Your Business the Winning Edge.* New York, American Management Association (2005).
20. Herndon, D.: Using Red Teams Effectively. *APMP Journal*, (4), 53–70.
21. Stockton, N., (2014, August 1). *What's Up With That: Why It's So Hard to Catch Your Own Typos.* Retrieved June 14, 2015, from http://www.wired.com/2014/08/wuwt-typos/
22. Pentland, A.: *Honest Signals: How They Shape our World*, Cambridge, MA., MIT Press (2008)
23. When discussing handling customer problems and dissatisfaction, both situations will be called problems for simplicity of discussing what the salesperson should do when these situations happen. The actions required for the salesperson to follow are the same for problems and customer's dissatisfaction.
24. Communications skills summary card can be found in the appendix of Chapter 4 and downloaded from http://www.b2bprofessionalsales.com.
25. Sutton, R., *Learning from Success and Failure.* Retrieved June 1, 2015, from https://hbr.org/2007/06/learning-from-success-and-fail/ (2007, June 4).
26. Dye, L., *We Learn More From Success, Not Failure.* Retrieved June 1, 2015, from http://abcnews.go.com/Technology/DyeHard/story?id=8319006 (2009, August 26).

SECTION 2

CONSULTATIVE SELLING SKILLS

This section has two chapters: "Sales Call Skills" and "Handling Customer Objections." Building on the concepts introduced in the earlier chapters, this section describes in detail how to have a consultative selling conversation with your clients.

The consultative selling process follows the total quality management process. All parts of the consultative selling process are covered and the tools available for you to use for planning, execution, reviewing, and coaching. When you follow the steps described in this section, you will be better prepared and organized for your sales calls and will gain much more from each sales call. Your customer will also find the visit valuable and a good use of their time. Too many salespeople will schedule visits with their clients without sufficient planning or review. The salesperson who masters these skills will become one of the differentiating factors why your customers will choose your company.

The sales call tools described in the chapters are available to you from the www.b2bprofessionalsales.com website.

Sales Call Skills

Applying the Basics

"Success is neither magical nor mysterious. Success is the natural consequence of consistently applying the basic fundamentals."[1]

In the previous chapter, it was shown that sales activities are what a salesperson does to manage their day-to-day responsibilities. Many times this requires having a sales conversation with their customers and prospects. In B2B sales, the most effective approach is consultative selling following the need-satisfaction process. Some people challenge the need for such a structured approach and argue that should be more relaxed and ad hoc less work. The reason for the structure is justified by the results. Successful professional salespeople strive to win in a competitive environment. They take luck out of the success equation by following a methodical and repeatable process and making conscious decisions of how to win their customer's business. As captured in the Jim Rohn quote above, success is the natural consequence of consistently applying the basic fundamentals. The consistency of effectively applying the need satisfaction process is achieved with basic sales call skills the topic of this chapter.

Chapter Objectives

After reading this chapter, you will be able to:

- Understand the structure of the sales call.
- Understand and use the sales call skills.
- Apply the total quality management (TQM) process to the sales call process and complete the preparation and analysis steps before and after each sales call.

The Need-Satisfaction Process

The sales call is the application of the need-satisfaction process, as shown in **Fig. 7.1**. The goal of the need-satisfaction process is to make mutually beneficial decisions for both the customer and the salesperson. Not all sales calls will go through all the steps of the need-satisfaction process and, depending on the type of sale, not all the steps have the same level of importance. See **Chapter Highlight 7.1: Fit for Purpose: I Will Take One of These, These, and These.**

Each part of the need-satisfaction process is briefly described below, and later in the chapter each part will be explained in detail.

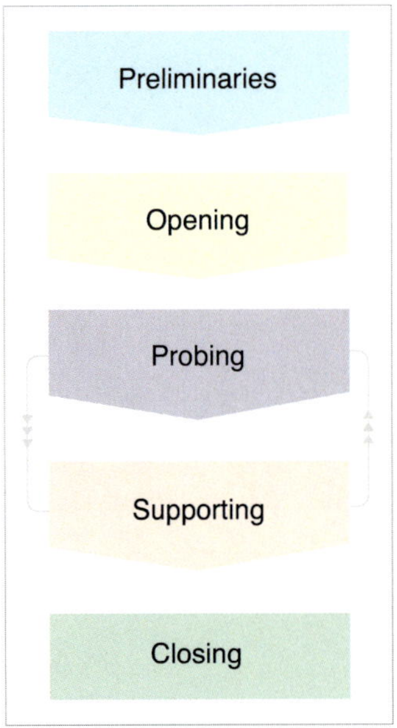

Fig. 7.1
The need satisfaction process is a five-stage process that the salesperson follows when conducting sales calls during the sales activities. The goal of the need-satisfaction process is to make mutually beneficial decisions for the customer and salesperson.

Fig. 7.2
The sales call TQM process: planning, execution, and analysis.

Preliminaries: Sales call will begin with preliminaries to start the conversation and build rapport with the customer.

Opening: An opening to start the business discussion of the meeting.

Probing: Asking questions to discover needs of the customer.

Supporting: After the salesperson understands the customer's needs, then they support explaining how their products and services will address the customer's needs.

Closing: The salesperson concludes the meeting, and customer agrees on the action items.

Preparing for the Sales Call

Sales calls are not ad hoc events. Successful sales calls apply the total quality management (TQM) processes of planning, execution, and analysis to ensure that the sales call is effective and efficient, as shown in **Fig. 7.2**. For each part of the TQM process, there are specific tools the salesperson will use to assist them to prepare, execute, and review.

For each sales call, there is a minimum amount of planning prior to the meeting, and analysis and action items that follow the meeting. For each sales call, there should be the following:

- CRM database information check regarding the account, opportunity, and name of the contact(s) with whom you will be meeting in the sales call
- Purpose, objective, and back-up objective
- Prepared opening statement, probing strategy, and support documents
- Post-call analysis of the execution of the sales call: processes, outcome, and action items

Customer Relationship Management (CRM) Database Information Check

Pre-call preparation starts by reviewing your company's CRM database. From the account corporate profile, you will find the required background account information regarding corporate goals, objectives, and strategies. This information helps you to know what the specific business drivers are for the opportunity you are trying to win. You will also need the organizational and buying center analysis, which provides insights into how to deal with the contact(s) you will meet in the sales call. If you have not previously met the person(s), it is a good idea to query your company's CRM database to see who entered or last made a change to the contact record and also check who entered the most recent opportunity in the CRM database for this account. You can then contact that colleague for information about the contact(s) you will be meeting.

The first tool a salesperson will use when preparing for a sales call is the sales call preparation worksheet. The complete worksheet is included in the appendix of this chapter and available for download from the textbook website. The basic information for the sales call is entered into the buying center profile section of the sales call worksheet and then aligning strategies based on the customers profile can be prepared and entered into the aligning strategies sections of the worksheet.

An example of completed worksheet sections are shown in **Fig. 7.3.** Once the entire worksheet is completed, it becomes a valuable tool for debriefing other

Chapter Highlight 7.1: Fit for Purpose: I Will Take One of These, These, and These

The consultative selling approach used in combination with the need-satisfaction process allows the salesperson to customize a sales call for a specific purpose.

Neil Rackham in 1988 completed a landmark study and published his results in a book entitled *SPIN Selling*.[2] His conclusions shocked many professionals in the sales profession; however, his study spanned ten years and Rackham and his associates observed more than 35,000 B2B sales meetings, identifying the difference between successful salespeople and less successful salespeople. A significant observation was the relative importance of the steps in the need-satisfaction process for large and small sales. From a customer perspective, the factors that drive what is considered large or small sales are:

- **Length of the sales cycle.** The bigger dollar value of the sales, the longer the sales cycle. This can be due to the approval process.
- **The risk of mistakes.** Generally having to get it right will cause the customer to treat a purchase like a big sale. They will want to take their time so as to not make a poor decision.
- **Number of people involved.** Sometimes a small sale will have only one person you will need to talk to. They can have all the responsibility to make the decision. This is not uncommon for repurchases. Larger sales can have people not only from one company, but also include partners and government organizations. Buying center roles may be committees of people rather than one individual.
- **Size of the customer commitment.** This is normally measured in dollars, but can also be defined by contract period and people commitment. The bigger the commitment, the better off you are to treat the sale as a large sale.

What Rackham discovered was the larger the sale, the more important the step of probing has impacting sales success. The smaller the sale, the more important the closing was. This shocked many people since, up to the time of *SPIN selling* the widely accepted belief was that for sales success the salesperson should always be closing or "ABC"—an acronym made famous by the movie *Glengarry Ross* when Alec Baldwin, who plays the sales motivator, informs a group of under-performing salespeople, "you must ABC!" What Rackham proved was ABC was true for small sales, but not for large, more complex sales.

In B2B sales, you can have both small and large sales. A common situation is to win a large opportunity and once you are in the implementation stage, there can be many smaller opportunities.

By considering the factors relevant to the sales call, the salesperson can create a fit-for-purpose sales call. This is done by choosing only the parts of the need-satisfaction process to meet the purpose of their specific sales call, at what speed they will cover all the steps of the need-satisfaction process, and what will be included in their closing. As shown in the figure above, the factors that influence the design of the sales call are as follows:

- **Time to Decision.** When will the customer make the award or choose their supplier
- **Small or Large.** Length of sales cycle, risk of mistakes, number of people involved, and size of commitment
- **Sales Activity.** Is the salesperson prospecting, qualifying, conducting a sales meeting, presenting proposals, or following-up
- **Opportunity Management Stage.** Account profile, identification of the compelling event, evaluation of options, submission of proposal, resolution of concerns, negotiations, monitoring, outcome analysis, implementation, or project review

Chapter Highlight 7.1: Fit for Purpose: I Will Take One of These, These, and These (cont.)

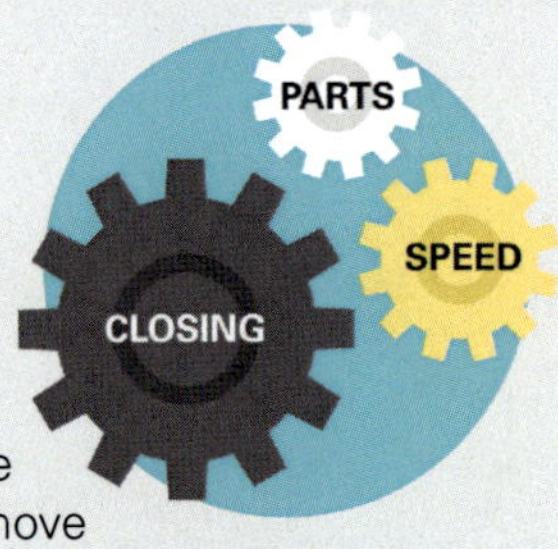

How the number of parts, speed, and closing are designed is explained below.

Parts

Preliminaries: Every sales call will begin with preliminaries to start the conversation and build rapport with the customer. The time spent on preliminaries varies depending on many factors, including culture.

Opening: Start the business discussion of the meeting. Every sales call will have an opening. Then, depending on the factors shown above, the salesperson may move to probing or supporting.

Probing: Asking questions and listening to discover needs of the customer. In smaller sales, the salesperson normally will go through each one of the need-satisfaction process steps in one meeting. Alternatively, they can collect the customer requirements and return with a proposal, at which time they would then support. Larger sales following the opportunities management process will have several sales meetings where the salesperson will only probe to discover needs for each of the people in the buying center. After this and selecting their competitive sales strategy, they will then have sales calls to support without the need to probe.

Supporting: Matching customer needs to your product and services. As stated above, small sales normally go through all the stages. In some B2B sales, the collection of customer requirements (probing) can be done by one group, such as online ordering, and then another group or salesperson will support and close. In larger sales as mentioned above, the supporting only happens after the sales team has met with all the buying center members and understands their needs, their competitive sales strategy is selected considering the competition's strategy. In large sales, not every sales call will have supporting. In fact, a problem for some salespeople is supporting too soon. This will be discussed in more detail in the supporting section.

Closing: Asking for the customer's commitment. Every sales call will have a closing.

Speed

The timing for how fast each part of the need-satisfaction process is covered is dependent on if the sale is large or small and the time left before the customer makes a purchase decision. In small B2B sales, the entire need-satisfaction process can be done in one sales call. The sales call could be carried out via the telephone, email, or web or in the customer's office. Large B2B sales can take from months to years, with the formal closing asking for the award happening as part of the customer's RFP process. If a customer needs to make a decision fast, the entire need-satisfaction process can be accelerated, even in a large sale. For example, the customer has a crisis and needs to fix the problem as soon as possible. In this situation, the salesperson could go to the customer's office and find all the buying center members in the meeting room and then be asked to wait outside while they make a decision. The speed for which a sales cycle is completed is largely controlled by the customer's buying processes. For example, do they negotiate after an offer has been made? Do they have partners or reviewing departments? All these issues were discussed in Chapter 4 "Opportunities Management."

Closing

In the closing, the salesperson concludes the meeting and agrees on the action items to be addressed after the meeting. Depending on the factors shown in the figure above, the closing can range from checking to see if the customer needs anything else to asking for the customer's commitment to award the work to the salesperson. In small sales, the closing is asking for the customer to buy your products or services. In larger sales, most closings are actions that will lead to the customer or buying center being convinced your offer is the best once they review your proposal and notify you of their decision.

Each one of the factors in the chapter highlight will be discussed in detail later in the chapter. The purpose of the highlight is to emphasize that not every step of the need-satisfaction process will be used in every sales call, but every successful sales outcome will have included each step of the need-satisfaction process. The sales call must be tailored to fit the purpose of the sales call.

Sales Call Preparation Worksheet

BUYING CENTER PROFILE

Date: 10/3 **Account:** BOC **Opportunity:** Exploration Program – wireline

Stage: Evaluation of options – early **Competitive Strategy:** Flanking – Alter

Reviewed Account Corporate Profile? ☑ Yes ☐ No Project part of BOC objective to improve reserves in region.

Contact	Position	Role	Social Style	Technology Adoption
B. Brown	Drilling Mgr	Decision-maker	Driver/Analytical	Conservative

CRM Database up-to-date and complete? ☑ Yes ☐ No Need to check social media for additional insights.

ALIGNING STRATEGIES

	Driver	Expressive	Amiable	Analytical
Preliminaries: Quick reference to Bruins, as he is a Bruins hockey fan.				
Likes	Control	Social	Supportive	Detailed
Opening Aligning Strategy: Proven techniques for his consideration.				
Measures personal value by	Power Results	Applause Support	Approval Attention	Respect Activity
Probing Aligning Strategy: Start with customer lead probing to get his view.				
Needs environment	Responds	Inspires to their goals	Suggests	Provides details
Supporting Aligning Strategy: References.				
Support their	Conclusions and actions	Dreams and intuitions	Relationships	Principles
Closing Aligning Strategy: If meeting goes well ask for his recommendation for next steps or ask for support.				
For decisions give them	Options and probabilities	Testimony incentives	Guarantees and assurances	Evidence and service
Take time to be	Efficient	Stimulating	Agreeable	Accurate

Fig. 7.3
Sales call preparation worksheet buying center profile and aligning sections.

people who join you on the sales call and to keep a record of sales calls made for a specific opportunity.

Setting the Sales Call Objective

Each sales call will have a specific purpose, tactics, and objective. The purpose is what you as the salesperson want to achieve on the sales call. As a result of your purpose, you will execute one or more sales call tactics to achieve the objective of the sales call. The objective is what you want the customer to agree to at the end of the sales call. The relationship between purpose, tactic, and objectives is shown in **Fig. 7.4.**

For example, when the sales activity is "Present Proposal," the opportunity management stage is "Resolution of Concerns" and the competitive sales strategy is "Frontal Solution." The purpose of the sales call could be to secure the opportunity, but in this scenario, your solution is not the cheapest. In this case, your sales call tactic would have to be "Prove Value" to justify the premium price. The objective would be to have the customer acknowledge the value and issue a purchase order for your products or services.

Fig. 7.4
Purpose, Tactic, and Objective.

One of your key decisions in the opportunities management process is to select the appropriate competitive sales strategy as discussed in Chapter 4 "Opportunities Management" and then decide which tactics to use. Common tactics for the sales call are shown in the sidebar "What is Your Purpose? Are You Tactful?" The execution of a successful opportunity plan includes all these tactics. **Chapter Highlight 7.2** shows some common purposes, tactics, and objectives for each of the sales activities and opportunities management stages.

For each sales call, there must be a purpose and clear objective as well as backup objective. Your backup objective is a lesser next-step commitment. This is your fall-back position if you don't accomplish your primary objective when the customer is reluctant to commit to your primary objective.

The process used to select your specific sales call objectives begins with making a list of all the specific actions the customer could take as a result of you successfully executing your sales call tactic. Then rank the list in order from the most feasible and desirable to the least feasible and desirable. Next, select the best action as your primary objective and your second highest ranked action as your backup objective. The feasibility factor is a function of the following:

- Contact's social profile
- Buying center role
- Procurement process being followed by the account for the opportunity
- Phase of the opportunity management process

An example of a completed objectives section is shown in **Fig. 7.5** and the actions section is shown in **Fig. 7.6**. With the objectives set, the next step in the sales call

▶ ***What is Your Purpose? Are You Tactful?***

Every sales call has a purpose and objective. The purpose is described by the sales tactic and supports your sales call objectives.

Over the complete sales cycle, all the PRIME^{3} sales tactics should be completed, starting first with Retrieve Information. If the salesperson has proved value, minimized weaknesses, and emphasized strengths, then they are insulated against the competition.

Being insulated against the competition is very important in the late

stages of an opportunity. The reason is when the customer makes the final decision in large sales, the salesperson will not be in the office of the customer in most cases. Therefore, it is essential that the customer be able to recall the reasons why he or she should choose you over the competition. If so, then you are insulated against the competition.

During the procurement stages, it is a good practice to visit the customer and review your proposal to reinforce (support) why your proposal is the best option for them.

Chapter Highlight 7.2: Sales Call Purpose, Tactics, and Objectives

Sales Activity	Opportunity Mgmt. Process	Purpose	Tactic	Objective
Prospecting	Account Profile	Understand what drives the account.	Retrieve information.	Customer agrees to meeting to determine needs.
Qualification	Identification of Compelling Event	Fully qualify the compelling event and determine if the project is worth winning. Determine buying center participants.	Retrieve information.	Customer to agree to accept proposal. Customer to agree to introduce key buying center members.
	Evaluation of Options			
Sales Meetings	Early Stages	Contact buying center members to determine decision criteria and evaluation model; determine can we win, can we compete.	Retrieve information.	Customer agrees to contact references to validate features and benefits.
	Middle Stage	Formulate strategy that maximizes perceived fit Select competitive strategy.	Prove value. Emphasize strengths. Minimize weaknesses.	Gain customer's agreement on value of features and benefits of solution.
	Late Stage	Demonstrate advantages of solution to buying center members. Apply relationship strategies.	Prove value. Emphasize strengths. Minimize weaknesses. Insulate against competition.	Confirm all needs have been addressed and no other questions or issues to be discussed.
	Procurement Phase			
Present Proposals	Submit Proposal	Submit organized proposal with clear value proposition statement and required information for each of the main buying center participants.	Prove value. Emphasize strengths. Minimize weaknesses. Insulate against competition.	Review proposal; answer any questions or concerns.
	Resolution of Concerns	Seek out risk and consequences that the buying center has and work to resolve them.	Prove value. Emphasize strengths. Minimize weaknesses. Insulate against competition.	Customer to confirm all questions and concerns have been addressed.
	Negotiations	Agree on final terms and conditions. Win-win agreement. Strengthen the relationship.	Emphasize strengths. Minimize weaknesses.	Customer to agree to terms and conditions of negotiated agreement.
	Monitor	Be prepared for late procurement phase tactics by competitor, customer and your attack strategies if required.	Emphasize strengths. Minimize weaknesses. Insulate against competition.	No further questions or concerns.
Follow Up	Outcome Analysis	Understand final decision and lessons learned.	Retrieve information.	Customer award to you.
	Implementation	Deliver on promises made. Strengthen the relationship.	Prove value. Emphasize strengths. Minimize weaknesses. Insulate against competition.	Confirm customer satisfaction with products and services. Customer to provide referrals and references as appropriate. Confirm customer satisfaction with handling problems and successes.
	Performance Review	Capture lessons learned and best practices. Reinitiate selling process.	Retrieve information. Prove value. Emphasize strengths. Minimize weaknesses.	Confirm product and services delivered, as promised. Confirm future needs of customer.

Sales Call Preparation Worksheet

Actions the *customer* should undertake to achieve the sales call tactics:	D Desirable	F Feasible	R Ranking
Agree to value as calculated and support decision to use BHA; support running demo job.	**High** Med Low	**High** Med Low	1
Agree to verify claims with internal groups.	High **Med** Low	**High** Med Low	2
Agree to verify claims with references.	High **Med** Low	High **Med** Low	4
Agree to review calculations used; contact later to verify.	High Med **Low**	**High** Med Low	5
Agree to BHA logging string but not to other benefits.	High Med **Low**	**High** Med Low	6
Agree to mobilization plans but not to BHA benefits.	High Med **Low**	High **Med** Low	9
Agree to pass information with one of their reports and set up contact.	High Med **Low**	**High** Med Low	8
Actions *you* could undertake to achieve the sales call tactics:			
Make presentation to drilling group on rig reduction ideas and mobilization plan.	**High** Med Low	**High** Med Low	3
Arrange shop tour and meeting with proposed rig personnel.	**High** Med Low	High Med **Low**	10
Meet with any suggested contacts.	High **Med** Low	**High** Med Low	7
	High Med Low	High Med Low	
	High Med Low	High Med Low	
	High Med Low	High Med Low	

Fig. 7.6

Example of a completed sales call worksheet actions section. The two top-ranked actions are selected as the main objective and backup objective for the sales call. However, depending on how the sales call progresses, the sales representative may ask for one of the lower-ranked objectives.

Sales Call Tactic(s):

- ✔ Prove value
- ☐ Retrieve information
- ☐ Insulate against competition
- ☐ Minimize weaknesses
- ✔ Emphasize strengths

Sales Call Primary Objective: 1. Get agreement on rig time savings for Big Hole Logging service. 2. Check for acceptance of emergency package and mobilization plan.

Backup Objective: Have Brown contact reference to confirm value. Agree to follow-up meeting.

Fig. 7.5

Example of a completed sales call objectives section.

planning process is to prepare your preliminaries and opening statements for the sales call. Both of these steps could be conducted over the telephone or via e-mail to schedule a sales call visit with the customer. Good objectives are well defined and very specific. Once you have your objectives set, ensure that they pass the SMART test as described the sidebar "SMART Objectives."

Preliminaries

This is the initial part of the discussion between you and the customer. The goal of the preliminaries is to reduce the tension levels to a level appropriate for the business discussion, as discussed in Chapter 5 "Communication Skills." The length and style of this phase of the conversation depends on relevant cultural norms and expectations. It will also be dependent on the individual customer's personality, as described by the person's social profile. Amiable and Expressive customers will engage in the preliminaries longer than Drivers and Analyticals. Most customers will give you a clear sign, either verbally or by using body language, when they want to begin the business discussion. Be alert for these signals.

Greeting

The greeting is very important as it sets the tone of the meeting. If this is the first contact with the customer it will also make your first impression, which of course you want to be positive. The greeting communicates a lot more than hello. It is also how the greeting is sent with body language, tone, and words.

When greeting the customer in person, arrive early and be dressed appropriately for the visit. When welcoming the customer, stand up straight, use their full name and thank them for taking time to visit with you. The last part of the greeting is the business card exchange.

▶ *SMART Objectives*

There is no argument when it comes to making your objectives SMART. If you Google SMART objectives, you will find lots of variations to choose from. A proven SMART test is below:

- **S**pecific actions to be taken.
- **M**easurable outcome that demonstrates the objective has been achieved.
- **A**ccountable. Someone is responsible to complete the objective.
- **R**ealistic. It is good to have stretch objectives but only if they can be realistically achieved.
- **T**ime bound. The objective has to be completed by a specific date.

If your objectives pass the SMART test, you won't look stupid.

▶ ***Preliminaries***

Goal

The goal of the preliminaries is to reduce the tension levels to a level appropriate for the business discussion.

When

The first part of the contact with the customer

How

- Greeting.
- Rapport building.
- Tell what you have done to prepare.
- Check for timing.
- Permission to take notes.

Rapport Building

Rapport building for some people can be confusing in not knowing who should lead this part of the preliminaries. It depends on the customers—your lead depends on the person's social style, as mentioned earlier.

The purpose of rapport building is to get the conversation started. Ask non-threatening culturally appropriate questions. Some examples are:

- How long have you been with the company or this department or in this position?
- Do you have family here?
- Ask questions or make comments regarding economy, industry, business, sports, or entertainment events.
- Compliment them on a recent accomplishment or milestone.
- Comment on obvious mentionable characteristics: model cars on front of the desk, a picture with a famous person, dogs on their computer screen.
- Use the person's full name (i.e., Mr. Smith). Start formal until invited to be less formal.

Tell What You Have Done to Prepare

Telling what you have done to prepare gives you credibility and helps the customer feel more comfortable with what you say. The customer will appreciate the fact that you have invested some of your time for this meeting and make them feel important. In some situations, the customer may also suggest other sources or contacts that you can use for future calls when preparing. If this part of the sales call is being conducted over the telephone or by e-mail, they may also suggest you do some other preparation to help make the visit more productive.

Check for Timing

Confirm how much time the customer has for this visit. Even if the visit was agreed upon via telephone or e-mail, always check once in the customer's office. It is better to adjust the sales call at the start then have the customer excuse themselves in the middle of the call before you have covered your critical points.

Permission to Take Notes

Always ask permission to take notes and offer to make a copy for the customer at the end of the sales call. This is essential when you are using the sales call worksheets, which will be discussed later in this chapter. To do this, you will need to explain the form being used and why and ask if they would like a copy at the end of the meeting. For example:

Salesperson: "Is it okay that I takes notes during our meeting?"

Customer: "Yes, no problem."

Salesperson: "I will use a Project Solution Worksheet, which helps me not miss any important details about your project. If you want, at the end, I can make you a copy."

Customer: "Yes, I would like a copy. Thank you."

When this phase of the conversation is complete, begin the business discussion by starting the next step of the sales call process: the opening. Shown in **Fig. 7.7** is a completed preliminary section from the sales call preparation worksheet.

PRELIMINARIES

Business Card ✔ Rapport Hockey game Bruins Preparation Reviewed last project Time 1 hr. Notes ______

Fig. 7.7
Sales call preparation worksheet preliminaries section.

Opening

The goal in opening is to reach an agreement with the customer on what will be covered or accomplished during the call. A meeting is opened after the preliminaries.

▶ ***Opening a Sales Call***

Goal

To agree on what will be covered or accomplished.

When

At the beginning of the sales call.

How

- After preliminaries.
- Propose an agenda.
- State the value proposition.
- Check for acceptance.
- Check for customer's agenda.

Propose an Agenda

Propose an agenda by saying how and what you would like to do or accomplish during the call. This sets a clear direction for the conversation. An example of a proposed agenda statement is:

"What I'd like to do today is discuss (how) with you some technology my company has developed for horizontal wells" (what).

The **how** part of the agenda is to let the customer know how you want to hold the communication and what your medium will be. For example, you might want to make a presentation, have the customer meet an expert you have brought along, or review a proposal. The **what** part of the agenda tells what, in general terms, you want to discuss. After the agenda, state the value proposition for the customer.

State the Value Proposition

By stating the value proposition, you get the customer's attention and prepare them to listen. The value has to be believable, relevant to the customer's field of experience, and presented in terms the customer can appreciate. In your value proposition statement, you might say:

"I believe you can reduce your drilling costs by 10% to 15%." The value proposition needs to be short and describe what your product and services mean to the customer as discussed in Chapter 6 (see the discussion on the Value Stairs).

In Chapter 1, buyer behavior was classified into four buyer groups: price, value, relationship, and convenience. One of the reasons value and relationship buyers migrate to price buyers is a lack of customer focus from salespeople. By clearly stating in your value proposition statement how your products or services will impact the customer's value drivers, you make clear the added value your company provides. Once you have stated your value proposition, you then ask for feedback by checking for acceptance.

Checking for Acceptance and Checking for Customer's Agenda

After proposing an agenda and stating the value, use the skill of confirming and make sure the customer accepts the agenda you have proposed and does not have anything to add or have his own agenda for the meeting. You might say:

"How does that sound?" or "Is there something else you'd like to cover?"

Checking for the customer's agenda demonstrates to the customer that you are also concerned about what they want, not just what you need. It also takes into consideration that in many situations with your customers, you have an ongoing business relationship or active projects they may want you to address while you are visiting with them. If the customer does have some additional items to be discussed, then decide with the customer the order in which the issues will be discussed.

▶ No, I'm Sorry, I Don't Have Time to Visit with You Today

A common mistake for many sales representatives is to state their sales call objective in the value proposition statement. Take the first example cited, but re-stated another way:

Sales representative: "I would like to visit with you to discuss our new technology. I think you should run it on this well."

Customer: "No, I'm sorry I don't have time to visit with you today."

In this exchange, the sales representative has just asked for the customer's time and only mentioned the sales representative's benefit—the customer agreeing to run the new tool. In most cases, this is not a very compelling reason for the customer to give you the time to meet with them.

With acceptance at this point, you start to deliver your message and hold the intended sales discussion. If the customer does not accept the agenda, use clarifying and confirming techniques to understand why. A common problem with new salespeople is that instead of stating the value proposition, they describe their objective for the sales call. However, the customer may not agree to the meeting, especially if the individual has other priorities. Remember that the purpose of the sales call is to have the customer agree to the objective at the end of the sales meeting in the closing. See the sidebar, "No, I'm Sorry, I Don't Have Time to Visit with You Today," for how not to open a sales call meeting.

Planning for the Preliminaries and Opening

Planning for the opening consists of four parts:

- Aligning strategies
- Ideas for preliminaries
- The agenda
- Value proposition

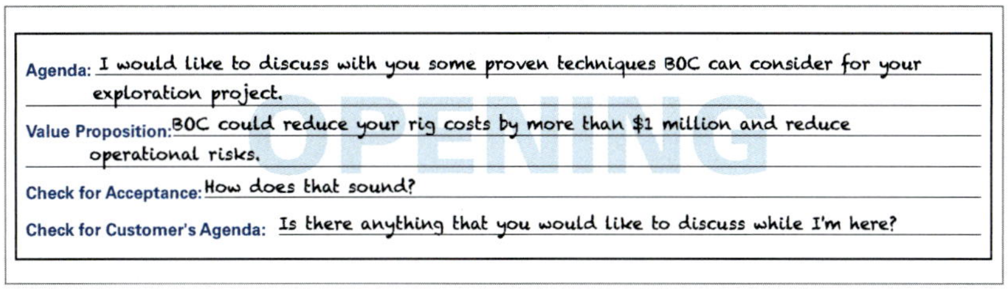

Fig. 7.8
Sales call preparation worksheet opening planning section.

Figure 7.8 shows a completed opening section of the sales call preparation worksheet. The four-step opening process is listed on the left-hand side.

Preliminaries

In this section, list ideas for discussion topics to use in the preliminaries stage before the opening. If you have met with the customer earlier, you should be familiar with the person's hobbies, interests, etc. Consider the customer's social profile. For some customers, the preliminaries may be no more than your personal introduction.

Agenda

In the agenda section, write what you are going to tell the customer. The reason for thinking about this prior to setting up the sales call is to ensure that you do not state your sales call objective and get an early rejection, as described in the previous sidebar.

Value Proposition

Write what you will explain as the value proposition. As discussed in Chapter 2 "Value Drivers," the value proposition statement clearly communicates how your services or products impact the customer's targeted value drivers or critical success factors. The value proposition can address the customer's corporate, project, or personal objectives. Stating the value proposition lets the customer know how the meeting will be useful, and further establishes your focus.

Check for Acceptance and Check for Customer's Agenda

In the check for acceptance section, write your confirming statement for the opening. A good practice is to check with the customer to see if there are any other issues the person wants to discuss in the sales call.

Sales Call Discussion

In the discussion part of the sales call, deliver a clear message—supporting your objective for the sales call. The communication skills used in the discussion part of the sales call are as follows:

- Probing
- Supporting
- Handling customer rejection (next chapter)

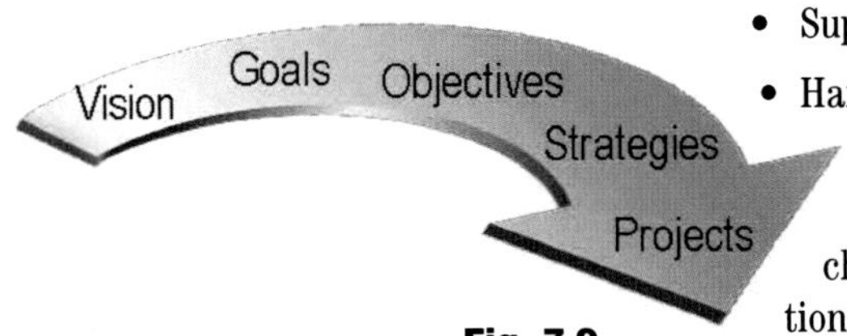

Fig. 7.9
The drivers of customer requirements. The corporate vision establishes the corporate goals. Goals establish corporate objectives and strategies for achieving the objectives. Typically, the objectives will result in projects being initiated. Once the projects have been initiated, the project requirements are established. It is critical for the sales representative to fully understand the connection from the corporate vision through to project requirements before beginning the selling process.

In all of the sales conversations you will have, whether it be probing, supporting, or handling negative reactions, always ensure that you are checking with the customer. Confirm and clarify throughout the conversations, and never assume that you know what the customer means if they make a vague statement or they understand what you have stated. Continuous checking will keep both you and the customer engaged throughout the conversation.

For a successful sales call discussion, you must anticipate how the customer will react to your message and be prepared to support and address any rejection behavior. This is done by preparing probing and supporting strategies and presentation materials that are customized for the specific customer you are meeting, based on the individual's profile (i.e., position, role, social style, and technology adoption). The specifics of how to handle customer rejection is the topic of the next chapter.

Probing

Prior to the sales call, prepare probing strategies based on your sales call purpose. To assist you in planning your probing strategy, review the opportunity management process and tactics listed in Chapter Highlight 7.1. Even in simple or smaller sales situations, apply the same probing strategies to make certain you understand the customer's business drivers and requirements. The only difference in a simple sales situation is the size of the sales team and less time involved to retrieve the information. In some cases, it may be as short as a one meeting. The challenge is always to make the connection between what you are providing to satisfy the customer's requirements and the higher-level goals and objectives that create the requirements. **Figure 7.9** illustrates the connection between the corporate vision and requirements.

Understanding this relationship is the first priority of any probing strategy. When you understand the goals, objectives, and strategies driving the project, you will be in a better position to propose a solution that best satisfies the requirements and contributes to the project strategies and objectives.

▶ ***Probing***

Goal

To build a clear, complete, mutual understanding of the customer's needs

When

You want to elicit information from a customer.

How

Use open and closed probes to explore the customer's:

- Circumstances.
- Requirements.

Open probe: Encourages a free response

Closed probe: Limits a response

Use *confirming and clarifying* after giving or receiving information.

Probing to Uncover Customer Requirements

When you understand the relationship between the business drivers and the project requirements, your goal in probing is to build a clear and complete mutual understanding of a customer's requirements. This means that you understand the objectives, concerns, or issues associated with those requirements. In probing, you may uncover many wants or problems that may not be connected to requirements. The customer may be telling you what is wrong, but does not want to take action or spend resources to change. By understanding the strategies and objectives for a project, you will be in a better position to identify what the real requirements are and where your can impact the value drivers. For example, a discussion between a salesperson and customer could proceed in the following way:

Salesperson: "What are your requirements for the program?" *(open probe)*

Customer: "A cheap, basic evaluation." *(requirement)*

Salesperson: "Why is that?" *(open probe, clarify)*

Customer: "The wells are low producers and we have to keep our costs under control in order to make a profit." *(strategy)*

Salesperson: "What are your profitability targets?" *(closed probe, clarify)*

Customer: "For this field, we want to keep our lifting costs at or below $3.50 per barrel." *(higher level objective)*

Salesperson: "Is that a corporate objective?" *(closed probe, clarify)*

Customer: "Kind of. The company has a goal of reducing lifting costs by 20% over the next five years in order to improve profitability by 10% over the same time period, so this is our target." *(business goal)*

In the above discussion, the salesperson does an excellent job of probing. The probing reveals a vague requirement, "cheap basic evaluation," and discovers that the strategy for the project is to lower the lifting costs to the target objective, driven by the corporate goal to improve profitability. The salesperson now understands that lifting costs and profitability are very important value drivers, in addition to the customer's basic evaluation. The salesperson still needs to probe to fully understand all the issues, concerns, and circumstances regarding the requirements of the evaluation. However, the salesperson can now explore all the possibilities of how he or she can provide a basic evaluation and help lower the customer's lifting costs and increase profitability—a total solution.

In addition to the business requirements, strategies, and objectives, the salesperson must also consider the customer's personal objectives and requirements. It is important to understand how the results of the project will affect the customer's personal objectives and strategies for success. The salesperson might ask:

Salesperson: "Do you personally have any concerns or expectations about the project?" *(close probe)*

Customer: "Yes, I have a big concern. Half my bonus is tied to lowering the lifting costs by 20%." *(personal objective)*

Salesperson: "Wow! That is a pretty serious objective." *(confirming)*

Customer: "Yes, and I will make it!" *(clarifying)*

Salesperson: "Anything else? *(closed probe)*

Customer: "Well yes, now that you ask. I don't want any problems this time. The last project in this field was plagued with major cost overruns and I looked pretty bad. I don't want that to happen again." *(personal strategy for success)*

The above exchange gives the salesperson the personal requirements of the customer that will also play an important part in the decision process. The salesperson has a good idea of the business and personal requirements he or she will have to address to secure the project.

One of the most effective probing techniques is the visualizing probe. There are two types of visualizing probes: open and closed (see sidebar "Two Types of Probes").

> **▶ Two Types of Probes: Long Version and Short Version**
>
> **Open Probes**
> - Encourages free response
> - Long version
>
> Visualizing open probe:
> Understand the customer's vision of success from his or her point of view and gain a deeper understanding of the client's primary objectives.
> - Short Version
>   - What can you tell me about your project?
>
> **Closed Probes**
> - Limits response to:
>   - Yes or no, choice among alternatives.
>   - Closed probe to confirm need.
> - Long Version
>
> Visualizing closed probe:
> Helps client draw conclusions.
> - Short Version
>   - Very effective if the customer has provided information by first using the open probe.
>   - When the customer has finished talking, ask "Is there anything else?"

Open Visualizing Probe

An open visualizing probe asks the customer to visualize what the ideal situation would look like or consist of. For example, after the opening, an effective first probe is:

"Can you describe for me what are the key factors for success in this project?"

Or

"Can you prioritize for me what the key factors for success are as you see them?"

This probe will usually get the customer to describe several of the key factors. When the customer stops talking, an effective yet simple closed probe is:

"I see. Anything else?"

If there is anything else to add, the customer will usually describe it at this time. If not, the customer will simply say:

"No, that about sums it up."

Closed Visualizing Probe

Another version of the visualizing probe is the closed visualizing probe. As you uncover the customer's requirements, it is helpful to show how your benefits will satisfy a requirement. You can do this with closed probes that allow the customer to visualize and acknowledge the outcome you have in mind.

"What if we could complete this for you in five business days? Would that help?" Or, *"If you could relieve your rig manager of routine supervisory tasks, would that allow them to focus on the more important issues?"*

The second type of closed visualizing probes encourages the customer to picture or imagine resulting benefits. For example:

"Picture how strong a position you'd be in with clear data showing exactly how much gas you are making from each zone." Or, *"Can you imagine what these integrated services efficiencies could do for your bottom line?"*

Planning a Probing Strategy

To make the most of what you know, it is useful to create a sales call probing strategy based on your pre-call planning, as described earlier. A probing strategy is simply a sequence of probes you can use to structure your questions. Probes help the customer recognize and confirm requirements you can satisfy. There are two types of probing strategies classified based on who is leading the discussion, the customer or the salesperson. Each is appropriate for specific sales call situations. The first probing strategy is the customer lead probing strategy.

Customer Lead Probing Strategy[4]

The customer lead probing strategy is used when the salesperson asks questions based on customer feedback. It can be considered more of an exploring probing technique from the customer's perspective. The customer lead probing strategy is based on SPIN© probing strategy developed by N. Rackham. Rackham's research was discussed earlier regarding the relative importance of the need-satisfaction process components for large and small sales. Another very important

▶ *Customer Lead Probing*

When

You want the customer to guide the conversation to discover facts and requirements about the opportunity.

How

Use open and closed probes to discover:

- Situational information of the customer's business.
- Problems or opportunities.
- Implication of the problem or opportunity.
- Need payoff of addressing the problem.

factor discovered in Rackham's research was the way successful salespeople probed in B2B sales. The title of his book, *SPIN Selling*, is the acronym for the probing strategy Rackham says most successful salespersons use. His research concluded that effective probing consists of the probes described in **Fig. 7.10.**

The SPIN probing strategy follows the opportunities management process. In the early phase of the opportunity management process, establish corporate goals, objectives, and strategies, or what Rackham calls "S," Situation probes. Next, identify the compelling event, which corresponds to the "P" or Problem probes in the SPIN strategy. At this point, you are confirming that the problem exists and the customer considers the problem or opportunity to be serious enough to take action to address it. Next are the "I," Implication probes, which correspond to the evaluation of options phase. Using these probes, position or align your offering in

Probe	Characteristics
Situation	• Achieve fact-finding objectives, client's business scenario • Have low selling impact • Useful in the Account Corporate Profile phase of the opportunities management process
Problem/ Opportunity	• Uncovering dissatisfaction or opportunity objectives • The client's current performance • Have moderate selling impact • Useful in the Identification of Compelling Event phase of the opportunities management process
Implication	• Achieve objectives of developing and aligning your offering to address dissatisfaction of opportunity • The implications of the current performance • Have high selling impact • Useful in the Evaluation of Options phase of the opportunities management process
Need Payoff	• Achieve objectives of rehearsing and selectively focusing customer attention • The client's suggestion and thoughts on what to improve and how to do it • Have high selling impact • Useful in the late stages of the Evaluation of Options phase and in the Procurement phase of the opportunities management process

Fig. 7.10
SPIN probing strategy. The SPIN probing strategy suggests that you should start with the situation questions, then proceed to the problem questions and implication questions, and finish with the need payoff. Once you have reached this stage, you are then ready for the demonstrating capabilities stage of the selling process.

the best way, so the perceived fit is considered a good fit to the customer's requirements. In the last probing stage of the SPIN strategy, use the "N," Need payoff probes that get agreement from the customer on the benefits received from using your products and services.

Example of a customer lead probing sequence:

Situation: "What can you tell me about your project?"

Problem: "As you see it now, what are your critical challenges or success factors?"

Implication:	"What if these factors are not addressed? What is the impact **to your project?**"
Need Payoff:	"What is the benefit if these factors are correctly handled?"

Another way to use the customer lead probing is to classify information as the customer responds to your questions. For example: You ask the customer "What can you tell me about your project?" and they say "The last time we ran over budget by 15%, and that was a disaster!" From this reply, even though the salesperson was asking for situational information, what the customer responded back with was implication. In this situation, the salesperson would recognize they have implication information, but no situation or problem information. Therefore, the salesperson would go backwards in the model and ask "And what caused that?" (a problem question). If the customer responds, "It was the lost circulation zone that we spent five days trying to fish the stuck tool from," now the salesperson knows what caused the problem and could ask, "So this year you want to ensure you have a plan to deal with the lost circulation zone, so you do not over-spend your budget fishing?" This is a need-payoff probe. If the customer confirms the need payoff, the salesperson can then go back to the first question again and ask what else the customer can tell them about the project to discover the situational information.

By classifying the information as the conversation progresses, it becomes very easy for the salesperson to stay at level 1 listening.

▶ ***Sales Lead Probing***

When

You want to guide the conversation to address anticipated problems and needs.

How

Use open and closed probes to:

- Determine that the problem or need exists.
- Quantify/qualify the situation.
- Identify consequences of inaction.
- Confirm willingness to look/listen.

Sales Lead Probing Strategy [5, 6]

The second probing strategy is used when the salesperson wants to lead the discussion and have the customer recognize and confirm needs you can satisfy for them. In this probing strategy, the salesperson leads by asking a set of pre-planned questions. This technique was developed by Learning International and evolved from the original Xerox Persuasive Communication Skills program **(Fig. 7.11).** The salesperson asks questions that:

- Determine a possible problem or requirement exists.
- Quantify/qualify the problem, learning additional facts.
- Identify consequences of failing to solve the problem or meeting the requirement.
- Confirm the customer's willingness to listen to, or look at, relevant features and benefits.

This technique is particularly useful for difficult situations when the customer may be indifferent or when your company is not well known by the account. It is also recommended when you suspect a problem or need exists, but the customer has not raised this as being a requirement or issue. Your first step is to verify your assumption by starting with an open probe. This lets the customer give you as much or as little information as they want to provide. For example:

"Since that zone is likely to be over pressured, how do you plan to drill it?"

Or

"I know a lot of local operators have been running into problems associated with abnormal overpressure. What has been your experience?"

Phrase your probe tactfully. Be sure your probe does not imply poor customer performance. Once you are sure a problem or need exists, continue probing to clarify the issue for yourself and the customer. If the customer does not have the need or problem anticipated, do not try to address it. Instead, probe for other needs or problems.

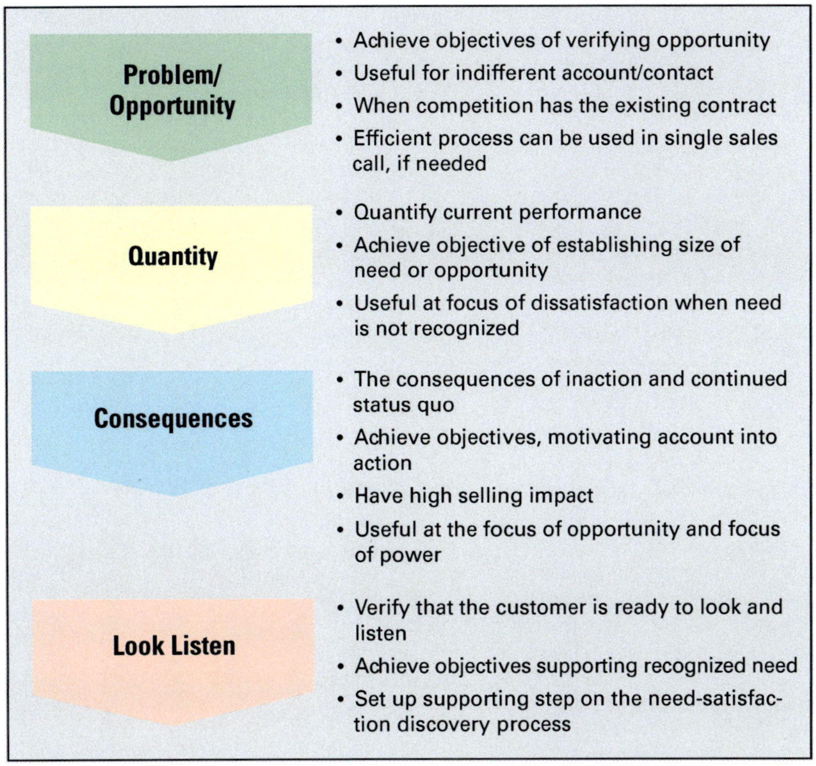

Fig. 7.11
Sales lead probing strategy.

Once you have confirmed that the problem or requirement exists, use open and closed probes to confirm additional details in quantifiable, measurable terms. Mutual understanding of the situation's size and scope helps you focus on what your company can do to help. Ask questions that define the size and scope, such as:

- "When does it occur?"
- "How frequently does that happen?"
- "How much does that cost you?"

With the size of the problem identified, ask questions to confirm the consequences of inaction as well as the potential cost of letting needs go unmet and problems unsolved. Consequence probes help you and the customer focus on these risks and costs. By doing so, the questions build momentum to take action. There are many ways to phrase consequence questions. For example:

- "What would happen if you did not?"
- "What are the potential cost consequences if you don't?"

Sometimes, your consequence probes include a viewpoint the customer may not have considered. For example:

- "Let's say the zone doesn't turn out to be commercial. What does that do to your development program?"
- "Assume that 3D could turn up information confirming your original assumptions. If that were true, how would you calculate the cost of not having that information?"

Once you have a complete understanding of the need or problem and the importance to take action, confirm the customer's willingness to look at or listen to suggestions that will address the issue. For example:

- "Would you be willing to look at some ideas about how to deal with that?"
- "I have an idea that should take care of the problem. Can you discuss it?"

You may also want to use a visualizing question to confirm the customer's interest in discussing features and benefits. For example:

- "If you could do away with that entire contamination problem, would you want to know how that works?"
- "Let's assume I could show you potential efficiencies that can address the cost-reduction objectives you've been discussing. Would you like to look at some specific examples of how an integrated services approach will bring down the total cost?"

Once the customer has expressed a desire to hear how you can address the issue being discussed, use the step of supporting, which is discussed in the next section.

Combining both probing strategies can be effective. Use sales lead probing as a backup to customer lead probing, if the customer does not raise the requirements you expected.

As a general rule, early in the opportunities management process strategy, as you gather and improve your understanding of the customer's situation, use customer lead probing and requirements. Later in the evaluation of options phase, as you begin to build your ideas and solution for the customer, confirm your solution by leading the discussion. However, as mentioned above, a customer may be indifferent to using your company. In these cases, as a backup to customer lead probes, use more specific probes to confirm an opportunity or requirement the customer has not raised. **Figure 7.12** illustrates the process to follow.

Fig. 7.12
Probing options during the of the sales call. The figure illustrates the options available to the sales representative when probing. The preferred pattern is to start by using a customer lead probing strategy, usually with a visualizing open probe, to discover the customer's requirements. The sales representative can choose to fully develop the requirement and then support or fully develop the requirement before probing again to uncover more requirements and support all requirements in one step. Once it appears that the customer has no more requirements to offer, the sales representative may use a sales lead probing strategy if there are still some unrecognized requirements that your company can satisfy. In some situations, such as with an indifferent customer, the sales representative can also start by using a sales lead probing strategy. These types of negative reactions will be discussed in detail in the next chapter.

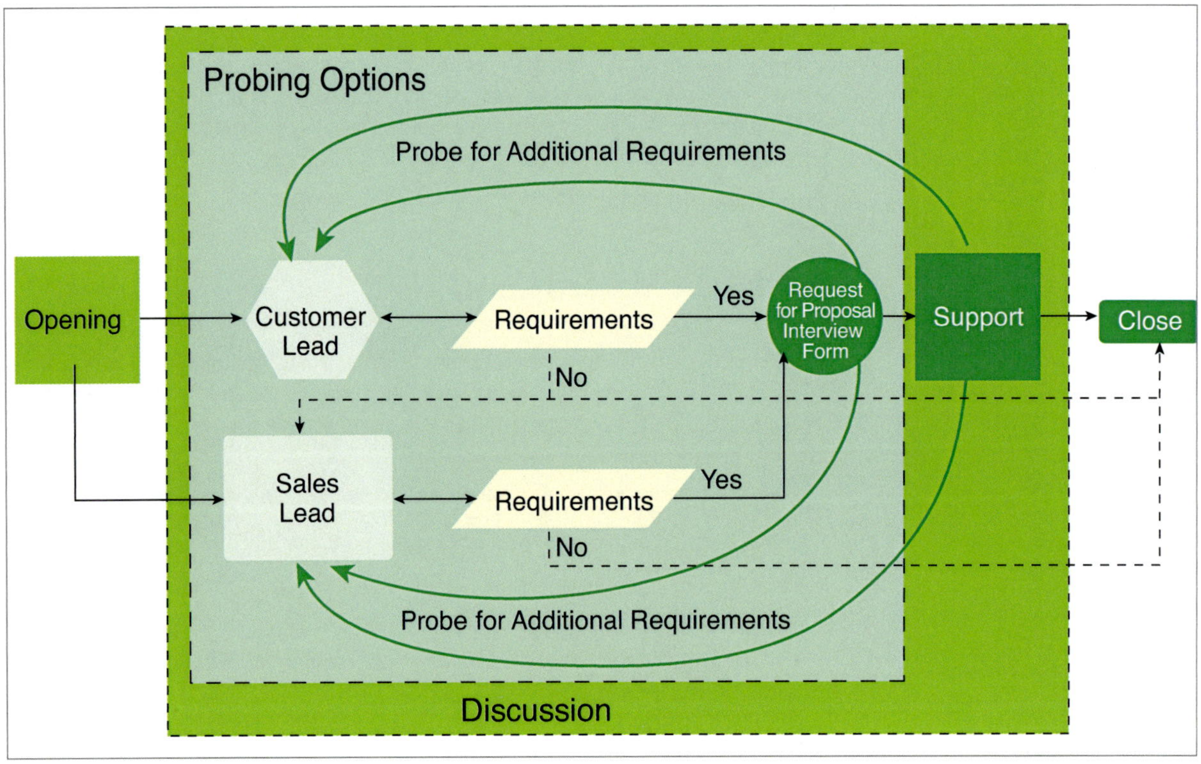

Preparing Probes

Prior to the sales call, complete the following five-step sales call preparation probing exercise:

1. Prepare a list of all the questions you would like to have answered.
2. Next, categorize the questions according to whether the questions are situa-

Questions you want to ask:	S Situations	P Problems	I Implication	N Need Payoff	✔ Answer
Where is this project in BOC's priorities?	•				
Are there any specific objectives you or your group have for this project?	•				
What is the cost for one day of rig time?			•		
What are your major concerns or issues for this project?		•			
Who will be involved in the selection of the logging company?	•				
Do you have any concerns about the project?		•			
Do you have any concerns about using my company?	•				
Do you believe there are advantages to combining multiple services from one company?				•	
If the project is delayed, what are the consequences?			•		
Are there any other ways the logging co. can assist BOC other than with logging services?		•			
Have you been involved in their projects? If so, which logging company did you use?	•				
How will you measure success for this project?				•	
What key operational metrics will you track for the project?				•	
What cost components make up one day of rig costs?	•				
Is there anything else I could do for you on this project?	•				
What is the budget for the project?	•				
Would you support a decision to use my company?	•				
Who will decide on the testing company?	•				

Questions Customer may want to ask you:
How many projects have you done like this?
What are the costs?
Can your competitors provide similar services?
Who else has used this technology?
What are our options if this fails?
Has anyone else from BOC used this?

Fig. 7.13
Sales call preparation worksheet questions section completed for the Chukchi Sea Exploration opportunity.

tion, problem or requirement, implication, or need payoff. **Fig. 7.13** is an example from the sales call preparation worksheet questions section.

3. Once you have completed the list of questions and categorized them. Review the lists to be sure that each type of question is asked, avoiding a high frequency of one type of question. As reported in the book *SPIN Selling*, implication and need-payoff types of questions have a higher correlation to successful selling.[4] Situation and problem questions do little to help customers solve problems or meet their objectives, so be efficient in gathering the situation and problem background information and move quickly to implication and need-payoff types of questions.

4. Prepare several general open probes to ask to make certain you uncover the required information you have listed in the first step and any other information the customer will offer that you have not thought of. The more general probes you should prepare are:

   - The visualizing open probe you will use at the start of the sales call.
   - Probes to find information about the customer's situation, problem or requirements, implication, and payoff used in the customer lead probing technique.
   - Probes used to confirm a problem or requirement, size of the problem, consequences of inaction, and more information in the salesperson lead probing technique.

With experience, you will develop a set of probes for each different situation that you will encounter and be able to reuse the next time you have a customer with a similar need or project. Two examples of effective visualizing open probes you can use in the majority of your sales calls are:

- "Can you prioritize for me the key success factors for this project?"
- "Can you describe to me the key issues for this project?"

Typically the response from the visualizing open probe will be sufficient to give you information regarding the situation and problem or requirements. If the customer has not answered all of your situation problem or requirement questions on your list, use the confirming and clarifying probes to ask the questions. From there, you can ask generic implication and payoff questions, such as:

- "For the most important factor you described, what would the implication be for the project if you didn't achieve this?" *(implication)*
- "For the most important factor you described, what is the measurable benefit if you achieve this?" *(payoff)*

If the customer does not offer a key factor that you believe is an important requirement, use the sales lead questioning technique to confirm this is a factor the customer should consider important.

By asking questions one step at a time and gaining agreement from the customer, you are adding value for the customer by helping them recognize important issues they were not aware of. This is one of the key aspects of the consultative selling approach. Once the customer confirms the need, you then ask the customer if they would like to hear more about how you can address this need.

For example, for an exploration project in which the salesperson is discussing the requirements for the borehole assembly (BHA), the customer's drilling engineer has stated they need directional and gamma ray information, but has not mentioned a need to reduce the chances of getting the BHA stuck. However, the salesperson believes this requirement is important, based on the last drilling program where the customer lost two BHAs. Supported by this belief, the salesperson should have prepared a sales lead probing sequence. The probing sequence might be as follows:

Salesperson:	"Do you mind if I ask you a few more questions regarding the program?" *(ask permission to probe)*
Customer:	"No, go ahead."
Salesperson:	"Thanks. In last year's program, weren't there two wells where you lost the BHA?" *(confirm the problem exists)*
Customer:	"Yes, now that you mention it, we did."
Salesperson:	"Each lost BHA and fishing operation cost in total about $500,000?" *(confirm size of the problem)*
Customer:	"Yes, and this year we budgeted $600,000 for each well for the fishing contingency plan."
Salesperson:	"If you don't do anything differently from the last program, you will probably have the same chances of losing a BHA."
Customer:	"Yes, this is why we have budgeted for it."
Salesperson:	"Would you like to hear how another company was able to reduce the fishing frequency for a similar project by 50%?" *(confirm the customer wants more information)*
Customer:	"You bet. Tell me how."
Salesperson:	"What the customer did was add to the BHA our downhole weight on bit and downhole torque sub this way . . ." *(support need with relevant feature benefit; see next section)*

Situation Probes: Probe about the current situation.
I have a basic understanding of your exploration project. Can you describe it from a drilling perspective?

Problem/Opportunity Probes: Probe for problems or key factors for opportunity. Visualize open probes.
Can you prioritize the key factors for success for this project?

Implications Probes: Probe about the implications of problem or opportunity.
How much of a drilling window do you have to get the two wells drilled and tested?

Need Payoff Probes: Probe about benefits of addressing problem or opportunity.
If you can reduce the drilling time per well, would that be of value to the project?

CUSTOMER LEAD PROBING

Problem/Opportunity Probe:
For the exploration project, you have a very short window to drill the wells. Is that correct?

Quantifying Probe:
How much time have you allotted per well?

Consequence Probe:
What would be the costs if you had to come back next season to drill the second well?

Look/Listen Probe:
What you be interested in knowing how my company was able to use a technique to reduce rig time to evaluate similar exploration wells by two days?

SALES LEAD PROBING 1

Fig. 7.14 (top)
Sales call preparation worksheet probing section—Customer Lead Probing.

Fig. 7.15 (bottom)
Sales call preparation worksheet probing section—Sales Representative Lead Probing.

The third step, as discussed earlier in Chapter 6 "Sales Activities," is to prepare questions and answers the customer may want to ask you as per the Ben Duffy story.

Planning probes before the sales call helps ensure that you do not miss any opportunities to uncover customer needs and requirements. As stated earlier, probing is the means by which you gather information so you have a clear, complete and mutual understanding of a customer's requirements. Shown in **Figs. 7.14 and 7.15** are the completed probing sections of the sales call preparation worksheet.

To help the customer make an informed buying decision, provide information about the ways in which you can address those needs. Following are supporting skills you can use to provide information about how your product and service features, and benefits, satisfy the customer's requirements.

Supporting

The goal in supporting is to help a customer understand the specific ways you can satisfy an expressed need. When you support, you provide information about your products, services, people, and organization. You provide this information by discussing features, benefits, and values. A feature is a characteristic of your product, service, or organization that provides a benefit to help satisfy a customer's requirements. The value is the specific impact the benefit will have for the customer's situation. This is what is referred to in Chapter 1 "Understanding the Role of Marketing and Sales" as having a customer focus. An important tool for supporting is the support worksheet, which is discussed in more detail in the supporting planning section.

How and when you support expressed requirements depends largely on the type of sale.

In small sales, you may support each need separately after you and the customer have discussed it in the same meeting. In large sales, you may need to contact other people in the buying center and gather competitor intelligence before you start supporting.

▶ ***Supporting***

Goal: To help a customer understand specifically how you can satisfy a need.

When

- The customer has expressed a need.
- There is mutual understanding of the need.
- You know how your product/organization can address the need.

How

- Acknowledge the requirement.
- Describe relevant features and benefits.
- Demonstrate capabilities.
- Check for acceptance.
- Test for value.

Feature: A characteristic of a product, service, or organization.

Benefit: How a feature helps a client.

Value: Specific benefit provided in the customer's situation.

In small sales, you can choose between supporting after each need is stated or probing for more requirements. To use this approach, you can ask the customer after they describe one requirement "Is there anything else?" Once the customer has no more to tell you, begin your support of the multiple needs.

To support a need:

- Acknowledge *(confirm or clarify)* the need.
- Describe relevant features and benefits.
- Demonstrate capabilities.
- Check for acceptance *(confirm the customer's understanding)*.
- Test for value.

Acknowledging the Requirement

An effective way to promote an open exchange is to acknowledge the customer's needs. Show you understand and respect expressed needs. A good time to do this is when you make the transition from probing to supporting. To acknowledge the need, either confirm or clarify the need based on your understanding. You might say:

- "It's always wise to involve people in decisions that affect them." *(confirming the requirement)*
- "And why is that a top priority?" *(clarifying the requirement)*

Acknowledging creates a sense of alignment. It lets the customer know you understand the expressed point of view, and empathize with those feelings. Acknowledging further supports the customer's desire to take action. It prepares the customer to hear what you have to offer and encourages the sharing of additional requirements. There are many ways to acknowledge needs. For example, you can agree the need is worth addressing:

- "That makes sense."
- "I think you're right to make that a priority."
- "That is important in an organization like yours."

Mention the importance of the need to others:

- "Many of the organizations we work with have come to similar conclusions."
- "I talk to a lot of drilling engineers who share that concern."
- "You're not alone in that viewpoint."

Show that you recognize the consequences of not satisfying the need:

- "Right. If you don't do something, it's bound to continue."
- "Sure. As it stands now, it will be hard to meet your objectives."
- "Definitely. You don't want to let those costs get out of hand."

Demonstrate your awareness of the feelings that surround the need:

- "That must be very frustrating."
- "Sounds like a very challenging mandate."
- "It's difficult when you have to involve so many people in the decision."

It is important to become comfortable acknowledging in a variety of ways, so you are not always saying, and the customer is not always hearing, "I understand."

Acknowledging prepares the customer to listen and helps you make a smooth transition from the identification of a need to an explanation of how you can help. There are other times when acknowledging is useful, such as when a customer expresses a need but you are not ready to support it or you are not yet sure how you can help. You can demonstrate your understanding by acknowledging the need.

Besides acknowledging needs, you can acknowledge the information a customer provides as well as the feelings or opinions the customer expresses:

- "That's quite useful to know."
- "I appreciate your concern."
- "That's an interesting way of looking at it."

You don't want to acknowledge everything a customer says. To be effective, your acknowledging statements must be sincere and reflect genuine empathy, understanding, and respect.

Describe Relevant Features and Benefits

Once you have acknowledged the requirement, describe relevant features, benefits, and value. When describing features and benefits in a support statement, you can start with the feature or the benefit. You might say:

- "The three-dimensional geovisualization application I'm talking about will increase the speed and accuracy with which you can define subsurface relationships for you. By doing that, you reduce your E&P costs and risks." *(feature first)*
- "You can reduce your E&P costs and risks by defining subsurface relationships more quickly and accurately with our three-dimensional geovisualization application." *(benefit first)*

The features and benefits you describe must be relevant to the customer's situation. Avoid spending time supporting potential or irrelevant benefits. It is your job as your company's representative to present only the features that address the customer's explicit requirements. It is tempting to elaborate, because your company offers many features and even more benefits. However, if you do not listen carefully and actively match your benefits to the needs expressed, you may find yourself describing benefits that do not apply. When this happens, it is called a "feature dump" and most customers will stop listening and other things. See the sidebar "Feature Dump." When you support, describe only those features and benefits that address the particular need you are supporting. For example:

▶ *Feature Dump*

When a sales representative tells a customer all the possible features and benefits without separating the implicit features from the explicit features, you call this a "feature dump," which is not a good sales practice.

"Dumping" potential features on the wrong customer is just as bad as ignoring benefits altogether. In most cases, you will encourage the customer to drop to level 3 listening level.

Customer requirement:	"I have a reasonable schedule, but I do have a budget to meet. I can't afford to have any surprises causing delays. That can lead to major unanticipated expenses. I need to have the data in hand before trouble hits."
Feature:	Logging while drilling real-time data transmission.
Relevant benefit:	Protects budget by providing data in time to help operator spot trouble before it happens.

After describing relevant features and benefits, offer relevant proof to demonstrate your product or service capabilities.

Demonstrate Capabilities

A relevant proof is determined by the customer's social profile, technology adoption preference and buying center role. In the logging while drilling example, a relevant proof to demonstrate capabilities with a profile of an Analytical/Amiable Pragmatist/User (social profile–technology adoption preference–role) is to show a professional society paper describing how another company successfully drilled and evaluated wells in a similar environment. Do not move ahead in your discussion until you know the customer has understood and accepted your explanation.

Checking for Acceptance

In checking for acceptance, you are confirming that the customer understands and accepts your support. Keep in mind you do not have to check verbally. Usually, it is sufficient to make eye contact, assess the customer's reaction to the information, and respond accordingly. If the customer gives any indication of not understanding your information or the benefits you have presented, find out why. Handle any confusion or concern right away. If you cannot tell whether a customer accepts the benefits you introduce, ask a confirming question, such as:

- "How does that sound?"
- "Would that be of interest to you?"

If the customer reacts favorably to a benefit, make a mental or written note. When it is time to close, you'll want to remember which benefits were accepted. Once the customer has acknowledged the feature and benefit, it is time to ask what kind of value this benefit would provide in the customer's operation. Referring back to the value stairs described in Chapter 6 "Sales Activities" the next step in the supporting process clearly articulates what the feature benefit means to the customer.

Test for Value

Testing for value is the final and most important step in supporting. Testing value ensures that the customer is able to make the connection of how the feature and benefit will impact their operation. When you test for value of a feature and benefit unique to your company, you are making sure the customer will be able to justify using your company in the final stages of the decision-making process. A test for value probe could be asked as follows:

Salesperson:	"If you could get the logging done while drilling, how much rig time could you save in your program by running the logging simultaneously?"
Customer:	"I would estimate with the total depth at 5,000 meters, it would easily be two days."
Salesperson:	"And how much is your rig time per hour?"
Customer:	"We use $6,000 an hour for this rig."
Salesperson:	"So 48 hours at $6,000 per hour is $288,000."
Customer:	"Wow. I never actually realized it would be that significant. I will have to bring this up at tomorrow's drilling meeting."

Not Prepared to Support

Before supporting, ask yourself if the customer has actually expressed a need. If not, use a closed probe to confirm the need. You have to be convinced that both of you clearly understand the "what" and "why" of the need. If not, keep probing. Ask yourself if you can satisfy the need. If you can't, acknowledge the need, but don't make a complete support statement until you can describe the relevant features and benefits and test for value. If the customer has a requirement or need you don't know how to satisfy, acknowledge it. Say you will get back with an answer after you consult with others in the office or at your company to learn if anyone else has had a similar request by other customers. See the sidebar "Supporting Early" for reasons why this is not a good idea.

Preparing to Support Customer Requirements

Effective and efficient supporting of customer requirements requires planning. Prior to making a sales call:

- Predict the customer's objectives and requirements—what are the needs and why are they important.
- Prepare the sales call supporting worksheet and support aids.
- Prepare a sales lead probing sequence for the requirements you are planning to support.
- Predict likely rejections and prepare to address them.

> ▶ ***Supporting Early***
>
> Supporting early is a common problem. You must be sure you support only after the customer has:
>
> - Expressed a requirement.
> - There is mutual understanding of the requirement.
> - You know how you can address the need.
>
> If you support before these conditions are met, the customer may feel you're interested only in pushing your product and may doubt your commitment to understanding and satisfying the expressed needs.

Predict the Customer's Requirements

Prior to the sales call, predict the customer's requirements and the level of importance placed on each requirement. You will recall in the opportunities management process that this was part of completing a vulnerability analysis and opportunity supporting worksheet in the evaluation of options phase. In addition, in the specific sales call, you also considered how your solution addressed the individual's personal priorities.

Prepare a Sales Call Preparation Support Worksheet

As discussed in Chapter 4 "Opportunities Management," for each opportunity, you will use your probing skills to interview the customers in the buying center and complete the project solution and request for proposal worksheets. These completed worksheets give you a complete understanding of all the customer's needs at both project and personal levels. This will allow you to addresses the customer's specific requirements. This worksheet will be used to organize your supporting of the customer's requirements.

For each feature and benefit, have an appropriate support aid to demonstrate capabilities. These can include an white paper, log example, success story, or list of references. Each support aid should be appropriate for the customer's profile. As part of the support process, also predict the possible types of rejections the customer might have and be prepared to handle them. We will discuss this situation in more detail in Chapter 8 "Handling Customer Rejection." For benefits that have a specific monetary value, estimate the value and list all the parameters needed or used to calculate the value. In the sales call, you will discuss the estimated value and parameters with the customer.

As discussed earlier in this chapter, the benefits with dollar values calculated are used in the "Prove Value" tactics. If you can't calculate the specific dollar value of the benefit, consider it a strength and use this in the "Emphasize Strengths" tactic. If you are more expensive than your competition, then you must justify your premium. There is no better way to do that than by quantifying your value. Once the customer has this information. It becomes a simple return on investment (ROI) calculation to justify the more expensive option.

Predict What Type of Rejection the Customer Could Have and Prepare to Handle It

Occasionally, the customer will reject what you are claiming regarding features, benefits, and the resulting value of your solution. By considering what the most likely rejection would be prepare an appropriate strategy to address it. When a customer does reject, it is best to deal with it immediately and then continue on with the sales call. An unanswered rejection can stop the whole sales process and minimize the positive impact of other features, benefits, and values you want to discuss. We will discuss this in detail in the next chapter.

Figure 7.16 shows an example of a sales call preparation support worksheet. This type of worksheet is especially helpful in pinpointing multiple benefits provided by the features you discuss. The worksheet helps you select the appropriate requirements to discuss, depending on your sales call objective and tactics.

Being prepared in advance makes the sales call much more efficient. You will not have to set up another meeting with the customer to find a demonstration of capabilities or to overcome any supports that were rejected. After effectively supporting you should ask for next steps, as identified in your sales call objective. This is done in the closing of the sales call, which is discussed next.

▶ ***Closing***

Goal

To agree on the appropriate next steps.

When

- Customer signals a readiness to move ahead.
- Customer has accepted the benefits you've described.

How

- Ask the customer if there are any other issues to discuss.
- Review previously accepted benefits.
- Propose the next steps for you and the customer.
- Check for acceptance.

Closing

You build the foundation for an informed, mutually beneficial decision by understanding a customer's needs, and by helping the customer to understand how you can address those needs. If you do an effective job of probing and supporting, your customer will be ready to move ahead, and closing will be a natural next step in concluding your discussion.

Your goal in closing is to reach an agreement for the next steps in moving forward on a mutually beneficial decision. Close the sales call when the customer signals a readiness to move ahead. This may be a verbal or nonverbal signal that the customer is interested in moving forward. Examples of closing signals are:

- "It all sounds good."
- "You've made some interesting points."
- "I like what I'm hearing."
- The customer smiles, nods, or looks at you expectantly.

If the customer has already accepted the supports you've described, but doesn't signal a readiness to move ahead, it is acceptable to use a test close and propose the next steps.

Check for Any Other Issues

The first step in closing is to ask if there are any other questions or needs to discuss before you begin to close. If there are none, start the second step of closing by reviewing the previously accepted benefits.

In the course of a call or several calls, you may support a number of needs with a variety of features, benefits, and demonstrated value. Ideally, make written notes of the benefits and value the customer accepts. This is a simple process if you use the sales call preparation worksheets. Mark the accepted benefits as the sales discussion progresses.

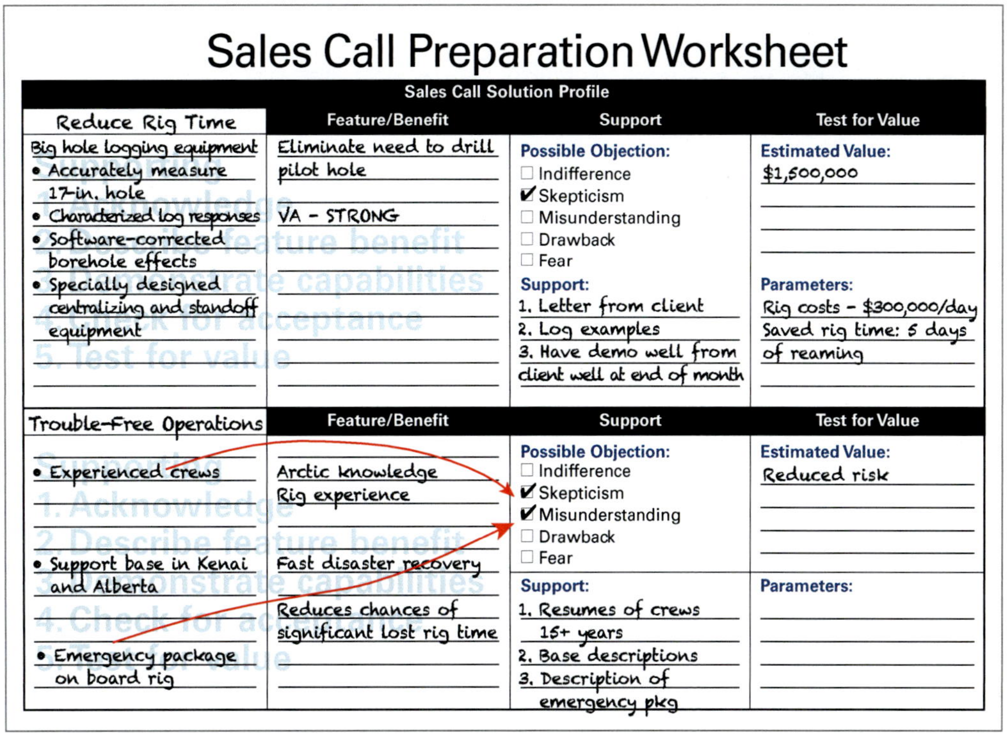

Sales Call Preparation Worksheet

Sales Call Solution Profile			
Reduce Rig Time	Feature/Benefit	Support	Test for Value
Big hole logging equipment	Eliminate need to drill pilot hole	Possible Objection:	Estimated Value:
• Accurately measure 17-in. hole		☐ Indifference	$1,500,000
• Characterized log responses	VA – STRONG	✔ Skepticism	
• Software-corrected borehole effects		☐ Misunderstanding	
• Specially designed centralizing and standoff equipment		☐ Drawback	
		☐ Fear	
		Support:	Parameters:
		1. Letter from client	Rig costs – $300,000/day
		2. Log examples	Saved rig time: 5 days of reaming
		3. Have demo well from client well at end of month	

Trouble-Free Operations	Feature/Benefit	Support	Test for Value
• Experienced crews	Arctic knowledge	Possible Objection:	Estimated Value:
	Rig experience	☐ Indifference	Reduced risk
		✔ Skepticism	
		✔ Misunderstanding	
• Support base in Kenai and Alberta	Fast disaster recovery	☐ Drawback	
		☐ Fear	
	Reduces chances of significant lost rig time	Support:	Parameters:
		1. Resumes of crews 15+ years	
• Emergency package on board rig		2. Base descriptions	
		3. Description of emergency pkg	

Fig. 7.16

Sales call preparation worksheet, sales call solution profile section. Tip: When you create a specific proposal that will include pricing terms and conditions, use the worksheet as described in Chapter 6 "Sales Activities" to organize your proposal components and select which requirements you will include in your proposal.

Review Previously Accepted Benefits

Reviewing previously accepted benefits reminds the customer of the benefits and expected value resulting when a purchase decision is made (or agrees to take steps toward such a decision). This review lets you convey your confidence in moving ahead. Position your review of benefits with phrases like:

- "Let me recap some of the ways we can help you achieve your goals . . ."
- "As you've discussed . . ."
- "Let's go over the highlights of what we have talked about so far . . ."

Begin your review of the accepted benefits. For example, when you are demonstrating the benefits and value of an integrated project management approach, you might say:

- "We've agreed that the integrated approach discussed will help you generate important savings. You estimated the savings as much as 20% similar to the company in the reference letter I showed you. Also, it will give you a single point of accountability, so you'll know exactly who to talk to when you have questions or concerns the moment they arise, and be sure of a fast response."

In many sales scenarios, both large and small, the salesperson will need to have several sales meetings. For each meeting there will be a close. The question becomes is that close with a big "C" or little "c"? See the sidebar "Is it a Big C or Little C?" to know the difference.

Propose Next Steps

Once you've reviewed previously accepted benefits, propose the next steps. These are either your primary or backup objective you had planned earlier. Depending on how the sales call has progressed, close with your backup objective if it is more appropriate. If the sales call has progressed well, ask what the customer would recommend as the next steps. If the suggestion is not what you had hoped for, you can still recommend considering your next steps.

> ▶ ***Is it a Big C or Little C?***
>
> This is a common question heard in the office of sales professionals, especially from their sales managers. The big "C" refers to whether the salesperson closed on the deal, winning the work. Or was it a little "c," meaning the customer agreed to the next steps that will move the opportunity forward, getting closer to an award. Some people may think the big "C" is more important than a little "c." But in fact, in large sales as concluded from the research of N. Rakham discussed earlier, asking too soon or often for the award in large sales lowers the chances of winning the work. As the saying goes "slowly, but surely." Some little "c" closes can go a long way to winning you the work. Don't rush the sale.
>
> Shown next are little "c" closes. You might ask the customer to:
>
> - Review a proposal.
> - Attend a demonstration.
> - Arrange for you to make a presentation.
> - Arrange a meeting with a decision maker.
> - Do some internal "selling."
> - Meet again with you.
> - Give you the specifications and submit an estimate for the job.
>
> You might offer to:
>
> - Prepare a proposal.
> - Set up/conduct a demonstration.
> - Make a presentation.
> - Meet with a decision maker.
> - Provide materials and ideas to prepare the customer to "sell" internally.
> - Meet again to further explore the client's needs.
> - Take immediate steps to begin the job.
>
> **Factors That Determine Use of Techniques**
>
> Some of the factors that may influence your choice of techniques include the following:
>
> - Successful past experience
> - Your level of rapport with the client
> - National/regional influences and preferences
> - Your personal style
> - Customer's personality
> - Products, services, or capabilities being offered

In some sales calls, you may have to revise your objectives in the middle of the call in response to new information from the customer. Your ability to improvise new sales call objectives based on that information will often be the key to a successful close. This is why it is important during planning to list as many possible outcomes that will advance the sales call, because you may have to use one of your lesser outcomes to advance the process.

Specifying what you'd like the customer to do next ensures that the commitment you're asking for is clear. Saying what you'll do next demonstrates your commitment to working with the customer. As discussed earlier, ensure that your objectives pass the SMART test.

However, do not to make commitments that are significantly more substantial than those you ask the customer to make. If the customer isn't willing to take some action, decide how that lack of interest affects the time and effort you invest. Over time, the commitments you and your customers make should reflect the mutual responsibilities that characterize any good relationship.

When closing a sales call, there are many ways of the customer to award you the work. The **Chapter Highlight 7.3: "Sign Here, Here, and Here"** describes several options for your consideration.

Checking for Acceptance

After proposing next steps, make sure the customer accepts the plan you've outlined. You might say:

- "What do you think?"
- "Can you arrange that?"
- "How does that sound?"

When the customer doesn't agree to your next steps, even after accepting the benefits and value you described, the reluctance to take the next step may delay the decision you seek. The customer might say:

- "I'd like to hold off on that for a while."
- "Sounds good, but it's too early to make a decision."
- "I'm just not sure. Let me get back to you in a couple of days."

If you have been listening carefully throughout the conversation, this reluctance should not come as surprise. Rather, it will reflect what's been discussed so far. However, a customer's reluctance to close is predictable.

Some common reasons why customers may unexpectedly (or not so unexpectedly) refuse the close are because they:

- Have needs that have not been uncovered.
- Have questions that have not been answered.
- Are skeptical about your ability to deliver the benefits you've described.
- Remain reluctant to accept the rigors of change.
- Object to some aspect of your solution, or to the action steps you've suggested.
- Are unable to make a commitment.
- Are too early or too late in the opportunities management process to take the requested actions.
- Do not have the required authority or are not at a level to make detailed decisions.

When a customer seems reluctant to move ahead, probe to find out why. You might ask:

- "Why is that?"
- "Is there something else we should talk about?"
- "What needs to happen before you'll be ready to make a decision?"
- "Can you tell me the reason for your hesitation?"

If the customer raises a concern that was not revealed during the sales call, or a concern that was not satisfactorily handled, address the concern and consequences at this time.

Handling customers' negative reactions is an important part of the need-satisfaction process and will be discussed in detail in the next chapter.

When the customer is satisfied the concern has been addressed, proceed with the closing. If the customer is willing to move forward but at a slower pace, propose a lesser commitment than the one you originally asked for. Get the best commitment the customer is willing and able to make. If you can't get a decision or commitment to a next step, set a date by which a decision or commitment will be made, or set a date for a future meeting.

When it is obvious from your probing that the customer has given you a well-considered refusal to move ahead or has decided to award the work to a competitor:

- Express your disappointment.
- Thank the customer for taking the time to meet with you.
- Ask for feedback depending on if it is a small or large sale.

If it is a small sale, ask immediately after the customer has stated they will award the work to another company. In this scenario, ask:

- What factors contributed to the customer's decision?
- What did your offer or proposal lack?
- What did you do—or not do—that affected the decision?

Chapter Highlight 7.3: Sign Here, Here, and Here

Techniques for Winning the Deal—Next Steps

Professional sales representatives use these nine techniques to close the deal, with the customer awarding them the work.

Success Story Narrative

Narrate a comparable situation to show why the customer should commit to moving ahead. When describing your success story, explain how the next steps resolved pertinent problems, doubts, or other issues you're proposing. For example: "We recently converted hard-copy data like this for an abandoned Baku field. The results were excellent, and we had no trouble doing it in five days. We can get it finished in less than a week, if I can have your permission to begin immediately."

Point of Urgency

This close motivates the customer to act quickly or risk losing an advantage (or being penalized in some way). For example: "I think it would be best for you to agree on the schedule now, while I can guarantee availability of the equipment for the dates you need."

Sign Here

To use this approach, rely on actions rather than words to get a commitment. For example, you might produce a service form and begin to fill it out. You should use caution with this technique; it works best with clients you know well. In less familiar relationships, it may appear presumptuous.

Provisional Order

This technique allows the customer to commit even when circumstances beyond your control would otherwise cause a delay. For example: "Assuming the others are available, I'd like to schedule the meeting for Wednesday, based on your agreement to give you a couple of hours in the morning."

What Do You Recommend

When the sales meeting has gone very well and you are dealing with Drivers or Expressives, an effective way to propose next steps is to ask, "We have covered a lot of ground today. What do you recommend you do next?" You may be surprised by what the customer recommends, and you can always add or suggest your next steps if you think your next steps are more appropriate.

Direct

The direct technique is short and to the point. You use it when the customer gives you a strong buying signal. For example: "You can give me the specification right now and I will have the products delivered by Monday afternoon."

Supposition

This technique produces a commitment that depends on conditions or criteria. For example: "If I can have the unit at the dock on the date you've asked for, can you agree to award us the work today and I will start the mobilization?"

Either/Or

This technique encourages commitment by assuming the decision has been made and inviting the customer to finalize the decision with a simple, either/or choice. For example: "We can run the service for either well. It's your call." Another example is: "All you need to do now is decide whether to go with the standard service or upgrade. Which one do you want?"

Chapter Highlight 7.3: Sign Here, Here, and Here (cont.)

Step-by-Step

The step-by-step approach allows you to direct the main decision by asking for a number of small decisions that the customer can easily accept. For example:

Sales representative:	"Then why don't you touch base with your contracts department and, if they have any questions regarding the contract, do you think you can get their commitment to send those to you by Monday?"
Client:	"Yes I think so."
Sales representative:	"If you send those to me on Monday afternoon I will get with my contracts person and we can review any changes on Wednesday."
Client:	"Sure. sounds perfect"
Sales representative:	"And then we have our executives sign the contract on Friday and we start the project the 1st of the next month."
Client:	"Great. Let's do it."

Remember, there is always potential for future business. Make it clear that you want to maintain a presence with the customer by asking permission to stay in touch. This can be done as part of the planned account management program activities, discussed in Chapter 13 "Pipeline Management." Another option is to make a special effort to send articles of interest or invitations to relevant events. Communicate your undiminished readiness to help the customer and organization. Encourage the customer to contact you as other opportunities arise.

If it is a large sale and you have presented your proposal, then follow the steps as described in Chapter 6 "Sales Activities," section "Outcome Analysis Customer Debrief."

Preparing for the Closing

Preparation for the closing is completed by thoroughly implementing the other parts of the sales call process. All the previous preparation, as documented in the sales call worksheet, should enable you to achieve a successful outcome. The sections of the sales call preparation worksheet already discussed are the:

- Buying center profile
- Aligning strategies
- Objective setting
- Developing a probing strategy
- Preparation of the sales call support worksheet

The final preparation for closing occurs during the sales call. As the discussion progresses, actively analyze the feedback and prepare a brief summary of the agreed-upon points to use in the closing. A tool you can use is the closing section of the sales call worksheet. Make notes on accepted benefits and value the customer acknowledges and use your notes to summarize accepted benefits. **Figure 7.17** shows a completed closing section of the sales call preparation worksheet.

Even when you don't make a sale, your commitment to a mutually beneficial decision will work to your advantage in the long run. The more professionally you respond to rejections, the more likely the customer will be to call you in the future. Once you finish the sales call, complete post sales call analyses, regardless of the outcome of the sales call, as discussed on the next pages.

Closing			
Customer agreed to $ value of BHL upon verification of exploration manager. If exploration manager supports using BHL, then he will support. Will also request emergency package be included in bid package.	**Objective Achieved:** ☑ Primary ☐ Backup ☐ Other ☐ None	**Accepted Benefits:** Eliminate need to drill pilot hole; Mobilization plan; Liked emergency pkg	**Total Value Accepted:** $1,500,000 + reduced risks

Closing
1. Check for any other issues
2. Review benefits accepted
3. Propose next steps
4. Check for acceptance

Fig. 7.17
Completed closing section of the sales call preparation worksheet, which is completed during the sales call.

Post Sales Call Analysis

At the conclusion of each sales call, complete a post sales call analysis. The post sales call analysis has two parts. The first is analyzed from a strategic point of view. The second is a level 1 sales call effectiveness review. In the next section, you will discuss the level 2 sales call analysis.

Sales Call Strategic Analysis

The sales call strategic analysis should answer the following questions:

- What was the outcome of the call?
- What impact does this have on the opportunities management process and your competitive strategy?
- What are the next steps?
- Update the opportunity sales plan (SSP). The SSP will be discussed in detail in a later chapter.

What was the outcome of the call?

In this analysis, decide if the sales call objective or backup objective was achieved, or if lesser but related actions were agreed to **(Fig. 7.18).** Did the actions agreed upon improve your chances of winning the opportunity? By answering these questions you categorize the sales call as successful or unsuccessful. See the sidebar, "We Will Call You..." for definitions of a successful and unsuccessful sales call.[5]

Opportunities Management Process

For large sales each sales call is part of a strategy to execute a tactic to win an opportunity. At the end of each sales call, analyze any additional information gained and update the competitive strategy for the opportunity. The analysis is completed by:

- Reviewing the opportunity plan.
- Summarizing next steps.

Reviewing the Opportunity Plan. After each sales call, review the opportunity plan and new information from the sales call to decide if the plan should:

- Have a tactic added or canceled.
- Have a tactic modified.
- Continue as planned.

Fig. 7.18
Post sales call analysis, next steps and process section of sales call preparation and analysis worksheet.

Post Sales Call Analysis

Sales Call Outcome Analysis:

Successful: ☐ Order ☑ Advance **Unsuccessful:** ☐ Continuation ☐ Rejection

Opportunity Management Process Review:

Probability of Winning Opportunity: 90+ %

Updated timing for opportunity management process milestones: Delayed 1 mo

Account Corporate Profile → Identification of the Compelling Event → Evaluation of Options → Submit Proposal → Resolution of Concerns → Negotiate → Monitor → Outcome Analysis → Implementation → Performance Review

Analysis: B. Brown agreed $1,500,000 of rig time savings is a conservative estimate of reduced rig time due to elimination of pilot hole. Needs to have method approved by exploration manager. B. Brown will ensure my company will have rig time in Cook Inlet to see demo job on Cook Inlet well.
*Request for tender has been delayed by one month. No supplier presentations will be possible. Good thing. We made direct award proposal for work. This also indicates that BOC has decided who they want to use. B. Brown said they are very pressed for time now to be able to spud the first well in June. Jun 89

STRATEGIC POST SALES CALL OUTCOME ANALYSIS

PRIME Tactic Response: ☑ Add a tactic ☐ Cancel a tactic ☐ Modify a tactic ☐ No change

Responsible	Description	Due Date
1. J Amlin	PE tactic; contact exploration manager	Nov 30
2. M. Gunther	Contact BOC Kenai operations manager to confirm date for demo job	Nov 15

NEXT STEPS ACTION ITEMS – TACTICS

CVR entered into CRM Opportunity ☑

CRM Account, Contact, Opportunity Information Updated ☑

B. Brown Adapt / Pragmatic / Supporter. Milestones – updated. Tactic – P.B. Brown completed.

▶ *We Will Call You...*

How do you know a good sales call from a bad one? Sales calls can be classified into two types: successful and unsuccessful.

A successful sales call consists of either a confirmed sale or advance.

A confirmed sale is a firm commitment to purchase, such as a signed contract.

An advance is when the sales call results in some agreed-to actions that improve your chances of securing the work.

An unsuccessful call is one that does nothing to improve your chance of securing the work. Unsuccessful sales calls consist of two types of calls: continuations and rejections.

A continuation occurs when no agreements are made to advance or improve your chances of securing the opportunity. You know this is the case when the customer says something like, "Thanks for the presentation. We will call you . . ."

A rejection is when the customer has refused to make any commitments, has awarded the work to another company, or has chosen to do nothing.

Information from the sales call gives you better insight into the customer's requirements and perception of your ability to satisfy those requirements, compared to competitors. Answering the above questions becomes even more critical when the sales call was not successful in achieving its planned tactic. A series of unsuccessful sales calls may suggest that the sales team should review their competitive position and strategy.

Chapter 9 "Strategic Sales Plan" will discuss creating and using a sales plan to manage an opportunity in more detail. At key decision points in the opportunity management process, the sales team should reassess the competitive strategies based on the progress of the plan and information collected. The key inputs for this activity are the client visit reports (CVRs) reported from earlier sales calls. Once you have finished your analysis, update the probability of winning the opportunity, based on your review of the plan and analysis of the new information from the sales call.

Summarizing Next Steps. With the above analysis completed, make a list of action items, namely the next steps. In this part of the post call analysis, document and inform the sales team members of any follow up action items that were agreed to, and other actions for the sales team, based on the outcome analysis. Be sure that for each action a person is identified who should complete the action by a target date. Figure 7.18 is an example of a completed sales call analysis section using the post sales call analysis form. Once the analysis is completed, the post sales call analysis should be entered into the company CRM system as a CVR attached to the opportunity.

Level 1 Sales Call Effectiveness Review

In the level 1 sales call effectiveness review, examine each process of the sales call and ask yourself:

- What was done well and what do I want to retain?
- What could be done better and what do I want to improve for future sales calls?

To answer these questions, systematically go through each process and ask a series of questions to determine your effectiveness for:

- Preliminaries
- Opening
- Probing, confirming, and clarifying
- Supporting
- Handling rejection
- Closing
- Level 1 listening and aligning

To determine what you want to retain and what to improve, go through each sales skill listed above and ensure that for each skill you used each step of the process, as discussed earlier in this chapter.

- Did you begin with preliminaries having a clear agenda and value proposition?
- Did you check with the customer for acceptance before beginning the sales call discussion?

During the discussion, did you feel that you aligned effectively with the customer? Was there a sense of tension in the meeting? Did the conversation flow smoothly?

Were you able to discover and give the information you intended with your probing strategy? Were there questions after the meeting you wished you had asked the customer but didn't think of before or during the meeting? What was the customer's reaction to your questions—irritation or interest?

During the supporting processes, did you acknowledge the customer's requirements by confirming or clarifying? Did you check for the customer's acceptance after each support? Did you explain how the features of your products and services result in benefits for the customer? Did you feel comfortable using the checking for value statement and how did the customer respond? Were your support aids adequate or do you need to modify or create additional support aids?

Did the closing come naturally or was time was running out and you could sense the customer wanted to finish the meeting? Did you review the accepted benefits and the customer's specific value? When reviewing, what was the interest level of the customer? Was it at level 1 listening or at lower levels at this point?

Did you encounter customer rejection at the beginning of the sales call—after supports or when trying to close? Were you able to adequately handle the rejection or did you need to return to resolve the rejection?

What percentage of the time were you at level 1 listening and what percentage of the time was the customer at level 1? What could you do to keep yourself and the customer at level 1 listening a higher percentage of time?

When completing the sales call effectiveness review, use the level 1 sales call effectiveness review analysis worksheet. As you review each sales call process, rate your performance as one of the following:

- Needs improvement
- Good
- Very good

The analysis of the sales call should be conducted as soon as practical after the sales call, so details are not lost with time. The benefit of doing the sales call analysis is that with time you can judge your progress in the targeted areas needing improvement. Improving your sales call skills will also impact other communications with the customer, within your company, and in your personal life. These same sales skills are used in many of the other sales activities, such as negotiations. **Figure 7.19** is an example of a completed post call process analysis section.

Level 1 sales call analysis should be done on as many sales calls as possible. It is part of your personal commitment to the total quality management processes to maximize the efficiency and effectiveness of the supplier–account relationship for each of the main sales activities.

Complete the post sales call analysis, preferably in the customer's building immediately after the sales call, before doing anything else. Doing this consistently requires that the post sales call analysis be scheduled as part of every sales call. Some salespeople prefer to do the post sales call analysis back at their office, but that is a mistake. To understand why, see the sidebar "What Happens If They See Me?"

Level 2 Sales Call Effectiveness Review

The level 2 sales call effectiveness reviews are observed sales calls. Completing a level 2 requires you to have assistance ideally from your sales manager or colleague trained in sales. If a sales manager is not available, find a colleague or peer who has been trained and uses sales skills on a regular basis. This individual takes an active coaching role in the level 2 review, as described below.

The purpose of the level 2 sales call is to develop a more detailed analysis of your sales call performance, starting with the planning stage through the execution and analysis stages. Having an independent observer assist in the sales call process may uncover areas for improvement you had not considered. These may be areas you are not able to recognize because of your involvement in the execution of the sales call. An important factor to remember is that level 2 sales effectiveness reviews are not a joint sales call. When soliciting your manager's or colleague's assistance for a level 2 review, that individual is present for coaching purposes. The level 2 review consists of the following:

- Level 2 review preparation
- Pre-call briefing
- Sales call observation

Fig. 7.19
Level 1 review completed section of the sales call preparation worksheet.

Level 1 Sales Call Effectiveness Review:

	Need Improvement	Good	Very Good	Comments
Preliminaries	✔			-Little nervous at first NO BUSINESS CARD!
Opening		✔		-Good value prop statement. Could skip preliminaries next time.
Customer Lead Probing		✔		-Picked up on higher svr. concerns and more expressive than driver.
Sales Lead Probing		✔		-This project is on B. Brown's personal objectives.
Supporting			✔	-Liked very much the reference letter.
Closing	✔			-Should have asked Brown what he suggested we do next instead of making recommendation first.
Objection Handling	✔			-Having reference letter easily resolved skepticism.
Listening/Aligning/Tension	✔			-A little too preoccupied with my preparation. Missed a couple of points Brown restated over lunch.

Support Documents:

☑ Need to develop
Once have the BOC demo job completed, need to create report and sales aid. Ask for reference from Brown regarding reduced rig time.

☐ Need to modify

> ### ▶ *What Happens if They See Me?*
>
> A sales manager was reviewing his sales team's client visit reports (CVRs) when he noticed his new salesperson had very few CVRs. But he was sure the salesperson was very active contacting clients and pursuing opportunities. The next morning the sales manager asked the salesperson to come to his office for a coffee and asked him how he was enjoying the new position. All was great. The manager then asked how many CVRs he was creating on average a week.
>
> The number was very low—only half the average number of CVRs entered by the other sales staff. When asked why his CVRs entered were low, the salesperson's explanation was he was trying to enter the CVRs, but when he arrived back at the office there would be telephone calls from customers to return and internal meetings. It was very difficult to make the contacts and take care of all the other responsibilities.
>
> The manager smiled and said, *"I know it is not easy. But your system is wrong. You do not do your CVRs here in the office. You do them immediately after your call."* The salesperson looked puzzled and asked, *"Where?"* The manager said in the customer's building, normally in their reception or coffee area. Now the salesperson looked shocked. *"You mean in the customer's building?"* The sales manager said, *"Yes."* The salesperson answered *"But what if the customer sees me?"*
>
> The sales manager smiled again and said *"Perfect. If the customer comes out of their office and sees you taking five or ten minutes to summarize your call, what will they think?"*
>
> The salesperson was silent for few seconds and then said *"I guess that the call was important to me."*
>
> The sales manager said *"I can't think of a better way to end a sales call, can you?"*

- Post-call debriefing
- Troubleshooting

Level 2 Review Preparation

To prepare for a level 2 review, complete the sales call preparation worksheet for the coaching call as described earlier in this chapter and review post sales call analysis worksheets from a previous sales calls. Previous reviews will determines your sales skill focus areas for this level 2 review. The sales call focus area is a specific sales call skill. Inform the observer to take detailed notes on how you execute the skill. For example, from the post-call analysis in Fig. 7.18, the sales call skill focus area for the level 2 review is to execute better listening. It is beneficial to have several of your last sales call preparation worksheets to refer to with the observer when doing the pre-call briefing.

Pre-Call Briefing

In the pre-call briefing with the observer, review the sales call preparation worksheet. Going over each section carefully will give the observer background information regarding the call in preparation for what to expect during the sales call. The observer should provide constructive criticism for areas of the pre-call preparation that might make the call more effective.

Also, review the roles in the observation call in the pre-call briefing. If you are doing the observation call with your sales manager, who has had the sales management training, the individual will understand the expected role and welcome your initiative to have a level 2 review. If you are conferring with a colleague, be certain the individual understands that the responsibility involves observing the call and recording the events of the sales processes as thoroughly as possible. Your colleague is not present to impress the customer. A completed sales call briefing section from the level 2 sales call observation form is shown in **Fig. 7.20.**

Sales Call Observation

At the start of the sales call, introduce the observer and the person's role. This is a simple process if the observer is your boss or the regional or HQ sales or marketing manager. In these situations, you might use an introduction such as:

- "This is Mrs. Lynn Wilson, our regional sales manager. She is accompanying me today as part of your account maintenance program and will take a notes on how I conduct and participate in our meeting."

If the observer is a colleague, you might use an introduction such as:

- "This is Jason Smith. Jason is the salesperson for other oil companies here in town. Today, Jason has accompanied me to observe the meeting as part of your account maintenance program and will take notes on how well I conduct and participate in the meeting."

Of course the exact introduction you use depends on many factors. Discuss the introduction before the meeting and agree with the observer on the introduction that you will use. With the introductions complete, begin the sales call following your plan. At this time the observer begins to take notes.

The observer records the interaction between you and the customer using the level 2 sales review observation form. An example of a completed sales call observation form is shown in **Figs. 7.21. 7.22, and 7.23.** When recording the events of the sales call, the observer should use as few key words as possible in order to remain unobtrusive. The observer should also avoid facial expressions or gestures that communicate personal feelings about the call. In general, the observer should maintain a low profile so that you can proceed with the sales call as normally as possible. At the end of the call, the observer should thank the customer for the opportunity to sit in.

Level 2 Sales Call Observation Form

The level 2 sales call observation form has been designed to guide the note taking of the observer for each sales skill. The top part of this form has the pre-call briefing, which has already been discussed. It is followed by the foundation sales call skills and each step skill is listed. The bottom part of the form has space for the observer to record general observations regarding the sales call dynamics that developed, including:

- Sales call tension
- Aligning
- Listening levels for you and the customer

These notes are to assist the observer in preparing the summary comments on page 2 of the form. When page 2 is completed, the observer reviews the comments with the salesperson, and both decide on the most appropriate improvements, if needed, as part of the post-call debrief.

Post-Call Debriefing

With the call complete, conduct the post-call debrief as soon as possible. In the post-call debrief, the observer will use the notes taken during the meeting to prepare summary comments. When this is completed, review them together.

The review should start with the salesperson reviewing how they perceived they did. The observer listens and compares the salesperson's analysis to their summary.

Fig. 7.20
Complete pre-call briefing section of level 2 sales call observation form from sales calls preparation worksheet.

Level 2 Sales Call Observations

PRE-CALL BRIEFING

Sales Engineer: Harry   Account: BOC   Contact: J. Jones   Observer: JPA   Date: 2/3/02

Sales Call Objective: Have customer agree to run new technology because of improved sampling and rig time savings.

Sales Call Skill Focus: Strength: Supporting Improvement: Level 1 listening and probing

Observer Introduction: JPA is the sales manager and is accompanying Rita today as part of our account maintenance program.

Sales Call Preparation Worksheet reviewed ✔ good   Account Profile ✔ not complete   Sales Plan ✔

PRELIMINARIES

Process	Greeting	Rapport	Preparation	Time Check	Notes
Preliminaries	good	✔	✔	✔	missed

OPENING

Process	Agenda	Value Proposition	Check for Acceptance	Check Customer's Agenda
Opening	✔	little weak	missed	missed
Comments				

PROBING CUSTOMER LEAD

Process	Situation	Problem	Implications	Need Payoff
Customer Lead	good	closed probe	missed	missed
Comments end of meeting		open probe	✔	missed

PROBING SALES LEAD

Process	Problem	Quantify	Consequences	Look/Listen
Sales Lead quality samples	good	✔	✔	✔
Comments rig time	good	Missed	✔	missed

SUPPORTING

Process	Acknowledge Requirement	Feature Benefit	Demonstrate Capabilities	Check for Acceptance	Test for Value
quality samples	good	✔	✔	✔	excellent
rig time	good	✔	✔	missed	✔

Fig. 7.21
Completed level 2 sales call observation section for the basic sales skills of opening, probing, and supporting.

Then the observer gives their feedback. First, the observer describes what they observed in terms of strengths and areas for improvement. The observer should give reasons for the assessment and address where their observation was different from the salesperson's feedback. Together, they agree on the cause of any problem areas and actions to improve them. As a guide to completing the post-call summary comments, the next section lists the seven most common sales call skill problem areas. The chances of you having one or more of the same difficulties are high. As the observer goes over the summary comments, listen carefully to see if the description of the observed problem fits one of the common problems. Discuss the applicable improvement actions listed with each performance problem. A completed level 2 sales call review form is shown in **Fig. 7.24** on page 256.

Sales Call Skills Performance Problems

The following pages describe seven common problems related to the misunderstanding or misapplication of critical selling skills. For each situation described, probable causes and recommended improvement actions have been outlined.

1. **Does Not Recognize Opportunities and Requirements When the Customer Expresses Them.** You don't recognize or respond appropriately to customer opportunities and requirements. In fact, you may seem almost oblivious to high-potential opportunities and requirements that would give the customer strong reasons to make a commitment. The customer gets annoyed because time is wasted in what appears to be an unsatisfying meeting and may not agree to another meeting.

Possible Causes

Sales Skills Deficiency: You may not hear the requirements and opportunities expressed. You may be too busy figuring out what to say next and may not be listening. Listening is, of course, an integral part of the skill of probing.

Technical Knowledge: You may lack knowledge about the products, applications and technical requirements, or account situation that would allow you to recognize an opportunity or need or you might not be applying this knowledge during call preparation.

You can determine if it is technical knowledge by reviewing your sales call preparation worksheet and interview forms (project solution and request for proposal) with the observer or technical expert in this area. If your supports are judged to

INDIFFERENCE

Process	Probe to Understand Customer's Position	Acknowledge Customer's Position	Ask Permission to Probe	✔Problem ✔Quantify ✔Consequence ✔Look/listen
Quality samples	Good	✔	✔	

MISUNDERSTANDING

Process	Probe to Understand Concern	Acknowledge Customer's Concern	Acknowledge Requirement Not Met	Explain Feature Benefit	Check for Acceptance
none					

SKEPTICISM

Process	Probe to Understand Concern	Acknowledge Customer's Concern	Offer Relevant Proof	Check for Acceptance
Rig time savings	Good	Good	Had reference letter but didn't use?	Missed

DRAWBACK

Process	Probe to Understand Drawback	Acknowledge Drawback	Handle Did excellent job at defining costs	Check for Acceptance
Customer said too expensive for quality samples.	✔	✔	☐ Research ☑ Redefine ☐ Trade-off ☐ Outweigh	✔

CLOSING

Process	Check for any other Issues	Summarize Accepted Benefits and Value	Propose or Ask for Next Steps	Check for Acceptance	Thank the Client
Customer said MDT too expensive for quality samples.	missed	missed	✔	✔	✔

SALES CALL DYNAMICS

Skill	Preliminaries	Opening	Probing	Supporting	Handling Objection	Closing
Aligning	✔	no	✔	too technical	good	OK
Tension	OK	high	OK	OK	high	OK
Listening	improvement	no	need improvement	customer was not	OK	OK

Fig. 7.22 (top)
Completed level 2 sales call observation section for the four customer rejection behaviors and appropriate handling steps.

Fig. 7.23 (bottom)
Completed level 2 sales call observation section for the closing, appropriate handling steps, and the sales call dynamics section.

be weak, discuss how to improve them. If the solutions are complete, the cause of the problem is a sales skills deficiency.

Improvement Actions

If sales skills are the problem, review the section on probing in this chapter and Chapter 5 "Communication Skills." In your next call, do more confirming and clarifying of the customer's feedback to identify expressed requirements.

If you believe that you have a good understanding of probing and listening skills, conduct a role-playing exercise in which the observer is assisting you as the customer. When you hear the "customer" express a requirement, stop the role-playing, paraphrase the requirement, and then support it. If the role-playing customer expresses a need you do not respond to, the customer should stop and explain what was just expressed, and then you support. If you have just returned from a sales call where this skill was a problem, replay the sales call in the form of role-playing.

In subsequent calls, take notes using your sales call preparation sheets as an aid to help focus your attention on listening to the customer and identifying requirements you can support.

If deficient technical knowledge is the problem, review your preparation support worksheet to improve and/or add features and benefits to the supports. In addi-

Level 2 Sales Call Review

		Comments
Sales Call Preparation	☑ Very good ☐ Satisfactory ☐ Improvement needed	Summary Harry had very good plan going into the sales call. He had a clear objective and backup objective with a good list of other possible actions. Good list of questions and sales call solution profile with supports.
Preliminaries	☐ Very good ☐ Satisfactory ☑ Improvement needed	Summary A little too long for the driver style of the customer. No business card and did not check for timing.
Opening	☐ Very good ☐ Satisfactory ☑ Improvement needed	Summary Suspect his social style for Jones is not amiable, but more driver. During preliminaries, Harry spent too much time with small talk. Jones getting a little irritated. Value was generic; could have been more specific to Jones' program.
Probing Customer Lead	☐ Very good ☐ Satisfactory ☑ Improvement needed	Summary Customer lead probing needs work even though Harry had written down probes beforehand. Perhaps role-playing would solve this.
Probing Sales Lead	☑ Very good ☐ Satisfactory ☐ Improvement needed	Summary Excellent job on sales engineer lead probing. Customer accepted value of MDT samples (see over).
Supporting	☐ Very good ☑ Satisfactory ☐ Improvement needed	Summary Overall very good, especially on sampling and the need for quality. Missed one check for acceptance on rig time.
Customer Objection	☑ Very good ☐ Satisfactory ☑ Improvement needed skepticism	Summary Brilliant job on customer indifference and drawback regarding sampling. Missed chance to offer reference letter for skepticism on rig time savings. Made another meeting to get back to Jones regarding this! Not efficient use of time.
Closing	☐ Very good ☐ Satisfactory ☑ Improvement needed	Summary Didn't check for any other issues before moving to next steps. Did not review accepted benefits, but this was OK as meeting was short.
Aligning	☐ Very good ☐ Satisfactory ☑ Improvement needed	Summary Could have been better as Jones wanted to get on with business, yet Harry was still making small talk. Some of Harry's features and benefits dwelled on the technical details, which did not interest Jones.
Listening	☐ Very good ☐ Satisfactory ☑ Improvement needed	Summary During Harry's sales engineer lead probing, he was not listening or confirming or clarifying what Jones was saying. During Harry's support, he was too technical; Jones was starting to drift to lower levels of involvement, which Harry didn't seem to recognize.

Performance Area	Improvement Actions	
☐ Technical knowledge ☐ Account knowledge ☑ Sales skill	☐ Observation ☑ Review ☐ Other ☐ Preparation ☐ Role play ☐ Research ☐ Training	In general, Harry is doing a pretty good job in most aspects of the sales call, as evidenced by his achieving his primary objective. Believe doing a role-play to improve in the areas in which he needs improvement would achieve the necessary focus and improvements on his next sales call. Look forward to the next Level 2. JPA
☐ Technical knowledge ☐ Account knowledge ☐ Sales skill	☐ Observation ☐ Review ☐ Other ☐ Preparation ☐ Role play ☐ Research ☐ Training	
☐ Technical knowledge ☐ Account knowledge ☐ Sales skill	☐ Observation ☐ Review ☐ Other ☐ Preparation ☐ Role play ☐ Research ☐ Training	

Fig. 7.24

Completed level 2 sales call review comments section.

tion, ask for supports you can use as sales aids. You may also have to attend technical training if you have not had sufficient technical training on the product or services.

As part of the service and product introduction of any new product, a sales toolbox should be provided. The toolbox has a generic customer presentation that lists the product or service details, theory, as well as key features, benefits and applications. Review the customer presentation in the toolbox and thoroughly understand the material so you can customize the features, benefits, and application to each customer.

When arranging meetings for your next sales calls, ask what the customers want as main requirements for the opportunities you are going to discuss (open visualizing probe). Make certain your sales call support worksheet addresses each requirement. Be prepared to support the requirements. It is a good idea to review your sales call support worksheet with the domain expert before going on the call.

2. **Over-controlling the Call.** A symptom of this problem is using too many closed probes. When this happens, the customer will tend to make brief responses. Even when the customer does talk, you don't respond to what's expressed as important. Instead, you provide support on the basis of untested assumptions. By failing to listen interactively for understanding or rapport, you do not align with the customer. As a result, the customer remains at a lower level of participation, possibly at a lower listening level, and may be reluctant to give any significant commitment for next steps.

   This approach is especially inappropriate when dealing with Expressive customers, who enjoy an active give-and-take and respond best when given a chance to talk. Over-control also alienates Driver customers, who want to control the conversation themselves. While Analytical customers expect a pragmatic approach, they resist any effort to force their attention. Amiable customers reject salespeople who try to force the conversation and fail to build rapport.

Possible Causes

Sales Skills Deficiency: You have not mastered the skill of probing, particularly the use of open probes, to uncover requirements and to align. You may also fail to listen effectively when the customer responds to probes. You make little effort to raise the customer from lower levels of participation and listen at higher levels. Thus, you conduct the call in a way that better complements your own personality type, rather than the customer's. You have little or no ability to recognize the customer's personality type.

Technical Knowledge: Sufficient product knowledge may also be lacking. As a result, you can't relate new requirements to product and service features and benefits, and you force the discussion into areas you are prepared to handle.

Improvement Actions

If deficient sales skills are the problem, review the section on probing in this chapter, and the aligning strategies for all personality types in Chapter 5 "Communication Skills." The result of effective probing and aligning is to have the customer talk freely and for you to listen to what is said. It's important for customers to state in their own words what's important to them.

If you believe you have a good understanding of probing and aligning skills, conduct role-playing in which you play the role of the customer and your colleague takes the role of the controlling salesperson. After the role-playing, debrief on how it feels to be on the receiving end of an overly controlled probing strategy.

This problem can also be the symptom of a very well-prepared salesperson. When you have done a very good job of preparing and researching the customer's needs, there can be a tendency to want to demonstrate how well prepared you are. Instead of using preparation to respond to expressed requirements, you conduct the sales call only to confirm your findings. Remember, this approach is a sales lead probing strategy and should be used only when appropriate. As suggested earlier, begin by using a customer lead probing strategy. Use the salesperson probing strategy only for requirements you believe the customer has, but they have not raised them as an issue.

In subsequent calls, be sure you are thoroughly prepared and use your aligning strategies for each sales call skill. Use your customer lead probing strategy immediately after the opening. Also check with another salesperson who knows the contact to confirm an accurate classification of the customer's social style.

If your preparation is sufficient, engage in role-playing in which you play the salesperson and practice using your customer lead probing and aligning strategies for the given scenario. Ask the observer to interrupt the role-play if you start to use too many closed probes or do not confirm the customer's expressed statements accurately.

If deficient technical knowledge is the problem, follow the same improvement action for technical knowledge, described in the first problem of this section, "Does Not Recognize Opportunities and Requirements When Customer Expresses Them." Seek technical support from a domain expert and determine how to correct the problem, either through better sales call preparation or training.

As you have already seen from the above improvement actions, the foundation to improving sales call performance is completing the sales call preparation worksheet. If all the preparation is complete from technical services—feature/benefit considerations—the problem is in the execution of the skill.

3. **Probing Without Apparent Direction.** You probe, but without the necessary focus to elicit meaningful responses. You may use too many open probes, even when not yielding relevant information. This unstructured approach causes an Analytical customer to doubt your competence and true concern. The Amiable customer, while welcoming questions up to a point, also wants feedback to responses. Driver customers quickly feel that endless probing is wasting time. Expressive customers want probes to culminate in discussion of how their ideas will be turned into reality. By not making clear the purpose or direction of extended probing, you risk irritating—and even alienating—all these types of customers.

Possible Causes

Sales Skills Deficiency: You are not comfortable enough with probing skills, aligning, and raising strategies to formulate logical questions quickly. You may also be concentrating on what you will say next, rather than listening actively for understanding and building rapport.

Technical Knowledge: You lack sufficient knowledge of the customer's requirements or personality type (or both) to ask appropriate questions and establish rapport.

Improvement Actions

If deficient sales skills are the problem, first make certain you have completed sufficient pre-call preparation, so your probes are directed toward the areas of highest potential need. By using a complete sales call preparation worksheet, your sales call meetings will have a much better defined purpose and logical flow from the opening to a natural conclusion at the closing.

If sales call preparation is not the problem, conduct a role-play in which you play the salesperson. This should help overcome the problem. Pay close attention to your opening and the early part of the sales call, as this part of the meeting provides the direction for the call. Record the role-play and play it back. Analyze your performance. Discuss any points with the person playing the customer. You should identify where better probing would have improved the effectiveness of the sales call role-play.

If deficient technical knowledge is the problem, follow the improvement procedures described earlier. Before going on your next sales call, review your sales call supporting worksheet with the domain expert.

4. **"You Tell Instead of Support"—Don't Ask Enough Questions.** You do most of the talking, and the customer is forced to listen most of the time. The Amiable customer dislikes this approach, preferring a collaborative give-and-take. The Analytical customer feels ignored and their input is not being considered. The Driver customer resents your attempt to control the conversation, plus the apparent lack of concern for the customer's ideas and objectives. The Expressive customer, standing ready to explain a preferred ideas, becomes frustrated when not given the opportunity to do so. In most of these cases, customers remain at low participation and listening levels. In this type of sales call, the probability of the customer making a significant commitment in the closing is low.

Possible Causes

Sales Skills Deficiency: You are not comfortable with the skill of probing, especially as part of the interactive listening process. You may not see the value in probing, feeling that it's easier and more efficient to tell someone about the product or service than it is to ask a lot of questions. Therefore, you choose to operate in more of a telling mode rather than probing and supporting the customer's requirements. You also may not recognize the customer's personality type, and can't probe in a way that achieves alignment.

Technical Knowledge: You are not sure of what questions to ask because you depend on the standard technical presentation, regardless of the customer involved.

Improvement Actions

If deficient skills are the problem, review this chapter's materials on probing and supporting. When you take the approach of "telling instead of selling," from a customer's point of view, it will appear as if your objective is to simply to sell your services and not help meet the customer's objectives and project requirements. This lack of customer focus may make it difficult for the customer to appreciate what is different about your solution. This is not the approach to take. As discussed several times in this textbook, the professional salesperson must apply the consultative selling approach. You are in the business of providing customer solutions and building strong business relationships.

Before each sales call, be sure to have thoroughly prepared your customer lead probing strategy. Start each sales call with a visualizing open probe and follow up with open probes, following the customer lead probing strategy. Also, pay close attention to your aligning strategies. In preparing for the sales call, check with your peers and discuss the social profile of the customer you are going to visit.

With your sales preparation worksheet complete, conduct a role-play in which you play the salesperson. Tape-record or videotape the role-play and play it back so that you can analyze your performance.

If possible, plan to accompany another salesperson on a sales call as part of a modeling sales call. Select a salesperson you believe is very good at using all the sales skills, or get the recommendation of your sales manager. Plan to have another level 2 sales call review to observe the use of probing and aligning skills to check for improvement in this area.

If deficient technical knowledge is the problem, follow the improvement procedures described earlier. Before going on your next sales call, review your sales call supporting worksheet with the domain expert.

5. **Supports Prematurely.** You support whenever the customer describes a problem or dissatisfaction, thinking it might be a need. You may also support vague

requirements that lack appropriate definition. As a result, you lose credibility by supporting issues you don't fully understand—issues that may not, in fact, be important to the customer or may not be real issues at all. The customer quickly loses interest, and you may be unable to establish rapport or gain any meaningful commitment.

Possible Causes

Sales Skills Deficiency: You don't know the difference between situational information and problem information, and/or opportunities and requirements, and you don't probe for understanding to confirm requirements. You might lack a probing strategy for developing background information on opportunities and requirements. Your supports, therefore, are premature.

Account Knowledge: You're not familiar enough with the customer's company to understand potential problems or specific requirements. You, therefore, tend to support vague requirements.

Improvement Actions

If deficient sales skills are the problem, review the probing and supporting sections of this chapter. Understand the purpose of each step of the probing and supporting processes. Before each sales call, make sure to fully complete the sales call preparation probing strategies for both the customer and sales lead.

Conduct a mini role-play in which you play salesperson. Your colleague plays the customer, making various statements of opportunities and requirements. The "customer" should prompt you when necessary to probe for understanding and to confirm requirements before supporting.

If deficient account knowledge is the problem, first review the materials in Chapter 2 "Value Drivers," Chapter 3 "Account Corporate Profile" and Chapter 4 "Opportunities Management." Then identify the higher-level business drivers for the customer's project. Before you go to the sales call, be sure you have reviewed and considered the information in the your CRM database.

Print the account corporate profile and review it with a customer from the accounting, ask for feedback.

Review the opportunity-specific sales supporting worksheets with other sales people who are familiar with the account and get their feedback on the business drivers for the opportunity. Make the connection for what your company is providing with a higher-level customer business drivers.

In your next sales calls, use a visualizing probe to ask what the main business drivers are for the opportunity.

6. **Weak Support Statements.** You neglect to acknowledge the customer's need (the first step of supporting), and instead start to tell the customer about the product or service. or you make support statements with features only, neglecting to introduce benefits that describe how the product's features will satisfy the customer's requirement. As a result, the customer may not listen to or understand the value of what you have to offer and will not be aware of the benefits or value to justify making a commitment if you are more expensive than your competitors.

Possible Causes

Sales Skills Deficiency: You have not mastered the steps of supporting or fully understanding the purpose of the supporting steps.

Account and Technical Knowledge: You do not have enough product or account knowledge to make strong, logical connections between the customer's requirements and the product or service you offer. Instead, you continue to rely on general benefits for all supporting situations.

Improvement Actions

If deficient sales skills are the problem, review the materials on supporting. Understand the reasons you are acknowledging the customer's requirement. Then support with features and benefits, explaining why you also test for value.

Review your sales call preparation worksheet to be sure you have thoroughly completed the sales call supporting worksheet with benefits and customer value estimates.

If preparation is not a problem, conduct a mini role-play in which you play the salesperson. Have your colleague play the customer, stating the requirements. Respond with support statements and have the role-playing customer prompt you if you forget any steps of supporting. If you support with only a feature (but no benefit), ask the role-playing customer to say, "So what?" Do this until you feel confident that you can apply the skill of supporting well.

If possible, plan to accompany another salesperson on a sales call as part of a modeling sales call. Select a salesperson who is very good at using all the sales skills, or get the recommendation of your sales manager. Plan to have another level 2 sales call review to observe the use of supporting skills to check for improvement in this area.

If deficient technical knowledge is the problem, follow the improvement procedures described earlier. Before going on your next sales call, review your sales call supporting worksheet with the domain expert.

If deficient account knowledge is the problem, follow the improvement procedures described earlier. Before going on your next sales call, review the account profile and have another salesperson familiar with the account comment on your opportunity-specific and sales call supporting worksheets. Also discuss the higher-level business drivers in relation to the opportunity and sales call.

7. **Makes Weak or Unrealistic Closing Statements or Fails to Close.** You fail to summarize the benefits and value that the customer has agreed are important, or you close with tentative language or language unsuited to the customer's personality type. You do not formulate a logical, realistic action plan that requires customer commitment. As a result, the customer is ready to accept and is waiting for you to close and recommend the next steps. This is risky because customers in this position are liable to slip from acceptance and back down into less positive attitudes.

Possible Causes

Sales Skills Deficiency: You may not have mastered the skill of closing. You may not be able to react appropriately to what happens on the call, or may not recognize the value of the skill steps. Also, you may be unable to close in terms that satisfy the customer's personality type.

Account Knowledge: You may not know enough about the customer's business to formulate a logical, realistic action plan. You may have neglected to think through the commitment in pre-call preparation. The result is either a tentative closing or an unrealistic request for commitment.

Improvement Actions

If deficient sales skills are the problem, review the materials on closing in this chapter. Review your sales call preparation worksheet and, in particular, the objectives for the sales call and your aligning strategies for closing.

Conduct a role-play in which you are the salesperson using the sales call preparation worksheet for an upcoming sales call. Have your colleague, acting as the customer, assume a particular personality type, telling you what that type is. Write out a full closing statement appropriate for that personality type. Assume the customer has accepted the supports you have listed in the sales call worksheet. Use one of the techniques listed in Chapter Highlight 7.2: "Sign Here, Here, and Here" or the sidebar "Is it a Big C or Little C?" Now conduct the role-play starting at the closing. Do this several times, each time having the role-playing customer take on a different social profile.

If possible, plan to accompany another salesperson on a sales call as part of a modeling sales call. Select a salesperson who is very good at using all the sales skills, or get the recommendation of your sales manager. Plan to have another level 2 sales call review to observe the use of closing skills and check for improvement in this area.

If preparation is the problem, closely review your actions and sales call objectives section of the sales call preparation worksheet. Be sure you are fully developing your list of possible actions that could advance the opportunity for both the customer and your company. Have another salesperson review your list to see if anything should be added.

If deficient account knowledge is the problem, follow the improvement procedures described earlier. Before going on your next sales call, review the account profile and have another salesperson familiar with the account comment on your sales call objectives. Also list possible actions that could advance the opportunity plan. In addition, review the role your contact has in the buying center to ensure that the proposed next steps are appropriate.

▶ ***Planning Sales Calls and Success***

In a large sales force in a very competitive market in North America, the most successful sales representative was a twenty year seniority employee with ten years in the sales role. He handled more accounts and had better sales results than most of the other sales representatives.

When asked how he was able to manage more accounts and achieve above-average results, as measured by higher key services sales ratios and lower discounts, he pointed to a binder on his shelf. On the spine of the binder was "Sales Call Preparation Work-sheets 1991." It was next to similar binders for 1990 and 1989. Every sales call he had made in 1991 was in chronological order. Each pre-call and post sales call analysis section was complete with a photocopy of any support aids he used. When questioned why he, as a seasoned sales representative, would go through the planning stages each and every time, and wouldn't that be a waste of his time, he grinned and said, "No, I think it would be a waste of the customer's time if I didn't."

Learning a New Skill

This chapter has presented the sales calls skills needed to successfully execute the need-satisfaction process and all the skills required to achieve the highest level of sales call effectiveness. To the new salesperson, all the concepts added together might seem overwhelming. If you try to apply them all at the same time in your next sales call, the results could be much less than you hope for. As in learning any new skill, following a few guidelines can help you be successful.

First, understand the concepts and feel comfortable in how to apply them. You can accomplish this by completing the "Applying the Concept" exercises. Next, before going on your sales call, prepare by using the sales call preparation worksheets described in this chapter. Successful salespersons make preparation part of their daily sales routine. See the sidebar "Planning Sales Calls and Success" for an example from one experienced and successful salesperson. Select one or two of the sales call skills to focus on in your next sales call. Chances are you are already in a sales position and making sales calls, so you need only to use the material in this chapter to modify your sales call routine and improve your effectiveness. As in any other activity that is new at first, it may feel awkward. You may stumble the first few times, but don't give up. If you are having a problem executing a sales skill, try doing some role-plays or single skill practice.

Review the seven common sales call skill deficiencies to learn if the one you are having a problem with is on the list.

If you are part of a sales team, include as part of your annual objectives a minimum of four level 2 reviews with your sales manager. You will benefit from having someone observe your sales call and from the sales manager's experience. Consider this practice as part of your personal TQM program. When selecting your level 2 review sales call, choose one that is in a low pressure, early in the opportunity management process, or in a sell opportunity during the execution stage, after you have been awarded the contract.

The sales call activity is one of several daily activities that occur between you and the account. The need-satisfaction process provides guidelines for how you conduct your sales calls. The sales call is a frequently used and important tool in the consultative selling approach. When properly conducted, the sales call can strengthen the relationship between you and your customer. It can also enable your company to provide services at a profit by capturing a portion of the added value that the customer recognizes you provide.

As stated at the start of the chapter, sales success is the natural consequence of consistently applying the basic fundamentals. For salespeople, the basic fundamental is the sales call.

Summary of Chapter Objectives

1. Understand the structure of the sales call.

The sales call is the application of the need-satisfaction process consisting of the **pre-call planning, execution, and review** immediately following the sales call. Sales representatives need to become proficient at every phase of sales call skills early in their careers. This is a five-step process consisting of preliminaries, opening, probing, supporting, and closing.

2. Understand and use the sales call skills.

The sales call is a key component of the sales representative's skills. Without good sales call skills, even a sales representative who has great products and services knowledge is unlikely to be successful. Sales call skills are built on the foundation of effective communication skills. The sales call structure starts with preliminaries; in this step, the salesperson reduces the initial tension that may exist early in the sales call and uses this time to build rapport, let the customer know what preparation you have done, confirming the time available for the meeting, and asking permission to take notes. After the preliminaries is the opening. In the opening the sales representative introduces the topic of discussion by stating the agenda and the means to be used to convey the messages. The means may consist of a presentation, showing examples, introducing another team member, and so on. After the agenda has been presented, the sales representative states the value the customer should receive from the meeting and, before beginning the discussion, confirms acceptance by the customer and checks for the customer's agenda.

The **discussion** part of the sales call delivers the message the sales representative wants to convey. This involves **probing** and **supporting** customer requirements. There are two main probing strategies.

The first and most common is **customer lead probing**. The sales representative primarily uses open probes to gain a deeper understanding of the customer's business **situation, problems, or opportunities,** plus **implications** of the problem or opportunity, which reveal **needs** and **payoffs** for addressing the problem or opportunity.

The second probing strategy is the **sales lead probing strategy**. It is used typically as a backup to the customer lead probing strategy, when the customer lead probing strategy does not uncover all the requirements for which you can provide a solution. The sales lead probing strategy uses a combination of **open** and **closed probes** to confirm the requirements the sales representative believes the customer may have. Executing this strategy requires several steps. The sales representative develops a probing sequence that confirms the **problem** exists, determines the size or **magnitude** of the problem, confirms the **consequences** of not addressing the problem, and finishes with a **look/listen** probe. The latter probe establishes whether the customer would like to have more information on how your company can address the problem or issue.

The sales representative should identify a requirement, have a complete and mutual understanding of the requirement, and know how his or her company can provide a solution. Next, the sales representative **supports** the requirement with a **feature** and **benefit.** In a supporting action, the sales representative **acknowledges the need, describes the relevant features and benefits, demonstrates capabilities, checks for customer acceptance**, and then **tests for a specific customer value**.

The sales meeting may involve a variety of probing and supporting sequences. These continue to the point at which the customer or the sales representative has no more to offer for expressed requirements. It is critical for the sales representative to be as efficient as possible during the discussion. The task is to quickly identify requirements the customer is prepared to address. The salesperson then supports, presenting only features and benefits relevant for the customer's requirements. To ensure that the discussion process is conducted as efficiently as possible, the sales representative uses the communication skills of **aligning**, monitoring **tension levels** during the discussion, and staying at **level 1 listening.** Every attempt should be made to keep the customer at the higher levels of listening and involved in the discussion. The sales representative must stay alert to recognize the customer's closing signals and know when to conclude the meeting.

The last step in the need-satisfaction process is the closing. In the closing, the salesperson starts by asking if there are any **other issues** the customer wants to discuss. This is followed by a **review of accepted benefits, asking for the next steps** and **confirming acceptance**.

3. Apply the total quality management (TQM) process to the sales call process and complete the preparation and analysis steps before and after each sales call.

The TQM process for sales calls consists of **pre-call planning, execution**, and **post-call outcome analysis**, followed by a level 1 sales effectiveness review conducted after each sales call and, finally, a level 2 sales effectiveness review conducted on a less frequent basis.

The pre-call planning is conducted before each sales call and consists of completing the sales call preparation worksheet. The worksheet facilitates pre-call planning, the execution of the call, and post-call analysis. The sections of the sales call worksheet are the **buying center profile**, a list of **possible actions** the customer could take, and agreed-to actions you could take to advance the sales strategy for the opportunity. The other sections are the **preferred objectives** for the sales call and appropriate tactic(s) for the sales call, a list of questions the sales representative wants to have answered by the customer, questions the customer may have for the salesperson, planned **probing strategies, sales call supporting worksheet, closing summary**, and **level 1 review form**. Using the sales call preparation worksheet, the sales representative is now well prepared to conduct a successful sales meeting.

Immediately after the sales call, the sales representative concludes the sales call processes by completing a **post sales call analysis**. In the post sales call analysis, the sales representative completes a **sales call outcome analysis** by summarizing and communicating the **action items** to sales team members who need know what was agreed on with the customer in the sales call. The sales representative also classifies the **outcome** of the sales call as a **success**, resulting in an **order or advance**, or as **unsuccessful**, resulting in a **continuation or rejection** of any next steps proposed by the sales representative. Based on the outcome of the sales call, the sales representative completes a **strategic review** and decides if the opportunity sales plan should have a **tactic** added, modified, or removed. The post sales call analysis should be entered into the CRM database as a **Customer Visit Report (CVR)**. The final step of the post sales call analysis occurs when the sales representative completes a **level 1 sales effectiveness review**. In this review, the sales representative evaluates the execution of each step of the sales call. The object is to identify strengths and improvement areas, and to develop a plan to leverage the strengths and simultaneously target areas for improvement in future sales calls.

On a less frequent but regularly scheduled basis, the sales representative should complete a **level 2 sales effectiveness review**. This review requires the presence of either the manager or other sales professional trained in the sales processes. This meeting observer will accompany the sales representative on a sales call and observe the interactions. The outcome of a **sales call observation** is a critical review of the sales representative's sales skill strengths and weaknesses as well as action plan for improvement. The **improvement areas** can be classified as **sales skills, account knowledge**, or **technical product or service knowledge**. The actions can include **practicing** specific skills, conducting **role-plays**, preparing better, **researching** the account, **observing** a modeling sales call, attending **training**, and completing **other actions** as agreed between the observer and sales representative.

Applying the Concepts

1. Complete a sales call preparation worksheet and level 1 review for an upcoming sales call you have planned. Be as thorough as possible when completing the different parts of the worksheet. Take time to develop your list of possible actions to advance the sales strategy and a list of questions you would like to have answered in the sales meeting a well as questions your customer may have of you. Show your sales call preparation worksheet to another salesperson who is familiar with the account. Ask for input regarding your plan and the social profile of the contact(s) you are going to meet. The electronic version of the sales call worksheet is available from the textbook website.
2. Develop a sales aid for one of your key services or products that you can use in an upcoming sales call to demonstrate capabilities. When developing your sales aid, be sure it fits onto one sheet of paper and is customized for the specific customer contact you are visiting. Be certain it is appropriate for the customer's social profile, technology adaptability, and role in the buying center. Develop a brief, clear feature benefit description and an example application. If possible, include a list of references and list of recent accounts who have used the product or service. On the backside of your sales aid, list information you would require to calculate the specific dollar value the benefits would create for the account. Refer to the guidelines in Chapter 6 "Sales Activities" for creating a proposal.
3. What processes should you have in the region to enable the sales team to consistently capture supporting materials and produce sales aids for use in your sales meetings? What additional steps would be needed to make the materi-

als ready for use in advertising in your local chapter of a professional society newsletter? Would this be a program that could impact the success of the region? Who would have to be involved in the program and what types of incentives would be needed to make the program a success?

4. Are there any changes you can recommend to improve the sales call preparation and outcome analysis worksheets?
5. Assuming you have completed a sales call using the sales call preparation worksheet, how beneficial would you rate this practice on a scale of 1 to 5, where 1 is no benefit to you and 5 is excellent?
6. Who in the region would be best qualified to assist in a salesperson's level 2 sales effectiveness review? How many level 2 reviews should a salesperson complete per year? Should the level 2 program be part of the salesperson's incentive program? Should it be part of the sales manager's incentive program?
7. Which of the sales call skills do you find the most difficult to execute? Why do you find these difficult? Which ones do you find the easiest? Why do you find these easy?
8. Discuss and compare the techniques you use to execute the sales call with other salespeople in your office.

References

1. Rohn. J. (n.d.). BrainyQuote.com. Retrieved June 5, 2015, from http://www.brainyquote.com/quotes/quotes/j/jimrohn122132.html
2. Rackham, N.: *SPIN Selling,* New York, McGraw-Hill (1988).
3. White Paper: The PRIME Actions to Win More Quickly. (n.d.). Retrieved June 10, 2015, from http://content.thetasgroup.com/white-paper/the-prime-actions-to-win-more-quickly?utm_source=Resources&utm_medium=image&utm_campaign=White Paper_The_Prime_Actions
4. Adopted from Rackham, N.: *SPIN Selling.*
5. There are many probing strategies that have been developed over the centuries, beginning with the Socratic method, also known as the method of elenchus, elenctic method, or Socratic debate. This technique is named after the classical Greek philosopher, Socrates. It is a form of inquiry and discussion between individuals, based on asking and answering questions to stimulate critical thinking and to illuminate ideas. One of the modern techniques developed by the PAR Group is explained in their book *Cracking the Code to Leadership: The PAR Skills.* Their technique uses the acronym, NIQCL (pronounced "nickel"), which stands for understanding how others feel about Needs, Importance, Quantify, Consequences, and Look/Listen.
6. Herrington, G., & Malone, P.: *Cracking the Code to Leadership: The PAR Skills*, West Conshohocken, PA, Infinity Publishing (2007).

Sales Call Preparation Worksheet

BUYING CENTER PROFILE

Date:__________ **Account:**__________ **Opportunity:**__________

Stage:__________ **Competitive Strategy:**__________

Reviewed Account Corporate Profile? ☐Yes ☐ No __________

Contact	Position	Role	Social Style	Technology Adoption

CRM Database up-to-date and complete? ☐Yes ☐ No __________

Social Style Preferences

ALIGNING STRATEGIES

Social Style	Driver	Expressive	Amiable	Analytical
Factors Likes:	Control	Social	Supportive	Detailed
Measures personal value by:	Power Results	Applause Support	Approval Attention	Respect Activity
Needs environment:	Responds	Inspires to their goals	Suggests	Provides details
For decisions give them:	Options and probabilities	Testimony incentives	Guarantees and assurances	Evidence and service
Take time to be:	Efficient	Stimulating	Agreeable	Accurate
Support their:	Conclusions and actions	Dreams and intuitions	Relationships	Principles

OBJECTIVES

Sales Call Tactic(s):

☐ Prove value
☐ Retrieve information
☐ Insulate against competition
☐ Minimize weaknesses
☐ Emphasize strengths

Sales Call Primary Objective:__________

Backup Objective:__________

Preliminaries

PRELIMINARIES

Business Card ___ **Rapport** __________ **Preparation** __________ **Time** ____ **Notes** ______
Video ______

OPENING

Agenda:__________

Value Proposition:__________

Check for Acceptance:__________

Check for Customer's Agenda: __________

Appendix A

Sales Call Preparation Worksheet

Actions

Actions the customer should agree to do to achieve the sales call objectives:	D Desirable	F Feasible	R Ranking
1	High Med Low	High Med Low	
2	High Med Low	High Med Low	
3	High Med Low	High Med Low	
Actions your company should take to achieve the sales call objectives:			
4	High Med Low	High Med Low	
5	High Med Low	High Med Low	
6	High Med Low	High Med Low	

ACTIONS

Questions

Questions you want to ask: 4 P's of Questioning, Prefacing, Phrasing, Pacing, Pursuing

		S Situations	P Problems	I Implication	N Need Payoff	✔ Answer
1	Preface Question					
2	Preface Question					
3	Preface Question					
4	Preface Question					
5	Preface Question					

Questions the customer may want to ask you: Capabilities, Personnel, Management, References, Pricing, Service, OSH&E, Problems, Successes

1 Question

Answer

2 Question

Answer

3 Question

Answer

4 Question

Answer

5 Question

Answer

QUESTIONS

Sales Call Preparation Worksheet

Customer Lead

Situation Probes: Probe about the current situation.

Problem/Opportunity Probes: Probe for problems or key factors for opportunity. Visualize open probes.

Implications Probes: Probe about the implications of problem or opportunity.

Need Payoff Probes: Probe about benefits of addressing problem or opportunity.

CUSTOMER LEAD PROBING

Sales Lead: short description of the problem or issue

Problem/Opportunity Probe: Probe to confirm if problem or opportunity exists.

Quantifying Probe: Probe to confirm the size and frequency of the problem or opportunity.

Consequence Probe: Probe to identify consequences of inaction.

Look/Listen Probe: Probe to confirm willingness to see or hear how you can assist with this issue.

SALES LEAD PROBING 1

Sales Lead

Problem/Opportunity Probe:

Quantifying Probe:

Consequence Probe:

Look/Listen Probe:

SALES LEAD PROBING 2

Sales Lead

Problem/Opportunity Probe:

Quantifying Probe:

Consequence Probe:

Look/Listen Probe:

SALES LEAD PROBING 3

Supporting Worksheet

Sales Call Solution Profile

Customer Need	Feature/Benefit	Support	Test for Value
Supporting 1. Acknowledge 2. Describe feature benefit 3. Demonstrate capabilities 4. Check for acceptance 5. Test for value		**Possible Objection:** ☐ Indifference ☐ Skepticism ☐ Misunderstanding ☐ Drawback ☐ Fear	**Estimated Value:**
		Support Documents:	**Parameters:**

Customer Need	Feature/Benefit	Support	Test for Value
Supporting 1. Acknowledge 2. Describe feature benefit 3. Demonstrate capabilities 4. Check for acceptance 5. Test for value		**Possible Objection:** ☐ Indifference ☐ Skepticism ☐ Misunderstanding ☐ Drawback ☐ Fear	**Estimated Value:**
		Support Documents:	**Parameters:**

Customer Need	Feature/Benefit	Support	Test for Value
Supporting 1. Acknowledge 2. Describe feature benefit 3. Demonstrate capabilities 4. Check for acceptance 5. Test for value		**Possible Objection:** ☐ Indifference ☐ Skepticism ☐ Misunderstanding ☐ Drawback ☐ Fear	**Estimated Value:**
		Support Documents:	**Parameters:**

Customer Need	Feature/Benefit	Support	Test for Value
Supporting 1. Acknowledge 2. Describe feature benefit 3. Demonstrate capabilities 4. Check for acceptance 5. Test for value		**Possible Objection:** ☐ Indifference ☐ Skepticism ☐ Misunderstanding ☐ Drawback ☐ Fear	**Estimated Value:**
		Support Documents:	**Parameters:**

Appendix B

Post Sales Call Analysis

Closing

Closing

1. Check for any other issues
2. Review benefits accepted
3. Propose next steps
4. Check for acceptance

Objective Achieved:
☐ Primary
☐ Backup
☐ Other
☐ None

Accepted Benefits:

Total Value Accepted:

Sales Call Outcome Analysis:

Successful: ☐ Order ☐ Advance **Unsuccessful:** ☐ Continuation ☐ Rejection

Opportunity Management Process Review:

Probability of Winning Opportunity: ____%

Updated timing for opportunity management process milestones:

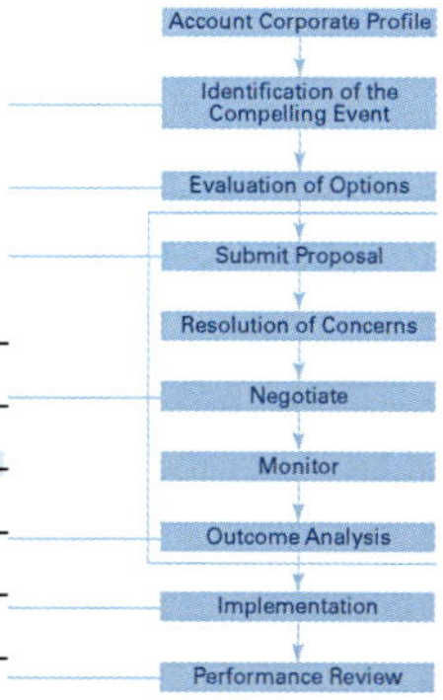

Analysis: ____

STRATEGIC POST SALES CALL OUTCOME ANALYSIS

PRIME Tactic Response: ☐ Add a tactic ☐ Cancel a tactic ☐ Modify a tactic ☐ No change

Responsible	Description	Due Date
1.		
2.		
3.		

NEXT STEPS ACTION ITEMS – TACTICS

CVR entered into CRM Opportunity ☐ ____

CRM Account, Contact, Opportunity Information Updated ☐ ____

Level 1 Sales Call Effectiveness Review:

Process	Need Improvement	Good	Very Good	Comments
Preliminaries				
Opening				
Customer Lead Probing				
Sales Lead Probing				
Supporting				
Closing				
Objection Handling				
Presence				
Relating				
Questioning				
Answering Questions				
Listening				
Checking				
Positioning				
Handling Tension				

PROCESS

CRITICAL COMMUNICATION SKILLS

Support Documents:
☐ Need to develop ____ ☐ Need to modify ____

Appendix C

Level 2 Sales Effectiveness Review

PRE-CALL BRIEFING

Sales Engineer: Account: Contact: Observer: Date:

Sales Call Objective:

Sales Call Skill Focus:

Sales Call Preparation Worksheet reviewed ☐ Account Profile ☐ Sales Plan ☐

PRELIMINARIES

Steps	Greeting	Rapport	Preparation	Time Check	Notes
Preliminaries					

OPENING

Steps	Agenda	Value Proposition	Check for Acceptance	Check Customer's Agenda
Opening				

PROBING CUSTOMER LEAD

Steps	Situation	Problem	Implications	Need Payoff Confirmation Probe
Customer Lead				

PROBING SALES LEAD

Steps	Problem	Quantify	Consequences	Look/Listen
Sales Lead				

SUPPORTING

Steps	Acknowledge Requirement	Feature Benefit	Demonstrate Capabilities	Check for Acceptance	Test for Value
Supporting					

Objection Handling

INDIFFERENCE

Steps	Probe to Understand Customer's Position	Acknowledge Customer's Position	Ask Permission to Probe	☐ Problem ☐ Quantify ☐ Consequence ☐ Look/listen
Indifference				

MISUNDERSTANDING

Steps	Probe to Understand Concern	Acknowledge Customer's Concern	Acknowledge Requirement Not Met	Explain Feature Benefit	Check for Acceptance
Misunderstanding					

SKEPTICISM

Steps	Probe to Understand Concern	Acknowledge Customer's Concern	Offer Relevant Proof	Check for Acceptance
Skepticism				

DRAWBACK

Steps	Probe to Understand Drawback	Acknowledge Drawback	Handle	Check for Acceptance
Drawbacks			☐ Research ☐ Redefine ☐ Trade-off ☐ Outweigh	

CLOSING

Steps	Check for Any Other Issues	Summarize Accepted Benefits and Value	Propose or Ask for Next Steps	Check for Acceptance	Thank the Client
Fear					

FEAR

Steps	Acknowledge Customer's Concern	Connect with the Customer (story, analogy, metaphor)	Recommend Options to Move Forward	Check for Acceptance
Closing				

Critical Communication Skills

SALES CALL DYNAMICS

Skill	Opening	Probing	Supporting	Handling Objection	Closing
Presence					
Relating					
Questioning					
Answering Questions					
Listening					
Checking					
Positioning					
Handling Tension					

Level 2 Sales Call Review

Sales Call Preparation	☐ Very good ☐ Satisfactory ☐ Improvement needed	Summary
Preliminaries	☐ Very good ☐ Satisfactory ☐ Improvement needed	Summary
Opening	☐ Very good ☐ Satisfactory ☐ Improvement needed	Summary
Probing Customer Lead	☐ Very good ☐ Satisfactory ☐ Improvement needed	Summary
Probing Sales Lead	☐ Very good ☐ Satisfactory ☐ Improvement needed	Summary
Supporting	☐ Very good ☐ Satisfactory ☐ Improvement needed	Summary
Customer Objection	☐ Very good ☐ Satisfactory ☐ Improvement needed	Summary
Closing	☐ Very good ☐ Satisfactory ☐ Improvement needed	Summary

COMMENTS

Presence	☐ Very good ☐ Satisfactory ☐ Improvement needed	**Questioning**	☐ Very good ☐ Satisfactory ☐ Improvement needed	**Listening**	☐ Very good ☐ Satisfactory ☐ Improvement needed	**Positioning**	☐ Very good ☐ Satisfactory ☐ Improvement needed
Relating	☐ Very good ☐ Satisfactory ☐ Improvement needed	**Answering Questions**	☐ Very good ☐ Satisfactory ☐ Improvement needed	**Checking**	☐ Very good ☐ Satisfactory ☐ Improvement needed	**Handling Tension**	☐ Very good ☐ Satisfactory ☐ Improvement needed

Summary

Action Plan

PERFORMANCE AREA	IMPROVEMENT ACTIONS	
☐ Technical knowledge ☐ Account knowledge ☐ Sales skill	☐ Observation ☐ Review ☐ Other ☐ Preparation ☐ Role play ☐ Research ☐ Training	
☐ Technical knowledge ☐ Account knowledge ☐ Sales skill	☐ Observation ☐ Review ☐ Other ☐ Preparation ☐ Role play ☐ Research ☐ Training	
☐ Technical knowledge ☐ Account knowledge ☐ Sales skill	☐ Observation ☐ Review ☐ Other ☐ Preparation ☐ Role play ☐ Research ☐ Training	

Appendix E

Sales Call Skills

Preliminaries

1. Greeting – Business card
2. Rapport building
3. Tell what you have done to prepare
4. Check timing
5. Permission to take notes

Opening

1. State agenda
2. Value Proposition
3. Check for acceptance
4. Check for customer's agenda or propose your agenda, or both

Probing

Customer Lead

1. Situation
2. Problem or Opportunities
3. Implication of problem or opportunity
4. Need payoff – Confirm your understanding of the problem or opportunity and implication.

Probing (cont.)

Sales Lead

1. Problem or opportunity – Confirm the issue exists for customer
2. Quantify the size of the issue
3. Consequences what would happen if the issue was not addressed
4. Look/Listen would the customer like to see or hear more on how you could assist them in addressing the issue

Supporting

1. Acknowledge the need
2. Describe feature and benefits
3. Demonstrate capabilities
4. Check for understanding
5. Test for value

Closing

1. Check for any other issues
2. Review accepted benefits
3. Ask customer for next steps or propose next steps
4. Check for acceptance
5. Thank the client

Handling Customer Objections

8

Getting to Yes!

Previous chapters have discussed the consultative selling approach and how to apply the need-satisfaction process in the key selling activities throughout the opportunities management process. By following this professional sales discipline, you have a better appreciation of customer requirements and higher business drivers. With these sales skills and customer knowledge, you will be able to prepare proposals that are aligned to the customer's requirements and demonstrate your solution's value. Even with your best efforts, however, there will be situations when the customer will have concerns or will not accept your recommendations. Such situations are classified as customer objections. See **Fig. 8.1.**

Chapter Objectives

After reading this chapter, you will be able to:

- Describe most common customer objections encountered during the consultative selling approach process.
- Understand how to react and overcome common customer objections.
- Prepare strategies to avoid customer objections.

Customer Objections

This chapter discusses how to handle the five most common causes of customer objections, as follows:

- Indifference
- Misunderstanding
- Skepticism
- Drawbacks
- Fear

The five types of customer objections can occur at any phase of the opportunity management process. The salesperson is responsible for trying to minimize customer objections by anticipating them and preparing strategies that address the customer's concerns. The best time to address customer objections is early in the opportunities management process—ideally in the evaluation

Fig. 8.1
Common customer objections.

of options phase. But sales staff should also be prepared to address customer concerns that arise later in the opportunity management process.

General Framework of How to Handle Objections

The standard approach to handling any customer objection is as follows:

1. Probe to understand the negative reaction
2. Acknowledge the negative reaction
3. Handle as per the specific negative reaction guidelines
4. Check for acceptance from the customer

By applying this model whenever you get a negative reaction from a customer, you will immediately become more confident and better at handling the situation. Each step will be discussed briefly below, and then the handling of each instance of customer negative response will be addressed in detail.

Probe to Understand the Objection

When the customer states an objection, such as "you are too expensive," the salesperson must probe to gain a better, more detailed understanding of why the customer is stating this before trying to address the response. As stated earlier, there are five main factors that can cause the customer to have an objection during your discussion, and you must identify the cause before attempting to handle the objection. For example, below are all possible answers to the common "you are too expensive" objection.

- **Customer:** "You are too expensive."
  Salesperson: "Can you help me understand why you say that?"
- **Customer response 1:** "What you are suggesting is interesting, but I think we are okay for now—doing it like we always have before." *(indifference)*
- **Customer response 2:** "All those benefits you described. I'm just not confident you will deliver." *(skepticism)*
- **Customer response 3:** "Well, your competitor is offering me the same thing at 20% less." *(misunderstanding)*
- **Customer response 4:** "I have verified that the competitor is offering the exact same product with the same specifications and delivery date." *(drawback)*
- **Customer response 5:** "Your product does not let have the same options as your competitor." *(technical drawback)*
- **Customer response 6:** "Look, I understand what you are offering. But not at this time." *(fear)*

The above examples are all possible responses in customer objection. If you do not understand the reason for the objection, continue to probe until you do and then move to the next step. When the customer does express an objection, ensure that you always express empathy and interest in what the customer has expressed. This can be done with:

- Speaking slower and with an emphasis on "help me understand."
- Using body language (nodding your head, leaning forward, looking concerned).
- Prefacing before you start questions. Prefacing is the statement of why you are asking questions and makes the customer feel comfortable with your

> ▶ ***Do You Care?***
>
> If you are being asked if you care, then you need to read this carefully. Empathy with customers is a very important part of demonstrating your understanding, and nowhere is that more important than when the customer has an objection you want to resolve.
>
> Below are some tips on how to be more empathetic:
>
> **Put aside your viewpoint, and try to see things from the other person's point of view.**
>
> When you do this, you'll realize that other people most likely aren't being evil, unkind, stubborn, or unreasonable. They're probably just reacting to the situation with the knowledge they have.
>
> **Validate the other person's perspective.**
>
> Once you "see" why others believe what they believe, acknowledge it. Remember: Acknowledgement does not always equal agreement. You can accept that people have different opinions from your own, and that they may have good reasons for holding those opinions.
>
> **Examine your attitude.**
>
> Are you more concerned with getting your way, winning, or being right? Or, is your priority to find a solution, build relationships, and accept others? Without an open mind and attitude, you probably won't have enough room for empathy.
>
> **Listen.**
>
> Listen to the entire message that the other person is trying to communicate.
>
> Listen with your ears: What is being said, and what tone is being used?
>
> Listen with your eyes: What is the person doing with his or her body while speaking?
>
> Listen with your instincts: Do you sense that the person is not communicating something important?
>
> Listen with your heart: What do you think the other person feels?
>
> **Ask what the other person would do.**
>
> When in doubt, ask the person to explain his or her position. This is probably the simplest, and most direct way to understand the other person. However, it's probably the least used way to develop empathy.

questions. An example of prefacing for the "you're too expensive" objection is "20% more expensive certainly needs to be explained. Do you mind if I ask you a few more questions?" For more pointers on showing empathy, see the sidebar "Do You Care?"[1]

Acknowledge the Negative Reaction

Once you have a clear understanding of what is causing the objection, then you acknowledge. As recommended in the "Do You Care?" sidebar, acknowledging does not mean you have to agree. You can acknowledge their concern: "Okay, now I understand why you say that we are 20% more expensive" or "I can see now why you think that." While it is possible to show acknowledgment through body language (eye contact, head nod), it is important for you to verbally acknowledge what has been said. The client at this point should be ready to listen to what you have to say about their objection.

Handle as Per the Specific Objection Guidelines

Following this section on the general framework of how to handle objections is a discussion for each one of the five types of objections, as listed earlier. As you handle the objection specifically, addressing the root cause for the objection, you must continually check with the customer that they understand and ask whether they have any questions or concerns.

Check for Acceptance

The customer's objection has been handled successfully when they agree. Failing to check for acceptance if the customer is satisfied with your explanation could give you the wrong impression that the objection has been removed. The other scenario is that the salesperson incorrectly identifies the negative reaction, such as a misunderstanding when the objection was skepticism. In this situation the customer can give very good feedback as you explain your product or service because they do understand and, as you explain, you are in fact reinforcing their understanding, but you have not addressed their skepticism. If you do not check after your explanation if the customer is satisfied with your answer and that the objection they had earlier has been resolved, you would not discover that the skepticism was still there. The first objection to be discussed is customer indifference.

Customer Indifference

For an open exchange of information on a sales call, the client must be interested in the exchange. Sometimes, sales staff must call on clients who are not strongly interested in meeting with them. This commonly happens when you engage with the customer before they have identified the compelling event, which is stage 2 of the customer project management process. Some of the reasons customers may be indifferent include:

- The customer does not realize it is possible to improve their company's current circumstances.
- The customer does not understand the importance of making an improvement, or the particular topic the salesperson wishes to discuss is low on the customer's list of priorities. See the "From Euphoria to Panic" sidebar for another classification of customer indifference.[2]
- The customer is currently in the implementation stage and is using and satisfied with a competitor's product or service. The competitor could be an internally supplied service. The customer assumes that, at the end of the current contract, the company will engage in a repurchase process.
- Previous experiences with your company have not met the customer's expectations.
- The individual customer feels that he or she may lose some control by working with your company.

Other clients may know that they need to improve their circumstances but may be indifferent because:

- They are unwilling to deal with the stress of change.
- They want to avoid decisions they perceive as risky.

Sales staff will know the client is indifferent when the client expresses satisfaction with their current circumstances. When clients are not interested in exchanging information, they may say:

- "We already use the competitor, and we're happy with them."
- "We like the way things are working. We don't need to make any changes."
- "We'd rather handle that internally. We have the resources for it."
- "Sorry. We're just not looking for any help in that area right now."

Overcoming Client Indifference

The process of overcoming indifference must be handled tactfully as the salesperson can do more harm than good by implying that the customer is uninformed. Also, as stated before, the sales model discussed in this textbook is based on the consultative selling process to satisfy the customer's expressed needs and requirements. To overcome a customer's indifference, sales staff must not "push" your company products or services that have not been requested by the customer. Sales staff must maintain a tactful yet searching response to overcome customer indifference and apply the model in a way that is consistent with local cultural norms and expectations. Your approach should consider your knowledge of the custom-

▶ *From Euphoria to Panic*

In the popular Miller-Heiman sales training seminar and book titled *Strategic Selling*, the author describes the buyer's perception of the need to change as being one of four states. These four states can also be compared to the degree of indifference as described by the probability of the customer taking action.

The four states of a customer's need for change, as described by Miller-Heiman, and the expected level of indifference are:

1. **Growth.** There is a gap between the results of today with the results needed for today and future expected demand. The probability of the customer taking action is high.
2. **Trouble.** The results today are projected to worsen in the future. The probability of the customer taking action is high.
3. **Even keel.** The results today and expected future needs are on track. The probability of the customer taking action is low. This customer may exhibit an indifferent attitude to any proposed changes.
4. **Overconfident.** The results today are better than expected, and the future appears to be under control. The probability of the customer making changes is low to none. This customer may exhibit an indifferent attitude to any proposed changes and, in fact, may consider any proposal for change as negative.

Each of these customers can cause the salesperson to have feelings ranging from euphoria to panic regarding the chance of making a sale.

er's situation and social style. The steps to overcome client indifference are shown in the sidebar "How to Overcome Client Indifference." The first two steps bring the client to a point where he or she is willing to exchange information. The third step guides that exchange.

> **▶ *How to Overcome Client Indifference***
>
> When a client expresses indifference:
>
> - Acknowledge the client's point of view.
> - Request permission to probe.
> - Use the sales lead probing process to create client awareness of needs.
> - Support confirmed needs.

Acknowledging the Client's Point of View

Clients who are satisfied with things as they are may think that you'll try to sell them something they don't need. You can reassure a client that this is not your intent by making it clear that you understand and respect theirpoint of view. The time you spend on this step will depend on how you read the client's social profile and, sometimes, on what's appropriate to the culture. You might say: "I understand that you're happy with your current supplier," or "I hear you and appreciate that you're not experiencing any problems right now."

Requesting Permission to Probe

After acknowledging the client's point of view, request permission to probe by making an opening statement with a limited agenda. Your agenda is limited both in scope (asking a few questions) and in time (a few minutes, just long enough to find out if there's a reason for you and the client to continue talking now or at some point in the future). By proposing a limited agenda, you further reassure the client that you aren't trying to apply pressure.

As with other opening statements, you want to state the value of proceeding to the client and check for acceptance. Because you are attempting to reverse indifference, you also want to avoid any appearance of moving ahead without permission, which may seem arrogant or presumptuous. Again, client sensitivity to this point will reflect cultural norms and personality factors. You might say:

"I wonder if I might ask you just a few questions about what you look for in terms of data acquisition. Even though you're satisfied with your current vendor, we might find ways in which we could help you at some future time. Would a few minutes be all right?"

Another example might be:

"If you could spare just a few minutes, I'd like to find out a little about your current plans with regard to the Bintang field, which a lot of people are talking about now. We've had a fair amount of experience out there, some of which could be of value to you. Can you spare another minute or two?"

Use the Sales Lead Probing Process to Create Client Awareness of Needs

Once you've tactfully acknowledged the client's point of view and requested permission to probe, and the client has agreed to exchange information, you probe. The purpose of probing is to build the client's awareness of things that they might want to improve or accomplish and that you can help improve or accomplish.

To probe to create client awareness of needs, use the sales lead probing strategy as described in Chapter 7 "Sales Call Skills." When you verify whether a current problem or opportunity exists, probe to focus quickly and certainly on an area of concern to the client. For example:

"What has your experience been with downtime using your current acquisition methods?"

Gather facts that quantify and qualify the problem in ways the client may not have done. Use these probes to "set up" the consequences questions you'll address next.

▶ No Thank You, We Are Happy with Our Current Supplier

The above statement is not uncommon when you are not the current supplier. Shown to the right is a graphic representation of the likelihood of change as a function of the customer's current level of satisfaction with a current supplier, from great to crisis.

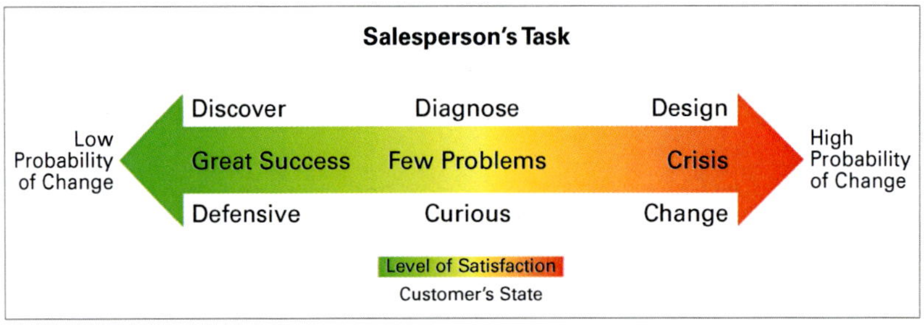

In this scenario customers are indifferent because they are very satisfied with their current supplier; in this situation the customer would be on the left-hand side of the continuum and will appear to be indifferent or defensive during the conversation. Knowing the customer's level of satisfaction gives you a good indicator of the likelihood of change.

The secret is the salesperson's task. If the salesperson wants to improve their chances of winning, then they need to fully understand what factors contribute to their current successes. In this situation, the customer will not want to lose or stop what they believe is a great success. The salesperson will need to support this need by demonstrating to the customer they will continue to enjoy the current successes.

The second task for the salesperson, once the customer is confident they will not lose anything they are enjoying now, is to discover what areas they would like to see improvement in and then support those needs.

For example:

"Could you estimate the number of unproductive hours that you're paying for in an average week in that field right now?"

Focus on the consequences of inaction. Whenever possible, ask about the potential impact of the problem on the individual client. For example:

"Over the course of the project, what impact does this have on your schedule in terms of the objectives you set for the project?"

Gain the client's agreement to look at/listen to your ideas for a solution. You may use a simple closed probe or a visualizing probe. For example:

"It sounds to me like you might want to think about ways to reduce that downtime. Is that correct? If I could show you a way to cut those downtime costs significantly, would you like to hear what I have in mind?"

Support Confirmed Needs

At this point, if the customer has agreed that this is a need worth discussing, you can begin to support the need as discussed in Chapter 7 "Sales Call Skills."

Sometimes a client's indifference takes you by surprise. Then, you depend on your ability to apply the technique to overcome indifference immediately. An important factor to remember when addressing the customer's indifference is if, at any point during the discussion, the customer does not acknowledge any step in the process, then you acknowledge the customer's feedback, stop the process, and either move onto another sales lead probing sequence or move onto closing the call.

It is not uncommon to discover indifference when prospecting or that you are not the current supplier for a company. See the sidebar "No Thank You, We Are Happy with Our Current Supplier." Knowing how to handle indifference and all the customer objections is an important sales skill. At the end of this chapter, there will be a discussion of corrective actions for salespeople having difficulties handling objections similar to the section on common problems in Chapter 7 "Sales Call Skills." However, when you discover indifference and if it is occurring frequently in your customer base, you want to ask why this is happening so often and what the root cause for the indifference is. If you are interested in the answer, read

Chapter Highlight 8.1: Is Your Marketing and Sales Plan Bulletproof?

If you feel like your customers are constantly shooting at you when you are trying to execute your sales activities, this chapter will help you dodge the bullets, but maybe a better solution is have the customers put their guns away.

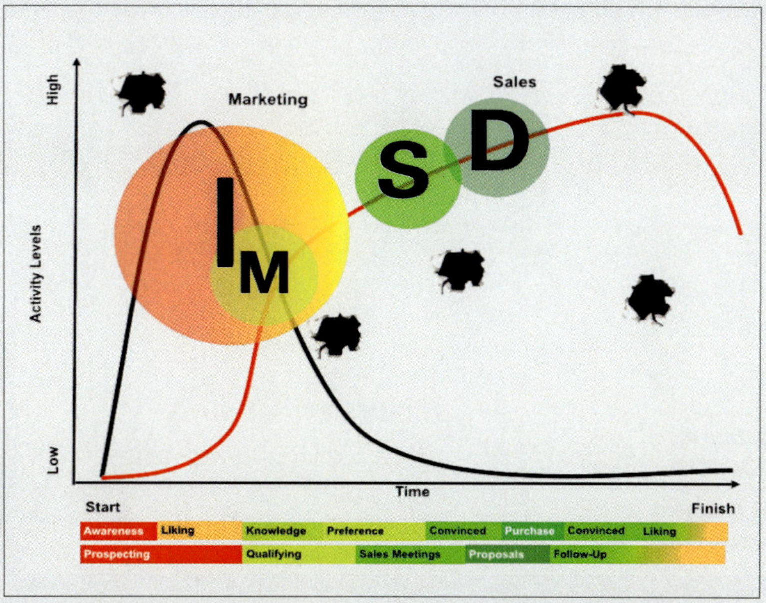

Shown in the figure on the right is a plot of marketing and sales activity levels for one opportunity on the Y-axis and the buyer readiness stages and sales activities as a function of time on the X-axis. In Chapter 1 "The Role of Marketing and Sales," however, the buyer readiness stages stopped at "Purchase". In the figure, after purchase the stages of "convinced" and "liking" are repeated. The reason for this is in B2B sales as part of the follow-up activities and as described in Chapter 4 "Opportunities Management," savvy salespeople know they should convince the people in the buying center again after the purchase that they made the correct decision by choosing their company. This will insulate them from their non-supporters during the implementation stage. Also in B2B sales at the end of the project as part of the follow-up activities, the salesperson should never miss the opportunity to say thank you to help build the "liking" opinion the customers have for your company.

The plot shows that, in the early stages of the buyer readiness stages, marketing activities should be high to target the buyer readiness stages of "awareness", "liking," "knowledge," and "preference" and supports the salesperson's activities of "prospecting" and "qualifying." As time goes by, "leads" become "confirmed opportunities," the sales activities increase, and the salesperson has sales meetings, presents proposals, and follows-up with their prospects. Based on this, a potential root cause of "indifference" can be your marketing communications program (MCP) not building "awareness" or making sufficient product comparisons to create "Preference" for your company. If this is the case, then adjusting the MCP may eliminate many of the indifference objections.

If there is a lot of "misunderstanding," then more effort should be made to educate your target audience. Perhaps less effort can be given to advertising and more to company-sponsored training seminars or lunch-and-learn sponsored events.

Once leads have been confirmed, salespeople become more active with the prospects as shown in the figure. Before the customer makes their "purchase" decision, the salesperson has to convince the customer their proposal is the best for them. If there is a lot of "skepticism" in sales meetings and when presenting proposals, then the marketing and sales collateral is weak or the supporting skills of the salespeople is weak—or a combination of both. Marketing and sales must work together to ensure that they have the appropriate demonstration of capabilities to convince the different buyer types they sell to.

If there are too many drawback objections, then either your pricing is wrong or the salespeople are not testing for value in the final step of supporting. The cause for this could be the marketing and sales collateral is not capturing documented references of customers enjoying real value as a result of using your product and services or salespeople's weak supporting skills. A high frequency of skepticism or drawback objections requires that the situation be reviewed by the sales manager and that level two sales effectiveness reviews be completed in order to confidently isolate the root cause for too many objections.

Chapter Highlight 8.1: Is Your Marketing and Sales Plan Bulletproof? (cont.)

The focus of this chapter is how to handle customer objections when you are confronted with this in the customer's office. If you are experiencing frequent objections, have a discussion with your sales manager and review your MCP and your supporting skills. Then maybe there will be less shooting.

Now for the bad news. If you discover indifference during the sales meeting, don't be surprised if you have to deal with misunderstanding, then skepticism to finally overcome a drawback. It is like a domino effect. The bottom line: Work as a team with marketing, do an excellent job of supporting, and you will have fewer bullets to dodge.

▶ *Resolving a Misunderstanding*

The customer expresses a misunderstanding when it's clear that he or she thinks you can't provide a feature or benefit you can provide. To resolve the misunderstanding:

- Probe to understand the concern.
- Acknowledge the concern.
- Confirm the need behind the concern.
- Support the need as per the supporting process.
- Check for acceptance.

Misunderstanding

With a misunderstanding, the client thinks you can't satisfy a particular need that you can satisfy. While there may be many reasons for the client's misunderstanding, it is often because the need hasn't been discussed and supported or the customer has made an assumption regarding your capabilities without having complete information.

Resolving a Customer Misunderstanding

You know the customer has a misunderstanding when they express dissatisfaction with a feature or lack of a feature of your product or service. For example, the customer may say something like "What you have said sounds good, except we need to be able to do more than what your tool does" or "We can't use that service because I've heard that it won't work in our conditions."

Eliminate a misunderstanding by taking the following steps:

Probing to Understand Misunderstanding

When the customer expresses a misunderstanding, you first probe to ensure that you fully understand the misunderstanding—as you did when the customer expressed skepticism—and let the customer frame the misunderstanding in their own words. You might use an open clarifying probe to have the customer describe the misunderstanding in more detail. For example, "You said that you can't use this service. Why is that?" or "You said the service will cost more than what you are using today. What do you mean by costs more?"

Acknowledging Customer Misunderstanding

Once you have a complete understanding of the customer's concern, address the misunderstanding. By acknowledging the customer's misunderstanding, you are providing feedback to the customer that you understand what it is that your product or service can or cannot do. For example, you might say, "Okay, I understand now what it is that you need" or "I see why that is important."

Once the customer acknowledges your feedback, move to the next step. If the customer does not acknowledge your understanding, you must keep probing until your understanding is confirmed.

Confirm the Need Behind the Concern

Next, probe to discover the need behind the concern. To confirm the need, use a closed probe that includes the language of needs. For example:

Client:	"Your approach is interesting, but there's a problem. I think it's too limited for our application."
Salesperson:	"Why is that?" *(probe to understand the concern)*
Client:	"Well, it sounds like a good way to do candidate selection more systematically. But that's not necessarily enough. What about during and after treatment? That doesn't seem to be on the program."
Salesperson:	"So you're looking for a way not only to identify wells, but, to evaluate the treatment during pumping, and then do a post-job evaluation, right?" *(confirming probe to transform the expression of a problem into an expression of a need)*
Client:	"Exactly."

Once you've confirmed the need behind the concern, as above, you may have to probe further about the "what" and "why" of the need to be sure you have a clear understanding before you support.

Supporting the Need

Once you've confirmed the need behind a misunderstanding and have a clear understanding of the need, proceed as you would with any need you can satisfy—that is, support it by acknowledging the need, describing relevant features and benefits, demonstrating capabilities, checking for acceptance, and testing for value.

▶ *Resolving Skepticism*

The customer expresses skepticism when he or she doubts a feature, benefit, or value you have described. To resolve the skepticism:

- Probe to understand the concern.
- Acknowledge the concern.
- Offer relevant proof.
- Check for acceptance.

Skepticism

When you make a support statement, clients sometimes doubt that your product or organization has the features or can provide the benefits you've highlighted. The client may say:

"I'm not convinced you can cut my costs combine significantly" or "You've done all that in conditions like the ones I'm looking at? I don't think so."

When a client expresses doubt that a product, service, or capability does what you've said it does, you've encountered skepticism. The steps to handling customer skepticism are described below.

Overcoming Customer Skepticism

When a client first expresses skepticism, the nature of the concern may not be clear. When you're not 100% sure why the customer is skeptical, probe until you are sure before responding. The customer may be skeptical for many reasons, including previous experiences with another organization or with your company.

Probing to Understand Skepticism

It is best to let clients frame issues in their own words. Once you have a complete understanding, you can respond appropriately and effectively. You might use an open clarifying probe to have the customer describe the skepticism in greater detail. For example:

"You said that you find that hard to believe. Why is that?"

"You seem skeptical about what I have said. Why is that?"

"What would you like to see to feel more comfortable with what I've shown you?"

Once you have an understanding of why the customer is skeptical, move to the next step of handling skepticism.

Acknowledging Customer Skepticism

By acknowledging customer skepticism, you provide feedback to the customer that you understand why they are skeptical. For example you might say:

"Okay, I understand now that you need more examples of where we have achieved similar cost reductions of this size"

"I see this is the first time you have heard of this service."

When acknowledging a client's skepticism (or any concern), be careful not to suggest that there are problems with your product or organization. In other words, don't say things such as "You're right" or "Many of our clients have that same concern."

Equally important, don't become defensive, argue, or debate the client. Depending on cultural sensitivities and social profile factors, taking an adversarial stance can quickly destroy rapport and undermine even a promising relationship. At this point, simply make it clear that you can appreciate the client's point of view.

Once the customer acknowledges your feedback you are ready to move to the next step. If the customer does not acknowledge your understanding, you have to do some more probing until your understanding is confirmed.

Offer Relevant Proof

Once there is a mutual understanding of the skepticism, offer proof by providing evidence that your solution does have the feature and/or does provide the benefit and value you've described. For example, suppose you told a customer that your company has considerable experience for companies operating in similar conditions. You might say:

"Here's a list of the jobs we've done in similar areas. As you can see, it includes several projects the same size as yours in terms of the number and condition of the wells."

In offering proof, make sure the proof you offer is relevant—that it addresses the specific feature or benefit the client is skeptical about. When you have several proof sources, use the one that best addresses the specific feature or benefit the client is skeptical about and is best suited for the customer's social profile. See the "Pick a Proof, Any Proof" sidebar for suggested resources.

Checking for Acceptance

After offering proof, check to make sure the client accepts it. If the client rejects your proof, probe to find out why and, if possible, offer a different, more appropriate proof if you can. Or ask the client what they need for them to be confident that you can do what you claim. Whatever you sell, it's important to know which features and benefits clients tend to be skeptical about and to identify credible proof sources for them.

▶ *Pick a Proof, Any Proof*

Below is a list of proof sources commonly used by sales representatives. Having a library of sales aids, or proofs, is a valuable resource for any sales representative.

- Professional society and other technical papers
- Anecdotal evidence/case histories
- Testimonials (written, on-the-spot calls)
- Technical journals
- Cost analyses
- Demos
- Certification sheets
- Brochures and other product literature
- Field tests and other reports
- Services team names and qualifications
- Statistics

Drawbacks

When the client is skeptical or has a misunderstanding, once the objections are removed the customer should agree to use your product or service because it satisfies their needs. Drawbacks are different in that your product or service cannot do what they need or has something they do not want. In this regard, your offering is not ideal. Drawbacks are usually expressed as a:

- Technical drawback. The client is dissatisfied because your company does not have a desired feature or has an undesirable feature. The technical drawback is easier to address during the evaluation of options phase. If technical drawbacks are expressed during the procurement stage, there may not be sufficient time to resolve the drawback, and the situation indicates that you did not fully understand the customer's requirements well enough early in the opportunities management process
- Financial drawback. "We would like to use you but you're too expensive." This is commonly expressed during the procurement phase and specifically during the negotiations stage.

▶ ***Resolving a Drawback***

The customer expresses a drawback when he or she is dissatisfied with the presence or absence of a feature or benefit. To resolve a drawback:

- Probe to understand the concern
- Acknowledge the concern
- Select the most appropriate technique or combination of techniques for addressing the drawback:
  Research
  - Request time to involve your company's technical resources
  - Make recommendation based on new technical solution

  Outweigh
  - Refocus on project objectives
  - Offset cost of drawback with value of previously accepted benefits

  Redefine
  - Suggest modified definition of evaluation criteria
  - Introduce benefits of your solution

  Trade-off
  - Refocus on project objectives
  - Offset drawback with strengths of your solution
- Check for acceptance

Resolving a Drawback

You know the customer has a drawback with your product or service when they express dissatisfaction with a feature or lack of a feature or benefit of your company's product or service. To handle a drawback, follow the steps described below.

Probing to Understand Drawback

When you encounter a drawback, it's particularly important to probe to understand the need(s) behind it—what the client wants and why. Even though you can't provide the particular feature or benefit the client is looking for, you can still position your response to show that the features and benefits you do provide contribute to the overall results he or she is looking for. When you encounter a drawback, it's important not to dismiss it as unimportant. Responding openly to drawbacks demonstrates your integrity and reflects positively upon both you and your company.

Acknowledging the Concern

As with the other types of concerns you've considered, you acknowledge a client's concern to let them know you understand and appreciate it. You might say:

"I can see why you'd want to work with people you've known and trusted over the years."

As before, once you acknowledge the customer's concern, check for acceptance and then move to the next step. You might say something similar to:

"Is that your concern?"

Tactics for Handling a Drawback

Once you complete the first two steps in resolving a drawback, decide how best to handle the specific drawback. Four tactics can be used for resolving a drawback:

- Research
- Outweigh
- Redefine
- Trade-off

Each tactic is best used for the drawback situations described next. However, there will be times when resolving a drawback to the customer's satisfaction may require using one or more of the tactics combined.

Research When the drawback is technical in nature and you are unsure as to whether an alternative technique or solution to the customer's technical requirement exists, ask the customer for time to research their requirement. You might say something like:

"That is the first time I have had a customer request that capability. If you agree, I can go back the office, make a request in our technical support system, and get back to you tomorrow on how we can address that need."

Requesting time for research serves two purposes. First and most important, you might find a technical solution to the customer's requirement that you were not aware of. By finding a solution you can go back to the customer and support the need as described in the supporting section in Chapter 7 "Sales Call Skills."

Second, it demonstrates to the customer that even though you may not have an immediate solution to the requirement, you have the support of your company's technical community.

If you cannot find a technical solution to satisfy the customer's requirement, or based on previous experience you are confident that your company cannot provide the customer with the feature, service, or benefit they need, then use one of the other techniques listed below to overcome the drawback.

Outweigh. Use the outweigh option when you can demonstrate financially to the customer that the cost of the drawback is more offset by the financial gains of the unique features and benefits of your solution the customer accepted earlier in the sales process. By using the outweigh technique, you are building the strength of other important criteria.

This tactic is commonly used when the customer objects to the cost of your product or service without taking into account the reduction in other costs, such as rig time, support, and installation. To implement this strategy effectively, you must understand the customer's objectives for the project, as discussed in Chapter 2 "Value Drivers," and demonstrate how your solution impacts the project objectives.

Outweigh is the preferred technique for addressing a drawback; it eliminates the danger of challenging crucial criteria (such as the techniques stated on page 290) and concentrates on building the importance of other criteria. However, for this technique to successfully overcome a drawback, you must have the customer's agreement on the dollar value of previously accepted benefits. Ideally, this agreement was obtained done during the evaluation of options phase of the opportunity management process.

To use the outweigh technique, probe to ensure that you fully understand the drawback from the customer's point of view and then acknowledge the client's concern. Next, help the client put the drawback in perspective—to consider it within the broader context of their other needs.

You can do this by inviting the client to step back and look at the bigger picture. You might say:

"From what we've discussed so far, there are other aspects of this project that are also important to you. Let's step back for a moment and consider everything together."

"Would you mind if we took just a few minutes to review some of the other factors we've discussed that will also be considered in your decision?"

In addressing a drawback, avoid using the word "but" between acknowledging and refocusing. If you say "but," the client may feel that you're minimizing the impor-

Chapter Highlight 8.2: We Would Like to Use You, BUT...

An effective way to introduce the outweigh tactic for handling a drawback is with the use of a spreadsheet analysis. The case histories described below all used a spreadsheet analysis to outweigh the customer's stated financial drawback:

"...we would like to use you, but you are too expensive..."

By presenting the accepted value and demonstrating the strengths of your solution against the weaknesses and drawbacks of the competitor's solution, you can outweigh the financial drawback and turn the "No" into a "Yes."

Case 1: Canada

Customer Negative Reaction: Financial Drawback
Handling Technique: Combination Redefine, Outweigh and Trade-off
Competitive Sales Strategy: Frontal Solution

Company A	Salt Mud Wells	Competitor
5	Logging Time	16
$634	Rig Cost/Hr	$634
$3,170	Total	$10,144
30	No. of Wells	30
$95,100	Rig Costs	$304,320
$450,000	Logging Cost	$300,000
$545,100	Total Cost	$604,320
150	Total Hours	480
13.75	Days Saved	

This example was shown earlier in Chapter 4 "Opportunities Management" as an example of how to influence the customer's decision criteria to make an incidental criterion more important and, therefore, put Company A into a stronger position in the customer's evaluation. The competitive sales strategy used was frontal-solution, based on superior service. The technique used to change the criteria was to redefine the customer's decision criteria to include rig time for logging as part of the logging costs, then to outweigh the financial drawback plus include a trade-off of days saved against the additional acquisition costs. The price differential between Company A and the competitor was overcome by considering the rig time savings that Company A provided due to its more efficient logging operations in the customer's drilling environment. In addition, the customer also profited from having more rig days for drilling (13.75) in the season than before when using the competitor to log the wells. The rig time savings in the salt mud environment was more than sufficient to outweigh the competitor's cheaper price. Company A was awarded the project based on this evaluation. Prior to the salesperson presenting the comparison logging times the customer, had not considered the impact of rig costs for logging the well in their decision-making process.

Had the muds been fresh, further research would have been necessary to quantify the financial benefit of how much the extra drilling days meant to the customer for the project, as the rig time savings from the more efficient fresh mud logging operations would have saved the customer only $19,000 in rig costs and while adding 1.25 days for drilling more wells. This clearly would not have been a sufficient value to overcome the $150,000 price differential between Company A and the competitor. Additional effort would have been required to discover and quantify other Company A features, benefits, and customer value. Perhaps a different competitive sales strategy—flanking, defend. or fragment—might have been required.

Case 2: Venezuela

Customer Negative Reaction: Financial Drawback
Handling Technique: Combination Outweigh and Trade-off
Competitive Sales Strategy: Frontal Reputation

Added Value Calculation	
Prevented LTIs compared to international standard	85
Cost per LTI	$ 30,000
Added value for customer	$ 2,550,000
Other benefits	Goodwill Best practice
Payback compared to alternative competitive proposals	< 6 months

This example was shown earlier in Chapter 4 "Opportunities Management" to highlight the power of tracking customer service indicators over long periods of time to demonstrate the benefits of an ongoing business relationship and the power of the performance curve. In this example, the value added to the customer's operation was the reduced cost due to lost time from accidents. The customer's QHS&E manager and Company A staff did the research jointly. With this information the customer was able to justify continuing to use Company A for the next contract period. There was a $1,000,000 price difference between Company A and the competitor. The competitive sales strategy used for this opportunity was frontal-reputation.

Chapter Highlight 8.2: We Would Like to Use You, BUT... (cont.)

Had the reduction in lost time incidents (LTIs) not been so significant or the price difference greater than $2,550,000, the sales team would have had to include goodwill in the decision criteria and use it as part of a trade-off technique in addition to the risk of switching service providers in a difficult operating environment. Also, the sales team would have had to do additional research to present and quantify other Company A features, benefits, and customer-specific value.

Case 3: Indonesia

Customer Negative Reaction: Financial Drawback
Handling Technique: Combination Outweigh and Trade-off
Competitive Sales Strategy: Flanking Alter

The customer required low-density cement slurries with high compressive strength in 7-in. production casing be-cause of the formation's low fracture gradient. The value proposition communicated by the sales representative was to replace the two-stage cementing system and associated extra materials and cost with the single-stage advanced cementing system. The sales representative presented the spreadsheet analysis for overcoming the customer's financial drawback. Because the calculated financial benefit was less than 10%, the sales representative thought it would also be best to combine the outweigh tactic with a trade-off tactic, emphasizing that in addition to the financial savings the customer would also benefit from lower rig costs. For future comparisons, the sales representative will turn the rig time savings into a value by calculating the cost per hour for the rig and, thus, the cost benefit. Company A was awarded the work and executed several successful jobs for the customer. The next step the sales representative took was to ask for a letter of reference so that, for future opportunities, the sales representative could update the demonstration-of-capabilities spreadsheet to include the customer's reference letter.

Item	Competitor	Company A
Technique	2 Stages	Single Stage
Costs		Not required
Stage collar	$6,000	Not required
External casing packer	10,000	$50,000
Cement slurry 1st stage	20,000	Not required
Cement slurry 2nd stage	15,000	Not required
Personnel costs for SC and ECP	6,000	Not required
Total cementing costs	$66,000	$50,000
Reduced cementing costs using advanced system		$16,000
Total rig required	18	8
Reduced rig time by using advanced system		10

tance of their concern. Instead, use words and phrases like "and," "it's also true," "let's look at," or "let's consider." To begin using the outweigh technique, you might say something like:

"I understand the importance of keeping costs as low as possible and that the proposed invoiced solution will be more expensive than the competitors—part of our additional cost comes from the fact that our solution provides you additional benefits. One of the more significant financial benefits you will receive is the reduction of rig time. As we discussed earlier, we will reduce rig costs by more than double the additional invoice costs for the service. This is achieved by eliminating the need to make multiple runs into the well to acquire all the data you need to evaluate the wells. Do you agree?"

When selecting benefits to review, ask yourself which ones would be most likely to outweigh the drawback. Consider reviewing:

- Benefits that address the highest priority needs of the client
- Benefits that impact the project objectives
- Benefits you know your competitors cannot provide

An effective way to present the outweigh technique is to use a spreadsheet presentation of the factors as shown in the **Chapter Highlight 8.2: "We Would Like to Use You, But . . . ."** The outweigh technique is the most effective technique

Chapter Highlight 8.2: We Would Like to Use You, BUT... (cont.)

Case 4: Alaska

Customer Negative Reaction: Financial Drawback
Handling Technique: Combination Outweigh and Trade-off
Competitive Sales Strategy: Flanking Alter

Company	Competitor	Company A
Rg costs/day	$300,000	$300,000
Days spent reaming	5	0
Days logging	3	2
Total days for logging	8	2
Logging irg costs	$2,400,000	$600,000
Evaluation costs	$800,000	$2,100,000
Total costs	$3,200,000	$2,700,000
Benefits		Fewer risks for bad hole conditions to develop

This example is taken from the case study used throughout the textbook. In this opportunity, Company A was competing against one of it's major competitors to secure an exploration program for the evaluation services. The operating environment is characterized as very expensive. Rig costs average $300,000 per day, the drilling window is very short (only two months), and the borehole conditions are unpredictable. The spreadsheet analysis was used in the negotiations when the contracts manager stated a financial drawback. Here is an excerpt from their discussion:

Contracts Manager: Based on our calculations, your company is more than double the cost of your competitors.

Sales Manager: What do you mean by costs?

Contracts Manager: We calculated the cost as per the example logging runs described in the request for proposal.

Sales Manager: Did you include rig time costs accrued during logging operations?

Contracts Manager: No, why?

Sales Manager: When you consider the rig time required for logging operations, due to our unique services as verified by your petrophysical and drilling departments, we are$900,000 cheaper than the competitors. Let me go through the calculations so you can see how.

The sales manager then reviewed the spreadsheet analysis with the contracts manager and resolved the financial drawback. Company A was awarded the project based on this discussion without having to make any movements on logging costs. Even if the competitor had decided to give the logging services away, they could not have overcome Company A's strong position.

to use in dealing with the customer's negotiation team, who is focused on your invoice costs and may not be aware of all the value your solution provides their particular project. When this is the case, you call it an apparent drawback. See the "Apparent Drawbacks" sidebar.

Redefine. This tactic alters the way the buyer defines a criterion so that it becomes easier for you to meet or resolve the drawback. The crucial criterion remains important to the customer, but its definition is altered so that you can meet or exceed it and therefore overcome the drawback. Use the redefine option when you can demonstrate that the customer's decision criterion is too narrow, does not adequately consider the benefits of your solution, or fails to capture all the negative impacts of the narrow definition used for the decision criteria. You might begin the redefine tactic as follows:

"I see in your services specification that you have requested a nuclear magnetic logging tool. However, in your zone of interest, the borehole size will be large. Unless the tool is decentralized, the data acquired through this section will be dominated by the borehole signal. This borehole-saturated signal will not give the formation readings you need to accurately evaluate the zone and could result in additional costs. Even worse, it could bypass a productive zone. Is this something that you want to take into account?"

Once the customer agrees, you are prepared to support the need and demonstrate

▶ *Apparent Drawbacks*

Apparent drawbacks arise when clients want to gain leverage for what they consider a better deal. Especially if they're trained or experienced buyers, they may agree with the dictum, "Never let the vendor leave smiling."

In that case, they may express drawbacks for tactical purposes—in order to win price or other concessions. If that's the case, you may eventually have to move out of the sales mode and into a negotiating posture—but not necessarily. The outweigh method will help you resolve the apparent drawback, eliminate the need for negotiation and clearly demonstrate the win-win aspects of the proposal.

the value of your solution. This technique is best used early in the evaluation of options phase when the customer is still developing the decision criteria.

Trade-off. This technique balances decision criteria where you are weak or cannot meet the limitations, penalties, or disadvantages of using the competitor. Trading off accepts the importance of a criterion, but shows other factors that must be balanced against it. This strategy requires that you have a thorough understanding of the competitor's capabilities. Use the trade-off option when you want to justify using your solution based on the agreed-upon strengths of your solution. Trading off is similar to the outweigh tactic, except that there has been no agreement on the dollar value of your solution. As such, this technique should be used as a last resort, either late in the evaluation of options phase or during negotiations if you cannot demonstrate the dollar value of the your solution's benefits. Trading off is typically used in conjunction with the other drawback tactics when the evaluation between your company and the competitor is close and could result in a lowest bidder selection.

A common drawback to using the trade-off tactic is when the customer wants to minimize the risks of an operation. Below is an example of a discussion where the customer expresses a drawback and the salesperson uses the trade-off tactic to overcome the pricing drawback.

Customer: "We would like to use you, but you are more expensive than the competitor."

Salesperson: "I certainly understand you want the best deal. Can you tell me how much more expensive are we?"

Customer: "You are 10% more expensive for all charges."

Salesperson: "Okay, that is what I expected. Can you tell me how concerned you are with the need to recover from a catastrophic event such as a unit failure?"

Customer: "That would be a disaster, as we have to have this project completed before the weather forces us to go into standby."

Salesperson: "Yes, in similar projects we have participated in, our clients had similar concerns. They considered the size of our in-country operation as an advantage as we could provide the resources needed to recover from any catastrophic failure. They felt the added security for continuous operations was worth the premium they paid for having Company A rather than the competitor on the rig."

Customer: "You're right. We need to consider this in the evaluation."

In the above example, the salesperson is now ready to support the ex-pressed need of the customer as discussed in Chapter 7 "Sales Call Skills." When using a trade-off to overcome a pricing drawback in a negotiation, you must have a supporter who can influence the buying decision to validate your claims of the benefits for the negotiating team.

Fear

This type of objection is an emotionally based. The phenomenon has been studied in neuro-linguistic programming (NLP). What happens is the customer will "anchor," or become stuck due to a negative emotional memory from the past. You know that the customer has anchored if after trying to address an objection such as indifference or skepticism, the customer accepts your explanation but will not agree to go forward. In Chapter 5 "Communication Skills," there was a brief dis-

▶ ***Resolving an Objection Resulting from Fear***

The customer expresses acceptance of your effort to resolve their objection, but is not agreeing to move forward. The customer has anchored due to a past negative experience. To resolve the misunderstanding:

- Probe to understand the real reason for the anchor.
- Acknowledge the concern.
- Connect with the customer through a story, analogy, metaphor, etc.
- Recommend options to move forward.
- Check for acceptance.

cussion regarding the parts of the brain that contribute to decision-making. These are the cortex, responsible for logic and complex thought; the limbic system, responsible for many functions including emotion; and finally, the brain stem, the oldest part of the brain, responsible for survival, the startle response, and the basic functions that keep you alive. In this situation, where fear is creating the objection, the old brain's survival instincts are dominating the cortex powers of reasoning. The fear of suffering a loss (could be business or personal) minimizes the potential gains. The key here is not to become impatient, but instead try to enlist the limbic system to move the anchor by following the steps below.

Probe to Understand for the Real Reason

Probe to understand the objection, concern, and consequences. What is the reality the customer sees? A good way to think of this is the three levels of why. When people offer a reason for an objection, you might get rapport or a vague answer.

Salesperson: "Why can't you confirm your purchase?"

Customer: "You are too expensive." *(rapport answer, first level of why)*

The problem is for some people this is a safe answer that can be used to easily explain why the customer did not buy from you. The key to probing for the type of fear-based objection is to dig beneath the rapport or vague answer get to the rational answer.

Customer: "You guys are 15% more than your competition." *(rational answer, second level of why)*

Salesperson: "But you get better answers with better measurements. I thought you agreed this is what you needed."

Customer: "Yes, that is true, and I have heard that many times. But unfortunately, it takes effort to extract that information and when it comes time to make the decision, no one has the time. This has been repeated many times. I looked like I was wasting the company's money, and I'm not going to do that again." *(real reason, third level of why)*

Acknowledge the Customer's Concern

Paraphrase back to the customer their reality, ensuring that you show empathy with your voice, body language, and words.

Salesperson: "Yes I understand why you are concerned. It is not just having better measurements, but using the measurements, and you're not comfortable the team has the resources when it comes time to making decisions to incorporate this information."

Customer: "Yes, that is correct. I don't want to be viewed as not able to control the spending."

Connect with the Customer

Connect with the customer using a story (personal or about another customer in a different industry), example from history, current event, quote, analogy or metaphor. What you are trying to do with the customer is have their perception change. Get them to look at possible outcomes to the objection they have from a different perspective. The use of a story can help them "pull-up" their anchor. It is like framing a picture. You first see it in a black frame and then in a gold frame; in the gold frame it looks so much better. The picture itself has not changed, but the way you see it does. The same is true with an objection resulting from fear. By reframing the objection, your customer may see the outcome differently.

▶ *What?* We Discussed This Already![3]

Pop quiz: You're nearing the end of a lengthy sales cycle with a large buyer, and so far it's been textbook perfect. When the prospect asks for one more meeting, you figure you'll be tying up loose ends and closing the sale. Instead, the prospect is somber and raises multiple doubts about moving forward. Do you a) offer a discount, b) start overcoming each objection, or c) relax, knowing you've got the deal?

The correct answer is "c." Surprised?

Less-experienced sellers often interpret a litany of last-minute objections as an indication that they have lost the deal. Observe the following:

- Panicked that a big deal appears to be slipping away, the inexperienced salesperson often makes "the potentially fatal mistake of dropping price," thinking it will make the buying decision easier. But the opposite is true. "The message you send by discounting is that the concerns about risk are valid," warn Holland and Young.
- The reality is that if a buyer is sharing their risk concerns at the end of the buying cycle, it means you are probably the vendor of choice. That's because final risk concerns can arise only if a buyer is envisioning a purchase being made. Holland and Young liken this natural process to a couple on the night before getting married. Last-minute jitters and cold feet are normal as the two wonder whether they've made the right choice, but these concerns can only arise with a firm commitment being imminent. The same is true for buyers; if they raise sudden concerns at the end, it's a sign a commitment is forthcoming—but only if you handle things right.

So how do you handle these last-minute objections? First, stay calm. Remember that these concerns are a good sign and that if you handle them with patience, the sale will be yours.

Second, recognize the objections for what they are—*fear,* an emotional hurdle for the buyer. As such, *do not try to tell the buyer why he or she shouldn't be concerned;* that's like telling buyers they're wrong to feel the way they do. Instead, be patient in allowing the buyer to work through the issues. It is likely they aren't looking for resolution, but simply wants to be heard. And since people only vent to those they trust, consider it a sign that you're trusted.

Once you've discussed the issues that are addressable, your best course of action, say Holland and Young, is to "summarize the potential value, the shortcomings of the current system, the capabilities needed, and the references that have been provided, and then gently ask the buyer to move forward." If you've done it right, the customer will say yes.

Salesperson: "You know, I had the exact same reaction when I wanted to buy decision analysis software for my team; all I wanted was a Monte Carlo plug-in for Excel because I did not have time to learn how to use the sensitivity analysis and decision tree tools. I knew it was better, but I was willing to do without it until the rep showed me the difference it made for two of his customers who are just like me. So what I had actually decided was I did not have time to make better decisions. That is not what I wanted. I wanted the best decisions. What we agreed on was for one of the team members to get trained on how to use all the modules. Now we have a much better and holistic approach to our decision-making and the rest of the team are being trained over the next twelve months."

Recommend Options to Move Forward

Small steps with a fear-based objection can be a big step towards gaining an agreement.

Salesperson: "If I can have one of our senior interpreters on site with your team during the data acquisition to run the analysis and go over the results, do you think that will help you get the most from your investment? After that we can look at setting up a real-time decision support access to our support center for future operations."

Check for Acceptance

Salesperson: "How does that sound. Will that help you get best of both worlds: data and decisions?"

Customer: "I like it. I think that will work."

In situations where fear is the cause of the objection, you must ensure that you keep in contact and continue to support their decision. Continued updates on the progress of making their decision a reality will keep the anchor up. In fact, last-minute objections are actually a good sign if you handle them correctly. See the sidebar "*What?* We Discussed This Already!"

When You Can't Resolve a Customer's Negative Objection

There will be times that you cannot resolve a customer's negative response. If you recognize this early in the opportunity management process at the beginning of the evaluation of options phase, you have a number of options available to you:

- Unresolved negative reaction is indifference or drawbacks. Uncover additional needs you can support with additional benefits. This may involve additional meetings with other members of the buying center and determining their requirements for the project.
- Unresolved concerns are skepticism or misunderstanding. Determine what actions the customer requires to address their concerns in addition to what you have already done to resolve them (for example, a demonstration job or additional proofs or meetings with experts or management to resolve concerns and consequences).
- Unresolved concern is a financial drawback due to imposed decision criteria that do not consider added value. Find a higher-level buying center member (high influence) who can change the decision criteria to consider added value. When meeting with the higher-level buying center member, use the outweigh drawback tactic. The value should result from one of your company's's unique products or services that impacts one or more of the customer's projects or corporate value drivers.
- You cannot resolve the client's concerns or fears, which will result in your company being evaluated in a weak position. Consider a weak position competitive sales strategy, as discussed in Chapter 4 "Opportunities Management," and either defend or fragment. In the defend strategy, where one of the key decision-makers has an objection anchored in fear, your supporter can talk to the person with the fear as a colleague and use the same approach to have them lift their anchor.
- You can only resolve a portion of the client's concerns, but believe you have supporters and strong evaluation. Consider a flanking competitive sales strategy that gives your company the strongest evaluation.

When you discover the customer's negative reaction late in the opportunity management process and are unable to resolve the customer's concerns, you have fewer options. In this situation, your strategy will be restricted to the procurement phase of the opportunities management process. Your options to indirectly overcome a client's negative reactions during the procurement process are:

- Plan a negotiation strategy to make sufficient trades to satisfy the concerns by having a well-prepared list of valuable, inexpensive trade-offs. This strategy is discussed further in Chapter 12 "Collaborative Negotiations."
- Prepare an attack strategy for late in the procurement process as described in the monitor stage section in Chapter 4 "Opportunities Management."
- Make a concession (last and most undesirable).

All the procurement phase strategies to overcome a customer's negative reactions to your proposal should be closely scrutinized and used only if the project is considered to have strategic value. The project's strategic value must be decided by your upper management and in discussion with the business manager. Finally, if it is determined that your solution will be evaluated as weak for financial considerations, then a competitive sales strategy of disengage, as described in Chapter 4 "Opportunities Management," should be considered.

Clients' Objection Prevention

The first section of this chapter discussed how to handle clients' negative reactions when you encounter them. This section discusses an overall sales strategy you can to implement to prevent the client from having negative reactions. The strategy consists of four actions:

- Continuous client marketing and sales communication program to build awareness and education of your solution's benefits.
- Opportunity planning and management.
- Pre-sales call planning, execution, and analysis.
- Proactive relationship management.

Each action, when taken together, greatly improves your chances of preventing customers from having negative reactions to your proposals and securing the desired customer's agreement during the opportunities management process. Failure to complete any one of the above actions results in more client objections during the pursuit of an opportunity, forcing the salesperson to spend more time resolving concerns and less time on other important matters, such as other customers or other opportunities.

Continuous Client Marketing and Sales Communications Program

Preventing client objections begins by proactively avoiding negative reactions to your proposals in the first place. Many of your customers' objections come from their lack of awareness of the benefits that your products and services can provide. A key component to every regional sales organization is a continuous client communication program to build awareness, liking, knowledge, and preference.

Such programs help eliminate many of the customer's objections, such as indifference, misunderstanding, and skepticism. Marketing and sales communication programs were described in the marketing chapter. With a continuous communications program in place, the sales force can target specific customers to address the early stages of the buyer readiness stages and help establish your company as the preferred company. With continuous client communication in place, you address the client's overall awareness of your company's benefits. These programs are planned outside the pursuit of specific opportunities.

Then, when new opportunities arise, the sales force can increase the customer's conviction to use your company by leveraging the success of past projects and demonstrating specific project value for the opportunity in question. If customers' unresolved negative reactions prevent your company from gaining a customer's conviction, your company may not be selected in the purchase decision.

Opportunity Planning and Management

Once you begin the opportunities management process, you analyze all the factors that impact the opportunity, starting with customer factors, such as project requirements, buying center dynamics, and competitive threats, to establish how your company will be evaluated in the decision-making process.

The goal of a completed opportunity analysis is to identify specific solution vulnerabilities and select your competitive sales strategy to leverage your strengths that best addresses the vulnerabilities and put your company in the strongest position to secure the opportunity. The competitive sales strategy will be implemented by the sales force using the tactics discussed in Chapter 4 "Opportunities Management" and Chapter 6"Sales Activities." A key factor in opportunity planning is your ability to understand your vulnerabilities. Vulnerabilities are predictions of customers' negative reactions to your proposed solution. The opportunity plan with the greatest probability of success and with the desired profitability is what the sales representative tries to build as early as possible in the opportunities management process. This makes time their advantage to adequately address vulnerabilities or demonstrate value.

As you execute your tactics, the competitors vying for the same opportunity will be executing their own tactics and counter-tactics. This is especially true in the late stages of the procurement phase. New negative reactions, such as financial drawbacks, skepticism, and misunderstandings that did not exist before, may suddenly appear as a result of competitors' influences during the procurement process. This means you have to be alert to and continually reevaluate and check the customer's reaction to your proposal throughout all the procurement stages until the contract is signed, and you must always be ready and available to respond to new concerns.

An important stage in the procurement phase of the opportunities management process is the outcome analysis stage. In the outcome analysis, as discussed in Chapter 4 "Opportunities Management," you need to analyze the outcome, whether negative or positive, from three perspectives: the customer's point of view, what you achieved, and what the competitors did. If you believe you lost on price, you know you were not successful in overcoming the pricing drawback. If you did not overcome the pricing drawback, you should try to determine why you were not successful. Did you overestimate or not confirm your unique value? Were the strengths you used in a trade-off tactic not considered? Was the customer skeptical, or was there a misunderstanding? Conversely, if you were awarded the project, why? If you were more expensive, what did the buying center use to justify the cost difference? How did they value your products and services? Did they award the project due to trade-offs? Did they contact the references you provided? If so, why?

Answers to these questions help you better prepare to prevent and resolve customers' negative reactions in future opportunities for the specific account and for similar projects for other accounts. The following discussion focuses on how to use opportunity management to prevent customers' negative reactions.

Pre-Sales Call Planning, Execution, and Analysis

Discovering objections during a sales call is not a good sign, but not being prepared to handle the objections can be fatal. Pre-sales call planning, execution, and analysis are also an absolute requirement in preventing customers' negative reactions. This is done by using the project supporting worksheet described in

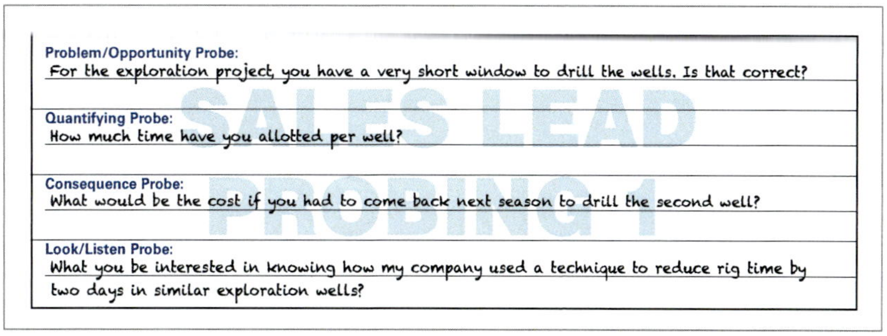
Problem/Opportunity Probe:
For the exploration project, you have a very short window to drill the wells. Is that correct?
Quantifying Probe:
How much time have you allotted per well?
Consequence Probe:
What would be the cost if you had to come back next season to drill the second well?
Look/Listen Probe:
What you be interested in knowing how my company used a technique to reduce rig time by two days in similar exploration wells?

Fig. 8.2
Sales call preparation worksheet probing section, Sales Lead Probing.

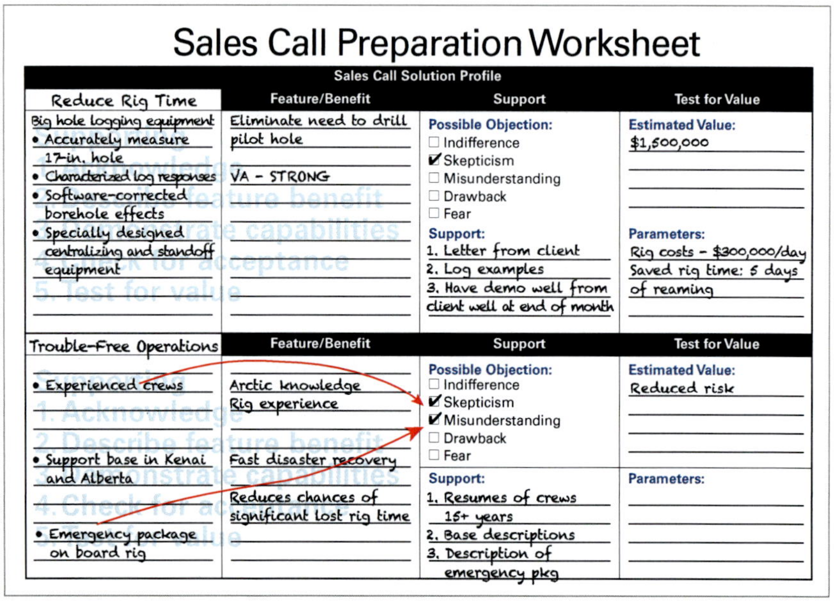
Sales Call Preparation Worksheet

Sales Call Solution Profile

Reduce Rig Time	Feature/Benefit	Support	Test for Value
Big hole logging equipment • Accurately measure 17-in. hole • Characterized log responses • Software-corrected borehole effects • Specially designed centralizing and standoff equipment	Eliminate need to drill pilot hole VA – STRONG	Possible Objection: ☐ Indifference ☑ Skepticism ☐ Misunderstanding ☐ Drawback ☐ Fear Support: 1. Letter from client 2. Log examples 3. Have demo well from client well at end of month	Estimated Value: $1,500,000 Parameters: Rig costs – $300,000/day Saved rig time: 5 days of reaming

Trouble-Free Operations	Feature/Benefit	Support	Test for Value
• Experienced crews • Support base in Kenai and Alberta • Emergency package on board rig	Arctic knowledge Rig experience Fast disaster recovery Reduces chances of significant lost rig time	Possible Objection: ☐ Indifference ☑ Skepticism ☑ Misunderstanding ☐ Drawback ☐ Fear Support: 1. Resumes of crews 15+ years 2. Base descriptions 3. Description of emergency pkg	Estimated Value: Reduced risk Parameters:

Fig. 8.3
Sales call preparation worksheet, supporting section.

Chapter 7 "Sales Call Skills." The sections of the worksheet specifically targeted when preventing customers' negative reactions are the sales call supporting worksheet and prepared sales representative probing pages. These pages assist you in preparing and rehearsing how you will begin discussions regarding benefits the customer may be indifferent to or unaware of. They also help you demonstrate capabilities with support aids for possible negative reactions. **Figures 8.2** and **8.3** show a completed probing page and sales call supporting worksheet section.

Thorough preparation and good supporting techniques should eliminate most customers' negative reactions. To prepare for a specific sales call, you should:

- Review previously completed sales call worksheets for sales calls made earlier in the opportunity, similar opportunities, or opportunities where the person(s) contacted were part of another buying center.
- Check the CRM database for recent opportunities for similar products and services and review the outcome analysis. Take special note of the opportunities for the same account and for opportunities where the main competitors are the same as the ones in your region.
- If the current opportunity is a continuation of a customer's multiyear project that was tendered earlier, review the service quality review meeting minutes and project review meeting minutes. Check for any performance issues that may have created the customers' negative reactions that you might have to resolve in this opportunity. Check also for outstanding performance that can be used to demonstrate value and strengths.
- Consider your own experiences and solicit input from the sales team, especially the region segment business manager. They may have information regarding the negative reactions clients tend to have for the type of solution you are proposing. Ask for relevant proof sources you could use to demonstrate capabilities that could address the customer's concerns.
- Find out which competitors the client may be talking to and determine what kinds of information the competitors might be communicating to the client that could lead to misunderstandings.
- Consider which features and benefits competitors offer that might result in the client expressing drawbacks about your product or organization. This is discussed in more detail in Chapter 9 "Strategic Sales Plan."

Chapter Highlight 8.3: The $200,000 Makeover

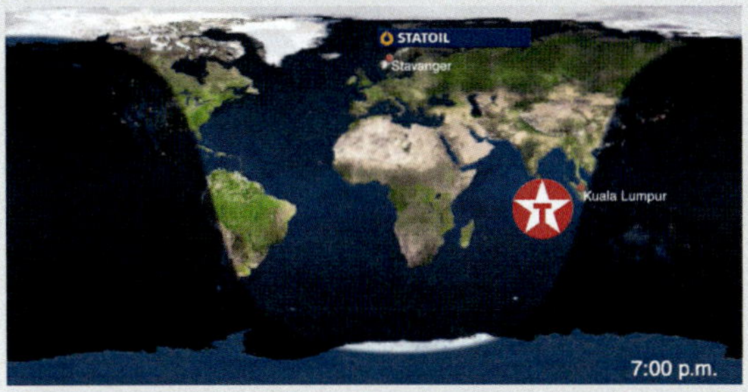

It was 7:00 p.m. on Sunday night June 7, 1993, when the Company A salesperson for the then-Malaysia–Thailand–Vietnam wireline division received a call from the Texaco drilling manager. The drilling manager asked the salesperson if he could be in the Texaco office on Monday morning for an urgent meeting. The time was set for 8:00 a.m. The purpose of the meeting was to describe to the customer's drilling and petrophysics teams, including the details and availability of the Company A's drill pipe-assisted logging system.

The phone call was brief, and the Texaco drilling manager did not provide much detail about why the meeting was urgent, as he was obviously concerned about other issues. Immediately after the phone call, the Company A salesperson called one of his golfing partners, a Texaco drilling engineer who worked for the drilling manager. When asked about the situation, the Texaco drilling engineer explained that on a rig Texaco was operating offshore in Malaysia, was experiencing problems getting wireline evaluation tools to the bottom of most wells. This frequently resulted in having to run drill pipe back into the well to do a clean-out trip with the drill pipe in after several attempts to get the logging tools to the bottom of the well. To make matters worse, even after doing the clean-out run with the drill pipe, the logging tools would become stuck when logging the well, and then an even more costly cut-and-thread operation was required to retrieve the logging string from the well—overall a very expensive procedure.

Texaco decided it was time to use the drill pipe-assisted logging technique, where the wireline tools are connected to the drill pipe and run into the hole, and then the wireline cable is connected once the tools reach the casing shoe. Although this is a time-consuming operation, it was still more efficient than a fishing operation. Competitor B was the wireline logging company on the current well, and Texaco had just finished cementing the drill string into the hole after Competitor B's drill pipe-conveyed system had failed. Then, the drill pipe became stuck. Texaco was preparing to sidetrack the well and switch out Competitor B with either Company A or Competitor A.

This was the purpose of the urgent Monday morning meeting. Company A and Competitor A were asked to present their drill pipe capabilities and equipment availability. Clearly, the customer was well advanced in the buyer-decision stages. They were aware of the competing options available and had a reasonable knowledge of each system's features and benefits. Both Company A and Competitor A were presently working for Texaco on different projects, but there was no clearly preferred system. The Texaco drilling engineer told the salesperson that the job would go to the company that could convince the Texaco team who had the most reliable and dependable system available to log the next section of the well.

With this background information, the salesperson quickly called a sales representative who he had worked with in Alaska and who was now in Stavanger working as a sales representative. The sales representative had recently been in Kuala Lumpur for a conference. Over dinner one night, the sales representative had described the success his division was having running "supper combinations" on drill pipe and, in fact, as a result of their recent logging successes, a North Sea customer had written a congratulatory letter to Company A. Using the advantage of the six-hour time difference between Kuala Lumpur and Stavanger, the salesperson was able to catch the sales representative at Sunday brunch. The sales representative in Stavanger faxed the letter that day to Company A's office in Kuala Lumpur.

This was just what the salesperson had been waiting for since the earlier discussion with the sales representative in Stavanger. He had been actively searching for a customer reference such as the North Sea customer letter after the meeting with Texaco two months earlier as Texaco began evaluating logging options for next year's program. The sudden turn of events on the current wells made the issue much more urgent. At the earlier meeting, the salesperson had just presented the table of recent jobs as part of his support and demonstration of capabilities. When he checked for the customer's acceptance, the drilling engineer asked if he had any client references or case studies. As a result of this sales call, the salesperson was actively looking for customer proofs, which prompted the discussion with the sales representative over dinner at the SPE conference.

Chapter Highlight 8.3: The $200,000 Makover (cont.)

With the North Sea customer letter, the salesperson knew he could improve his support document.

On Monday morning, the salesperson put together a copy of what he was going to present to the Texaco team, including the reference letter from the North Sea customer and a table of the most recent drill pipe-conveyed logging jobs done by Company A globally. The meeting went as planned, and the salesperson presented the Company A drill pipe-conveyed logging system features and benefits, supported with the combination job history table and reference letter. Texaco told the salesperson they would make a decision within a few hours. As he left the meeting, the drilling manager called in the Competitor A salesperson, who was waiting in the reception area. Two hours later, the Company A salesperson received a call and was instructed to arrange to have the Company A drill pipe logging system on the dock by 4:00 p.m. that day. The drill pipe-conveyed logging job was done a week later without problems. The revenue was $200,000!

Location	Tool String Top-Down	TD Meters	Deviation	Temperature	Operating Time
Norway	Tool string 1	4,003	80°	75° C	43 hours
Norway	Tool string 2	4,760	71°	135° C	35 hours
Norway	Tool string 2	5,700	81°	90° C	36 hours
Oman	Tool string 1	2,270	90°	90°C	18 hours
Oman	Tool string 2	1,942	90°	90°C	19 hours

To: Company A
Attn: Company Rep

Date: 27.04.93
TMC/tmc

From: Manager Reservoir Technical Operations

Subject: Improved combinability of openhole logging tools.

Customer A would like to take this opportunity to commend and congratulate your recent efforts in the area of improving the combinability of your openhole logging tools. We regard the success of the recent reservoir logging operations on Offshore A and B platforms as an important technological achievement, one that has a tremendous potential for improving the economics of logging in highly deviated wells.

The savings made possible by your modifications to the tools, in the form of reduction of rig-time plus accelerated production, are considerable. We estimate that the most recent operation alone, where a standard tool string and services for pressure sampling and dipmeter logging were combined into a single run, resulted in a savings to us on the order of 1 million dollars.

Due to rapid developments in high-angle drilling technology over the past three to four years, Customer A has been drilling a steadily increasing proportion of long-reach and horizontal wells. This trend is expected to continue in the future. Because of the high costs and risks involved with reservoir data acquisition in these wells, we have been experiencing a steadily increasing pressure to reduce our level of data acquisition to an absolute minimum. Our acquisition strategy was heading in the direction of replacing openhole wireline logging with a minimum suite of MWD/LWD logs.

With your improved combinability, drill pipe-assisted logging once again becomes an economically feasible logging method. In addition, we are no longer in a situation where marginal data acquisition and data quality must be pitted against the abnormally high rig-time costs involved with multiple logging runs.

It is our strong belief that this project has and will have a profound effect upon the market for logging services in the North Sea. We hope, therefore, that Company A can give the support and development of these techniques the priority that they deserve.

Once again, we would like to thank Company A managers, engineers, and technicians who have devoted their time to this project. We feel that it has taken a relatively short period of time for them to find a successful solution to our problems with logging in high angle wells, and this expediency should be commended. The ability to address our special problems in a fast and effective manner, as seen by us, is one of the most important elements of total service quality.

Thank you,

Manager Reservoir Technical Operations

On the next golf outing with the Texaco drilling engineer, the salesperson asked why Company A had been selected. The drilling engineer replied:

"You came in and did a good job at explaining the system and then showed us the job history table and the letter from the North Sea customer—that impressed everyone since the logging string we wanted you to run was much simpler than what you had been doing in places like the North Sea and the Middle East. Competitor A's sales representative came in and did a pretty good job as well in telling us about the system. But when asked if he had anything else to leave with us to help us make the decision, he gave us tool diagrams and a brochure! This didn't make anyone feel comfortable that they could do the job because this was the same type of proof Competitor B had given us!"

Fig. 8.4
Completed closing section of the sales call preparation worksheet, which is completed during the sales call meeting in preparation for the closing. In the Shell Chukchi Sea opportunity, one of the buying center members from procurement raised a financial drawback during negotiations. The price differential between Company A and the competitor was resolved using an outweigh tactic by presenting the accepted value from the sales call with the drilling manager in the evaluation of options phase.

Closing			
Customer agreed to $ value of BHL upon verification of exploration manager.	**Objective Achieved:** ☑ Primary ☐ Backup ☐ Other ☐ None	**Accepted Benefits:** Eliminate need to drill pilot hole	**Total Value Accepted:** $1,500,000 + reduced risks
If exploration manager supports using BHL, then he will support.		Mobilization plan	
Will also request emergency package be included in bid package.		Liked emergency pkg	

Late in the opportunity management process, you will want to keep track of the contacts being made with people in the customer's buying center in support of the opportunity to ensure that you have a record of the accepted benefits and value. This record will be invaluable for overcoming drawbacks late in the procurement phase. **Figure 8.4** provides an example of a closing summary from the sales call preparation worksheet for sales calls made in the case study referred to throughout the textbook. It clearly shows the accepted benefits and value.

Level 1 Sales Call Effectiveness Review

Part of the sales call process is the evaluation of how well you executed the supporting and handling of customers' negative reactions. Again, the worksheet facilitates your personal review of the sales call with the Level 1 Review section of the worksheet. In particular, consider how effective your sales supports were in demonstrating capabilities and satisfying any concerns the customer may have had. Ask whether you need to modify any support aids used in order to make them more effective or make a support aid the customer asked for and you didn't have.

Many times the customer will also offer what they would like to see if they are not totally satisfied with your proof. In this case, ensure that you check the need to develop box in the support documents section.

You should complete a Level 1 Sales Call Effectiveness Review (**Fig. 8.5**) after each sales call and keep good records by completing the project supporting worksheet and entering the information into a client visit report in the CRM database.

Fig. 8.5
Level 1 Sales Call Effectiveness Review section from the Post-Sales Call Analysis page of the Sales Call Preparation Worksheet.

Level 1 Sales Call Effectiveness Review:

	Need Improvement	Good	Very Good	Comments
Preliminaries	✔			-Little nervous at first NO BUSINESS CARD!
Opening		✔		-Good value prop statement. Could skip preliminaries next time.
Customer Lead Probing		✔		-Picked up on higher svr. concerns and more expressive than driver.
Sales Lead Probing		✔		-This project is on B. Brown's personal objectives.
Supporting			✔	-Liked very much the reference letter.
Closing	✔			-Should have asked Brown what he suggested we do next instead of making recommendation first.
Objection Handling	✔			-Having reference letter easily resolved skepticism.
Listening/Aligning/Tension	✔			-A little too preoccupied with my preparation. Missed a couple of points Brown restated over lunch.

Support Documents:

☑ Need to develop
Once have the BOC demo job completed, need to create report and sales aid. Ask for reference from Brown regarding reduced rig time.

☐ Need to modify

This part of the sales total quality management process will assist you in making ongoing improvements in your sales skills. To see how one salesperson made his company $200,000 by completing his level 1 review, see **Chapter Highlight 8.3: The $200,000 Makeover.**

The most effective way to determine how well you handle customers' negative reactions is to ask someone such as your sales manager to observe you regularly in sales calls as part of your development program. The level 2 review form includes sections for taking notes on handling customers' negative reactions in the sales call observation page, as shown in **Figs. 8.6** and **8.7**.

The next section discusses common performance problems with recommended improvement actions if the problem is determined to be one of sales skills, technical knowledge of products and services, or account knowledge. You should review these lists if you have difficulties handling customers' negative reactions or if you are going to be observing someone in a sales call.

Handling Customers' Objection Performance Problems

The following pages describe three common problems related to the misunderstanding or misapplication of critical selling skills for handling negative customers' reactions. For each situation described, probable causes and recommended improvement actions have been outlined.

1. Doesn't Recognize or Handle Skepticism Effectively

You have difficulty recognizing skepticism when it occurs, or you do not respond to skepticism with proof sources that are relevant to the client's business or suitable to the client's personality type. The client who has an Analytical social profile, for example, requires several proof sources, preferably of a technical nature—specifications, data, and case histories. Amiable clients want experts' reports and testimonials. Clients who are Drivers want facts. The Expressive client likes anything that confirms the sales representative's ability to turn their ideas into real-

INDIFFERENCE

Process	Probe to Understand Customer's Position	Acknowledge Customer's Position	Ask Permission to Probe	✔Problem ✔Quantify ✔Consequence ✔Look/listen
Quality samples	Good	✔	✔	

MISUNDERSTANDING

Process	Probe to Understand Concern	Acknowledge Customer's Concern	Acknowledge Requirement Not Met	Explain Feature Benefit	Check for Acceptance
none					

SKEPTICISM

Process	Probe to Understand Concern	Acknowledge Customer's Concern	Offer Relevant Proof	Check for Acceptance
Rig time savings	Good	Good	Had reference letter but didn't use?	Missed

DRAWBACK

Process	Probe to Understand Drawback	Acknowledge Drawback	Handle Did excellent job at defining costs	Check for Acceptance
Customer said too expensive for quality samples.	✔	✔	☐ Research ✔ Redefine ☐ Trade-off ☐ Outweigh	✔

FEAR

Process	Acknowledge Customer's Concern	Connect with the Customer	Recommend Options to Move Forward	Check for Acceptance
Probe to understand real reason.	✔	Story, analogy, metaphor.		✔

Fig. 8.6
Completed Level 2 Sales Call Observation Section for the five customer objections and appropriate handling steps.

Customer Objections	✔Very good ☐ Satisfactory ☐ Improvement needed	Summary Brilliant job on customer indifference and drawback regarding sampling. Missed chance to offer reference for skepticism on rig time savings. Made another meeting to get back to Jones regarding this!

Fig. 8.7
Completed Level 2 Sales Call Review comments section for customer objection.

ity. By not providing the kind of proof that each personality type demands, you fail to raise clients from skepticism to higher, more positive attitude levels.

Determine Cause(s)

Sales skills deficiency: You may not know how to recognize skepticism when the client expresses it. Generally, this happens when you fail to listen or probe for understanding of an attitude or simply assume understanding of an attitude. You may also try to use the same demonstration of capabilities for all customers regardless of social style.

Technical knowledge: You may not know enough to offer meaningful, relevant proof sources or to anticipate those benefits about which the client is likely to be skeptical. This often occurs because you have not done the necessary pre-call planning.

You can determine if this is the cause by reviewing your sales call preparation worksheet and, in particular, the opportunity-specific supporting worksheet page. This could also be reviewed by another person who has technical expertise in this area. If the observer finds your supporting worksheets to be weak, discuss how to improve them. If they are complete, then the cause of the problem is a sales skills deficiency.

Improvement Actions

If deficient sales skills are the problem, you should review the materials on recognizing and handling skepticism. In your next sales call, be sure to complete the sales call preparation worksheet for the features and benefits you want to introduce. Try to predict which of the features and benefits the customer is most likely to express skepticism about and ensure that you prepare an appropriate demonstration of capabilities for the specific customer's social profile. If you still encounter skepticism after you've revealed your proof source, remember to probe for understanding of the attitude rather than assuming understanding or ignoring the concern. Review the section on how social style affects how customers make business decisions in Chapter 5 "Communication Skills."

If preparation is not a problem, then conduct a mini role-play in which you play the sales representative. Have the person playing the customer state the client's requirements while you make support statements. Have the person playing the customer use expressions of skepticism and encourage you to probe for understanding. Then, once you believe you understand, acknowledge the skepticism, explaining the customer's position and why they are skeptical. Once the customer agrees, then support again—this time with a different demonstration of capabilities that will satisfy the customers objection.

If deficient technical knowledge is the problem, review your preparation worksheet, opportunity supporting worksheet, and sales call supporting worksheet pages to improve and add supports to address the features and benefits included in the supporting worksheet. You may also have to attend the appropriate key services seminars given by the segment if you have not had sufficient technical training on the product or service. During the key services training, time is set aside to practice supporting customer requirements with the features and benefits from the key services.

The sales toolbox, as part of the introduction of any new product, includes a generic customer presentation that lists the product or service details and theory as well as the key features, benefits, and applications of the service or product. Review the customer presentation to thoroughly understand the material as you must be able to customize the features, benefits, and application for your customer base.

2. Difficulty Handling Indifference

You do not adequately handle the attitude of indifference. Perhaps you simply fail to probe for unrealized needs, or do so ineffectively. As a result, the indifferent customer with a Driver social profile who is goal oriented and values time is never convinced that continuing the conversation will be worthwhile. The Expressive client starts off feeling no need for your company's help and ends up the same way, despite being normally receptive to help in realizing a personal ideas. The Analytical client, whose indifference is based on technical assumptions, is never made to question these assumptions and thus never changes them. The Amiable client talks freely about his indifference, but you fail to capitalize on this client's open and candid nature by probing to discover more needs. The result is the same with all personality types: The client's attitude remains negative, indifferent to the end.

Determine Cause(s)

Sales skills deficiency: You may not understand or recognize the attitude of indifference as clients typically express it. This may be due to a lack of understanding about what indifference is, or to an inability to recognize the indifference expressed by each personality type. It is also possible that you may not have mastered the strategy of uncovering unrealized needs when dealing with indifference, or of doing so in a way that fails to achieve alignment with the client's personality type.

Technical knowledge: You may not have sufficient knowledge about the client's needs, the competitive situation, or of the service in question, to know which opportunities to probe for when handling indifference.

Account knowledge: You're not familiar enough with the client's company to understand the client's specific problems or requirements. You, therefore, tend not to target their requirements for your sales call discussions. Instead, you remain at the application level, never focusing on the specific account's situation, and therefore do not offer specific dollar value for the solution's unique features and benefits.

Improvement Actions

If deficient sales skills are the problem, review the materials on handling indifference, plus the material on personality types and how to align with each one. After reviewing the material, you should be able to explain the strategy for uncovering unrealized needs, paying attention to how that strategy is modified to help reach an area of alignment with each personality type.

If an understanding of indifference or how to handle indifference is not a problem, conduct a mini role-play in which you play the sales representative. Have the person playing the customer provide expressions of indifference in words that each one of the four personality types would use. You should respond to each expression by probing for understanding, then identifying which opportunities to pursue in order to confirm unrealized needs. Be sure to probe in a way that aligns with the personality type you've assumed.

You may also need to practice delivering a sales lead probing sequence to uncover unrecognized customer needs. Prepare a set of sales lead probing questions for specific situations where you commonly encounter client indifference. Then, conduct a mini role-play in which you play the sales representative and the other person plays the client. Use the scenarios you developed and have the customer respond in role as a typical customer would to the probing sequence. At the end of the mini role-play, ask the person playing the customer for feedback on how well you were able to address the indifference. Repeat this exercise until you are comfortable with the use of the sales lead probing sequence.

If deficient in account knowledge, ask your sales manager to analyze with you one or more of your accounts where the client has been or probably will be indifferent. Discuss why the client is indifferent, the client's personality type, and what questions you can ask to uncover unrealized needs. Describe how you will tailor your probing to align with the client's personality type and what specific sales lead probing sequence you will use to uncover unrealized needs and align with the client.

If deficient technical knowledge is the problem, then follow the same improvement action for technical knowledge as described above in the first problem. Seek technical support from a domain expert, and determine how to correct the problem either through better sales call preparation or technical training. As you have already seen from the first problem area, technical knowledge improvement actions start by completing the sales call preparation worksheet. If all the preparation is complete for technical services—features and benefits considerations—the problem is in the execution of the skill, as discussed above.

Be sure to discuss with a domain expert (using a completed sales call preparation worksheet) all aspects of the sales call preparation. Ask for feedback on the completeness of the sales call preparation worksheet from a technical perspective. With the domain expert, discuss the following:

- The most common reasons for indifference and what kinds of information are needed to handle this attitude
- Where to obtain the necessary competitive information and review any information that is new to you
- Which customer requirements the competitor has unique features and benefits for that could cause the customer to identify drawbacks in the solution proposed
- How competitors try to overcome your unique features and benefits that create drawbacks for them

After the discussion, compile a list of future opportunities and customer requirements. For each opportunity and requirement for which your solution has unique products or services, develop a sales lead probing strategy to uncover needs satisfied by these features and benefits.

With your sales manager, select two or three accounts where the customer has been or probably will be indifferent and develop strategies for handling those clients. Review the strategies with other sales representatives who deal with the respective account(s) and ask for their feedback. Also, review the region marketing and sales communications program to create awareness of your company's unique features and benefits. Ensure that enough buying center members from your accounts attend or are included in the program. If their attendance is missing, you may have to be more pro-active to gain their commitment to attend. You may also have to use a more direct, low-pressure awareness technique, such as courtesy informational flyers, as discussed in Chapter 1 "Understanding the Role of Marketing and Sales."

If deficient account knowledge is the problem, first review the materials in Chapter 2 "Value Drivers" and Chapter 3 "Account Corporate Profile" These resources assist in building an understanding of the customer's value drivers. Print the Account Corporate Profile and the Project Solution Worksheet and review these with a customer in the account who is a supporter and ask for their feedback.

Review your opportunity-specific worksheets with other sales representatives who are familiar with the account, and get their feedback on the business drivers for the opportunity. Be sure you can make the connection between what your company is providing and the value drivers of the customer.

In your next sales calls, make your first probe a visualizing probe to determine the main business drivers for the opportunity. If there are specific accounts in particular where you have frequent cases of indifference, ask someone who is familiar with the contacts in the buying center to conduct a role-play in which they play the indifferent client. Ensure they adopt the appropriate personality type of the customer for the role-play. Practice handling their indifference with appropriate probes.

3. Difficulty Handling Misunderstandings

You have difficulty recognizing customer misunderstandings. You either don't probe to understand the misunderstanding, or you treat it as a different type of negative reaction by the customer. By not handling the misunderstanding correctly, the sales call is not efficient, the customer becomes impatient, and unmet needs or requirements are not addressed. As a result, the sales call ends and you fail to resolve the clients' misunderstanding.

Determine Cause(s)

Sales skills deficiency: You may not know how to recognize a misunderstanding when the client expresses it. Generally this happens when you fail to listen or probe for understanding of an attitude or simply assume understanding of an attitude. You may also try to use the same demonstration of capabilities for all customers regardless of social style.

Technical knowledge: You may not know the complete range of features and benefits of the products and services you are offering and, therefore, cannot identify the misunderstanding as a lack of customer knowledge about the features and benefits of your company's products and services. This happens when you have not done the necessary pre-call planning.

You can determine if this is the cause by reviewing your sales call preparation worksheet and the sales call supporting worksheet section with a person you consider to have technical expertise in this area. If they find your supporting worksheets to be weak, discuss how to improve them. If they are complete, the cause of the problem is a sales skills deficiency.

Improvement Actions

If deficient sales skills are the problem, review the materials on handling misunderstanding. After reviewing the material you should be able to explain the strategy for handling a misunderstanding. A common reason for not handling misunderstandings properly is insufficient probing to gain a full understanding of why the customer has expressed a negative response.

Conduct a mini role-play in which you play the salesperson. Prepare a set of sales aids for specific situations where you commonly encounter client misunderstanding. Then, conduct the mini role-play in which you use the scenarios you have developed and have the person playing the customer provide expressions of misunderstanding. You should respond to each expression by probing for understanding, and then confirm the customer's unmet needs. Once you have confirmed the unmet need, then support as you would normally for a customer need. Make sure that you support in a way that aligns with the customer's personality type you've assumed for the role-play. At the end of the mini role-play, ask the person playing the customer for feedback on how well you were able to resolve the misunderstanding. Repeat this exercise until you are comfortable with handling the misunderstanding process.

If deficient technical knowledge is the problem, follow the same improvement action for technical knowledge, as described above. If all the preparation is complete for technical services—features and benefits considerations—the problem is in the execution of the skill.

When a new salesperson is confronted with a customer's objection and is not sure how their solution can address the objection, a good strategy is to use the research tactic to seek expert advice before treating the objection as a drawback. This assumes that you started preparing your solution according to the standard sales procedure early in the opportunity management process in the evaluations of options phase and have used the initial sales call to discover all the critical buying center members' requirements. Based on these requirements, prepare a proposal that best meets these needs. Review your solution with your sales manager or technical expert before returning to the customer to present it. This way, you get a second opinion on how to improve the proposal and address areas in which you are lacking in technical knowledge. Attend the appropriate technical training to improve your technical knowledge and familiarity of supporting collateral you can use to better explain technical features, such as videos, web pages, and released examples. All these will help make it easier for the customer to understand.

4. Difficulty Overcoming Objections Due to Drawbacks

You don't handle drawbacks effectively. You tend not to deal with the drawback directly and are unable to present offsetting benefits that outweigh the drawbacks.

Determine Cause(s)

Sales skills deficiency: You may not have mastered the strategy for handling drawbacks, or you may be unable to tailor the strategy to suit the personality type of the client. You may try to "explain it away" or handle the drawback directly by negating it. Sometimes this happens because you don't recognize the need as a drawback. When this happens, you are unsure how to support and continue to probe for ideas on how to support. From the customer's perspective, the probing seems to go nowhere, and they find themselves repeating information.

Technical knowledge: You may lack the knowledge of specific features and benefits of your company's products and services as well as the application of these benefits in different environments. Therefore, when presented with a financial drawback, you cannot use outweigh or redefine tactics. You may also not be very familiar with competitors' offerings and, therefore, cannot use the trade-off technique effectively. As a result of all the above, you are not able to apply any of the drawback handling techniques effectively or efficiently.

Account knowledge: You're not familiar enough with the client's company or environment to understand the client's specific problems or requirements. You, therefore, tend not to target their requirements for your sales call discussions, stay at the application level, and never focus on the specific account's situation. You also do not offer specific dollar value for the unique features and benefits of your solution. Therefore, you cannot use the outweigh tactic to handle drawbacks and must limit your tactics to trade-offs, which for non-technical customers is not very effective.

Improvement Actions

If deficient skills are the problem, review the materials on handling drawbacks. Select one or two calls that you made in the past where a drawback was not successfully handled and construct a list of benefits that could have been used to minimize the importance of the drawback. Also, construct a list of sales lead probes that could have been used to remind the client of these benefits if the customer exhibits indifference to the benefits when using the outweigh or trade-off tactics. Review the lists with your sales manager and ask for feedback.

If deficient technical knowledge is the problem, follow the same improvement action for technical knowledge as described in problem 1. During your discussions with the domain expert, be sure to discuss:

- Why do clients in your region typically express drawbacks?
- For the products and services you sell in your region, which product and service features result in benefits that can logically outweigh various drawbacks?
- Ask them to review your sales support materials and provide examples what they have used as supporting materials.
- What are the sources and who are the experts they use to keep current with technical developments and applications?

During the discussion, be sure to construct a list of the most common drawbacks and reference the sales aids you can use to overcome the drawbacks, not how these be adopted for the different customer social profiles you serve.

If deficient account knowledge is the problem, follow the same improvement action for handling indifference as described above in problem 2. Analyze from an account perspective where a drawback has blocked progress in making a sale. Discuss these questions:

- Why is the client raising this drawback?
- What benefits might logically outweigh the importance of this drawback to the client?
- What probes might you use to remind the client of these benefits or to uncover opportunities that will lead to these benefits?

After this discussion, conduct a mini role-play with another person in which they, as the client, present you with commonly expressed drawbacks. As the sales representative, probe to handle the drawbacks. Ask the other person for feedback.

Sales Call Preparation for New Sales Personnel

For new sales representatives, in addition to the actions already discussed, this section may prove useful when you have difficulties handling customers' objections.

Understanding Requirements

When arranging the sales call meeting with the customer, as much as possible ask the customer to describe the main requirements for the opportunity that you are going to discuss during the sales call (open visualizing probe). Depending on which stage opportunities management process stage you are at, ensure that you use the client interview worksheets to guide your conversations with the customer. If you are qualifying an opportunity and in stage 2 "Qualifying the Compelling Event," use the project solution client interview worksheet; in early stage 3 "Evaluation of Options," use the request for proposal worksheet.

Completeness of Supporting Worksheet

Ensure that your sales call supporting worksheet addresses each requirement, and be prepared to support the requirements during the sales call and demonstrate capabilities. It is a good idea to review your sales call supporting worksheet with the domain expert before going on the call. Compile a list of the most common negative customer reactions for each product or service and review it with the domain expert.

Domain Expert

Ask your sales manager for the domain experts for technical services, applications, and specific account knowledge. Discuss with the domain experts why clients express negative reactions and the most appropriate ways of handling them. Compare your library of different types of proof sources, references, and sales aids for each product or service with those the domain experts use. You may find they have a more complete library of sales tools, depending on the customer's social style and type of negative reaction.

Sales Library

As a standard practice, compare your sales aids with those of others selling the same products and services and share the proof sources among the sales team members in the region and globally. Over time, your team will have an ever-expanding library of support worksheets (features, benefits, and proofs) that can be used to customize new supports for future sales opportunities.

Level 1 and 2 Reviews

If possible, ask your manager or the domain expert to accompany you on one call a month or every other month and conduct a level 2 review as described in Chapter 7 "Sales Call Skills." Complete the pre- and post-call review and ask for feedback.

Modeling Coaching Calls

Ask your sales manager to recommend another competent salesperson in the region that you can accompany and observe on a sales call. Review the sales call preparation worksheet of the salesperson you will accompany. Closely review all parts of the sales call preparation worksheet and how they are prepared to support according to the type of possible rejections they expect for each feature and benefit.

Prior to going on the modeling sales call, discuss the importance of recognizing and handling drawbacks. During the sales call, use the level 2 review form to follow the salesperson's progression through the sales call and, in particular, how the salesperson handles the customer's negative reactions.

Role of the Purchasing Department

To conclude, this chapter explains the role of the purchasing department or the individual who has been assigned the responsibility of soliciting and evaluating a request for services (evaluator). Some salespeople believe that customers go out of their way to simplify the bidding process and make the selection of the preferred supplier a lowest bidder decision. This is not an accurate interpretation of the purchasing manager's role.

In procurement seminars, purchasing personnel are taught that they can never prove they got the best price; what they have to prove is that they tried to get the best price. They are taught that, to get the best price, they should have a well-defined procurement process that:

- Ensures that they (customer) have the correct technical requirements and a request for proposal that clearly describes the minimum bid specification for products and services, as agreed to by the operations staff.

- Has a list of qualified suppliers that is reviewed and updated regularly.
- Makes each new or significant procurement a competitive bid process that covers the most likely scenarios, with calculated costs for each scenario and costs for any products or services that may be required.
- Has an evaluation technique that is simple, consistent, quantitative, and reviewed.
- Transfers risks that don't increase their (customer) costs.
- Negotiate only with the preferred suppliers.
- Compare evaluated costs against invoices and challenges any variances.
- Uses their (customer viewpoint) terms and conditions for contracts and closely reviews and challenges any requests for changes.

Most procurement departments try to have three or more acceptable suppliers. If the operations or technical staff has verified the suppliers as having similar capabilities, the procurement decision becomes much simpler and can be made by comparing each supplier's quoted prices. In fact, many bid requirements today include a very well-defined spreadsheet in which prices are to be entered to facilitate bottom-line analysis.

Strange as it may seem, this is not at odds with what the salesperson is trying to do, which is to demonstrate value and then share in the value generation, which to the customer represents a premium over the competitor. As long as the value is proven or the customer's required operation staff validates the strengths of your solution, then most customers will pay a premium for value-creating products and services.

Closing Comment

Now you have seen the fundamental sales skills of the consultative selling approach and need-satisfaction process, including handling customers' objections. You should be equipped to successfully manager your opportunities.

Problems arise for mainly two reasons:

- You start too late in the opportunities management process to get your differentiated, value-added products and services included in the decision criteria. Therefore, if you begin to offer this only in the procurement process, the non-technical people will react negatively and have concerns such as those discussed in this chapter. There may not be time for you to address all the concerns the technical staff may have.
- You don't discover the customer's objections to your sales proposals until late in the opportunities management process or in the procurement phase after the proposals have been submitted.

Both issues can be resolved by applying the concepts of opportunities management and consultative selling approach following the need-satisfaction process and handling customers' objections.

The focus will turn to selling in a competitive environment specifically for large sales engaged in competitive bidding following the customers' procurement processes.

Summary of Chapter Objectives

Previous chapters discussed the consultative selling approach skills and the need-satisfaction process. With these sales skills and customer knowledge, you should be able to prepare proposals that are aligned to the customer's requirements and demonstrate your solution's value. Even with your best efforts, however, there will be situations when the customer will have concerns or will not accept your solution. Such responses are classified as customer objections.

1. Describe the most common customer objections encountered during the consultative selling approach process.

There are five typical types of objections. These are indifference: The customer is not motivated to support the selection of your company and sees no need to change their current mode of operating. Misunderstanding: this is when the customer incorrectly assumes that you cannot provide a feature and benefit they require. Many times the customer may express skepticism about your claims regarding features and benefits. The most common negative response is that of the drawback. Two drawbacks are common: A technical drawback, where your solution cannot provide a feature or benefit the customer needs or the solution includes a feature the customer does not want, or a financial drawback, which is the more common drawback. Often you will hear, "I would like to use you, but you're too expensive." The fifth objection is fear. The client had a bad experience in the past that causes them to minimize the benefits they could enjoy because the fear of a loss is greater. The fear objection is well known and studied by neuroscientists. The fear objection causes the customer to anchor, and the old brain's survival instincts will discount logical explanations to move forward.

2. Understand how to react and overcome common customer objections.

Each type of negative response by customers is best handled by following specific tactics for each type of response. Because the indifferent customer doesn't see the benefits of doing business with your company, the salesperson must first acknowledge the customer's point of view and then ask permission to probe to understand their circumstances. This is a delicate process, and you do not want to infer that the customer is uninformed. Your probing should be brief and efficient. The best technique to follow in this circumstance is the sales lead probing strategy. Once you confirm a need the customer has, you are in a position to support the need. If at any time during the probing sequence the customer does not confirm the need, then you drop the probing sequence and move to the next step in the sales call—either another probing sequence or concluding the meeting.

For the next three types of customers' negative reactions, you always begin by probing to ensure that you understand the nature of their reaction. Never assume that you do, and once you have a thorough understanding, acknowledge the customer's point of view before beginning to try to change the customer's position. For a misunderstanding, the most important aspect is that the customer perceives they have a need that is not being met by your solution. As a result, an important step in handling a misunderstanding is to first confirm the need before you begin to re-explain or support the assumed need. When the customer has expressed skepticism, you must identify what the customer would consider an acceptable proof in order to accept your claims. For the drawback, if it is technical, the tactic to use if you are unsure a solution exists or that their requests cannot be met, you should research the customer's requirement before you assume it is not possible and then treat drawback as a financial drawback. For the financial drawback, there are three tactics. The most successful is to outweigh the drawback with previously accepted benefits and value the customer has accepted or to trade off the financial difference between your company and the competitor. You do this by ensuring that the customer understands the features and benefits they will not get from the competitor's lesser offering or the additional costs or risks the competitor's solution has compared to yours. The last tactic for handling a drawback is to try to have the customer redefine the evaluation criteria so they more accurately evaluate the benefits of your solution.

When handling the fear objection, you must have the customer view the fear from a different perspective. You do this by connecting with the customer through stories, analogies, and metaphors to help the customer reframe the fear and allow them to move forward. Give the client options to choose from for next steps. In this situation, you also want to be readily available after you have closed the meeting in case the customer has any questions or clarifications in order to keep them committed to going forward.

The best strategy for handling customers' negative reactions is to prevent them from happening. This is achieved by having proactive marketing and a sales–customer–communication program that uses all aspects of the promotional tools available to the marketing and sales team—tools such as advertising, personal selling, direct marketing, and public relations. Successful programs create awareness in the target markets or customers about your company's benefits and help educate the customer about your company's offerings. These are the first two stages in the buyer-readiness stages. The salesperson must guide the customer through these stages so that the final purchase decision is in your company's favor.

3. Prepare strategies to avoid customers' objections.

You discussed the opportunities management process by starting early to understand what negative reactions a customer may have to your solution. You can decide where you are vulnerable and define a competitive sales strategy that puts you in the strongest position to secure the project. This will drive your tactics, which eliminate predicted negative reactions among customers by leveraging your strengths. Included in the opportunities management process is the monitoring of the decision process all the way through to the end. You must fully analyze any decision to understand where you were not successful in handling customer concerns, why you were successful, and the value the customer gave you to justify their decisions. Also, when you execute tactics, competitors will react; as a result, a customer may develop negative reactions late in the procurement process. You have to be prepared to react to these late reactions.

By improving your sales call planning, execution, and analysis, you can also avoid many of the customer's negative reactions. The project supporting worksheet and eight-page document were designed to assist the salesperson in methodically planning, executing, and analyzing each sales call. In addition, the salesperson should use sales management and domain experts to help develop the skills and techniques for handling and preventing customers' negative reactions.

Lastly, a salesperson should not be upset or surprised when a customer seems to push the decision toward the low-cost bidder. If the customer has not given you the benefit of your added value, you first should examine whether you have effectively used the opportunity management process to prove your value or whether you waited too late in the process to introduce your value-added solution. You might also be discovering the customer's concerns too late in the opportunity management process, not leaving you many options to deal with them effectively. Remember the customer's procurement process is there to prove that the department or individual responsible for the procurement tried to get the best solution for their company. It is your job to demonstrate that your company has the best solution. Sometimes the customer will ignore or make unreasonable demands because they believe this is the best way to get the best deal. They believe they are being a good buyer for their company. The best way to effectively deal with these "good buyers" is for the salesperson to be a "good seller," to know and prove the added value your solution brings to the customer.

Applying the Concepts

1. What are the most common negative reactions that you experience in your day-to-day sales?
2. What are the best sales aids you use in your sales calls, particularly during the demonstration of capabilities?
3. What is the largest financial drawback that you have successfully overcome?
4. How can you ensure that there is a good exchange of success stories and sale support tools within and between regions?
5. How much of your time is spent handling customers' negative reactions?

References

1. Hill, R.: *Empathy at Work: Developing Skills to Understand Other People.* Retrieved June 15, 2015, from http://www.mindtools.com/pages/article/EmpathyatWork.htm (n.d.).
2. Heiman, S., and Sanchez, D.: *The New Strategic Selling: The Unique Sales System Proven Successful by the World's Best Companies,* revised and updated for the 21st century (Warner Books ed.), New York, Warner Books (1998).
3. Holland, J., and Young, T., *Rethinking the sales cycle: How superior sellers embrace the buying cycle to achieve a sustainable and competitive advantage*. New York, McGraw-Hill (2010).

Appendix A

Handling Customer Objections

Indifference

1. Probe to understand indifference
2. Acknowledge customer's position
3. Ask permission to probe
4. Use Sales Lead probing sequence to build awareness:
   - Problem–need confirmed
   - Quantify–size of problem confirmed
   - Consequence–of not addressing issue confirmed
   - Look/listen–confirmed customer wants to:

     a. Support confirmed need

Misunderstanding

1. Probe to understand misunderstanding
2. Acknowledge customer's position
3. Acknowledge need not met
4. Support need as per supporting process

Skepticism

1. Probe to understand skepticism
2. Acknowledge customer's concern
3. Offer relevant proof
4. Check for acceptance

Drawback

1. Probe to understand drawback
2. Acknowledge customer's drawback
3. If technical, research
4. If financial, use one or combination of below:
   - Outweigh spreadsheet analysis. Cost of drawback compared to your proposal's value
   - Redefine definition of price to include other associated cost not include in price analysis
   - Tradeoff–review benefits customer will not be receiving if he or she chooses competitor
5. Check for acceptance

Fear

1. Probe to understand the real reason for the Anchor
2. Acknowledge the concern
3. Connect with the customer through a story, analogy, metaphor etc.
4. Recommend options to move forward
5. Check for acceptance

Appendix B

Communication Skills

Active Listening

1. Make eye contact
2. Sit straight or lean forward
3. Nod in agreement
4. Use facial and body language
5. Ask questions
6. Take notes
7. Classify the information as you hear it

Exploring for Ideas

1. When you invite a suggestion -> Give a reaction
2. When you make a suggestion -> Invite a reaction
3. When you use/build on the ideas of others -> Acknowledge the connection
4. When you need to be innovative or imaginative -> Temporarily alter restrictions

Crediting

1. Give a specific example of performance.
2. Mention personal qualities that contributed to performance.
3. Mention resulting benefits to the customer or and or you

Triangulating a Concern

1. Use neutral tone
2. Don't state your opinion
3. Refer to problem or concern as "It"

Managing Difference of Opinion

1. Define the difference
   - Probe to understand the customer's position
   - Confirm what is important to the customer
   - State what is important to you
2. Explore for ideas for an acceptable solution for both parties and or handle as drawback
3. Conclude the discussion
   - Summarize next steps
   - Check for acceptance
   - If difference of opinion remains
   - Acknowledge customer's point of view and state you still hope your solution has sufficient value even with difference of opinion and if not you understand why he or she has taken this position.
   - Thank them for their time.

Constructive Criticism

1. Introduce the subject in a neutral tone
2. Confirm your understanding of the situation
3. Give balanced feedback
   - Specify what you want to see retained.
   - Specify what you want changed.
4. Explore next steps.
   - Invite ideas; offer feedback.
   - Offer ideas; invite feedback
   - Acknowledge connection to others ideas
   - Temporarily alter restrictions
5. Summarize next steps you've agreed to

Sales Call Skills

Preliminaries

1. Greeting – business card
2. Rapport building
3. What preparation
4. Check timing
5. Permission to take notes

Opening

1. State agenda
2. Value Proposition
3. Check for acceptance
4. Check for customer's agenda

Probing–Customer Lead

1. Situation
2. Problem or Opportunities
3. Implication of problem or opportunity
4. Need payoff – Confirm your understanding of the problem or opportunity and implication

Probing–Sales Lead

1. Problem or opportunity confirm the issue exists for customer
2. Quantify the size of the issue
3. Consequences what would happen if the issue was not addressed
4. Look/Listen would the customer like to see or hear more on how we could assist them in addressing the issue

Supporting

1. Acknowledge the need
2. Describe feature and benefits
3. Demonstrate capabilities
4. Check for understanding
5. Test for value

Closing

1. Check for any other issues
2. Review accepted benefits
3. Ask customer for next steps or propose next steps
4. Check for acceptance
5. Thank the client

Customer Objections

Indifference

1. Probe to understand indifference
2. Acknowledge customer's position
3. Ask permission to probe
4. Use Sales Engineer Lead probing sequence to build awareness
   - Problem–need confirmed
   - Quantify–size of problem confirmed
   - Consequence–of not addressing issue confirmed
   - Look listen–confirmed customer wants to see or hear more
   - Support confirmed need

Misunderstanding

1. Probe to understand misunderstanding
2. Acknowledge customer's position
3. Acknowledge need not met
4. Support need as per supporting process.

Skepticism

1. Probe to understand skepticism
2. Acknowledge customer's concern
3. Offer relevant proof
4. Check for acceptance

Drawback

1. Probe to understand drawback
2. Acknowledge customer's drawback
3. If technical–research
4. If financial use one or combination of techniques below:
   - Outweigh spreadsheet analysis cost of drawback compared to your proposal's value
   - Redefine definition of price to include other associated cost not include in price analysis
   - Tradeoff – review benefits customer will not be receiving if he or she chooses competitor
5. Check for acceptance

Fear

1. Probe to understand the real reason for the Anchor
2. Acknowledge customer's position
3. Connect with the customer through a story, analogy, metaphor etc.
4. Recommend options to move forward
5. Check for acceptance

Made in the USA
Monee, IL
25 March 2025

525b401e-742c-40a3-8f20-1b9ca2c44b6cR03